AF940888

Italian Constitutional Law in the European Context

Italian Constitutional Law in the European Context

Diletta Tega (coordinator)
Giorgio Repetto
Giovanni Piccirilli
Stefania Ninatti

Wolters Kluwer

Published by:
Kluwer Law International B.V.
PO Box 316
2400 AH Alphen aan den Rijn
The Netherlands
E-mail: lrs-sales@wolterskluwer.com
Website: www.wolterskluwer.com/en/solutions/kluwerlawinternational

Sold and distributed by:
Wolters Kluwer Legal & Regulatory U.S.
920 Links Avenue
Landisville, PA 17538
United States of America
E-mail: customer.service@wolterskluwer.com

ISBN 978-94-035-3059-8

e-Book: ISBN 978-94-035-3069-7
web-PDF: ISBN 978-94-035-3079-6

© 2025 Kluwer Law International BV, The Netherlands, and/or subsidiaries, its licensors, and contributors. All rights are reserved, including those for text and data mining, AI training, and similar technologies.

No part of this publication may be reproduced, stored in a retrieval system, or transmitted in any form or by any means, electronic, mechanical, photocopying, recording, or otherwise, without written permission from the publisher.

Permission to use this content must be obtained from the copyright owner. More information can be found at: https://www.wolterskluwer.com/en/solutions/kluwerlawinternational/rights-and-permissions

to our students

Table of contents

© Wolters Kluwer Italia

Part II
Italy and the EU

 © Wolters Kluwer Italia

Part III
Democracy and Pluralism in Italy

Part IV
Rights and Duties in the Italian Constitution

 © Wolters Kluwer Italia

Foreword

When it comes to studies in Comparative Constitutional Law the 'usual suspects' belong to a demoralizingly narrow group of jurisdictions: First and foremost, English speaking jurisdictions. This is the result both of the lamentable linguistic capacities of scholars in the Common Law countries but not only this. English is, for better and for worse, the most common 'second language' in the world. So also, scholars from non-English speaking countries when they come 'to do' comparative law frequently turn to English speaking jurisdictions. And when they want their work to have a global reach they are pushed to publish in English.

The malaise does not stop here. There is still a persistent 'scholarly Euro-centrism' which dominates the field of comparative constitutional law. But even within small puddle of the European legal space, two jurisdictions dominate – France and Germany.

There are, of course, shining exceptions but no one will deny the relative paucity of engagement with, say, Italy, Spain let alone important Eastern European jurisdictions and scholarship.

We pay a dear price for the narrowness of the comparative law endeavor. These other jurisdictions are not only important in their positivist particularity. They enrich our very understanding of public law since there are different sensibilities, hermeneutic and otherwise, which one disregards to one's own peril.

Making a virtue out of a vice, the publication in English of this volume by Tega et.al. covering comprehensively the Italian constitutional legal order is, thus, a cause for celebration. It is not exactly *Terra Incognita*. There is the early work of Cappelletti and Perillo and the more recent excellent volume by Cartabia and Lupo to give but a couple of examples.

But the current volume has its own identity and specificity which make it particularly welcome.

First and foremost it has in mind a readership not only of scholars but, perhaps even principally, of students. It presents, in English, the kind of material which an Italian student studying the material and preparing for an exam would be using in an Italian university. This is rare. If nothing else, given programs such as Erasmus which bring a host of students to different countries where the language of instruction, in a concession to reality, is in English this book will be indispensable.

The doctrinal comprehensiveness and detail are truly impressive and judiciously selected will prove, too, an invaluable resource in any comparative public law course wherever this may take place and whenever one wishes to descend from the Olympus of general principles to the nitty gritty of actual positive constitutional law.

And there is a second virtue. Oftentimes, and I am guilty of this too, public law comparativists tend to focus on systemic issues such as the system of judicial review to give here the most common example. Naturally, this aspect of the field is not neglected in the current volume. But substantive law, the true meat of legal discourse, richly receives the place it deserves.

Taken together then, the authors of this volume, alongside Cartabia and Lupo, provide hitherto unknown access to the hugely important, rich and instructive legal system – the Italian legal *Bel Paese*.

Joseph H.H. Weiler

© Wolters Kluwer Italia

Foreword

During the short course of a few years, the breadth of scholarship about the Italian Constitution written in English has expanded significantly. This textbook, authored by a distinguished group of Italian scholars based at a range of universities, is a new and important link in a chain that we hope will continue to grow over time. Its predecessors have all been carefully considered by the authors of this volume and are mentioned in their *Preface*.

Yet, every book has a different purpose and its own peculiarities. Every book has its own unique personality. This one focuses on the European dimension of Italian constitutionalism. Therefore, after presenting, in the first part, an essential overview of the Italian constitutional system, it expands, more specifically, on a number of topics which clearly demonstrate the interconnection between the national and the supranational. The second part is devoted to analyzing the relationship between Italy and the EU, considering not only the EU's influence on Italy, but also the Italian contribution to the European integration process. Democratic procedures, viewed from the perspective of pluralism, are examined in the third part of the textbook, while the fourth part deals with rights and duties, in relation to which the intertwinement between legal orders is particularly evident.

Particular attention is devoted to the case law of not only the Italian Constitutional Court, but also the Court of Justice of the European Union, and the European Court of Human Rights, and in some limited cases other national Constitutional Courts.

In brief, this book examines the Italian Constitution from a European lens and sheds light on the European dimension of the Italian Constitution. Since its entry into force, on 1st of January, 1948, the Italian Constitution has been transformed not only by constitutional amendments but also thanks to the profound and pervasive effects of the European integration process, commencing in the 1950s and making even more of an impact during the last decade of the twentieth century.

This approach reflects the new wave of constitutional scholarship, which naturally transcends borders, applying comparative and transnational methods.

As the co-authors explain, this book is not only an educational tool, although it clearly relies upon multiple teaching experiences. Indeed, while it addresses a range of audiences, it is particularly useful for students and young legal researchers. Moreover, it pursues the objective of establishing and consolidating a common language and an approach to Italian specificities that renders them comprehensible worldwide.

One of the valuable aspects of such a work is to provide university professors with an appropriate teaching resource, suitable for constitutional law classes offered in English. Teaching in English is becoming more and more common in Italian universities. English spoken classes appeal to Italian as well as international students, including Erasmus and exchange students hailing from all over the world. This book perfectly suits this audience and addresses the many challenges connected to this endeavor.

Until very recently, a number of objections were raised in relation to teaching legal courses in English at Italian universities and especially within Italian law schools. The most common was the insistence on the peculiarity of each legal system, that was reflected in the specific legal language and terminology adopted by every individual country. Today, Italian law professors teach and write in both English and Italian, thus contributing to the global scientific debate – in which they inevitably offer Italian solutions and sensibility – and to the formation of lawyers (and of other professionals) required to work across multiple, intertwined legal systems.

The next step in this development, and the indicator of success of the interaction between scholars of all countries that has developed over the past few decades, is the inclusion of the Italian constitutional experience among the more relevant models to be duly taken into account in comparative and transnational constitutional law studies.

Marta Cartabia and Nicola Lupo

© Wolters Kluwer Italia

Preface

The purpose of this book is to present topics that are distinctive of Italian Constitutional Law. The authors have chosen to address the most significant issues in contemporary European and global legal discourse: the separation of powers, the protection of rights, the role of constitutional adjudication, the transnational judicial borrowing and dialogue between constitutional courts, as well as democracy, pluralism, constitutional identity, and national sovereignty *vis à vis* the EU. By analysing Italian Constitutional Law through the lens of the most pressing challenges, students will be equipped with a comprehensive framework that enables them to understand the intricacies and complexities of this field within a broader and multifaceted context. Faced with the realities of complex societies, constitutional law comes up against numerous challenges that arise from multiple horizontal and vertical governance interactions. At the international level, domestic constitutional law must navigate the impact of European integration and engage with the global context. Meanwhile, at the domestic level, constitutional law grapples with a range of pressing issues pertaining to the distribution of powers and the protection of individual rights. Many of the solutions that Italian Constitutional Law developed with regard to these matters fit perfectly into the ongoing debate between scholars and constitutional courts across all Western democracies. However, although the Italian Constitutional System shares features and experiences that are common to many contemporary legal systems (norms are converging and the distance between legal systems and practices is increasingly shrinking) it still retains its own peculiarities.

These peculiarities can be traced back to the birth of the Italian Republic. In the aftermath of World War II, a State which had just emerged from a totalitarian experience, with a bureaucratic and economic organization inherited from the nineteenth century and which was, moreover, impoverished and dependant on foreign aid, underwent the strongest 'constitutional discontinuity' of its history: the meeting of the Constituent Assembly and the adoption of the first truly democratic Constitution, with its many innovative principles and institutions. These included the establishment of a Constitutional Court, an innovation with respect not only to national history, but also to European tradition, which until then had only seen the short experience of the Austrian Constitutional Court. In the subsequent decades, rather than fading away, this 'democratic discontinuity' became increasingly present at a societal level. As well as experiencing considerable industrial growth, for example, the country became one of the wealthiest Western democracies. In this context, the judiciary became entirely independent from the political framework: the liberties proclaimed by the Constitution were implemented by the legislature and the courts, both ordinary and constitutional, and the Italian Parliament was able to pass important reforms such as those regarding the national public healthcare system. All this happened despite significant government instability and a frail political system.

The Constituent Assembly was itself heavily influenced in its choices by two factors. The first was the 'tyrant complex'. Following the fall of fascism, the members of the Assembly were apprehensive with regard to the potential return of authoritarian regimes, and they feared a strong executive in particular. The second was the 'veil of ignorance': political elections were to follow shortly after the entry into force of the Constitution; their outcome was uncertain, and so was the future position of Italy with respect to the two ideological blocks into which Europe was being divided. This division would linger on in national political and institutional life until the 1990s: Italy was a democracy but also the home of the largest Communist Party in the Western world. By the end of the 1970s, the political system had entered a phase of further crisis, which imploded in the 1990s with the «Bribesville» scandal (*Tangentopoli*) and the emergence of new political forces. To this day, the system struggles to reach a steady pace in terms of its overall functioning, while the Constitution still operates as an effective compass of the life of the Republic.

There are two intended audiences for this book. It has been conceived firstly for the benefit of non-Italian students interested in understanding how the national constitutional system works and its similarities with their own legal systems. The work has not been conceived as a general introduction to public law, or to the basic features of Italian Constitutional Law. Other handbooks fulfil this task admirably (see below). Rather the book aims both to provide students with the potential insights or even the lessons that Italy may present, and to offer them a method with which they may grasp the peculiarities of the Italian constitutional experience within the European legal landscape, even in order to understand, though in a constitutional law perspective, what Merryman defined as the «Italian Style of Law, Doctrine and Interpretation».

It has also been designed to present both Italian and foreign colleagues with an overview of how the Italian legal system is embedded in a constitutional and political fabric which has recurrent patterns common to many Western countries. The various issues are contextualised from the perspective of the main strains of constitutional thought, with reference to international literature on the subject to

 © Wolters Kluwer Italia

be found for the most part in English. The authors have endeavoured to present the issues succinctly but in all their often significant complexity without dilution. It is for the reader to judge whether these challenges have been met.

The four authors have worked closely together since the start of this project. Their first step was to agree upon an overall view of the index of the topics to be discussed. Giorgio Repetto took responsibility for the first Part, Giovanni Piccirilli for the second, Stefania Ninatti for the third and Diletta Tega for the last.

They proceeded to work together discussing, amending, and re-writing the entire volume. All the authors involved in this project possess solid experience in teaching Italian Constitutional Law in English. They may be affiliated with different Italian Universities, but they have all studied and taught abroad, and have all published in international academic journals. They share the conviction that Italian Constitutional Law and its methods deserve to be analysed from a perspective that transcends national borders. All four work in the field of European Constitutional Law.

This work follows in the wake of other valuable contributions in English on the Italian legal system, although much of the volume departs from these models. When Mauro Cappelletti, John Henry Merryman and Joseph M. Perillo wrote *The Italian Legal System: An Introduction* (Stanford University Press) in 1967, little had been written on the topic. Over the years, however, this has gradually changed. In the 1990s, Alessandro Pizzorusso edited the yearbook *Italian Studies in Law*, which contained a selection of studies on Italian Law edited by the Italian Association of Comparative Law. The real pioneer of the *genre*, however, was Valerio Onida: at the end of the same decade, he collaborated with some of the most gifted scholars that he had tutored in preparing his *Constitutional Law in Italy*, a volume still in print today with relevant updates (Kluwer). In 2008, Giuseppe Franco Ferrari and his contributors published their *Introduction to Italian Public Law*, also periodically updated (Giuffrè and now Giuffrè Francis Lefebvre). In 2009, Marta Cartabia and Giacinto della Cananea launched the *Italian Journal of Public Law* which aims to serve as a bridge between the Italian and other legal cultures. In the same period, Carlo Fusaro, editor-in-chief of *Quaderni Costituzionali*, one the most renowned journals of constitutional law in Italy, began to publish essays and short commentaries in English, Spanish and French. In 2014, Alessandra De Luca and Alessandro Simoni edited *Fundamentals of Italian Law* (Giuffrè) which contains an overview of the constitutional system by Giovanni Tarli Barbieri and Veronica Federico. More recently, in 2016 and 2020, Vittoria Barsotti, Paolo G. Carozza, Marta Cartabia and Andrea Simoncini edited *Italian Constitutional Justice in Global Context* (OUP) and *Dialogues in*

© Wolters Kluwer Italia

Italian Constitutional Justice: A comparative perspective (Giappichelli/Routledge). Finally, in 2022, Marta Cartabia and Nicola Lupo edited *The Constitution of Italy: A Contextual Analysis* (Hart), a volume which has deeply inspired the overall structure and the method of this handbook as envisaged by the authors.

Although the content of this book is original and differs from the works mentioned above, it shares a great deal with them, in particular as regards its international perspective and its collaborative methodology. It is no accident that many of the authors of the works mentioned above, as well as those of this book, are active participants in the International Society of Public Law (ICON·S) and its young and vibrant Italian Chapter (ICON·S Italy).

References have been selected in the light of the following criteria. Together with several works considered classics of Italian scholarship on public and constitutional law, the authors have cited the most important publications that have been written in English by Italian authors. In line with the objectives of the book and the target readership, these references offer readers the opportunity to delve further into the literature on Italian Constitutional Law, with the aim of proposing a list of the most representative contributions.

On the assumption that particular attention has to be paid to the case law of the Italian Constitutional Court, each Part deals extensively with its decisions, in order to highlight their contribution to the development of the Italian legal order and the cross-border significance of some of its doctrines and techniques. An English translation of a selection of the most important decisions of the Italian Constitutional Court is available and constantly updated on the Court's website (www.cortecostituzionale.it).

In addition to the contributors listed below, the authors would also like to thank Stefano Civitarese, Adriano Dirri, Pietro Faraguna, Massimo Fichera, Silvia Filippi, Justin O. Frosini, Nicola Lupo, Stefano Osella, Simone Penasa, Cesare Pinelli, and Mario Savino, for their very useful readings, comments, feedback and suggestions. The English used by the authors was revised by Interlanguage s.r.l. and Traducendo Ltd. The final overall reading by Patrick Leech was invaluable.

As it has already been noted, this work emerged from the extensive teaching experience of the authors. Giovanni Piccirilli expresses his gratitude to Leonard Besselink, who teaches Constitutional Law 2 with him at LUISS University. Special thanks to Carolina Moretti and Vittorio Leozappa, who attended the course that Giovanni and Leonard taught and provided an extensive and systematic version of the notes taken during the academic year 2021/2022. Diletta Tega wishes to thank Micol Pignataro, passionate and generous tutor of the Constitutional

 © Wolters Kluwer Italia

Law and Global Perspectives course, for the inspiring exchange of ideas regarding the conception of Part IV. This Part is also the result of research carried out under the project Prin 2017 'Where is Europe going? Paths and perspectives of the European federalizing process' (2017PFF2SN).

Stefania Ninatti, Giovanni Piccirilli,
Giorgio Repetto and Diletta Tega

Contributors

Alberto Arcuri is Adjunct Professor of Constitutional Law at the University of Bologna and Post-doc Researcher at the Sant'Anna School of Advanced Studies of Pisa. He is the Author of Part IV, Section C, §§ 3, 3.a., 4., 4.a.

Francesco Bilancia is Full Professor of Public Law at the Sapienza University of Rome. He is Author of Part I, Section B.

Maria Elena Gennusa is Associate Professor of Constitutional Law at the University of Pavia. She is the Author of Part III, Section B, § 1.

Barbara Guastaferro is Associate Professor of Constitutional Law at the University of Naples Federico II. She coauthored together with Diletta Tega Part IV, Section C, §§ 1., 5.e., 5.f.

Giacomo Menegus is Assistant Professor of Constitutional Law at the University of Macerata. He is the Author of Part II, Section B, §§ 4-4.d., and Section C.

Stefania Ninatti is Full Professor of Constitutional Law at the University of Milano-Bicocca. She is the Author of Part III, Section A, § 1, Section B, § 3.

Giovanni Piccirilli is Associate Professor of Constitutional Law at LUISS University of Rome. He is the Author of Part II except for Section B, §§ 4-4.d., and Section C.

Micol Pignataro is PhD candidate and Teaching tutor at the University of Bologna. She is the Author of Part IV, Section C, § 2.a.

Giorgio Repetto is Associate Professor of Public Law at the University of Perugia. He is the Author of Part I, Sections A, C, D and E.

Palmina Tanzarella is Associate Professor of Constitutional Law at the University of Milano-Bicocca. She is the Author of Part III, Section C, § 1.

Diletta Tega is Full Professor of Constitutional Law at the University of Bologna. She is the Author of Part IV, Sections A, B and C (except for §§ 2.a, 3, 3.a, 3.b, 4., 4.a). She coauthored together with Barbara Guastaferro Part IV, Section C, §§ 1., 5.e, 5.f.

Paolo Zicchittu is Associate Professor of Constitutional Law at the University of Milano-Bicocca. He is the Author of Part III, Section A, § 2., Section B, § 2., Section C, § 2.

AUTHORS

Stefania Ninatti (1968) is Full Professor of Constitutional Law at the University of Milano-Bicocca. She taught in English Public Law, Advanced Constitutional Law and Transitional Justice and State Building. She received a 2-year postgraduate fellowship at the Albert Ludwigs University of Freiburg and was Emile Noël Fellow at the Jean Monnet Center for International and Regional Economic Law & Justice, New York University. In 2015 she was awarded the role of Module Leader on the Jean Monnet Module pertaining to «Religious Pluralism and European Integration». Her first book, *How do our judges conceive of democracy? The democratic nature of the community decision-making process under scrutiny of the European Court of Justice* [*Giudicare la democrazia? Processo politico e ideale democratico nella giurisprudenza della Corte di giustizia*] was published in 2004. Her second monograph, focusing on family matters that are analysed from the perspective of the interaction between different constitutional traditions and the EU legal system [*Ai confini dell'identità costituzionale. Dinamiche familiari e integrazione europea*], was published in 2012.

Giovanni Piccirilli (1981) is Associate Professor of Constitutional Law at the Department of Law at LUISS Guido Carli University of Rome, where he teaches Constitutional Law 2, in English. In 2016 he was awarded the role of Module Leader on the Jean Monnet Module pertaining to «Legislative drafting in implementing EU law in Italy». He was Emile Noël Fellow at the Jean Monnet Center for International and Regional Economic Law & Justice, New York University. He has written two monographs; the first, on amendment procedures in the Italian Parliament [*L'emendamento nel processo di decisione parlamentare*], was published in 2008 and won the annual prize of Italian Constitutional Law Association in 2010, whilst the second, focused on the role of legislation in the European public space [*La «riserva di legge». Evoluzioni costituzionali, influenze sovrastatuali*], was published in 2019. In collaboration with Nicola Lupo, he edited the collection *The Italian Parliament in the European Union*, published in 2017.

Giorgio Repetto (1978) is Associate Professor of Public Law at the Department of Law at the University of Perugia, where he teaches Constitutional Law and, in English, European Constitutional Law. Law clerk at the Italian Constitutional Court, he has been a visiting scholar at the Universities Humboldt (Berlin) and Freiburg im Breisgau. He is co-director of the *Rivista di diritti comparati* and is member of the Editorial Board of *Diritto pubblico*. His first monograph

© Wolters Kluwer Italia

examined the role of comparative law in the case law of the courts of Luxembourg and Strasbourg [*Argomenti comparativi e diritti fondamentali in Europa. Teorie dell'interpretazione e giurisprudenza sovranazionale*]: published in 2011, it won the annual prize 'Sergio Panunzio' of the Italian Constitutional Law Association in 2011. He authored a second monograph on the transformations of constitutional justice in Italy [*Il canone dell'incidentalità costituzionale. Trasformazioni e continuità nel giudizio sulle leggi*], published in 2017.

Diletta Tega (1973) is Full Professor of Constitutional Law at the Department of Legal Studies of the University of Bologna where she teaches in English Global Constitutional Law and Constitutional Law and Global Perspectives. She is co-president of ICON-S Italy. She clerked at the Italian Constitutional Court. She was also Emile Noël Fellow at the Jean Monnet Center for International and Regional Economic Law & Justice, New York University. She held a *Max Planck Fellowship* at the Max Planck for comparative public law and international law in Heidelberg. She has held the position of Italian legal junior expert for the EU Fundamental Rights Agency. Her first book, *Rights in Crisis* [*I diritti in crisi*], published in 2012, presented a critical appraisal of the relationship between constitutional courts and the ECtHR. Her second book, *The Constitutional Court in Context* [*La Corte nel contesto*], published in 2020, proposed an original analysis of the role played in the legal system by the Court.

Part I

Italy and its Constitution
A Survey on the Fundamentals

The Italian Constitution of 1948 historically and conceptually belongs to the category of **democratic and pluralistic constitutions**. The commitment to popular sovereignty, established in Article 1, is made effective by a wide set of rules, principles and institutions aimed at safeguarding the primacy of **popular will** while firmly maintaining the centrality of the protection of **fundamental rights** and the **separation of powers**. The defining trait of the Constitution is its higher law nature, which is rooted in both its formal character (rigidity, as a device guaranteed by the Constitutional Court) and its material contents, the inviolability of rights (Article 2) and the principle of equality (Article 3), above all.

This Part deals with its characteristics by focusing on the regulation of different constitutional matters, so as to give a wide account of the functioning of the constitutional system and to introduce the reader to the following parts of this Handbook.

The main scope of the following analysis is to critically outline the main topics of Italian Constitutional Law, in order to show the mutual **implications** between the evolution of democracy in Italy and the capacity of the Constitution as a legal rule to both regulate the **political process** and to safeguard the conditions for making **fundamental rights** and the **separation of powers** effective.

Compared with other European countries like France, Germany and the UK, Italy turned into democracy relatively late: the right to vote was granted to women only in 1946.

The Constitution entered into force in 1948 has to regulate a mass democracy with legal devices which were quite unprecedented in the Italian system, like the President of the Republic, the Constitutional Court, the regional system and a fully-fledged catalogue of fundamental rights, including civil, political and social rights.

This required the Constitution to progressively gain an autonomous role in both the political and the legal debate.

On the one hand, the success of the Italian Constitution is closely linked with its capacity to reflect the different aspirations and value-systems of different **political cultures** represented in the Constituent Assembly (the Christian-catholic, the socialist and the liberal), while not entirely coinciding with a pre-given set of political, cultural and religious beliefs. On the other hand, the Constitution has proved to be a viable set of rules and principles able to progressively change and transform the Italian **legal landscape**, thanks to the combination of parliamentary enhancement of constitutional principles and of judicial enforcement of fundamental rights, in particular after the establishment of the Constitutional Court in 1956.

On these premises, in **Section A** a brief outline of Italian constitutional history is made, moving from the assumption that the Constitution of 1948 was adopted as a reaction to both the liberal era and to the fascist regime.

Section B deals with the basic principles of the Constitution and focuses on the value-system established therein as the normative core of the Constitution itself.

In **Section C**, the Constitution is considered from the perspective of its legal force: as a source of law that has deeply transformed the entire system of legal sources, moving from a renewed notion of legality and the attribution of law-making power to different entities.

Section D explores democracy and the separation of powers as the main features of the Italian form of government, in which the leading role of Parliament has to coexist with a wide range of further political and neutral institutions.

In **Section E**, the role and the functions of the Judiciary and the Constitutional Court are taken into account, in order to shed light on the lively contribution of judges in the enforcement of the Constitution.

 © Wolters Kluwer Italia

A) CONSTITUTIONAL HISTORY

1. The Unification Process and the 1848 Charter

From its early beginning, the Italian constitutional experience has been strongly intertwined with European history and legal culture. Even before emerging as a unitary state in 1861, Italian constitutional foundations were deeply rooted in several efforts aimed at activating a process of **national state-building**. Such efforts, which took place on different occasions (from the intellectual adventure of Niccolò Machiavelli to the different ephemeral *repubbliche* established in the aftermath of the French Revolution), have always been inspired by the idea that any constitutional regime was dependent on the issue of the establishment of a national unity (Saitta 1964). While striving for unification, great attention has been constantly paid to the constitutional settings that emerged and developed in different European countries (principally France and Britain), where the basic premises of modern constitutional law (from the separation of powers and the rule of law to the protection of individual rights) have been the object of wider and more intense discussion.

The struggle for a constitution and the quest for unification converged in the Kingdom of Piedmont/Sardinia, whose King, Carlo Alberto, decided to concede a newly established constitutional charter, the **Albertine Statute** (*Statuto Albertino*), in the aftermath of the 1848 revolutions. This Constitution belonged to the group of 'conceded' constitutions (*constitutions octroyées*), in that they had been introduced by the sovereign in order to find a compromise with new social classes (the *bourgeoisie*) claiming rights such as liberty, property and political representation. The *Statuto Albertino* was drafted by seeking a direct connection with the French (1830) and Belgian (1831) constitutions, whose main contents in the field of the relationships between the King and the Parliament and of individual rights were, for the most part, slightly adapted to the characters of a (then) small regional entity.

When the Kingdom of Sardinia became the Kingdom of Italy in 1861, the *Statuto Albertino* operated as the constitutional charter for the **newly established State** and remained formally in force (or, at least, some of its clauses) until the end of the Monarchy, in 1948.

© Wolters Kluwer Italia

The *Statuto* aimed originally at codifying the basic governmental structures of a **constitutional monarchy**, according to which the **King** enjoyed a preeminent position *vis-à-vis* other institutions, with particular regard to the Parliament elected by the people. According to Article 3, the legislative function was exercised by the King jointly with the two Chambers of Parliament, the *Camera dei deputati* (elected by the people with very limited suffrage), and the *Senato*, whose members were appointed by the King himself. The King had both a right of veto (*sanzione*, Article 7) and was fully entitled to dissolve the *Camera dei deputati* (Article 9). Moreover, the King was exclusively charged with executive power, in that he appointed and revoked the Ministers (Article 58), who were politically responsible since every governmental act, though formally pertaining to the King, had to be countersigned by them (Article 67). Lastly, even the Judiciary was not an autonomous power: judges were appointed by the King and were organisationally dependent upon the executive.

Although the Preamble of the Albertine Statute defined itself as the «fundamental, irrevocable and perpetual law of the Monarchy», its rules and its function showed a high degree of **flexibility and adaptation** to the changing contexts. The *Statuto*, like the other constitutional charters adopted in the same period, belongs in the category of those constitutions that remained open to every amendment contained in the ordinary legislation, since it did not prescribe any *ad-hoc* amendment procedure. The flexible nature of its rules had to coexist with the unchangeable structure of the constitutional agreement enshrined therein; *i.e.*, sovereignty belonged to the King (and not to the people), although he was deemed to be bound not to reintroduce the structures of the absolute State (MARTUCCI 2002).

The flexible nature of the *Statuto* proved to be a tool that could adapt the legal framework established by it to the reality of a new State. In the years that followed the unification process, the above-mentioned structure of the constitutional monarchy was called into question by the emergence of **social classes and regulatory problems** arising from the new national entity. This led to a reshaping of the previous balance of powers, in that the Parliament (though elected by a small percentage of the population) sought to find an institutional relationship with the Government by transforming the responsibility of Ministers before the King into a **parliamentary responsibility**. Although this transformation was not unchallenged, it paved the way to an evolutionary approach to the Italian form of government, which remained basically centred upon the dual structure of a **parliamentary monarchy**, in which the exercise of political power is shared between the King and the *Camera dei deputati*, as elected directly by the people (FIORAVANTI 2021).

© Wolters Kluwer Italia

An analysis of the rights and liberties protected by the Albertine Statute suggests that partial responses and shortcomings are more evident than the ones concerning the form of government. According to its liberal premises, the *Statuto* focuses on **equality before the law**, individual **liberty** and the 'sacred' nature of **property** as the three cornerstones of the relationships between the individual and public authority. Despite the proclamation of 'equality before the law', in many different ambits, the ordinary legislation could freely limit the enjoyment of (mainly) political rights to a certain part of the population. The right to vote, in particular, remained largely confined to a small percentage of the (male) population: in 1882, only 2% of Italian citizens were entitled to vote in the election of the members of the *Camera dei deputati*. Moreover, within the small range of protected rights, no attention was paid to **collective liberties**, such as freedom of association, which was deemed to be largely incompatible with the need of the liberal State to disadvantage the creation of collective entities acting between the individual and the State.

More generally, the flexible nature of the *Statuto*, the limited range of individual protected rights, and the dualist structure of government converged towards a certain idea of liberty that the liberal State in Italy was called to preserve. Many rights were protected by the *Statuto* by simply demanding that the legislation established limits to their enjoyment; exceptions to citizens' equality (Article 24), limits to individual liberty (Article 26), to the inviolability of the home (Article 27) and to the freedom of the press (Article 28) could all be settled 'pursuant the law'. Such a guarantee was crucial in that, while **reserving these ambits to the ordinary legislation** (*riserva di legge*), it prevented the executive power and its regulations from intruding on the lives, liberties and properties of citizens. On the other hand, this guarantee remained almost virtual, since the *Statuto* could be derogated by ordinary laws, to the extent that no effective **access to justice** was given against parliamentary acts infringing upon individual rights.

The enforcement of the *Statuto* showed, over the decades, a growing distance from the liberal model that it was originally called upon to enhance. The role of Parliament was challenged on several occasions and several efforts were made to **restore the exclusive power of the King** to appoint and revoke Ministers, as well as to dissolve Parliament without any restrictions. The most acute crisis took place between 1897 and 1900, when social protests spreading over the country led to the declaration of a state of *siége* and the re-establishment of the traditional authority of the King was invoked as a strategy to mitigate against incoming social crisis originating in workers' movements. Against this background, a new liberal-authoritarian model entered the scene; moving away from the influence exerted by the French and Belgian *Chartes*, the legal approach to rights and liberties showed a growing commitment to the German approach according to which they are nothing but a reflex of the autonomous will of the State to limit itself (*i.e.* the exercise of public power). Citizens could invoke the respect of the rule of law against governmental acts before the **administrative tribunals** (established in 1889) but were deprived of any possibility to challenge the constitutionality of parliamentary legislation (ALLEGRETTI 1989).

2. Mass Democracy and the Failure of the Liberal State

The adaptive capacity of the Italian constitutional system was only partially able to deal with the changing social and political conditions related to the transformations of European national systems before and after **World War I**.

As Santi Romano, a prominent legal theorist, wrote in 1909, the whole edifice of the modern State, as defined by the legal conditions of sovereignty, autonomy and self-sufficiency, was shaken from the inside by the vast array of **associations and workers' unions** that sought to promote the interests of given classes and groups. In this way, they were suspected of dismantling the (fictitious) general interest related to the sovereignty of the State. The emergence of these groups and classes, while advocating political representation, called for legal and political responses that made public intervention more and more necessary, with the result that the unitary nature of the State was endangered by the necessity to give sectional responses to unprecedented problems.

In the same years, dominated by the political figure of Giovanni Giolitti, Italy faced a process of modernisation of its **administrative** and **economic structure**, largely depending upon legislative reforms and stronger state intervention in the economy. New legislation in the field of state schools (1904) and of the judiciary (1907), along with the establishment of public organisations charged with the task of carrying out public services (railroads, social assistance, insurance), significantly enlarged the State's action and favoured the inclusion of new social categories within public structures.

Moreover, the enlargement of the right to vote to the generality of male citizens in 1912 and the adoption of a proportional voting system in 1919 paved the way for a deep transformation of both the political system and the institutional machinery. Political representation proved to be able to include groups and categories (like Catholics and workers) that had remained, until then, outside of the political arena. These sudden transformations could only partially be reconciled with a legal framework that was not designed to be compatible with **mass democracy**.

 © Wolters Kluwer Italia

Against this background, the response given by the political *élites* of the time was a further effort to restore the traditional authority of the Monarchy by entrusting the Fascist Party with the power to lead a government in 1922. In a few years, the weak structure of the liberal State, legally based on the Albertine Statute, was entirely replaced by an **authoritarian regime** that progressively eliminated other political parties and suppressed rights and liberties.

Even though the *Statuto Albertino* remained formally in force until 1948, the **fascist regime** introduced significant modifications into the constitutional framework. The law-making power of the Government had been increasing since 1926, along with the progressively decreasing role of Parliament, whose election (with regard to the *Camera dei deputati*) amounted (from 1923 onwards) to plebiscitary suffrage because of the suppression of other political parties and the hyper-majoritarian rule of voting. The constitutional ambitions of the fascist regime were fully coherent with its authoritarian premises in that they aimed to substitute liberal structures with new institutions representing the Fascist Party, such as the **Gran Consiglio del Fascismo** (which substantially superseded the Parliament in many important functions) and the **corporatist system**, a newly established set of rules and bodies that were called to regulate economic life in accordance with the basic needs of the autarchical State.

3. The Constituent Assembly: Method and Legacy

The **collapse** of the fascist regime in 1943 led both to a temporary re-expansion of the role of the King and to the re-emergence of political parties. In the last years of World War II, those parties that had been more actively engaged in the fight against fascism gained increasing importance in that they became *de facto* institutions whose main task was to provide basic organisation to those parts of the country where the traditional authority of the State had disappeared.

Primarily because of their role in promoting the ***Resistenza*** against Nazism and Fascism, **political parties** suddenly became the main actors in the process leading to the election of the Constituent Assembly.

On 2nd of June, 1946, the Italian people voted by universal **suffrage (including women)** for the election of the members of the Constituent Assembly and the dissolution of the Monarchy and the creation of a Republic. Such a doubly popular decision ratified the central nature of those political parties which were most actively engaged in the fight against fascism (such as Christian Democrats, socialists and communists, and liberals) who were, for the most part, in favour of a new **republican setting**.

The discussion taking place in the **Constituent Assembly** (*Assemblea costituente*) was entirely dependent upon the **method** that the different parties converged upon to establish the principal framework of the new constitutional system. Despite sharp ideological and political conflicts running between these parties, they proved to be able to find a wide-ranging **compromise** between different cultural and political options, including the main ideological tenets that were common to the Christian (in particular), liberal and socialist political and social thought.

Two good examples of this can be identified in the debates concerning two of the main pillars of the constitutional order which was introduced: the **system of rights and liberties** and the **form of government**.

Concerning the system of rights, the sharp contrasts between the parties and the respective solutions that they lobbied for, in terms of the balance between individual liberty and social equality, found mediation in a resolution (*ordine del giorno*), advanced by **Giuseppe Dossetti** in the First Subcommittee of the Constituent Assembly on September 1946:

> The Subcommittee,
>
> after examining the possible systematic approaches to a declaration of human rights,
>
> after excluding the one which is inspired by a purely **individualistic** vision, after excluding that which is inspired by a **totalitarian** vision, which traces the attribution of the rights of individuals and communities to the State, believes that the only approach that is truly compatible with the historical data that the new statute of democratic Italy must comply with is the one which:
>
> a) recognises the substantial **precedence of the human person** (understood as the whole of his or her material as well as spiritual values and needs) as opposed to the State and the purpose of the State to serve the human person;
>
> b) recognises, at the same time, the necessary **sociality of all of the people**, who are destined to complement and perfect each other, through mutual economic and spiritual solidarity: first of all, in various intermediate communities arranged according to natural gradualism (family, territorial, professional, religious communities, etc.) and secondly, for everything in which these communities are not enough, in the State;
>
> c) affirms the existence of both the fundamental **rights of persons** and of the **rights of the communities** before any concession by the State.

This statement proved to be a viable compromise because it favoured the convergence of the different parties on a framework of rights and liberties that, while rejecting the previous liberal non-interventionism as well as State-dominance,

 © Wolters Kluwer Italia

was centred upon the pre-eminence of the **human person** and upon **social pluralism** to create the necessary preconditions to pursue **social equality**.

In terms of the form of government, the main debate centred upon the need to eschew the problems associated with classical, liberal parliamentarism (which was historically charged with powerlessness before the rise of authoritarian regimes) and the fear of a disproportionately strong executive power.

A compromise was found in the Second Subcommittee of the Constituent Assembly, also in September 1946, thanks to a mediation proposed by **Tomaso Perassi**:

> The Second Subcommittee, […],
>
> considering that neither the presidential government nor the directorial government would respond to the conditions of Italian society, pronounces itself for the adoption of the **parliamentary system** to be regulated with constitutional devices capable of protecting the needs of stability of government action and to avoid the **degenerations of parliamentarism**.

This statement was not meant to provide a general solution to the many regulatory problems of a parliamentary democracy that Italy had, until then, never experienced. As will become apparent in Section D, many issues concerning the relationships between political institutions have given rise to several disputes, with peculiar regard to the claims concerning the stability of government action and the centrality of Parliament. Despite this, the solutions regarding the form of government provided by the Constituent Assembly proved to be able to adapt to a changing context and favoured the affirmation of Italy as a mature **representative democracy**.

The discussions and conflicts emerging from the Constituent Assembly, and the related centrality of political parties left a significant **legacy** for the subsequent constitutional experience in Italy, involving the irreversible nature of the achievements related to the general principles of the Constitutions, such as popular sovereignty, the coexistence of liberty and equality, and social and institutional pluralism. The legacy of this experience is the awareness that democratic self-governance is possible from opposing starting points and cultural positions on condition that the balance between liberty and authority is achieved by following the Constitution's principles and procedures (Cheli 1978).

4. The 1948 Italian Constitution Today: Continuity and Transformation

Though Italy, unlike other European countries, lacked any democratic background in 1948, the Constitution delivered by the Constituent Assembly gained

© Wolters Kluwer Italia

a steadily increasing level of institutional and popular **acceptance**. Due to its rigid nature (*i.e.*, the provision of an *ad-hoc* amendment procedure), it has been capable of offering guidance in the renewing and adaptation of a legal order that was, from the beginning, largely inconsistent with the basic principles enshrined therein.

In the early decades of the Republic, the Constitution operated as a fundamental legal yardstick to activate a process of the legislative and judicial **enactment** of its main principles. The vast array of constitutional principles and values established in the first 12 articles (Fundamental Principles) and in Part I of the Constitution (entitled 'Rights and Duties of Citizens') have enabled both parliamentary law-making and the Constitutional Court to find a reference for their respective roles of legislative enhancement and judicial enforcement of the Constitution (Bartole 2012).

This process has been progressively influenced by the membership of Italy in the **European Union**, from the beginning. As will be extensively considered in Part II, both in law-making and (especially) in judicial applications, the basic choices enshrined in the Constitution have had to interact with the politico-institutional and judicial machinery established by the European Treaties. From the 1970s in particular, the 1948 Constitution worked increasingly as an **entrenched Constitution**, in that its enforcement and application were strongly influenced by European Union law, particularly after the Constitutional Court declared (in 1973) that Article 11 of the Constitution, by accepting «limitations of sovereignty» in view of the establishment of a legal order promoting «peace and justice among Nations», can be referred to the EU legal order (Judgment No. 183/1973).

The **adaptive capacity** of the Constitution is even more demonstrable if one refers to its Part II, which is dedicated to the 'Organisation of the Republic'.

The form of government and, indeed, the discipline of the relationships between political institutions, have undergone massive evolutionary transformations affecting both the structure and the function of political parties. As the experience of the Constituent Assembly faded, and the political leaders acting within it left the scene, **compromise-driven politics** has been progressively substituted by a highly **competitive party system**, that has increasingly raised many concerns about its capacity to grant stability to the political system (Ragone/D'Amico 2023 at 284).

Despite the growing weaknesses of political parties, the evolution of an institutional system has emphasised the increasing role played by **neutral institutions** such as the President of the Republic and, more recently, the Constitutional Court, as well as the growing importance of the actors of territorial pluralism,

 © Wolters Kluwer Italia

such as Regions and local authorities (particularly after the 2001 constitutional amendment affecting Title V).

B) THE BASIC PRINCIPLES OF THE CONSTITUTION

1. Introduction

A constitution is many things at the same time. In a focused consideration of the State constitution in the aftermath of World War II, attention must be paid to at least three different issues. The *constitution* is what *constitutes* the nation State after death and disruption and, in the Italian case, after a civil war and a revolution as well as the dissolution of the liberal Monarchy. The constitution is, then, at the same time, the **fundamental law** of the new republican order and a legal tool for the foundation of the new legal system. Additionally, of equal importance, it is a political document: an instrument of social, political, legal and economic transformation of civil society and political systems. As many other constitutions implemented after the end of the World War II, particularly in contexts in which the end of the war also meant the end of a totalitarian state, the Italian Constitution was the founding instrument for a new **republican democracy**, born through a popular insurrection, but driven by a legal process, framed by political parties and organised in a transitional legal path. The Italian Constitution was born as a consequence of a democratic process, based on significant popular participation, the first real appearance of **mass democracy** evidence in Italy.

This popular movement was ruled by a **legal framework** designed to drive the transition from the fascist regime to the new legal order through an appropriate constitutional process. The legal and political contents of the Italian Constitution were founded on these premises, and also on the fact that the occupying Allied Forces allowed the Italian political parties, formed in continuity with the resistance struggle (*Lotta di Resistenza*) against fascism and nazism, to be fully involved in the writing and approving the new constitutional instrument.

As a political document, therefore, the Italian Constitution contains a range of fundamental principles, framing the new legal system and calling for a radical transformation of the material order and the concrete living conditions of the populace. Political, fundamental and constitutional principles were now married to a **normative structure**, yearning for a radical transformation both of the social and the legal system; **freedom**, civil **liberties**, **equality** and **social transformation** tied together in an institutional framework inspired by **democracy** and individual participation, political rights and **pluralism**, characterising, at the same time, the social and the institutional layers. This was a constitutional system open to the international legal order, founded on **multilateralism**, **peace**, common values, the international **rule of law**, **popular sovereignty** and the self-determination of nations.

The content of the Italian Constitution is, then, from its first articles, substantially inspired by these principles, inscribed as legal commitments and binding together the institutional system. In the next few paragraphs, the most important of these principles will be considered: **popular sovereignty**, the primacy of the **human person** and her inviolable **rights** of **liberty and equality**, social **pluralism** and collective liberties, **constitutional democracy**, institutional pluralism, regional and local autonomy, protection of **minorities**, multilateralism and the **international dimension** of the constitutional order and the protection of **peace**.

2. Popular Sovereignty

Denis Galligan, while dealing with the important issue of the relationship between political representation, democracy and the constitution, observed that «the universal problem is how a people can both govern itself and have effective government» (Galligan 2013 at 154). The question arising from this point is how to relate the democratic issue with the capacity of constitutional institutions to rule the people through an effective system of government. The challenge lies with popular sovereignty and **democracy** on the one hand, with **effective government** and the constitutional rule of law on the other. This needs to be addressed to design an institutional machinery and a constitutional system of government that should be at the same time, both effective and democratic.

Firstly, what is meant by the expression '**popular sovereignty**'? Article 1 of the Constitution reads: «Italy is a democratic Republic, founded on labour. Sovereignty belongs to the people, which shall exercise it in the manner and forms and within the limits of the Constitution». Sovereignty, then, which traditionally defines power, force, domination and statehood as State sovereignty, has transitioned to *popular* sovereignty. What does this shift from State to people mean?

The transition from state sovereignty to popular sovereignty was a profound movement of political power from an historical entity (*i.e.*, the Monarch), to the State and then on to the people. More precisely, this power (also strength, force, *krátos*) while being allocated to a different subject, the people, undergoes a transformation depending upon the substance and nature of its destination. Moving from a monocratic to a pluralistic structure, from the King to the people, the distribution of power becomes something completely different. Such power, strength, force, once concentrated on a single entity, the monarch, and then the

 © Wolters Kluwer Italia

State, become fragmented and distributed among millions of people; the citizens (FERRARA 2000). What was once a concentration of material strength in one single entity, is now a collective bargaining among **the many**. Moved by the dissemination of that force and power among the people, a distinctive idea of sovereignty must be established by a necessarily collective reality of individual **political liberties**.

The understanding of sovereignty which emerges can be clearly inferred in the wording of Article 1, which, after saying that popular sovereignty belongs to the people, then specifies that it has to be exercised «in the forms and within the limits» of the Constitution. To reflect the will (perhaps better defined as the 'interests') of all the individuals that form the people to let the people rule, procedural machinery has to be implemented, with decision-making processes established through legal constitutional instruments. This brings attention to a very important consequence of the transformation of sovereignty within a constitutional framework: **democracy**, in a constitutional legal context, meaning the power of the people itself, has to be necessarily shaped and limited by functioning legal arrangements to be, and remain, **'constitutional'**. One of the most important tools that constitutionalism has been fostering through the last two centuries has been the limitation and **separation of powers**, meaning any power, beginning with the legitimate institutional organs of the State. This includes any institutional instrument legally in force, even if democratically legitimised. People sovereignty, designed by the Constitution, therefore, has to be framed within the institutional machinery, organs and procedures of the State and respect the constitutional limits provided for any power involved.

It should be briefly noted that, while criticising **populism** from a legal point of view, scholars generally agree on the specific character that all of the varied and diversified experiences of populist movements around the world have in common: they interpret the role of the will of the people, the abstract idea of the people ruling the political system, as something distinct from any constitutional ideology. No legal framework, no limitations, and no instruments implementing the principle of division of powers are ever considered possible if they threaten the people's power and the popular will. Populism is, therefore, characterised by the idea that popular sovereignty must be represented without any legal constitutional boundaries.

3. The Primacy of the Human Person

As already considered, the historical origin of the Italian Constitution and its implementation, due to the convergence of different political cultures and ideologies, has brought together different political patterns and values as the foundations for its basic principles. Italian constitutional scholarship generally recognises that the central role of the individual, the primacy of the **human person**, both in the social and the political system, is a derivative of Catholic culture alongside liberal ideology. This is especially true because of the preceding totalitarian regime: to dispose of the deplorable ideology and 'legal' consequences on human rights of fascism, the framers of the Constitution chose to build the new constitutional regime and its institutional framework based upon the centrality of the human person. This is why, for example, personal rights and individual liberties are framed in the first part of the Constitution, ahead of considerations about the Republican institutional order, in Part II (Articles 55, ff.). From a symbolic perspective, this also demonstrates the ideological primacy and the constitutional prevalence of the human person over the republican State and institutions; the human person is first and is central in the constitutional normative hierarchy itself.

This fundamental principle is clearly established in Article 2, which expresses that «[t]he Republic recognises and guarantees the **inviolable rights** of man, both as an individual and as a member of the social groups in which his personality finds expression, and it requires the compliance with unavoidable political, economic, and social duties». The expression 'recognises and guarantees' points back to a sense of natural law: the pre-existence of personal rights, even in democracy and the republican legal system. The centrality of the human being, the very fundamental position of **individual rights**, termed as inviolable, constituted one of the cornerstones of the Italian form of state, defining the entire institutional system as an instrument for implementing and protecting the individual and his or her fundamental rights. This is the set of driving principles from which the Constitution then built the basic relationships between individuals and **authority**.

Alongside the central position of the person, Article 2 also gives rise to the maximum extension of **social pluralism**. While the fascist regime allowed no room for any institutional arrangement between the individual and the State (or the 'single party'), leaving each citizen as an isolated addressee of state sovereignty and government power, the Constitution became open to the widest importance of every intermediate body, providing significant protection to individual liberties with collective exercise, beginning with the **freedom of association** (see especially Articles 18, 19, 31, 33, 39, 45 and 49) and any other associated body, from **family** to **school**, to **trade unions** and **political parties**, through religious communities, universities, and so on. Everything that a single person can do can also be done through associations (Article 18; on this, see *III.C).1.b*).

 © Wolters Kluwer Italia

Before analysing the communitarian and social relevance of constitutional rights, it is worth mentioning the last part of Article 2, in which individual unavoidable **duties** are also claimed. The role and position of each and every citizen within the social and political system designed by the Italian Constitution not only provides for the centrality of the human person and her protection from any kind of power, no matter whether public or private, it further guarantees against aggressions and restrictions of both individual and collective rights. The Constitution is aware of the importance of the social projection of the human being. As the Article 2 provision warns, being part of a social community, calling for the guarantee and respect of personal individual rights, cannot be intended as a formulation to design the position of every citizen as a selfish and self-referencing entity.

Rather, the new Constitution planned to build a new idea of **social community** along with a renewed institutional and political system, within a liberal legal order completely inspired by the most advanced doctrines of contemporary constitutionalism. Every citizen should make his or her part in designing an open society, inspired by their own personal involvement in the construction of a renewed social commonwealth that is participatory and open. This is why the Constitution also emphasises the **duties** with which citizens should comply, some of which are formally specified in other articles. As stated in the second part of Article 4, «[e]very citizen shall have the duty, according to personal potential and individual choice, to perform any activity or function contributing to the material or spiritual progress of society». In this context, it is also important to note Article 23, referring to the «obligations of a personal or a financial nature»; Article 52, detailing the duty of every citizen to defend the Motherland, Article 53, which establishes that «every person shall contribute to public expenditure in accordance with their capabilities» and Article 30, pointing to «the duty and right of parents to support, raise and educate their children».

4. Liberty and Equality

When speaking of liberty, the mind goes back to the bourgeois revolution of the eighteenth century, and the American and French revolutions. An initial interpretation of the term is that of freedom from the State's power and the monarch's sovereignty, tying freedom, instead, to the autonomy of the individual from any interference in individual **property** and **liberty** by the State. The importance of **independence** should also be noted, especially if the American revolution is taken into account as well as the significant consequences of the self-determining political rights that America claimed when separating from England. However, although very important and related to the conquest of individual liberty, the history of American nation-building and the federalist issue present in this specific political experience, will not be dealt with here.

The first point to consider concerning liberty, is its negative dimension; a theoretical issue that has to do with an absence, a space empty of State-related power actions – a citizen (better, still the subject of a State's) is free because the State's institutions do not interfere within the personal domain, allowing that domain to remain at the autonomous determination of that (male) individual. In considering the origin of 'freedoms' theory in European public law doctrine, going back to the works of Paul Laband and Georg Jellinek in the ninetenth century in which this **liberty** was interpreted as an untouched space, an **empty domain**, in which the State's institutions would not apply any restrictions to individual rights, it is clear that the very meaning of liberty is a concession given by the State's sovereignty. These doctrines used to speak of individual rights as the **State's self-limitation**, giving them their original 'negative' dimension. Going a little further, it is possible to see that to enjoy one's freedom as a space empty of legal State rules, a person should have needed the possibility to use a law-empty space, which meant being able to enjoy some **land property**. Therefore, in his own property, for that small minority of the populace enjoying land property, an individual could be protected from State's interference in her own rights, because of the irrelevance, in that space, of the legal order of the State and its acts of power. For this reason, these rights were called *Subjective Public Rights* (*subjektive öffentliche Rechte*), building a kind of peer reciprocity between the State and some of the individuals, while those liberties would have been understood, in more recent times, as belonging to the combination and interdependence of two different prerogatives: States and **landlords**.

As is clear, there was no room for State intervention to transform socio-economic reality, and no attention to **equality**, since the only way to enjoy individual rights was to be part of the landlord social class (as defined by later Marxist ideologies). What distinctively characterises the contemporary notion of constitutional rights and liberties is, on the contrary, the idea that they are fundamentally depending upon binding legal prescriptions, which make it compulsory for the State's legal system to guarantee and implement them through legislation and administrative action. Following the contemporary doctrines of constitutionalism, therefore, State institutions now have the duty to extend the enjoyment of these rights to **everyone**, regardless of the position held in the social community, thus prescribing a binding commitment to ensure that everyone obtains the **concrete entitlement** of these rights. The overcoming of the doctrine of subjective public rights by contemporary constitutional arrangements is one of the most evident consequences of the equality engagement that constitutionalist ideology

 © Wolters Kluwer Italia

began to deal with, challenging constitutional law to strengthen its responses to the claim of this principle. Equality started to be the background to constitutional rules, ensuring that the legal instruments were able to guarantee that the rights and liberties described by constitutional documents could become true for everyone within the polity.

It is usual to find the turning point of this very important constitutional evolution, both symbolically and historically, in the Weimar Constitution of 1919, the 'unfortunate' Constitution (Mortati 1946) born after the German revolution of 1918, and soon to be eclipsed by the advent of Nazism. In Article 153, dedicated to the protection of private property, it was stated that 'property obliges', bringing with it the necessity to legally consider, with the interests of the owner, the interests of those who do not have property. For the first time, it was established to entrust Parliament to **rule by law** on the contents of this right, to consider not only the interest of the owner, but also those of the **others** (and, indeed, the **general interest)**. It is not possible, however, to understand the importance of this prescription if account is not taken of the fact that Parliament, the legislature entrusted with the task to define the meaning of **property rights**, had now become a body representing all the people, not only the bourgeoisie and the landlords. This is worth noting, as legislatures, from then on (with the exceptions of the European dictatorships of the twentieth century), consist of representatives of **the entire people**, being transformed from a single-class institution into a **mass-democratic** one, representing every social class (although, still for some decades, only half of the real population had the right to vote, as women were precluded, despite the fact that Germany had provided for the electoral suffrage for women in 1918). This is how equality started to evolve through the Constitution, entrusting the institutional system with stronger and more adequate instances of democracy. Mass democracy began to challenge the State's sovereignty, while those once excluded from Government started to develop a voice, to be centrally considered in terms of their needs, both legal and material.

This also marks the point where **liberty** encountered **equality,** bringing with it, together with the dissemination of its values and contents, a transformation of its real substance, implying the necessity of the State's intervention to ensure entitlement and guarantees to **every citizen and person**. It can be seen that, at the end of this evolution, the meaning and essence of rights and liberties became a ***positive*** **commitment** of the State's legal order. In this sense, with a new positive structure substituting the old negative one, once the contents of these rights turned out to be the substantive prescription of **binding legal rules**, the simple absence of State's interference in the property space was over.

Here is where the real meaning of the words of Sandro Pertini, once leader of the Italian Resistance Movement, then President of the Republic, can be found:

> There cannot be true freedom, without social justice, as well as there cannot be real social justice without any freedom… How can a man be considered really free, when he starves, lives in poverty, is jobless, and is humiliated because he cannot feed and give an education to his own children? That is not what we can call a free man.

From this formulation of the principles of equality and social justice, many political and social conflicts would arise during the years of constitutional enforcement and implementation, when many pieces of legislation and Constitutional Court decisions would become the living Constitution of the first decades of Italian republican history (see *IV.C).1.*).

This is the point at which political and social **'equality'** started to overcome its traditional interpretation, as an objective principle called upon to characterise the legal system as a whole and became, first and foremost, an **individual right** (FERRARA 1974), an individual claim to be empowered, to become a real citizen, entitled with the same opportunities than others as a matter of chance.

Another issue of great importance to be noted is, of course, that **freedom from** all interference of public powers and institutions is still the first guarantee of individual liberty. In this sense, the call for **liberty** is also a call for **autonomy**, intended as the autonomy of each person in defining her own personal interests and decision-making. In this sense, moral agency brings with it legal agency, as free **self-determination** of the individual, and where no obstruction can legally be opposed by any power, whether public or private. The **protection** of liberty and its **implementation by law** is, however, even more important, in light of the true meaning of equality and for democracy to become reality as a system of conflicting interests to be selected, confronted and settled together as shared interests of the entire commonwealth. This is where **democracy** impacts upon liberty to give it the real sense of an egalitarian entitlement. Where, once again, the insight of one's autonomous rights and liberties becomes aware of the same rights and liberties of every other individual, the **equality** of all individuals is recognised. Constitutional rights are legally applied within a discourse of equality, which is why it is understood that equality is a constitutive element of democracy to be realised, and **solidarity** is an instrumental tool for it (reading together Articles 2, 3 and 4).

5. Pluralism

As the previous paragraph describes, the Constitution has at its core the human being, the person in every possible declination, regardless of the many possible

 © Wolters Kluwer Italia

facets and personal conditions. Of central importance is the relevance given to the **social dimension of the human being**, arising from the general attention given to the natural condition of individuals as existing within groups of different forms and significance. The reason for the particular attention given to intermediate groups and entities has already been attributed to the positive attitude assumed by the Constitutional Assembly regarding the importance of these bodies in the implementation of a multivarious and **plural citizenry**, moving in the opposite direction of fascism, which framed the individual in an isolated entity, subservient to the State and the single-party will. The totalitarian regime intended to control the entire life of every single person, and fight every kind of associated initiative to avoid letting individuals strengthen their position against the State and the 'single party': fascism banned political parties, unions and freedom of association, together with freedom of expression, the press and free involvement in public and political life. In sharp contrast, the framers of the 1948 Constitution were determined to give as much importance as possible to any form of socialisation and **group building** on any possible grounds.

The social dimension of rights and liberties is secured in Article 2, which clearly states that inviolable human rights shall be guaranteed both as individual rights, and «in the social groups where human personality is expressed». Therefore, the associated form of the exercise of civil liberties and constitutional rights, as well as the legal relevance of the social dimension of the human being, are guaranteed, protected and implemented in many different articles of the Italian Constitution. See, for example, Article 6, safeguarding **linguistic minorities;** Article 18, on **freedom of association**, together with Articles 39 and 49, on the freedom to form **trade unions** and **political parties**; Articles 19 and 20, on "the right to profess freely **religious faith** in any form, individually *or in association*, to disseminate it and to worship in private *or public*"; Articles 29 and ff., on the protection of **family rights;** Articles 33 ff., on the right to establish schools and institutions of education, and so on (see *III.C).2.b.1.*). The Italian Constitution gives the widest importance to every kind of association-related rights and liberties, whether they be trade unions, sporting associations, commercial companies, families, **universities** or **churches**, thereby protecting the rights and liberties of each individual within, and even against, those social group entities (*formazioni sociali*).

It is now important to point out that by designing a world composed of all kinds of associations and private entities that was not only allowed to exist but even promoted and implemented by the Republic, the Constitution fostered a very open and pluralistic society to be turned into reality through its rules, principles and values. This is a seminal issue to note when describing the Italian

Constitution's basic principles: it first creates a complex and **pluralistic social system**, to provide for a multifaceted (and plural) **institutional system**, interpreting the principle of the **separation of powers** in the most wide and structured way. In doing this, the Constitution establishes **local autonomies** and **Regions**, implementing autonomy and **decentralisation** in the State's services and legislatures (see Articles 5 and 117) and promoting **subsidiarity** and **differentiation** (Article 118).

Pluralism is designed as a structural pattern, and a value characterising both the social and the institutional systems. At the same time, a qualifying feature of the political life of the country is that it is to be enriched by giving space to any kind of interest and social and political attitude, and the Constitution allows social, cultural, religious, political and economic (see Articles 41 to 45) conflicts to be freely testified and promoted, to be synthesised and absorbed throughout its institutional and representative machinery. This specific element of the Italian constitutional design will be further analysed in Part III, which will also consider the importance of the **freedom of expression** and rights to form unions and political parties, to freely profess individual religious faiths, the freedom of the arts and sciences and the freedom to teach them.

Moving from Article 2 of the Constitution to Article 3, it is worth considering the very dimension in which any individual person's position within the constitutional system is conceived, in relation to others and the republican institutions and constitutional organs. The manner and form of political representation through the legislatures, both national and regional, will be analysed later. At this point, attention is paid to the importance of relating individual liberties with the principle of **equality**, to identify the importance of the interdependence between the **autonomy** of the individual and public intervention in the social domain, through the implementation of equality-related rights.

6. Democracy and its Variables: 'Founded on Labour'

As has already been described, Article 1 of the Constitution states that Italy is a **democratic Republic**, founded on labour. The meaning and content of the principle of popular sovereignty has already been considered, especially in relation to the expression «in the forms and within the limits of the Constitution». We have also clarified why, and to what extent, democracy has to be interpreted within the legal framework of the constitutional rule of law, in which political sovereignty may only be read as a plain constitutional issue if and when a process of legal settlement for controversial issues is provided. In this sense, we call it a 'constitutional democracy' (Carlassare 2005; Ferrara 2009). But, still, what is democracy?

 © Wolters Kluwer Italia

It should be remembered that, on 2nd of June, 1946, the Italian people voted with universal suffrage (eventually, and for the first time in Italian constitutional history, also including women) for both the election of the **Constituent Assembly** and for an **'institutional' referendum** to choose the form of the future Italian State. The Italian people voted for the republican form of State, with the consequent dissolution of the Monarchy. Thus, it can easily be inferred that the **Republic**, as opposed to **Monarchy**, means that the Head of State would have initially been elected, while the reign of the Savoia family was rejected by popular suffrage, and then neglected. With an elected President of the Republic to substitute the King, the new constitutional order provided for the old ruling class and aristocracy, once related to the royal house, to be dismissed and moved away from State institutions and political life (Articles XIII and XIV of the transitory and final provisions of the Italian Constitution). The meaning of the constitutional expression **'democratic Republic'**, which is used in Article 1 to establish the fundamental institutional arrangements of the Italian State, should also be considered. This formula must be read in strict connection with what is stated in Article 139, the final constitutional provision, as a set of legal limitations to the constitutional amendment power (see below *C).2.*). There, it is expressly stated that «[t]he Republican form shall not be a matter for constitutional amendment», calling again for a legal definition of what has to be meant as 'Republic'.

It is easy to understand that democracy and republic are sometimes used as near synonyms, where each comes to better define and specify the other, both having a reciprocal importance. In this way, a democratic Republic is a constitutional system in which not only the Head of State but every constitutional body involved in the system of government, starting with the legislature, shall have a democratic foundation, which means, in a mass democracy, a representative design and structure. Not only any constitutional amendment trying to reinstate the Monarchy, but also any attempt to eliminate or reduce the representative foundation of the system of government, should be qualified as unconstitutional.

But, still, what is democracy? As is widely known, the origin of this concept goes back to classical thought, to both classical Greece and Roman legal culture. In Aristotle's works, though, the actual word that is used to describe what we now call democracy, *isonomia*, was a term mostly related to the concept of equality. The literal etymology of the word 'democracy', instead, (the Greek word being *dēmokratia, δημοκρατία*) rests on the combination of the word *dêmos* (*δῆμος,* could be used to indicate people) with the word *krátos* (κράτος, which means force, power, even violence), and is described as one of the degenerated systems of government, together with tyranny and oligarchy. Within its substantive meaning, the concept was able to bring together a combination of different layers:

free elections, **accountability**, political **responsibility** and deliberation by **open discussion** in a public assembly, and respect for the wellbeing of the commonwealth and the interests of every citizen. Although *isonomia,* in Athens, was an entitlement only important for those citizens who were free (and) men, it was an institutional and political device of the constitution, much more desirable than the harsh *dēmokratia*, through which the power of the people had to be intended as limitless and bloodily driven by a possible demagogic leader, with no space left for individual, or for minority rights, **constitutional limits**, accountability and self-restraint. The idea of a wide democracy still had to be refined by constitutional instruments and be shaped by what, centuries later, would be called the **'rule of law'**.

For the time being, the theorists of the democracy of classical Athens, were, in this sense, already aware of the dramatic risks of the degeneration of powers based on people's consent and support, if not yet their 'will' or, at least, acquiescence. The conceptual dissociation between the people's will, on the one hand, and the government, on the other, to be mediated by some institutional machinery set out by the Constitution, was still to come. A late inheritance of the advent of the mass democracy in the nineteenth century is, therefore, the awareness that government by the people could not be a real thing, as a public assembly could not be set up anything other than in a metaphoric sense. Therefore, the most important substance of democratic government is its dependence upon general, free and periodical elections to found legislature and government as **representative bodies**. And, somehow even more important is to let the legal system lead by the principle of the rule of law (this time in the meaning of *stato di diritto, Rechtsstaat*, *état de droit*), provided that government and legislature shall always act under **the gaze of the people**, being open, transparent and legally conformed. To allow real democratic control over political power to be effective, the institutional machinery must be shaped through legal rulings and judgments and act thoroughly within the framework and limits of a constitutional assessment.

It is, however, still a question of people's consent to let **'the few'** (as J.S. Mill described it) govern over **'the many'** in an effective way while, at the same time, fulfilling the interests of the latter. For a small group acting as the people is, on the contrary, a commonly degenerated feature of authoritarian regimes vested as acting 'in the name of the people'. This question cannot be considered now, but this is what is called direct democracy, meaning **identitarian democracy**, a term used to describe the power of those governments in which a single entity, person or constitutional body, purports to be the only original interpreter of the substance and spirit of the people, unified through the artificial construction of an existential identity. No room is left, consequently, for anyone but 'the people', who

 © Wolters Kluwer Italia

remain outside, and fight against those who are stigmatised as not citizens (or as **strangers**), as if they were not even persons (Azzariti 2005). This is a theoretical perspective not in line with the doctrines of constitutionalism, which move from a mistaken idea of popular sovereignty, and give rise to political perspectives that lead to **authoritarian** solutions. Historically speaking, all dictators claim to be the real interpreter of the only and true 'will of the people'.

Recalling the main features of **democracy** within the Constitution, it is now clear how these two concepts have to be taken into account simultaneously and in terms of their reciprocal interdependence, as contemporary constitutionalism is well aware of the extreme importance of this interrelation if the main issues implied by its implementation are to be achieved. Where democracy needs to be fulfilled as the best, although imperfect, **system of government**, it is only by framing it within a constitutional instrument that can be made effective as a **people-driven** instrument of political participation. Furthermore, it is through the manner, forms and limits of the Constitution that a democratic government can have a concrete and adequate attitude towards the wellbeing of the entire commonwealth, while also protecting and implementing **individual rights** and **liberties**. A democratic government is, therefore, strongly empowered and legitimised, but also well-oriented by a **constitutional framework** that also provides for counter-majoritarian and independent bodies to prevent it from abuse, or misuse, of power, that is legally committed to safeguarding individual rights and freedoms and that fulfils equality and justice within society.

This is where the second part of the first paragraph of Article 1 becomes most relevant. Among the foundational principles of the Italian Constitution, special attention should be given to the **labour principle**. The final draft of this part of Article 1 was approved by the Constitutional Assembly on 22nd of March, 1947, when the wording 'founded on labour', proposed on behalf of the Christian Democratic Party by Amintore Fanfani, was preferred to the alternative solution presented by Lelio Basso for the Socialist Party, which insisted on a different formulation, based on 'the effective participation of *all workers* in the political, economic and social life of the country', thereby proposing to add the final part of Article 3 to Article 1. Lelio Basso and the Communist Party intended to strengthen the relation between the workers' involvement in politics and democracy, as this was also the basic idea of another, different proposal of the Communist Party, which was to substitute the formula 'founded on labour' with the more direct expression 'founded on workers' (political forces and movements of labour). A third option was also presented, as proposed for the Republican Party by Ugo La Malfa, with the wording «Italy is a democratic Republic founded on freedoms and labour rights». This was also rejected. It is notable that during the discussion,

Palmiro Togliatti, leader of the Communist Party, had already indicated that his party was in favour of the formulation of Fanfani, which would shortly become the final wording of the second part of Article 1 of the Constitution. It can easily be said, therefore, that this formulation enjoyed, on the whole, a fairly wide consent within the Constituent Assembly. Although no room was left for class-related conceptions of democracy, **popular involvement and participation** had been successfully conceived as the cornerstone of the constitutional order.

It can be concluded that, on this issue, the Italian Constitution claims to be an **open democracy**, **inclusive**, participatory and **rights-oriented**, inspired by and featuring the principle of **equality**, in a substantive sense. It was an idea of democracy that was much more dependent upon its **constitutional legitimation** than on an outdated doctrine of unlimited sovereignty. Nation states still claim, however, that their territory is a sovereign space, acting to limit the right to claim citizenship only to national individuals. Furthermore, where the Constitution recognises and safeguards the 'inviolable' human rights, there is no role for an old-fashioned national identity giving rise to a militant, ethnically-oriented idea of popular sovereignty. This brings us to the discussion of the relevance of the international and multilateral inspiration of the Italian Constitution, which was the appropriate characteristic which could help overcome the citizen/stranger divide, an inheritance of the violent twentieth century.

7. Openness to International Cooperation and Peace

One of the most important events influencing the new-born system of international relations after the dramatic conclusion of World War II and the terrible findings of the Auschwitz camps, is the radical redefinition, meaning from its very basic essence, of the international order. This redefinition was inspired by the burgeoning principles of **equality among Nations** and **self-determination**, **international rule of law**, **human rights protection**, the **ban of the war** and the use of force in international dispute settlement and peace as a cross-fertilising feature on a world scale. To achieve such ambitious goals, in 1945 the **United Nations Organisation** (UN) was created, with the intention of building a new world order, in a sort of constitutional international legal framework. The UN Charter, the founding document of the new international order, posed a system of rules and principles, binding the states, in an attempt to **ban the use of force** in international relations and to set up a legal dispute resolution mechanism, inspired by the principle of the rule of law. The aftermath of WWII, therefore, was characterised by the innovative spirit of political **multilateralism** and cooperation between States. In Europe, this gave rise to the foundation of two new and important international organisations: the **Council of Europe** (1948),

 © Wolters Kluwer Italia

within which was formed the European Convention on Human Rights and Fundamental Freedoms (1950), and the **European Coal and Steal Community** (1951), which was to develop, over the next seventy years, into the European Community and the **European Union**.

The framers of the Constitution were aware of the new world order, and the open international perspective, as the value of **peace** was extensively debated during the sessions of the Constituent Assembly. Of course, the consciousness of the discussion of the peace treaty imposed by the allies was in the background of all debates, as Italy was a defeated country, although still free to write its own Constitution thanks to the role played by the Resistance during the final stages of the war. The very spirit of the framers, in fact, was deeply present in the writing of Article 11 within the international vocation of the new order, thus inspiring the final wording of the Article. In its first part, it states that «Italy rejects war as an instrument of aggression against the freedom of other peoples and as a means for the settlement of international disputes», then concludes without interruption that (Italy) «agrees, on conditions of equality with other States, to the limitations of sovereignty that may be necessary to a world order ensuring peace and justice among the Nations», and then «promotes and encourages international organisations having such ends». It is worth observing that, in the wording of this article, there are no full stops, giving the sense that its three sentences should be read and understood as a *continuum* in which the **rejection** of **war** as a form of **aggression** and as a **dispute settlement** tool have to be achieved through **limitations of sovereignty**, to implement and enforce the new international legal order and the international organisations necessary to fulfil these goals.

Article 11 speaks of 'rejecting' the war as an 'instrument of aggression' and as means of international dispute settlement in an attempt to give rise to a different system of international relations, in which the ban on the use of force lies comfortably with the construction of a legal mechanism and **procedural machinery** to deal with conflicts among Nations. Reading the reports of the Constituent Assembly, it is clear that the forthcoming UN international order was in mind and present in the debates among the framers, even with some evocation of the incumbent European Communities around some kind of union among the states of Europe. To be more precise, however, what the Constituent Assembly had in mind was to prepare the new Italian constitutional order to be **open** to an **international legal framework**, through **limitations of states' sovereignty** and direct involvement in the building of the new international system. In the debates of the framers, it was clearly pointed out that the starting point was the political fact that the United Nations had waived a part of States' sovereignty for the new international law to become an institutional reality. As Zagari clarified, the phrase «Italy gives its consent to limit its sovereignty» means that «Italy expressly wants these limitations. It is Italy itself, conscious of a new peaceful order, it is Italy which puts itself as part of the grounds of this new international organisation for peace, which does manifest great interest in this organisation to come».

The most interesting parts of the Constituent Assembly Reports are those dedicated to the first part of Article 11, in which the word 'reject' with regard to war was eventually chosen. These are the words of Meuccio Ruini, President of the Commission for the Constitution:

> The first question at stake is the choice among different verbs, 'renounces', 'rejects' and 'condemns' which appear in the various amending proposals. The Commission [of the 75] found that where 'condemns' has an ethical more than a political or legal value, and 'renounces' presupposes, somehow, giving up a good, a right, the right to war (something we want, on the contrary, protest against), the word 'reject', even if it could seem for some reason not a fully satisfactory choice, has a kind intermediate meaning, a more significant connotation implying both 'condemning' and 'giving up' war.

Where, of course, the settlement of any international crisis or conflict over State sovereignty has to be reported to the international organisation, it is, first and foremost, war that has to be avoided and, where this is not possible, it must be dealt with through the direct involvement of the UN institutions, starting with the Security Council, and the rules and procedures set out in the UN Charter, the reason for this being the attempt to manage any international conflict using legal procedures and institutions, even where the use of the force is unavoidable. Conducted under the control and command of the UN Security Council, this could represent the only **legitimate use of force** within the international legal system. No clearer sign of the **international perspective** of the Italian Constitution, and no stronger statement of the self-determined legal **limitations to state exclusivity**, could be imagined than those written in the final drafting of Article 11.

C) SOURCES OF LAW

1. Supremacy of the Constitution

Article 1 of the Constitution establishes a mutual relationship between **popular sovereignty** and **supremacy of the Constitution**.

Unlike in the previous regimes explored in Section A, the will of the people is here recognized as the **highest source of legitimacy of every public power**. The

 © Wolters Kluwer Italia

exercise of the popular will, and the limits thereof, must, however, comply with the Constitution, *i.e.,* with its rules and its principles.

From both a historical and theoretical background, there are valid reasons for claiming that the value of the Constitution as a legal rule cannot be detached from its **source of legitimacy**.

In the liberal state (as the *Statuto Albertino* demonstrates), the flexible nature of the constitution is not simply related to the procedure regulating its amendment procedure. On a deeper level, liberal constitutions were equated with ordinary legislation, in that they were mainly addressed to the political institutions, and regulated the relations between them, without the capacity to directly influence the law-making processes or to provide individuals with enforceable rights *vis-à-vis* the public authority (COSTA 1985). According to this view, the Constitution remains separated from the general body of law, since it works as an **agreement between political actors** that deprives constitutional rules of the capacity to effectively bind legislation. Therefore, a direct connection can be established between the (political) **sovereignty of the King** (or of a limited sector of society) and the (legal) **sovereignty of the legislation**, thus reflecting the will of the majority sitting in Parliament. There are no individual rights outside of the legislation, and any limit to the law-making power of the Parliament is groundless.

Against this backdrop, the Constitution claims, from the outset, a legal sovereignty that is intimately connected to its **higher law nature**.

Articles 1 and 138, which regulate the **special procedures** for constitutional amendments, have to be jointly taken into account since they make clear that the Constitution has a higher value than ordinary legislation, a supremacy that means that every instrument of law-making, whatever the political institution is charged with, must respect the Constitution, *i.e.* the procedures it establishes and the substantive contents it prescribes.

In this way, the Constitution is the **formal source** of all public power in that it establishes a framework of powers and legal acts, whose exercise cannot conflict with the limits and the conditions established by it. The ordinary legislation itself, which had a crucial importance in former constitutional settings, loses its nature of a legal act provided with a **general competence** and turns into an instrument of law-making whose ambits of intervention are limited by the Constitution in favour of other actors and instruments (ESPOSITO 1948).

Even more importantly, the Italian Constitution traces the **substantial requirements** that the ordinary legislation must comply with, in that its normativity is directly related to the objectives laid down in its fundamental principles. Thus, the 'higher law' nature goes far beyond its being the formal source of every public power, since it establishes some material value-choices (such as liberty, solidarity, equality and the promotion of social policies) that operate as the substantial yardsticks with which every legal act must comply. All of these principles are strictly connected to the fundamental rights enshrined in Part I of the Constitution and represent the basic choices concerning the relationships between the **individual** and **authority** that run across the entire constitutional text.

Constitutional principles, and the related clauses on fundamental rights, have therefore a two-fold legal value.

On one hand, they operate as **limits** to public power, in that they prescribe what the law is prevented from doing. Among the fundamental rights, crucial importance is given, for example, to personal liberty (*habeas corpus*) and Article 13, para. 2, states that «[n]o one may be detained, inspected, or searched nor otherwise subjected to any restriction of personal liberty except by order of the Judiciary stating a reason and only in such cases and in such manner as provided by the law» (for further details see *IV.C).3.*).

On the other hand, fundamental principles do set out **programmes** for public power, by establishing goals and objectives that the legislator is under a constitutional mandate to carry out. In the field of social rights in particular, the Constitution is binding because of its capacity to steer the action of the legislator in pursuing some objectives: according to Article 31, para. 2, «[t]he Republic shall protect mothers, children and the young by adopting necessary measures».

Such fundamental principles can be consequently seen as the grounds upon which the Constitution is assigned the nature of **legal rule**, because it relies on the basic choices that have been taken by the different parties sitting in the Constituent Assembly.

Therefore, the Constitution is **legally supreme**, in that it is the source of every public power and sets the material requirements that every instrument of law-making has to comply with in order to be legitimate.

One cannot enjoy the full meaning of constitutional supremacy if, however, a procedure for ascertaining the respect of the constitution by every other legal act is not regulated. A constitution can fulfil the requirements described so far, but such supremacy risks ineffectuality if an **independent (judicial) body** is not given the power to verify whether the constitution has been respected by ordinary legislation.

According to the Italian Constitution, this power is vested, first and foremost, in the **Constitutional Court**. Its power to verify whether and to what extent

 © Wolters Kluwer Italia

ordinary laws respect the Constitution gives a further dimension as to where its normativity can be improved.

Without the constitutional review procedure delegated to an independent constitutional court, the validity of the Constitution and its supremacy are at risk, since there are no effective legal instruments aimed at preventing its infringement by ordinary legislation. The establishment of judicial review of legislation affects, therefore, the very essence of the Constitution, because its validity depends upon its capacity not to be derogated or violated in concrete circumstances. An effective constitutional review of legislation is what makes rigidity effective and confers the Constitution a peculiar **normative strength** (PALADIN 1996).

The establishment of the Constitutional Court has paved the way for the **consolidation** of the Constitution as higher law. Since its first ruling, delivered in 1956 (see *IV.C).1.*), it has declared that every rule and principle enshrined therein has the same legal value, and even those constitutional clauses containing programmes are binding since they lay down goals and objectives that ordinary legislation should not contradict. Moreover, the possibility for the Judiciary to activate judicial review before the Constitutional Court has made it possible for judges to interpret ordinary rules in accordance with the Constitution, conferring to it an even more general legal value (on the Constitutional Court, see *I.E).2.*).

2. Constitutional Amendment Procedure and its Limits

The Constitution is a higher law, since it is the outcome of an extraordinary power, vested in the Constituent Assembly between 1946 and 1948: according to modern legal and political thought, this power is called **constituent power** (or *pouvoir constituant*, in the words of its main interpreter, *Joseph-Emmanuel Sieyés*).

Because of the extraordinary nature of the power leading to its approval, the Constitution risks that its value remains separate from every other source of law. A legal text whose content cannot be changed or adapted to shifting legal reality is under the constant risk of remaining **ineffective**. For this reason, the Italian Constitution regulates the procedure of constitutional amendment in Article 138 and states that the power is given to **constitutional amendment laws** (*leggi di revisione costituzionale*) to modify the clauses of the Constitution. Such a legal instrument, even though it must comply with procedural requirements that are more complex than ordinary legislation, cannot be equated with the exercise of constituent power: whereas the latter is extraordinary and unrepeatable, the former is bound to follow both the formal and substantial requirements established by the Constitution itself.

The power of constitutional amendment has to be qualified as **constituted power** (*pouvoir constitué*) because its exercise does not call into question the most intimate nature of the Constitution and it falls within the legal empire of this one, that sets **procedures** and **limits** for modification.

The main feature of the constitutional amendment procedure is that the ordinary procedural requirements are, in many aspects, **aggravated**, that is made more elaborate, in order to safeguard the existing Constitution against modifications supported by occasional parliamentary majorities.

The first aggravating element is that both Chambers of Parliament have to **vote twice** on the same draft, and the second deliberation has to be taken after a **delay** of a minimum of three months. Even though the Constitution is silent on this point, a long-standing practice prescribes that after the first two deliberations, the draft cannot be modified.

The second aggravating element regards **qualified majorities**: whereas, in the first deliberation, the decision of both Chambers is taken with a simple majority (as for every other legislative vote), in the second deliberation, more than half of the members of each Chamber (an absolute majority) have to agree on the same draft.

The third aggravating element to be considered involves the possible need for a parliamentary vote to be confirmed by a **popular referendum**. If a parliamentary majority does not approve the constitutional amendment bill with an highly qualified majority (two-thirds of the members of each chamber), the possibility is given to 500,000 citizens, to five Regional Councils and to one-fifth of the members of any chamber of Parliament to ask for a referendum on the issue, to be held before the constitutional amendment enters into force. The main scope of this referendum is to allow minorities (in society, at a local level or even in Parliament) to promote a popular vote against the risk of a constitutional amendment approved by a parliamentary majority that may coincide with the one supporting the Government. This objective is even clearer if one considers that no majority yardstick (*quorum*) has to be reached in a popular vote for the referendum to be validly won, so that even a narrow percentage of voters can prevent a constitutional amendment from entering into force.

One further feature of the constitutional amendment procedure that should be explored is that Article 138 does not delegate the constituted power only to constitutional amendment laws (*leggi di revisione costituzionale*), but also to **other constitutional laws** (*altre leggi costituzionali*). Both categories of laws have the

 © Wolters Kluwer Italia

same legal effect, while their functions differ. Whereas constitutional amendment laws are those acts aimed at modifying the text of the Constitution, other constitutional laws are those sources of law whose main scope is to regulate sectors and functions that the Constitution does not directly regulate, even though they are inextricably connected with constitutional domains. Two clear examples of this can be found in Article 116, according to which the statute of Regions vested with a special autonomy has to be adopted with a constitutional law, and in Article 137, for which the same legal instrument is necessary to establish «conditions, forms, terms for proposing judgments on constitutional compliance, and the safeguards on the independence of constitutional judges».

The room for other constitutional laws, however, is not only related to constitutional clauses enabling their intervention. It is widely accepted that the instrument can be used to give a constitutional form to regulations that are not directly connected with the ambits covered by the Constitution since the legislator is not prevented from **constitutionalising** (*i.e.*, giving constitutional value to) every ambit it deems to be necessary.

According to its nature, while directly stemming from the Constitution, the power of constitutional amendment is **not boundless**.

Article 139 reads: «The form of Republic shall not be a matter for constitutional amendment». In the intention of the framers, this provision is directly linked with the popular vote held on the 2nd of June, 1946, when the majority of voters opted for the Republic and against the Monarchy. Following this approach, the form of Republic mentioned in the last article of the Constitution can be referred to as the **republican setting**: the presence of a temporary Head of State, who is not appointed by inheritance, but by the will of the people (mediated by parliamentary voting).

The meaning of this clause has gone far beyond this merely historical argument, and the (abstract) notion of Republic mentioned therein has been associated with the concrete type of **democratic Republic** that Article 1 aims to establish. In this vein, Article 139 identifies those characters of the Italian constitutional system that are held to be intrinsic to its quintessential nature (Mortati 1975).

Those characters have been interpreted in different ways, and no definitive consensus has emerged as to those rules and principles that should not be suppressed or even modified, even with the procedure regulated by Article 138. The ‘democratic Republic’, implied jointly by Articles 1 and 139, refers to both **fundamental principles** and **inviolable rights**, in that they define the irretractable

© Wolters Kluwer Italia

core of the Constitution (see *IV.B).1.*). Among the former, a special mention must be made of those principles laid down in the first articles of the Constitution, but also to those rules and institutions that embody the peculiar form of political democracy emerging in the Italian system that are committed to the centrality of political representation. The inviolable rights mentioned by Article 2 can be identified with those basic guarantees, which protect the individual against public authority and enable citizens to jointly cooperate in the attainment of political, social and cultural goals.

The Constitutional Court has contributed on several occasions (Judgments Nos. 30 and 31/1971, 12 and 195/1972, 183/1973, 214/1983, 238/2014, 24/2017) to the emergence of this wider interpretation of Article 139, particularly when it endorsed the idea that law stemming from **other legal orders** (such as the Catholic Church, the EU or customary international law) has to respect the basic characters of the constitutional system to be applicable by the Judiciary. In very few cases, and in a quite piecemeal fashion (for example, in Judgment No. 1146/1988), the Constitutional Court has evoked the possibility that a **constitutional amendment law** could be declared **void** whenever it runs counter to those basic principles of the Constitution and to the inalienable rights indirectly implied by Article 139.

3. The Constitution and the Ordinary Legislation: Rule of Law and the Principle of Legality

One further consequence of the higher law character of the Constitution is that it must be considered as the legal source that is called upon to determine the types and the ambits of intervention of **every other source of law**. The move from the classical notion of the rule of law, which implies the pre-eminence of parliamentary legislation, to the **constitutional rule of law** means, therefore, that the fundamental decision as to the formal and substantial characters of law-making, and the limits thereto, is demanded to a legal act that does not depend upon the will of the majorities.

Against this background, a crucial role is played by the meaning and scope of that particular notion of the rule of law defined as **reserve of legislation** (*riserva di legge*) that is associated with the relationships between the Constitution and ordinary legislation.

Whereas the Constitution establishes that the legislative function is vested in the Parliament (Article 70) and that other law-making instruments shall be equated with parliamentary legislation, many clauses of the Constitution **reserve**

 © Wolters Kluwer Italia

to ordinary legislation the ability to regulate topics such as those related to several fundamental rights.

Article 13 explains that «No one may be detained, inspected, or searched nor otherwise subjected to any restriction of personal liberty except by order of the Judiciary stating a reason and *only in such cases and in such manner as provided by the law*». Article 16 further indicates that «Every citizen has the right to reside and travel freely in any part of the country, *except for such general limitations as may be established by law for reasons of health or security*». According to these articles, and many others, **ordinary legislation** has to establish the conditions under which a certain right can be enjoyed, and such a duty implies, first and foremost, that governmental acts shall not be allowed to encroach upon the same topic.

The supreme nature of the Constitution confers to the rule of law principle a **binding nature** that is more effective than it was in the previous regimes that were characterised by the flexible nature of constitutional documents. In those systems, the rule of law clauses could be derogated by subsequent legislation, so that the protection of individual rights was left in the hands of political representatives and, consequently, the rule of law did not have any distinctive guarantee differentiating it from a general **principle of legality**. Protection of rights met no enforceable limits since parliamentary legislation was deemed to act as an intrinsic guarantee for individuals and groups.

On the contrary, where the Constitution is a higher law, the rule of law bears a clearer and legally **enforceable value**, since the ambits of intervention of the ordinary legislation and the limits thereto are not in the hands of Parliament or of any authority entrusted with law-making power, since any legal provision conflicting with constitutional clauses has to be declared void.

Against this background, the Constitution prescribes that the rule of law shall generally guide legislative activity, with particular regard to the **limitation of fundamental rights**. This general principle makes fundamental rights' protection effective because the limitation of rights has to be decided by the Parliament on the basis of a public debate, where participatory rights of minorities are safeguarded, and because any measure infringing rule of law guarantees can be challenged before the Judiciary, and even ordinary laws can be reviewed by the Constitutional Court.

The peculiar nature of the **reserve of legislation clauses** in the Italian Constitution ascribes to the ordinary legislation the power to regulate the aforementioned ambits, albeit such intervention can take place in different forms:

© Wolters Kluwer Italia

a) **Absolute** reservation (*riserva di legge assoluta*): only ordinary legislation can regulate a certain topic (e.g., personal liberty, freedom of domicile, freedom of communication, criminal penalties).

b) **Relative** reservation (*riserva di legge relativa*): the legislature has competence for the establishment of general principles, while the power to lay down more specific rules within the limits set out by the law is left to governmental acts (freedom of circulation, power to levy taxes).

c) **Reinforced** reservation (*riserva di legge rinforzata*): ordinary legislation is demanded to regulate a certain topic, with a limited appreciation power as to the objectives that have to be pursued. Article 16, protecting freedom of circulation, prescribes, for example, that citizens can be limited in their power to freely circulate exclusively «for reasons of health or security». Article 18, concerning freedom of association, states that citizens have the right to freely associate «for any ends that are not forbidden by criminal law» (in so doing, the law could not set a limit to freedom of association that does not coincide with a criminal prescription binding for individuals).

Such a central role assigned to the **rule of law**, and the different meanings of the reserve of legislation, make the distinction with the **principle of legality** even clearer. This is to be considered a general principle that is implied by the Constitution, according to which every exercise of public power must find its legal basis in a legislative prescription. The core meaning of the principle of legality is not only to confer to the Executive power only those tasks that are provided for by the ordinary legislation, but more significantly, to limit its discretion when carrying out its functions. Such a *substantive* notion of legality implies, therefore, that the legislation has to generally lay down the basic substantive criteria that the Government should comply with when regulating a certain ambit.

4. Parliamentary Legislation

Legislation pertains to **Parliament**. Article 70 states that «The law-making function shall be exercised collectively by both Houses». With these clear words, it establishes a close connection between the legal source, aimed at prescribing general and abstract rules, and the centrality of Parliament. Within the framework of a rigid Constitution, ordinary (parliamentary) legislation remains the main legal act that is vested with the power to set out **general legal rules**, since Parliament is the institution through which the representatives of the people are called upon to activate those processes of political integration leading to decisions that bind everyone. By the interplay between majority and minority, and by virtue of

 © Wolters Kluwer Italia

public debate, legislative decisions are taken, and their content is the outcome of a process that leads to general acceptance of legal rules.

The legislative procedure, which is regulated by the Constitution and, in more detail, by parliamentary standing orders, is divided into five steps:

a) **Initiative**: according to Article 71, legislation may be introduced by the Government, by a Member of Parliament and by those entities and bodies so empowered by constitutional laws.

The people may initiate legislation by proposing a bill drawn up in sections and signed by at least 50,000 voters. The Government is in a particular situation, in that it may propose a bill following a preliminary procedure, that starts with the proposal of a Minister or the President of the Council of Ministers, and is deliberated upon by the Council of Ministers and validated by the President of the Republic (Article 87). Moreover, only Government can propose bills concerning the budget and the conversion of decree-laws.

b) **Examination**: once the bill is presented at one of the two Chambers, it is up to the parliamentary committees to initiate the legislative process. Through a process of examination and inquiry, a detailed assessment is made as to the impact of the draft proposal, with particular regard to budgetary requirements.

c) **Voting**: every legislative draft must be approved by both Chambers. In each of these, the voting procedure is split between the committee and the Assembly, which has the final word as to the amendments and the final vote, taking place regularly and on a simple majority basis. Even before the entry into force of the Constitution, a practice emerged as to the possibility that a law could be passed by the committees of both Chambers. According to Article 72, para. 4, such an accelerated procedure is possible with the exception laid down therein (constitutional and electoral laws, delegated legislation, authorisation to ratify treaties, and budget matters).

d) **Promulgation**: after the vote of Parliament, the President of the Republic has the task of promulgating the law, so as to confer legal effect to it. In exceptional circumstances, the President of the Republic may decide to block (or repeal) the law: constitutional practice suggests that such a power does not entail a proper (political) veto function, since its requirements mostly rely on constitutional reasons (such as a manifest conflict with the Constitution or a lacking budgetary assessment). In recent years, an increasingly important reason for repeal is manifest conflict with EU rules. Both Chambers remain free to confirm the repealed

© Wolters Kluwer Italia

law with a new deliberation; in such cases, the President of the Republic is under a duty to promulgate it.

e) **Publication**: a law must be published within 30 days of promulgation to be binding. It normally enters into force 15 days after its publication in the *Gazzetta Ufficiale*.

Traditionally, the province of legislation is to be found in the **general** and **abstract** nature of its provisions. This requirement is strictly related to the principle of equality, according to which everyone should be treated alike. Dealing with the equality principle in this way reflects the liberal category of parliamentary legislation, which is influenced by the absence of social and political pluralism (parliaments are elected by a limited sector of society) and, even more importantly, by flexible constitutions. In legal systems in which constitutions have a higher law nature and claim for a normative project for society, the reference to generality as the defining feature of parliamentary legislation **does not suffice anymore**.

For this reason, Italian Constitutional Law still refers to parliamentary legislation as the most important legal source, although it has lost its previous monopoly in ordinary law-making (Bradley/Pinelli 2012).

On the one hand, parliamentary legislation cannot be substantively **identified** with those rules that have a general and abstract content. In other words, legislation is outweighed by the Constitution, so that the need to comply with different (and often conflicting) constitutional principles gives no single indication of what legislation should be.

The legislative function is exercised even when concrete provisions do regulate concrete cases, as in the case of **legislative measures** (*leggi provvedimento*). In response to different needs, parliamentary legislation can be called upon to give a legal basis to concrete provisions, a form of regulation that pertains to public administration. A vast array of regulatory powers is exercised by ordinary legislation on a daily basis in the field of public sector economics (public companies and public services). The same concrete attitude of legislation is made clear even when **retroactive laws** (referring to pre-established situations) are adopted, or when the law lays down a binding interpretation of a previous legislative clause (*leggi di interpretazione autentica*); this may be legitimate when judicial opinions radically differ as to the interpretation of a certain legislative clause.

 © Wolters Kluwer Italia

In all of these situations, the general and abstract nature of legal provisions cannot be guiding principles in establishing what ordinary legislation should be. Consequently, the inherent limit to the legislative function no longer coincides with the traditional principle of equality ('everyone should be treated alike'), but with the principle of **reasonableness** (*principio di ragionevolezza*). This represents a legal concept forged by the Italian Constitutional Court, closely linked to the principle of equality set out in Article 3, in that it is inspired by the idea that the legislator is under a duty not to treat differently what is alike and not to treat in the same way situations that are intrinsically different. In its basic meaning, a legislative provision is reasonable whenever a legislative clause is coherent with the decisions taken by the legislator in similar circumstances. To make such an assessment, the Constitutional Court has developed a **judicial doctrine**, according to which reasonableness (a kind of proportionality *à l'italienne*) implies an ongoing assessment of the relationship between the legal clause at stake and a similar legal provision, taking into account the objective that the legislator aimed to pursue in both cases. When this comparison satisfies a basic coherence test, the legislative clause at stake can be defined as reasonable. Moving from the equality principle, the principle of reasonableness has progressively turned into a far-reaching constraint for legislators (strict scrutiny), even more so when legislation regulates concrete situations like legislative and retroactive measures (on this, see *III.A).2.b.1* and *IV.B).1.c.4.*).

5. Legislative Acts Equated with Ordinary Legislation: Decree-laws and Delegated Legislation

Parliamentary legislation has lost its previous **centrality** because the Constitution has introduced more legal sources that are on an equal footing and that reflect a pluralism in law-making that goes beyond parliamentary representation.

Within this context, one should distinguish those legal acts that have the **same sphere of competence** of parliamentary legislation and those legal acts that enjoy a **separate sphere of competence**.

Within the first category, the Constitution establishes that two distinctive legal acts concur with the parliamentary legislation and are called upon to intervene in the same situations that may be dealt with by the ordinary laws: **decree-laws** and **delegated decrees**. Both involve the Government and confer to it a law-making power that has the same legal rank as parliamentary laws. This does not mean that the Government is fully entitled to act as a legislative body because, in any case, the Parliament has a legal and political 'final word' on the exercise of these executive powers.

According to Article 77, in case of necessity and urgency, the Government may adopt, under its responsibility, «**temporary measures** having force of law». On the same day, the Government shall present a bill to the Chambers to enable the Parliament to transform the decree-law into a parliamentary law. This must happen within 60 days from the entry into force of the decree-law, otherwise, it is deprived of any legal effect from the beginning (*ex tunc*).

The adoption of a **decree-law** has its requirements in the **emergency reasons** that the Government can invoke to regulate a certain situation in a prompt manner (*i.e.*, without waiting for the parliamentary legislative process to be activated and concluded). Once adopted, the decree-law has a temporary nature, because the Parliament has a limited time (60 days) to **validate** it, thereby making its effect stable. This is made possible thanks to the incorporation of its content in a *sui generis* parliamentary act, whose scope is to transpose the decree-law.

Decree-laws are a **powerful instrument** in the hands of the Government since the practice has shown that very few limits can be drawn with regard to the 'necessity and urgency' test. The consequence is that the executive power uses this instrument whenever it holds that a certain legislative intervention is politically necessary, placing **pressure** on the Parliament to validate the political decision lying behind the required measure or to enter into a conflict with the Government (which only happens in very rare circumstances). Such political pressure can be even greater if the Government decides to force parliamentary validation through the decision to make the **trust relationship** between the legislative and the executive power dependent upon the approval of the decree-law.

A first balancing factor can be found in the power of the **President of the Republic** not to enact the decree-law. According to Article 87, the President is entitled to enact those decrees that are equated with the law. It is widely accepted that presidential powers in this field are not influenced by the limits affecting the promulgation of parliamentary laws. The consequence is that the President may refuse to enact decree-laws that are adopted outside of the conditions laid down in Article 77, and a subsequent decision of the Government to propose the same decree-law is not deemed to be binding for the President of the Republic.

Despite this, presidential powers have, indeed, been exercised in very **limited cases**. For a very long time, governmental powers in this field led to an alleged abuse of decree-laws, which found its culmination in the mid-1990s, with the so-called **reiteration**: if Parliament did not transform a decree-law into a validating parliamentary law, the Government adopted a (formally) new law decree,

 © Wolters Kluwer Italia

whose content coincided with the former, a few days before the expiry date of sixty days. The consequence was a sort of chain of decree-laws, that substantially ended up depriving the Parliament of any legislative power in favour of Government.

This situation called for reactions, initially from the Constitutional Court. With Judgment No. 360/1996, the Constitutional Court declared the practice of reiteration unconstitutional, since it was openly against the word and the spirit of the separation of powers and, in particular, it infringed the exclusive power of the Parliament to adopt ordinary laws (Article 70). From that moment on, the Constitutional Court has reinforced a set of **limits** to governmental legislative powers, in that the necessity and urgency test have not been left exclusively to the political evaluation of Parliament, since their obvious deficiency makes the decree-law unconstitutional. This consequence affected only the decree-law, with the consequence that parliamentary validation had the effect of politically and legally confirming the evaluation made by the Government (Judgment No. 29/1995). In later instances, the Court declared that the «obvious lack» of necessity and urgency made both the decree-law and the parliamentary validation unconstitutional (Judgment No. 171/2007), since Parliament also is not entitled to modify the balance of powers set out in the Constitution.

A further limit to the power of the Parliament to amend the content of the decree-law during the parliamentary validation process has been introduced by the **Constitutional Court**. The fast-track procedure, if compared with the much longer ordinary legislative process, has often pushed political forces in Parliament to amend decree-law considerably in terms of their content, and to take advantage of the need to validate decree-laws within 60 days. Even though this practice has not been declared unconstitutional as such, the Court has warned members of Parliament that these amendments have to be coherent with the ambits covered by the decree-law (Judgments Nos. 22/2012 and 32/2014).

The other legal act that the Government can use to adopt legal rules that have the same legal status as ordinary law is **delegated legislation**.

According to Article 76, the exercise of the legislative function may not be delegated to the Government unless **principles** and **criteria** have been established and, even then, only for a limited **time** and for specified **ambits**. In comparison with the relationship between decree-law and (subsequent) parliamentary validating act, in delegated legislation, Parliament and Government enter the scene in different ways. The initial action is made by Parliament, which can decide to delegate the task to regulate a certain ambit to the Government. Such a decision must be taken in the form of a **delegating law**, which is bound to comply with some basic requirements by Article 76:

a) **Principles** and **criteria** have to be laid down to steer governmental discretion in the directions decided upon by the Parliament. As a matter of principle, Parliament should reserve the power to take fundamental decisions as to how a certain topic has to be regulated, whereas the Government is called to implement those decisions (taken in the form of principles and criteria) in an operating form.

b) The power of the Government should be exercised within a given (limited) **time**. It is necessary to limit the discretionary intervention of the executive, even more so because the delegation does not imply a transfer of legislative powers (the Parliament may decide at any moment to autonomously legislate in the same ambit).

c) Delegation should cover a **specific object**.

Within these limits, the Government is under a duty to adopt a **delegated decree** to implement the principles and criteria laid down in the delegating law.

Since both acts have the same legal value, a crucial question has been to understand how the **infringement** of the principles and criteria by the delegated decree could be remedied. The delegated decree remains valid as long as it does not infringe on the Constitution, but the violation of the requirements set out in the delegating law does not entail, as such, a direct conflict with the Constitution, with the consequence that the Constitutional Court might not be entitled to review its content.

This puzzle has been solved thanks to the emergence of a judicial doctrine according to which whenever the Constitution prescribes that the content of a legislative act should depend on the requirements set out by further acts, the infringement of the latter necessarily relates to the invalidity of the former, since constitutional provisions have the duty to lay down constitutionally enforceable limits to other law-making activities to these legal acts (so-called **interposed rules** technique).

Although decree-laws and delegated legislation procedures are conceived by the Constitution, in terms of **exceptions** to ordinary parliamentary legislation, the practice shows that the overwhelming part of law-making activity in Parliament is related to legislative decisions taken by the Government. During the eighteenth legislature (2018-2023), 66.3% of the parliamentary bills approved were related

© Wolters Kluwer Italia

to the validation of law decrees, whereas 31.5% involved bills initiated by the Government (mainly concerning laws of delegation). Approved bills stemming from the initiative of single MPs are quite exceptional (2.1%) (CAMERA DEI DEPUTATI 2022).

These statistics should not, however, ignore the fact that governmental legislation increased in the 2018-2023 legislature because of the urgency to cope with the **COVID-19** emergency and the massive problems it raised in almost every aspect of society. The response strategy of Italian authorities was to entrust the Government with the power to promptly regulate the emergency, by overly extending the recourse to regulatory instruments such as decree-laws and other governmental decrees, but without recurring to a codified emergency procedure that is not provided for by the Constitution (CIVITARESE MATTEUCCI ET AAL. 2021).

By further governmental decrees, usually defined as **regulations,** are meant acts which the Government may adopt to execute or somehow implement legislative rules. Even though they are not codified by the Constitution, their status can be negatively inferred by the rule laid down in Article 77, para. 1, of the Constitution, according to which «[t]he Government may not, without a delegation from Parliament, issue a decree having force of law». Apart from decree-laws and delegated legislation, which are the only codified exceptions to this prohibition, further governmental regulations are, therefore, deprived of legislative effect, and are thus bound by legislative provisions. A typology of these acts is legislatively codified in Article 17 of Law No. 400 of 1988.

In recent years, and as a reaction to the pandemic, the Government has made extensive use of regulatory instruments such as the **decrees of the President of the Council of Ministers** (d.P.C.M.), which have sometimes been required to intervene in critical issues such as the limitation of fundamental rights (the right to work, freedom of movement and assembly, religious freedom). With Judgment No. 198/2021, the Constitutional Court qualified this kind of decree as general acts whose scope and ambit of intervention have to be regulated by primary legislation, but whose flexibility makes them able to rapidly cope with changing situations such as the evolution of the pandemic.

6. Popular Abrogative Referendum

Among those legislative acts that are equated with ordinary legislation, the abrogative **referendum** regulated by Article 75 is to be included.

As the first two paragraphs of this article prescribe, a general referendum may be held to repeal, in whole or in part, a law or a measure having the force of law,

© Wolters Kluwer Italia

when so requested by 500,000 voters or five Regional Councils. No referendum may be held on a law regulating taxes, the budget, amnesty or pardon, or on a law ratifying an international treaty.

The essence of this legal instrument is to **abrogate** a legislative measure and not to amend it or to add any rule provided with legislative effect. Such a merely abrogative (*i.e.*, negative) effect is not incompatible with the fact that a referendum is to be held as a legislative source. In the words of Vezio Crisafulli, «abrogation is not to be counted as a lacking regulation, but it aims at 'differently regulating', and therefore it is the exercise of a normative power» (CRISAFULLI 1984 at 116).

The goal of the referendum is that the citizens may decide to abrogate in whole or in part a legislative act, according to the intention of the promoters of the initiative. As already said, some **categories of legislation** cannot be abrogated through a referendum. The Constitutional Court has increasingly expanded these categories to encompass every legal provision somehow connected with the aforementioned precluded areas. In this vein, 'budget' means that a referendum cannot have, as its object, budgetary laws or legal provisions that regulate incomes or public expenditure. Similarly, laws ratifying international treaties encompass every legislative act that is called upon, directly or indirectly, to implement or to comply with international obligations (such as EU regulations and directives). Moreover, a popular referendum cannot be directed against either constitutional laws or governmental regulations.

This wide set of limits sheds light on the **intimate nature** of the referendum, which is not the pure expression of direct democracy, even more so because this would challenge the parliamentary and representative nature of Italian democracy. Thus, there is no dualism as to the source of legislative power, since the popular will is to be counted as a constituted power, which coexists with Parliament because it can occasionally correct the decisions taken by representatives. Indeed, the popular abrogative referendum has played a crucial role in the evolution of Italian democracy, above all in those phases in which the basic premises of the agreement between political parties have seemed to be weaker and it has thus paved the way to new political equilibria.

This limited nature can become clearer if one considers the **procedure** laid down by Law No. 352/1970 for requesting a popular referendum. The initiative is left to citizens or five Regional Councils. In the first case, a group of promoters can collect no less than 500,000 signatures, which have to be validated by a specific office of the Court of Cassation (*Ufficio centrale per il referendum*),

© Wolters Kluwer Italia

which is called upon to verify whether the procedural requirements laid down by the law have been respected. As a second step, it is up to the Constitutional Court to declare the admissibility of the referendum request (even those presented by Regional Councils). Such an evaluation ensures that the request complies with the requirements set out in Article 75, and can be clearly understood and decided upon by the citizens.

The Constitutional Court has repeatedly insisted on the need to not turn the popular referendum into a **plebiscitary instrument**, which would happen if the people are called to vote on a request that may appear contradictory or even incomprehensible. The Court has highlighted that the vote on the referendum must be free (according to Article 48), in that the citizen must be able to give an opinion leading to a clear and self-standing legislative outcome.

As to the voting procedure, Article 75 prescribes that the referendum shall be considered to have been held if the **majority** of those eligible have voted. A referendum is successful if a **majority** of 'yes' votes have been achieved.

Once a referendum has been held and if the majority has voted in favor of the abrogation, the President of the Republic formally declares that the law at stake has been **abrogated**. Consequently, Parliament is under a duty not to circumvent popular will by reintroducing the abrogated provisions; indeed, any infringement of this rule can be challenged before the Constitutional Court.

7. Parliamentary Rules of Procedure (Standing Orders)

Decree-laws, delegated decrees and the popular referendum are the most important sources of law whose enactment involves actors other than Parliament and whose ambit of intervention coincides with the **competence** of State legislation.

A further category of sources of law includes those acts that are equated with ordinary legislation, for which the Constitution itself establishes a dedicated sphere of competence. According to many scholars, the Italian Constitution's contribution to the regulation of legal sources lies in its capacity to create **different domains of competence** rather than a fully-fledged hierarchy of laws (CRISAFULLI 1960). The growing importance of competence, as opposed to hierarchy, in coordinating law-making activities has a crucial importance in testifying to the importance of **pluralism** and the connected need to **distribute powers** among different entities. Moreover, the connection between competence (as opposed to hierarchy) and pluralism has made the Italian system quite sensitive to issues related to the incorporation of EU law into the domestic legal order (see *II.B).2*).

From both the internal and the external perspective, the pluralistic attitude of Italian Constitutional Law can be seen as the outcome of the institutional theory of law of Santi Romano, which focused on the 'plurality of legal orders' as a way to make state's authority compatible with the dispersal of law-making power at infra and supranational level (ROMANO 1946)

A category of internal sources of law with a dedicated sphere of competence are **parliamentary standing orders**, which regulate the internal organisation of both Chambers of Parliament and the procedural rules dedicated to different parliamentary activities. In so doing, parliamentary standing orders must respect the rules and principles laid down by the Constitution, primarily in the field of the legislative process. No other source of law (or even parliamentary legislation) is entitled to deal with the same issues.

According to Article 64, each Chamber of Parliament adopts its standing order with an **absolute majority** of its members.

A highly debated issue is whether these peculiar sources of law can be overseen by the **Constitutional Court**. Given their equation with ordinary legislation, no preclusion should be raised as to the possibility of being challenged before the Constitutional Court, whenever they conflict with the Constitution. On several occasions (Judgments Nos. 9/1959 and 154/1985) the Constitutional Court has denied such a possibility, based upon the assumption that Parliament enjoys a wide and unchallengeable **autonomy**. This implies that other institutional actors should not intrude on the choices made by peoples' representatives as to the internal organisation of the Chambers. In more recent times, the Constitutional Court has not excluded the possibility that scrutiny over standing orders could be exercised within the framework of a conflict of powers among constitutional organs, whenever such parliamentary regulations infringe a sphere that is reserved to the Judiciary (Judgments Nos. 120/2014 and 262/2017).

Another much debated topic is related to the possibility of standing orders being referred to as **legal yardsticks** in the control of legislative procedure by the Constitutional Court. Even in this area, the Court opted for a negative response, by repeatedly stating that parliamentary legislation can be declared void for procedural reasons only when it runs counter to a constitutional provision.

8. Regional Laws

Among the fundamental principles of the Constitution, **Article 5** states that the Italian Republic recognises and promotes local autonomies and implements the

© Wolters Kluwer Italia

fullest measure of administrative decentralisation in those services that depend on the State. The Republic itself is called upon to adapt the principles and methods of its legislation to the requirements of autonomy and decentralisation.

The regional character of the Italian State, which is neither federal nor strictly unitary, implies that the exercise of legislative power has to be intended in a pluralist fashion, which means that the State should not be held as the exclusive owner of law-making power. The use of the term '**Republic**' means that the Constitution guarantees the coexistence between State, Regions and further local entities and, in so doing, confers to every level of government a power of self-government that has to be reconciled with unitary interests. Within such self-government, besides organisation and finance, crucial importance is given to law-making, so that all the entities listed in **Article 114** («The Republic shall be composed of municipalities, provinces, metropolitan cities, regions and the State») have a basic set of normative powers. Municipalities, provinces, and metropolitan cities have their own statutes as well as the power to adopt regulations. Only the **Regions** are vested with the power to adopt laws that are formally equated with state legislation.

The relationship between State and regional legislation is regulated by **Article 117**, which, in its first paragraph, prescribes that both State and Regions are bound by the Constitution, and by the constraints stemming from EU law and international obligations.

Although both forms of legislation are hierarchically on the same footing, mutual relationships are regulated according to the principle of **competence**. In later paragraphs of Article 117, a wide set of ambits of intervention is detailed, related to the different competence rules accorded to both levels of government.

With regards to the fields in which the State enjoys an **exclusive competence**, such as (among others) foreign politics, the army, money, public safety, competition, the environment and basic standards concerning civil and social rights, only the State is entitled to legislate.

Article 117, para. 3, lists the areas of competence in which **State and Regions concur** in the legislative regulation. Within these ambits of concurring competence, the State is required to establish the general principles of a given issue (such as public instruction, health protection, urban and land planning, and cultural property), whereas the Regions are called to enact those principles by adopting a detailed regulation. In these areas, whenever a regional law conflicts with the general principles laid down by a state law, it can be declared void by the Constitutional Court. Even though both laws are equated, this is a further example of the legal technique described earlier with regard to delegated legislation (**interposed rules**).

According to Article 117, para. 4, Regions have legislative powers in all matters that are **not expressly reserved** to State legislation. This residual clause has been referred to ambits such as, among others, agriculture and the organisation of regional offices.

The constitutional reform of regional and local government adopted in 2001 aimed at conferring a wider set of powers to Regions and local governments than in the previous regime. As to law-making powers, the distribution of competences laid down in Article 117 has been significantly reshaped by the case law of the **Constitutional Court**, which has interpreted the State's legislative powers expansively. Many ambits of intervention listed in Article 117, para. 2 (such as environment and competition), have been interpreted to not simply identify a field of action. Rather, according to long-standing jurisprudence, they establish a **scope that has to be pursued**. Protection of the environment is a scope that may affect several other areas not directly pertaining to the State's powers (such as agriculture or urban planning). When this happens, the Court has admitted that unitary interests must be satisfied, and the pursuance of such fundamental goals cannot prevent the State from interfering with other regional competences. Such an expansion of the State's powers, however, has to be counterbalanced by **loyal cooperation**: State and Regions must reach an agreement as to the procedures and instruments that are necessary to execute these laws (Judgment No. 303/2003).

D) DEMOCRACY, SEPARATION OF POWERS, FORM OF GOVERNMENT

1. The Principle of Pluralist Democracy

As already said, the principle of **popular sovereignty** enshrined in Article 1 of the Constitution is the source of both a qualified role of the Constitution as higher law and a new way to conceive the relationships between individuals and public authority. By stating that sovereignty «belongs» to the people, and not simply 'originates from' the people, the drafters of the Constitution highlighted the necessity that every manifestation of public power should be traced

© Wolters Kluwer Italia

back to the expression of popular will, albeit within «the forms and the limits of the Constitution».

A first basic step that has to be taken to understand the democratic nature of the Italian constitutional order is, therefore, to link the principle of popular sovereignty established by Article 1 with the **right to vote** and the universal suffrage enshrined in Article 48, according to which «[a]ny citizen, male or female, who has attained the age of majority, shall be a voter». This link firstly makes it clear that the whole body of the Constitution, both in the political rights it protects and in the functioning of the institutional machinery it regulates, is based on the concept of **representative democracy**. Citizens are sovereign, in that they, whatever their sex, age and social conditions, have the equal right to elect their representatives within those constitutional organs that are called upon to take fundamental political decisions, firstly (but not exclusively) in the national Parliament.

The democratic principle cannot, however, be equated with the idea that its meaning and scope fully coincide with the exercise of the citizens' right to vote. To avoid the risks of a plebiscitary democracy, the «forms and limits» of popular sovereignty are formulated in the Constitution so as to give rise to a **pluralist setting**, which is aimed at promoting more structured and articulated forms of expression of the popular will. 'Forms and limits' of popular sovereignty are not the external constraints of a fictional unitary will of the people, but rather the instrument aimed at making that sovereignty effective, by being organised, acknowledged and made possible by legal rules.

Pluralist democracy means, therefore, that the political choices of individuals have to be expressed in diverse ways and forms in order to guarantee that the establishment of a political majority can be checked and balanced by contrary opinions expressed at different institutional levels or animated by organised social groups.

Italian democracy is thus committed to a pluralist setting in that, firstly, citizens are called to exercise their right to vote to appoint their representatives at a national level, as well as at **regional and local levels**. The basic principle that protects the autonomy of territorial entities, enshrined in Article 5, is a cornerstone of the democratic principle since it makes clear that there is no single institution in which popular will find its proper expression and, in so doing, it gives rise to the «other face of sovereignty» (Berti 1975). In the words of the Constitutional Court (Judgment No. 106/2002):

> Article 1 of the Constitution, by establishing, with a clear and definitive formulation, that sovereignty «belongs» to the people, prevents from believing that there

are single places or offices of the constitutional organisation in which it can be exclusively found. The forms and ways in which the sovereignty of the people can take place, in fact, are not resolved in representation, but permeate the entire constitutional framework: they are refracted in a multiplicity of situations and institutions and assume a configuration so broad that it certainly includes recognition and the guarantee of territorial autonomy. As far as the latter are concerned, the vision according to which the people are participants in the paths of the articulation and diversification of political power is closely linked, both historically and ideally, to the affirmation of the democratic principle and of popular sovereignty.

From another perspective, secondly, pluralist democracy is enhanced by the introduction of several forms of direct **popular participation**, such as referenda, both at the central (Article 75) and local level (Articles 123 and 132), and popular initiative in legislation (Article 71). Against the background that has been briefly outlined above, such instruments do not have to be properly considered as an alternative to representative democracy, but rather as a correction that paves the way for the direct involvement of citizens within the deliberative process, without infringing the overarching nature of the representative principle (Paladin 1995). On a closer look, the use of the category of 'direct democracy' may appear not entirely correct, since none of these instruments implies the autonomous capacity of voters to take a decision that is detached from an ongoing procedure. Either when a referendum takes place, or when a legislative process is initiated by a popular bill, the intervention of voters is deeply entrenched with the activity carried forward by representative institutions. The relevance of direct democracy must, therefore, be understood not as an alternative to representative democracy, but rather as a further circuit that is aimed, via popular participation, at correcting and controlling the activity of representative institutions (Panunzio 1979).

From a third perspective, pluralist democracy is qualified by the **special conditions** that the Constitution specifically associates with the principle of representative democracy.

With particular regard to the election of the members of the two Chambers of Parliament, taking place with «direct and universal suffrage» (Articles 56 and 58), the right to vote of the citizens is qualified by two concurring principles.

According to Article 67, «[e]ach Member of Parliament shall represent the Nation and carry out their duties **without a binding mandate**». This means, at a more general level, that elected representatives do not exclusively represent their voters, because MPs are called upon to serve the Nation by representing different opinions and beliefs with regard to what is deemed to be the general interest. Since every MP is called to represent the Nation, his or her political action must not be evaluated by those who voted for them in the previous election, and who

© Wolters Kluwer Italia

may pretend to recall him or her from the office, but by the potential future voters, who are called to verify whether they meet their standards of political conduct. The right to vote is the essential element of political responsibility, which improves and enhances the representative nature of the Italian democracy.

The prohibition of a binding mandate is closely connected to a further principle, according to which «[a]ny citizen shall have the right to freely establish political parties in order to contribute to the development of national policies through the democratic process» (Article 49). Italian democracy is animated by **political parties** both for historical reasons and because of their capacity to promote and represent political pluralism within the public sphere. The referral to the 'concurrence' of parties in determining national policies is the clearest evidence that Article 49 attaches major importance to the activity of a plural system of parties, rather than to the exclusivity of their action as public actors. This is further demonstrated by the well-established opinion that political parties are and must remain private subjects not directly vested with public tasks (RESCIGNO 1966), particularly because the 'democratic method' is an external limit to their action, and is aimed at safeguarding external pluralism, rather than at introducing a binding internal democratic organisation.

The role of political parties is, therefore, inextricably connected with the **model of democracy** that the Constitution aims to establish, in which they are called to channel different political, social and cultural strains into the institutions, with particular regard to national and local elections. This centrality does not entail, however, that political parties are the ultimate actors of the political process since Article 49 confers to the **citizens** the right to activate political initiatives whose main scope is to promote the broadest participation in the political, economic and social organisation of the country.

2. Separation of Powers and the Form of Government

A pluralist democracy implies both that the exercise of popular sovereignty is articulated in various forms and that the Constitution provides for a separation of powers, by stating that some of these can be detached from direct popular suffrage.

Although it is not expressly regulated by the Constitution, the principle of the **separation of powers** permeates most of its clauses and principles, since it reflects the will of the framers to prevent the establishment of an overarching power that could endanger individual freedom. The separation of powers should, therefore, be recognised as a general and unwritten principle, in that it specifies the pluralist principle at the institutional level, once it prescribes that the exercise of different public powers has to be referred to different institutional bodies, albeit in more complicated forms than the ones forged by the classical approach of Montesquieu.

At an initial level, such a major complexity is related to the different relationships that may develop between the **structure** of the institutions and bodies and the **functions** that they have to carry out.

In the case of **judicial power**, the guarantee of autonomy and independence by other powers (Article 104) and the attribution to the High Council of the Judiciary (*Consiglio superiore della magistratura*, CSM) of the exclusive competence to decide about assignments and transfers, promotions and disciplinary measures concerning judges (Article 105) are inextricably linked with the prohibition that other institutions may interfere or influence the judicial function. By stating that «[j]udges shall be subject only to the law», Article 101 reaffirms that the exercise of judicial power is bound by normative decisions taken in due form by political institutions (and mainly by Parliament) and transformed into legal rules.

There are, however, situations in which the same power can be exercised by **different organs**.

In the case of **legislative power**, Article 70 states that the legislative power «shall be exercised collectively by both Houses ». Although this clause establishes the principle of the centrality of Parliament in law-making, other clauses of the Constitution confer a certain quota of legislative powers to the Government, with particular regard to the adoption of decree-laws and delegated decrees (see *I.B).5.*). Such an exercise of governmental powers in the field of legislation does not alter the principle according to which the titularity of law-making powers is basically vested in the Parliament. Both decree-laws and delegated decrees require the necessary involvement of Parliament, and the exercise of autonomous law-making powers of the Executive, as in the case of regulations, must abide by the principle of legality. Despite this, it is undeniable that the exercise of the legislative function is not solely reserved to the Parliament.

On a second level, the powers and functions that are required to be balanced and separated are **many more** than only the legislative, executive and judicial ones.

One may make reference here to the **President of the Republic**, who is not directly involved in any of the aforementioned powers, even though its role implies an ongoing process of non-partisan influence *vis-à-vis* each of them. Article 87 confers the President of the Republic the task to «represent national unity»,

 © Wolters Kluwer Italia

which is the ultimate yardstick against which he is called to exercise his powers, particularly when they require a certain degree of flexibility and political leeway (Judgment No. 1/2013). Even the judicial review of legislation put forth by the **Constitutional Court** can be intended as an autonomous power, although it is exercised in a judicial form, but outside the organisation of the judiciary.

A further widely debated function that implies the exercise of an autonomous power, is the power of **political direction** (*indirizzo politico*). This may be summarised as an institutional circuit that can be called upon to express the ultimate and more general political goals that the national community might seek to achieve (CRISAFULLI 1958). Beyond the disputes around whether this is an autonomous function or not, it must be remembered that its essential notion aligns with the form of government, intended as «the rules regarding how the function of political direction is distributed among the different constitutional bodies» (CARTABIA/LUPO 2022 at 65).

In the following pages, a brief overview of the Italian form of government will be presented, in order to illustrate the basic elements about the structure and the functions of the Parliament, the Government, and the President of the Republic, and the transformations affecting their mutual relationships.

3. The Parliament

The second part of the Constitution, dedicated to the 'Organisation of the Republic', begins with a detailed regulation of Parliament (Articles 55-82). In comparison to the limited rules applied to both the President of the Republic and the Government, the extensive nature of the prescriptions for Parliament demonstrates that the Italian Republic is a **parliamentary democracy**, because the will of the people is expressed in parliamentary elections, thereby ensuring that the Parliament is the central institution within the national form of government.

The **centrality of Parliament** is, therefore, a defining feature of the Italian system. The Constitution makes it clear that the function of political direction originates in Parliament as the only institution legitimated by popular vote (**representative democracy**) and indicates Parliament as the place where the executive power is summoned to be held ultimately accountable for its actions (**political responsibility**). As will be seen, governmental power finds its legitimacy in the relationship of confidence with Parliament and its appointment and its enduring need to be validated by the vote and the consistent confidence of the two Chambers of Parliament.

As to the structure of Parliament, it is firstly characterised by the equal (or symmetric) nature of the **bicameral system**. The two Chambers (namely, the Chamber of Deputies and the Senate of the Republic), albeit composed of a different number of MPs (respectively, 400 and 200), are fully equal in both structure and functions.

Despite the efforts undertaken in the Constituent Assembly to provide for a **specialised Senate**, whose representative nature would reflect either different social and economic categories or territories of the Republic, the final drafting of the Constitution converged along a line of compromise, according to which the two Chambers had to be equipped with the same functions to mutually reassure the political forces that the majority in one Chamber could be tempered by the other. Over recent decades, even minor organisational **differences** (like the legislative terms and the age requirements for the electors) have been progressively eliminated, so that the main difference is currently one related to the presence, in the Senate, of a maximum of five life-senators appointed by the President of the Republic, among those «who have honoured the Nation through their outstanding achievements in the social, scientific, artistic and literary fields» (Article 59).

Both Chambers share a similar **internal organisation**, whose importance within a parliamentary democracy centred upon the action of political parties was clearly perceived during the discussions of the Constituent Assembly. The main organisational structures are:

- **Joint Chambers**.: Article 55 prescribes that «[p]arliament shall meet in joint session of the members of both Houses only in cases established by this Constitution». Unlike the two Chambers, which carry out their tasks according to the principle of continuity, the joint sessions take place when the Parliament acts as electing body (for the President of the Republic, including regional delegates [Article 83], for one third of the members of the High Council of the Judiciary and for five members of the Constitutional Court, [respectively, Articles 104 and 135]).

- **President** (Speaker): Article 63 states that «[e]ach House shall elect a President and a Bureau from among its members». The Presidents of the two Chambers have a crucial role since parliamentary standing orders and a well-established tradition confer upon them a vast array of powers related to the internal life of the Houses, since they take part in almost every parliamentary procedure and have the power to represent the Chambers. Moreover, the Constitution states that their advice is necessary whenever the President of the Republic intends to dissolve one or both of the Chambers (Article 88), as well as when a new

 © Wolters Kluwer Italia

Executive is going to be nominated by the President of the Republic. Few other constitutional topics have the same fluid nature as the role of the Presidents of the two Chambers, which has significantly changed over the years, ranging from a neutral figure emerging from the opposition parties to a more active and engaged arbiter of parliamentary life. Since he or she is elected by an absolute majority of the Chambers, his or her role remains associated with a function of guarantee.

- **Parliamentary groups**: These entities are indirectly regulated by the Constitution when it prescribes that standing committees of both Chambers have to be «composed so as to reflect the proportion of the Parliamentary Groups» (Article 72, and, similarly, Article 82). Parliamentary groups are fractions reflecting political parties, even though the traditional fragmentation of the Italian party system and the high level of mobility among parties in Parliament (often critically associated with *trasformismo*) have favoured the establishment of parliamentary groups that do not find correspondence with organised parties. Groups have a crucial relevance in the internal organisation of both Chambers, since their chairpersons, sitting together in the Conference of groups' chairpersons with the Chamber's President, is asked to programme and coordinate the activity of the Houses.

- **Standing Committees**: As a permanent internal articulation of both Chambers, the role of Standing Committees is to steer the first stages of the legislative process (see *I.C).4.*), with the possibility that some bills are approved by the Committees themselves (with the exception laid down in Article 72, para. 4). Besides these organs, a vast array of other committees are involved in non-legislative functions, such as those charged with the internal organisation of Houses (such as the Committee on the Rule of Procedure, on the elections and parliamentary immunities) and with *ad-hoc* tasks (these are often established by law, such as the Committee on Public Broadcasting).

The fundamental principles concerning the functioning of Parliament can be summarized as follows:

- **Publicity**: Even though secret deliberations are not excluded, every deliberation of Parliament takes place under the eye of the public, as well as every vote cast by the MPs (a secret ballot is foreseen by the standing orders for votes regarding specific persons or matters on fundamental rights). To put it briefly, in a democratic Parliament, public is the rule, secret is the exception. This explains, together with the role reserved to minorities, why the Constitution accorded a great significance to parliamentary legislation to safeguard fundamental rights via reservation to legislation (*riserva di legge*; see *I.C).4.*).

- **Continuity**: Unlike previous Parliaments, both the Chamber of Deputies and the Senate of the Republic do not cease their action with the legislative term (five years). Even though «[t]he term for each House may not be extended, save by law and only in the case of war» (Article 60, para. 2), to avoid the interruption of the representative function, Article 61 prescribes that until the new Houses meet, «the powers of the previous Houses are extended».

- **Autonomy:** Both Chambers enjoy a wide margin of autonomy in the regulation of those internal affairs that are not directly and explicitly regulated by the Constitution. Whereas an explicit delegation to the standing orders (see *I.C).7.*) is foreseen for the «internal functioning», a similar autonomy is recognised with regards to financial aspects, to the internal police and domestic jurisdiction. In these fields, only internal rules can be applied and enforced.

Once the organisation and the principles of functioning have been taken into consideration, a focus has to be made on the most important **functions** carried out by Parliament. These can be divided into three groups:

- **Legislative function**: The law-making power identifies a core function of every Parliament. In the Italian case, this task is even more central if attention moves from the assumption that the Constitution (Article 70) reserves the legislative function exclusively to the Parliament, unlike other countries where a quota of legislative power is reserved to the Executive (Article 34 of the Constitution of the French Republic). The basic tenets of the legislative process have been summarised above (*I.C).4.*).

- **Control and supervision**: Since Parliament is the only institution that directly represents the people, a further function assigned to it by the Constitution is to control the Executive's action and to promote public inquiries on every political, social and economic issue that is deemed necessary. Within the control functions, every MP is entitled to put questions to single Ministers (*interrogazioni, interpellanze*) and the Chamber can deliberate with a differentiated set of acts to make use of the power to get information from the Executive and to steer its action. The supervisory function includes mainly parliamentary inquiries, that may be conducted by each Chamber «on matters of public interest» (Article 82). Inquiries have often been established to ascertain politically sensitive issues and they are a powerful instrument since the *ad-hoc* created Committee enjoys the same powers as the Judiciary (Griglio 2022);

- **Political direction**: As previously mentioned, the function of political direction (*indirizzo politico*) pertains to the establishment of those ultimate political

© Wolters Kluwer Italia

and social goals that should be attained through the exercise of political power. In a a parliamentary form of government, this function is rooted in the basic decisions taken by Parliament, first and foremost in its relationship with the Executive, whose action is bound by the decisions of the majority sitting in Parliament.

Given its unwritten and somehow undefined nature, the exercise of the function of political direction does not have a **predetermined boundary**, therefore every decision of the Parliament in its legislative role, as well as in its control and supervisory function, can potentially qualify as a necessary condition for the continuation in office of the Executive. The approval or denial of some politically sensitive legislative measures (such as the budget or the ratification of an international treaty) implies, *ipso facto,* confirmation or end of the **confidence relationship** between the Parliament and the Government.

The main field in which Parliament's political direction role operates is, therefore, the one concerning the establishment, the persistence and the end of the **confidence relationship** (*rapporto di fiducia*) between the Parliament and the Executive.

To take and to continue in office, the Executive (*i.e.*, the President of the Council of Ministers and the Ministers *jointly*) «must receive the confidence of both Houses of Parliament» (Article 94, para. 1). This principle is at the core of the **parliamentary form of government**, and its concrete regulation will be dealt with when discussing the Government and the evolutions of the mutual relationships among these organs.

4. The Government

Unlike the detailed regulation of the structure and functions of the Parliament, the Constitution dedicates a very **narrow normative framework** to the Government (Articles 92 to 96). This stems the intention of the framers to circumscribe the executive power while making its structure and concrete functioning strongly connected with the role of Parliament in the form of government.

Although one of the fundamental guidelines of the Constituent Assembly was to preserve the stability of the executive function within the parliamentary form of government (*ordine del giorno Perassi*, see above, Section A), the institutional devices aimed at **rationalising** the relationships between Parliament and Government have played in practice a relatively ineffective role in ensuring the stability of the latter.

The defining feature of Italian parliamentary democracy is the **confidence relationship** that must exist between Parliament and the Government. This has to be established within ten days of the appointment of the President of the Council and the Ministers by the President of the Republic (Article 94, para. 3; formally, by their oath). The entry of the Government into office before the formal vote of confidence of both Houses of Parliament is a peculiarity of the Italian form of Government (Elia 1961), and is aimed at ensuring the continuity of governmental action, even though the powers of the Government before the vote of confidence (as well as after a vote of no confidence) are, by constitutional convention, limited to the ordinary administration.

According to Article 94, para. 2, «[e]ach House shall grant or withdraw its confidence through a reasoned motion voted by roll-call». The **motion of confidence** is the act with which both Houses confer to the Government the power to exercise the full range of its prerogatives and marks the material date of birth of the newly established Executive. The motion of confidence is voted by both Houses after the President of the Council delivers her or his speech alternatively before one of them, according to the fully symmetric nature of Italian bicameralism. The presidential speech contains the programme of Government's action, around which the parliamentary majority has found an agreement during the appointment procedure led by the President of the Republic. Henceforth, the motion is «reasoned» in that the vote of Parliament refers to the programmatic speech, and the public vote, with the roll-call system, is aimed at granting a clear assignment of responsibility between the newly formed Government and the MPs belonging to the groups that express the **parliamentary majority**. The rationalisation of the parliamentary form of government and the necessity to protect «the needs of stability of government action and to avoid the degeneration of parliamentarism» has thus been realised, at the beginning of the relationship of confidence, through a clear identification between parliamentary majority and the Government, which implies the **institutional responsibility** of the latter before the former, but with the assumption of a diffuse political responsibility of MPs before public opinion in case of a withdrawal of confidence (Rescigno 1967).

The **motion of no confidence** is the act that one or both Houses may adopt in order to legally force the Government to resign, whereas «[a]n opposing vote by one or both the Houses against a Government proposal does not entail the obligation to resign». The motion of no confidence is somehow symmetrical to the motion of confidence and marks the closing of the relationship of confidence that has to continuously take place during the term of office of the Government. Even the motion of no confidence is, then, regulated in a way that it is aimed at avoiding governmental instability: according to Article 94, para. 5, it «must be signed by at least one tenth of the members of a House and may be debated at least three days following its submission». Both requirements (subscription and

 © Wolters Kluwer Italia

term for presentation) have been referred to as elements capable of showing the willingness of the framers to ensure governmental stability, even though their effective function has been, rather, to deter parliamentary minorities from taking *impromptu* initiatives. In fact, with very few exceptions, Executives have always resigned because of internal weaknesses of majority coalitions, which led to parliamentary crises taking place **outside Parliament**.

Strictly connected to the motion of no confidence established by Article 94, is the possibility for one or both Houses to withdraw confidence in **a single Minister**. Even though this possibility is not directly regulated by the Constitution (which refers the relationship of confidence to the Government as a whole), it has always been considered a constitutional convention that is intrinsic to parliamentary democracy, centred upon the collective (or rather collegial) nature of the Executive, within which the President of the Council has no formal power to force Ministers to resign, whereas single Ministers «shall be individually responsible for the decisions of their own ministries» (Article 95, para. 3). In practice, with the only exception being the motion of no confidence approved by the Senate against the Minister of Justice Filippo Mancuso in 1995 (validated by the Constitutional Court with the Judgment No. 7/1996), every effort of parliamentary minorities to force a Minister to resign has to be dealt with by the President of Council, which often declares that the challenged act of a Minister falls under the responsibility of the whole Government, so as to defuse the political conflict.

Much more frequent is the use of another instrument which is not regulated by the Constitution: the **question of confidence**. Moving from a constitutional custom, later codified in the standing orders of both Houses, the question of confidence is a procedural mechanism enabling the Government to «pre-alert the Parliament as to the crucial effect to which a future parliamentary vote could give rise on the existence of the confidence relationship» (Cartabia/Lupo 2022 at 102). Whenever the Council of Ministers (which is competent, according to Article 2 of the Law No. 400/1988) decides, upon the initiative of the President of the Council, that a certain parliamentary vote is politically decisive for the Executive, it may pre-alert the Parliament that a contrary vote may lead to the end of the relationship of confidence and, thus, to the resignation of the whole Government. The practical effect of the question of confidence, which has become more frequent in recent decades, is both to reinforce the majority coalition (a roll-call vote is adopted) and, even more evidently, to force the Parliament to speed up the procedure of approval, since the question of confidence brings procedurally the chronological priority of the vote at stake and the impossibility of amending the text deemed by the Government to be politically crucial.

© Wolters Kluwer Italia

In recent years, increasing criticism has emerged concerning the practical use of the question of confidence, since it has become an instrument that is too often associated with so-called **maxi-amendments**, i.e., legislative initiatives on the part of the government aimed at resolving, with the submission of a text which substitutes an entire bill, a situation of political conflict within the majority coalition. The Constitutional Court has repeatedly criticised the combination of maxi-amendments and questions of confidence (among others, Order No. 17/2019), whose main effect is to limit the discussion of MPs and to contravene the constitutional provision according to which every bill should «be referred to a Committee and then to the plenary, which shall consider it section by section and then put it to the final vote» (Article 72, para. 1).

Both the **structure** and the **functions** of Government are not extensively provided for by the Constitution.

As to the former, the drafters clearly decided to move away from the predominance of the President of the Council of Ministers, which was a defining feature of the fascist regime, particularly after its authoritarian turn in 1925-1926 (see *I.A).2.*). Despite this, constitutional provisions did not sketch out a fully-fledged alternative in that they lay down three main principles from whose interaction and combination of different models of Government structure may emerge:

1) The **President of the Council of Ministers** enjoys a kind of primacy within the governmental structure since he or she «shall conduct and be accountable for the general policy of the Government» and «shall ensure the consistency of the political and administrative directions, by promoting and coordinating the activities of Ministers» (Article 95, paras. 1 and 2).

2) The **Council of Ministers** is the collegial body formed by the PM and Ministers and it legally has the ultimate power to declare the will of the Government; every act or decision that formally pertains to the Government as a constitutional branch has to be referred to the Council because both the PM and Ministers are subordinated to this body (Article 95, para. 3: «The Ministers shall be collectively responsible for the decisions of the Council of Ministers»).

3) The **Ministers** are assigned to an administrative structure with a proper domain (Ministries), and are held «individually responsible for the decisions of their own ministries» (Article 95, para. 3).

These three pillars of the governmental structure are left to different kinds of interactions, mainly ranging from a collegial focus to a clearer guidance for action on the part of the President of the Council.

 © Wolters Kluwer Italia

During an initial phase, coinciding with the dominance of the **proportional system** and the '**governments of coalition**', supported by a political majority emerging after the elections, government action was mainly guided by single Ministers, each one reflecting a single political party (or a fraction thereof), so that their high degree of autonomy left the role of a *primus inter pares* (lit. *first among equals*) to the President of the Council, mainly called upon to coordinate government policy, but not to direct it (CHELI/SPAZIANTE 1977). Against this **collegial background**, the instability of governments was compensated by the continuity of political forces that supported the majority (from 1948 to 1981, when Giovanni Spadolini, a prominent figure of the Republican Party, was appointed President of the Council of Ministers, every PM belonged to the Christian Democratic Party), and the persistent exclusion of some parties from that area (such as the Communist Party, according to the *conventio ad excludendum*, a formula coined by ELIA 1970). Continuity was granted, however, by the continuity of the appointment of Ministers to certain ministries, which reflected the political will to establish a link between certain political areas and some administrative domains (including agriculture and education, traditionally dominated by leading figures of the Christian-Democratic Party).

In a second phase, instigated by the **majoritarian turn** and coinciding with governments led by distinctive figures, the main role of the President of the Council was to guide the action of the whole Government, so that the role of Ministers became less relevant and even the collegial principle faded in favour of an emerging presidential trend. In this framework, the role of the PM is not only to ensure the coherence of political and administrative action through the coordination of Ministers, but also to assume a leading function according to his being responsible «for the general policy of the Government».

The increasing importance of the President of the Council, albeit in the framework of a government system that formally maintains a balance with the collegial principle (as is clarified by the relationship of confidence, running through the Parliament and the Government as a whole), is dependent upon **different reasons**, that do not entirely coincide with the majoritarian electoral system.

After a long time in which the formal relationships between the PM, the Council of Ministers and the Ministers remained mainly undecided, it was only in 1988 that the law establishing the organisation of the Presidency of the Council was enacted (**Law No. 400/1988**), in order to fulfil the obligation stemming from Article 95, para. 4 («The law shall establish the organisation of the Presidency of the Council, as well as the number, competence and organisation of ministries»). Even if adopted before the turn to the majoritarian system in 1993, this seminal piece of legislation provided a clarification of the variables emerging from the

Constitution, by stating that it is mainly up to the interaction between the PM and the Council of Ministers to sketch out the guiding lines of government action. In this light, the Council of Ministers remains the organ expressing the ultimate will **within** the Government and the PM enjoys a distinctive role in promoting and coordinating its action and in settling disputes among Ministers (Articles 2 and 5). Besides this, the President of the Council was given new and (mainly) unprecedented powers by the law, concerning governmental action **outside** of Government, such as in the field of the EU and the relationships with Regions (Article 5). This pre-eminence is demonstrated by the later **Delegated Decree No. 303/1999**, which created two *ad-hoc* structures (the *Department of the Presidency of the Council of Ministers for European Policies* and the *Department of the Presidency of the Council of Ministers for Regional Affairs*) dedicated to coordinate the PM's action in European and regional affairs.

The more significant role of the President of the Council is, then, only partially dependent upon the turn to a majoritarian system, something which has not significantly affected the instability of Governments: indeed, this role is much more connected with the need to coordinate internal, supra- and international policy (Rivosecchi 2018). Both the representative role at the international level and the growing quest for unity and coherence in the implementation of EU-related policies have favoured the leading role of the President of the Council, who has an administrative structure at his disposal (**Presidency of the Council**), whose role has grown in recent last years, with particular regard to the implementation of the NextGen Programme, launched by the EU in the aftermath of the COVID-19 outbreak.

A further area of transformation in the role of governments is related to the so-called **technocratic governments** (*governi tecnici*), which have been appointed on several occasions since 1993 because of the particular prestige of the technical figures acting as PMs (Ciampi 1992-1993, Dini 1994-1995, Monti 2011-2013, Draghi 2021-2023) and the need for less partisan politics in times of economic or political crisis. Although such governments are undoubtedly atypical because of their being led by figures who are not MPs and who drive forward an agenda that has not been entirely set by political parties, they have to be seen as a variant within parliamentary democracy, since they have always relied on the confidence of parliamentary majority and their appointment shows, if anything, the growing role of the President of the Republic within the form of government (Lupo 2015).

5. The President of the Republic

Coherently with the characteristics of parliamentary democracy, the President of the Republic is not elected by the people, but by the Parliament in its Joint

 © Wolters Kluwer Italia

Chambers. Several aspects of his election and mandate show that the Constitution moved away from the idea of a republican monarch vested with the titularity of executive powers, but has maintained some external traits of the previous figure since the President is defined «Head of State» with the main function to «**repre-sent[ing] national unity**» (Article 87).

The President of the Republic is **elected** by the Joint Chambers of Parliament with the addition of three delegates for each Region (except for the Valle d'Aosta Region which has one delegate). This integration of the elective body is aimed at conferring the President a wider representative basis, which includes territorial and linguistic minorities and reinforces the pluralist character of the Republic, as formed by regional and local entities in the framework of unity and indivisibility established by Article 5. The required **majority** for the election of the President is two-thirds of the members in the first three votes, and 50% plus one vote in all subsequent votes. Votes are delivered in a **secret ballot,** and a constitutional convention precludes any application. The presidential mandate covers a period of **seven years** and **re-election**, although not expressly prohibited by the Constitution, was excluded on a customary basis for a long period, until Giorgio Napolitano was re-elected in 2013, followed by Sergio Mattarella, in 2022.

All of these characteristics show that the President of the Republic is situated and works **'above'** party politics, but **not 'outside'** it; his legitimacy relies on a wide representative basis, which tends to exclude that the activity of the President can be identified with only one part of the political spectrum. The guiding principle of the office is thus to act formally as a Head of State (first and foremost in international relationships), and to undertake whichever action, whether formal or informal, he or she deems necessary to preserve and promote the balanced and correct functioning of the institutional system. The Constitutional Court, in Judgment No. 1/2013, has summed up these features in the following way:

> Given the above methodological premises, when describing the overall powers of the President of the Republic within the Italian constitutional system, it will become clear that he has been placed by the Constitution outside the traditional branches of state, and naturally above all political parties. He is thus vested with powers that impinge upon each of the aforementioned branches of the state, to safeguard both their separation and their equilibrium. This singular characteristic of the President's position is reflected by the nature of his powers, which do not imply the power to take decisions concerning specific issues, but give him the means to induce other constitutional powers to fulfil their functions correctly, thereby bringing about the relative decisions on the merits. The special nature of the Head of State's position is based on the nature of his powers, which set him

apart from other constitutional authorities, without however impinging upon the principle of parity between them.

And furthermore:

The President of the Republic «represents national unity» (Article 87(1) of the Constitution) not only in the sense of the territorial unity of the state, but also and above all in the sense of the cohesion and harmonious functioning of the powers, policies and guarantees comprising the constitutional framework of the Republic. The President is an authority for ensuring moderation and stimulus for the other branches of the state, which may be assumed to tend to an excessive exercise of their powers or inertia. Therefore, all of the powers of the President of the Republic have the goal of enabling him to direct appropriate efforts at the occupants of the offices that must take decisions on the merits; he must not act as a surrogate for them but encourage and support their operation or, in situations of stalemate or blockage, take measures aimed at relaunching the ordinary mode of operation of constitutional authorities.

Among the different presidential functions, the **appointment of the Government** is, therefore, one of the most sensitive, because it affects a central feature in the functioning of the form of government. According to Article 92, para. 1, «[t]he President of the Republic shall appoint a President of the Council of Ministers, on whose proposal the President of the Republic shall appoint Ministers», but no further element is given as to the procedure or the yardsticks against which the President of the Republic should exercise such a delicate task. The main task that the President has to fulfil is to appoint a President of the Council and, on his or her proposal, Ministers who can receive the confidence of the parliamentary majority. Such an objective can be easier to attain in all circumstances in which a clear majority is given, *e.g.*, immediately after elections (in this case, the discretion of the President is limited by the necessity to appoint a Government that, more or less directly, corresponds to the majority sitting in both Houses of Parliament). In all cases in which, on the contrary, the need to appoint a new Government derives from the dissolution of a governmental majority (as frequently happens), the discretion of the President of the Republic is increased since he or she is called to verify whether a new majority may arise in Parliament, and, in so doing, may favour a reassessment of the political landscape.

The **appointment procedure** is entirely regulated by conventional rules and customs, and is divided into three phases: consultations, mandate conferral and formal appointment. In the first phase, the President runs one or two rounds of **consultations**, during which he or she is informed by different figures (the Speakers of two Houses, leaders of parliamentary groups and party leaders,

 © Wolters Kluwer Italia

former Presidents of the Republic and representatives of social organisations) about which political options are available in view of a new majority, and which political figures may find a consensus in the parliamentary majority as PM and Ministers. Whenever this consensus is hard to find, assistance can be offered to the President of the Republic by other institutional figures (normally, the Speakers of the two Houses) who can negotiate with political parties to favour the emergence of a governmental majority. Once a possible consensus on a governmental formula emerges, a **mandate** is conferred by the President of the Republic to a candidate PM, who accepts the office on a provisional basis and takes some time to accept, during which he or she entertains a confrontation with political parties to sketch out a common programme and to identify the Ministers. When the mandate is finally accepted, the President of the Republic **formally appoints** the President of the Council with an *ad-hoc* decree, and, with a further decree, the Ministers proposed by the PM. All of these presidential decrees, along with the one accepting the dismissal of the previous Government, are countersigned by the new PM.

The countersignature of these acts sheds light on a general feature that qualifies the role and the status of the President of the Republic. According to Article 89, «[a] writ of the President of the Republic shall not be valid unless signed by the proposing Minister, who shall be accountable for it». This clause is strictly connected with the one laid down in Article 90, which states that «[t]he President of the Republic shall not be responsible for the actions performed in the exercise of presidential duties, except in case of high treason or attack on the Constitution». In line with the traditional assumption that has excluded any kind of responsibility for monarchs (*the King can do no wrong*), even the President of the Republic is shielded from both **legal** and **political responsibility**.

Regarding the former, the President may be held **responsible** only in the case of **high treason** and of a manifest attempt to **infringe on the Constitution**. Should this happen, he or she may be impeached by Parliament in joint session, with an absolute majority of its members, and her or his responsibility is decided upon by the Constitutional Court, sitting in an *ad-hoc* composition enlarged to 31 members, 16 of whom are randomly selected from within a list of 45 candidates proposed by the Parliament in joint session every nine years (Article 135, para. 7).

The rule is, therefore, that the President of the Republic cannot be held responsible for all of those acts that are carried out in the execution of his duties and functions, whose flexible and occasionally informal nature implies that the spectrum of legal responsibility has to be circumscribed to purely personal affairs. As the Constitutional Court clarified (Judgment No. 1/2013), the President is required «to liaise with all holders of the highest public office, exercising the powers of stimulus, persuasion and moderation referred to above, which necessarily require discretion and confidentiality».

As to **political responsibility**, the President of the Republic is formally vested with significant political powers (promulgating laws, appointing the Government, dissolving the Parliament, etc.), whose exercise may endanger his or her role of an arbitrating institution placed above, but not outside of, partisan politics. For this reason, Article 89 states that each and every act has to be countersigned by the Ministers, or even by the President of the Council, in the case of acts having the force of law or being indicated by the law itself. The role and effect of the **countersignature** aim, at the same time, at transferring political responsibility from the President to the Government (which is, by default, responsible before Parliament), and at preventing the President from exercising powers that may imply substantive political direction. In light of these concurring reasons, the nature and the scope of the countersignature are to be grasped within the diversified category of presidential acts. As the Constitutional Court stated in Judgment No. 200/2006, the countersignature

> takes on a different value depending on the type of procedure which it completes or, more precisely, for the validity of which it is a prerequisite. It is of course clear that the countersignature plays a substantive role when the act presented for signature by the Head of State is governmental in nature and therefore an expression of the powers vested in the Executive, whilst it must be recognised as having a merely formal value where the act is an expression of the powers vested in the President of the Republic [...]

It is thus necessary to differentiate the categories of presidential acts, to better understand the role played by the President and of the Government in their adoption:

a) **Formally presidential and substantively governmental acts**: This is the widest category that includes all of those acts that are formally adopted by the President, but whose content is decided upon by the Government. With regards to these, the countersignature clarifies who is to be held politically responsible for any decision (the President of the Council and/or the «proposing Minister»). Among others, such categories include:

- the enactment of legislative decrees and decree-laws;
- the authorisation to submit the Government's legislative bills to one of two Houses;
- the convening of parliamentary elections and referenda;

 © Wolters Kluwer Italia

- ratification of international treaties;
- the act of appointment (civil servants, prefects, and ambassadors) following deliberation of the Council of Ministers.

b) **Formally and substantively presidential acts**: In this more restricted category of acts, the President is called both to determine the content of the act and to formally adopt it. Against this background, the countersignature aims to demonstrate that the act originates with the President of the Republic and to verify that its essential constitutional and legislative requirements are satisfied. This category includes:

- the appointment of life senators and five constitutional judges;
- the power to send messages to the Houses;
- the power to grant pardons and to commute punishments (which was included in this category by the Constitutional Court with Judgment No. 200/2006, after having been traditionally referred to as a substantive governmental power);
- the power to refuse promulgation and to send Parliament a reasoned opinion invoking a reconsideration of a law passed by Parliament.

c) **Dual acts**: This much-debated category includes those presidential acts whose content is deliberated by the converging decisions of both the President and the Government (more accurately, the President of the Council). Only two acts are traditionally linked to this category, but they are among the most important powers exercised by the President of the Republic: the appointment of the Government (already considered) and the **dissolution of Parliament**. According to Article 88, para. 1, «[i]n consultation with the presiding officers of Parliament, the President may dissolve one or both Houses of Parliament». This act has a *sui generis* nature if compared with other presidential acts, since the President is procedurally bound by the necessity to hear the two Speakers, although their opinion is not binding for the President. The absence of clear criteria that justify dissolution is only partially compensated by the clause that prevents the President from dissolving Parliament during the last six months of the presidential mandate (Article 88, para. 2) and has, therefore, to be grasped within the low degree of formalisation that the whole procedure entails. The decision of the President of the Republic must converge with the opinion of both Speakers and with the President of the Council, in that the dissolution of Parliament is necessary whenever it is not able to express a clear governmental majority. The countersignature assumes, here, a very special nature, since it «confirms that the Government has resigned and that, at least *rebus sic stantibus* (things standing as they are), there is no alternative parliamentary majority in sight» (Cartabia/Lupo 2022 at 135).

© Wolters Kluwer Italia

Even more clearly than in the case of Government, the few clauses dedicated by the Constitution to the President of the Republic have favoured the emergence of this role as **fluid** and **open-ended** and, therefore, largely dependent upon the different personalities that carry out such a task. The presidential role has been reconstructed in accordance with different and often diverging paradigms as it could be alternatively associated with the role of the supreme holder of the Republic in times of crisis (Esposito 1960) or with the *super partes* guarantor of balances intrinsic to the parliamentary form of government (Paladin 1986). The evolution of the institutional system shows that the President of the Republic can be both, in that his sphere of action is limited to a *super partes* role whenever parliamentary democracy works in accordance with the *inputs* given by party politics, whereas his or her functions enlarge in situations in which political process is not able to be self-sufficient (because of governmental instability or exceptional crisis) and the need of unity can be satisfied only with presidential inputs. In recent years, this enlargement of function has been strictly connected with the **European engagement** of Presidents, such as Ciampi, Napolitano and Mattarella, whose formal and (more frequently) informal powers have been guided by the necessity to align fundamental political decisions to the commitments arising from the membership of Italy in the EU (Piccirilli 2018, and *II.B).1.b.*).

6. The Italian Form of Government as an Adaptive Framework

It is commonplace, in legal literature, that the constitutional regulation of the form of government in Italy is not clear-cut and leaves significant **room for *manoeuvre*** for institutions and political parties to adapt concrete functioning to changing contexts (La Palombara 1987). The rules, principles, customs and constitutional conventions described above are, then, to be intended as an open framework which sets the boundaries of what is precluded according to the Constitution, rather than a fully-fledged set of rules that impose a pre-given institutional arrangement.

Many factors may be invoked to obtain a clearer account of the transformations and the adaptive mechanisms that have shaped the Italian form of government in the recent decades.

Among others, a crucial significance is to be accorded to **electoral legislation**. Although the Constitution does not prescribe a certain electoral formula, the political parties that drafted the Constitution converged on the idea that the parliamentary form of government had to materially coincide with a proportional voting system, since this, more than others, could guarantee the functions of mutual reassurance and political counterweight that several institutional devices

© Wolters Kluwer Italia

were meant to preserve (the centrality of Parliament, symmetrical bicameralism, the limited coordinating role of the President of the Council). Except for the first republican legislature (1948-1953), which worked in a majoritarian fashion and culminated in the approval of a corresponding new electoral system that failed to maintain its premises and was quickly repealed, in the next 40 years, a **proportional voting system** gave rise to a parliamentary system based on a coalition model. In this framework, Parliament was at the centre of the political process, and the relationships between political parties were mainly aimed at differentiating *governmental* politics (led by coalitions agreements guided by the Christian-Democratic Party) from *parliamentary* politics (animated by those political parties that were, by default, outside of government coalitions, such as the Communist and post-fascist parties).

Such preclusions and their related institutional underpinnings were left behind when a popular referendum in 1993 induced political forces to introduce a **majoritarian voting system**. In line with major transformations taking place in the same period (the fall of the Berlin Wall and the collapse of an entire political class with the *Tangentopoli* or 'Bribesville' scandal), the movement to a different voting system induced a more general reassessment of the form of government. In such a different scenario, the coalition model and the centripetal party system (FARNETI 1983) were superseded by a bipolar pattern of electoral system which bolstered the presidentialisation of Government and the downgrading of parliamentary legislation to the inputs given by the Government. In this new landscape, the need to erect a counterbalance has been occasionally transferred to *super partes* institutions, such as the President of the Republic and the Constitutional Court (REPETTO 2018).

Two other factors that produced a transformation of the form of government can be briefly considered.

As has been the case with many other European countries, the Italian institutional system has undergone a process of polycentrism and internal differentiation, mainly because of the combined effects of both Europeanisation and the regionalisation of politics (see, respectively, *II.B).1.d.* and *III.B).1.*).

The ratification of the Treaty of Maastricht in 1992, with its stricter rules on public debt and the initiation of a new stage in supranational integration, triggered a relocation of public powers from the national to the **European Union** level, whose effects on the national form of government could not but alter those balances and *formulae* shaped in a period during which the State (and Parliament) were supposed to have the last word on public expenditure. Since European politics is (and remains) part of international relationships, it is quite inevitable that the transferral of more and more competences to the EU has taken place alongside the increased role of the executive power, whose members sit in the Council and whose Head contributes to the fundamental political inputs given by the European Council. As will be considered in Part II, the main challenge is thus to cope with the main features of the Italian system (democracy, the separation of powers, the centrality of Parliament and representative democracy) with the complex requirements of a **composite constitutional model**, such as the one set out at EU level, moving from the assumption that such a process has its constitutional basis in Article 11 of the Constitution and in the related necessity to promote international and supranational cooperation aimed at establishing «peace and justice among Nations» (LUPO/PICCIRILLI 2017).

Even the ongoing and pervasive process of **regionalisation** has affected the concrete functioning of the form of government since the transferral of significant legislative powers to Regions has quantitatively (if not qualitatively) eroded the role of the national Parliament. Moreover, the failure to establish a second Chamber in which Regions and local entities are represented at the national level has increased the role of Government, which is called upon to play a coordinating role with regional executives in the so-called 'system of conferences'; *i.e.*, bodies set up by ordinary legislation, whose main scope is to favour agreements between state and regional levels in all those ambits in which competences and powers are inextricably connected.

E) THE JUDICIARY AND THE CONSTITUTIONAL COURT

1. The Judiciary

To give a full account of the separation of powers, a section has to be dedicated to the guarantees that the Constitution reserves to the Judiciary.

Moving from the pervasive interference that the Government had previously exercised towards the Judiciary in the liberal state and, with an even higher degree of authoritarianism, in the fascist era, the drafters of the Constitution decided to establish an extensive set of guarantees for the judicial power, with the aim of preserving its **autonomy** and **independence**.

These guarantees are conferred to both the **single judge** and to the **Judiciary** as a whole and can be divided into **functional** and **institutional** ones.

A key principle is the one laid down in Article 101, para. 2, according to which «[j]udges shall be subject only to the law». This principle, which may seem a

© Wolters Kluwer Italia

codification of judicial activity in terms of the formal application of legal rules, entails a wider meaning and scope, in that it preserves the autonomy of judges in their activity of legal interpretation so that they are shielded from whatever influence may come from within or outside the Judiciary. This provision is thus closely connected to the institutional arrangement of the Judiciary, whose organisation does not reflect any formal hierarchy as to the effects of judicial decisions (Article 107, para 3, reads: «[m]embers of the Judiciary shall be distinguished only by their different functions»). This contributed to depicting the Judiciary as a **diffuse power** since even the Court of Cassation is not able to adopt decisions which, as a rule, binds the judges of lower degrees.

Special functional independence is then prescribed for **public prosecutors**, which are part of the Judiciary and are thus not dependent upon the executive power; their action is guided by the principle according to which they have «the obligation to institute criminal proceedings» (Article 112).

Individual judicial guarantees are strongly intertwined with the rules and principles that the Constitution dedicates to preserving the autonomy and independence of the **Judiciary** from «all other powers» (Article 104, para. 1). Judicial autonomy and independence are preserved through the establishment of an *ad-hoc* institution, the High Council of the Judiciary (*Consiglio superiore della magistratura*, CSM), whose composition and functions reflect the intention of the Constitution to reserve to the Judiciary itself all those administrative tasks that impact on the concrete exercise of judicial activity.

According to Article 105, the **High Council of the Judiciary** exercises **jurisdiction** over employment, appointments and transfers, promotions and disciplinary measures of judges, which have to be carried out following the legislative provisions laid down in the general law on the Judiciary (*ordinamento giudiziario*), whereas Article 107, para. 1, states that judges shall not be removed, and not «be dismissed or suspended from office or assigned to other offices or functions save by a decision of the High Council for the Judiciary, taken either for the reasons and in compliance with the defence rights established by the law regulating the Judiciary or with the consent of the member of the Judiciary concerned».

As these provisions show, judicial guarantees are aimed at ensuring that the judicial function is preserved against any kind of undue pressure, and assigning these tasks to the High Council of the Judiciary reveals a two-fold objective. **Firstly**, no other power, be it legislative or executive, can influence or endanger the exercise of judicial functions by removing or somehow interfering with the activity of judges in certain proceedings. **Secondly**, the judges are protected from the pressures from within the Judiciary, since every act pertaining to their *status* does not depend upon the will of the office's director, but has to be adopted by the institution that is supposed to serve the general interest of the judicial branch.

The **composition** of the High Council of the Judiciary shows that the notion of 'judicial self-government' does not meet with the rules concerning the organisation and the functions of this institution. The High Council is chaired by the President of the Republic and its members are selected from two different constituencies. Two-thirds of them are elected by the ordinary judges themselves (**'gowned'** members, currently 20), and one-third are elected by the Parliament in joint session with a qualified majority from among university professors of law and lawyers with 15 years of practice (**'lay'** members, currently 10). The First President and the Prosecutor General of the Court of Cassation are *ex officio* members of the High Council. The Vice-President, who *de facto* chairs the High Council in coordination with the President of the Republic, is elected by the High Council itself from among the lay members. The system of election of the 'gowned members' has been recently modified (legislative decree No. 71/2022), according to a majority voting mechanism in a larger number of constituencies, to prevent the risk of internal politicisation associated with the role of organised groups (*correnti*) supposed to reflect different cultural and political orientations. All of these complex mechanisms show that the autonomy and independence implied by the Constitution for the Judiciary are meant to be a guarantee against undue intrusions rather than a detachment of it from the rest of the constitutional organisation; the chairmanship of the President of the Republic, the presence of lay members and the principle of legality in the organisation of judicial offices reveal the qualified distance that should separate the Judiciary from other powers.

In the Italian judicial system, the unity of the jurisdiction is proclaimed by Article 102 («judicial functions shall be exercised by ordinary members of the Judiciary as shall be established and regulated by the law concerning the Judiciary»), which precludes the establishment of **extraordinary** (*i.e.*, *ad-hoc*) or **special judges**. This prohibition is the institutional corollary of the overarching value accorded by other clauses of the Constitution to the right of access to justice (Article 24: «Anyone may bring cases before a court of law in order to protect their rights under civil and administrative law») and to the right of defence (Article 111). The importance of these guarantees is emphasised by the right not to be «removed from the court seized with it as established by law» (Article 25), which embodies both a safeguard for the individual and a binding institutional guideline for the organisation of courts and tribunals.

 © Wolters Kluwer Italia

At the same time, the unity of jurisdiction is partially counterbalanced by further constitutional provisions, which delegate specific tasks to **specialised courts**.

Article 103, para. 1, establishes that «[t]he Council of State and the other administrative justice bodies shall have jurisdiction over the protection of legitimate interests before public agencies and, in particular matters laid out by the law, also of subjective rights». Administrative justice is currently exercised by the Council of State and by the Regional Administrative Courts, which respectively serve as appellate body and first-instance tribunals in the case of an application raised against (mainly) administrative decisions taken by public authorities. The Italian system of **administrative justice** is framed in accordance with the dual system forged by the French tradition, although it has been largely remodelled in recent years, with increasing importance given to those situations in which administrative courts are called upon to adjudicate exclusively on a certain field (*giurisdizione esclusiva*) involving individual (and sometimes even fundamental) rights.

Further specialised courts are regulated by paras. 2 and 3 of Article 103, with regards to the **Court of Auditors** (which has «jurisdiction in matters of public accounts and in other matters laid out by the law») and to **military courts**, which in times of war «have the jurisdiction established by law», whereas «[i]n times of peace they have jurisdiction only for military crimes committed by members of the armed forces».

2. The Constitutional Court: Nature, Composition and Functions

The Italian Constitutional Court (ItCC) is not placed by the Constitution inside the organisation of the judiciary (regulated in Title IV, Articles 101 to 113), but is included in Title VI of the Second Part of the Constitution, dedicated to '**constitutional guarantees**' (Articles 134 to 137), jointly with the constitutional amendment procedure (Articles 138 to 139). The reasons for this choice should not be of surprise, since the drafters of the Constitution were aware of its novelty, and demonstrated caution against the risk that the power to review legislation could fall into the hands of the judicial power. The ***gouvernement des juges*** had to be avoided since the vast array of new rights and values enshrined in the Constitution could remain undeliverable if its judicial enforcement was made dependent upon a generation of judges trained and appointed during the fascist regime.

Moreover, despite criticisms stemming from some areas of the Constituent Assembly, a vast majority agreed that the establishment of the ItCC as a specialised body was necessary in order to preserve the new edifice and its values against the risk of a downgrading, such as the one put forth by fascism against the institutions of the liberal state. Thus, constitutional justice is a **guarantee of the Constitution**, in that the normative force of the latter is reinforced, and its rigid nature is made effective, *vis-à-vis* threats coming from parliamentary majorities.

At the same time, the action of the Constitutional Court is largely shaped by judicial forms, and this reflects its nature as a **special centralised court**, which owes much to the elaboration of **Hans Kelsen**, in the context of the emergence of the Austrian model in the second decade of the twentieth century. The idea that a dedicated court had to be vested with the power to quash ordinary legislation whenever this ran counter to the principles and the rules of the Constitution was established by Kelsen within a complex theoretical and institutional framework, according to which the court acted as a 'negative law-maker', by exercising a para-legislative activity based on rules and limits of a judicial body. As will be made clear, the main indication of the judicial nature of the ItCC is given by its constant and necessary interaction with the Judiciary, which has the most important role in activating the Court's jurisdiction within the incidental proceeding. Besides this, a significant part of the ItCC's activity is not strictly dedicated to judicial issues but involves instead its role of arbitrator between other constitutional organs or between the State and the Regions.

The Italian system of constitutional justice, therefore, like many others established in other European countries, «draws inspiration from, but not faithfully reproduce the Kelsenian model» (Cartabia/Lupo 2022 at 191), since it shows a quite peculiar **mix of jurisdiction and politics**, regarding both its composition and its functions.

Unlike High Courts (at least in continental Europe), the judges of the ItCC are not necessarily judges by career, and their appointment procedures reflect the will of the framers to establish an indirect link with three constituencies of the newly established Court.

According to Article 135, para. 1, the 15 judges are **elected or appointed** in equal part (five for each) by the President of the Republic, by the Joint Chambers of Parliament and by the highest ordinary and administrative courts (three judges are elected by the Court of Cassation, one judge is elected by the Council of State and one judge is elected by the Court of Auditors).

The appointment of judges by the **President of the Republic** falls within the category of formal and substantive presidential acts (see above *I.D).5.*), which means that the President of the Council of Ministers shall exclusively verify whether the formal requirements for the appointment are met, without any possibility of challenging the decision on the merits. According to Article 135, para. 2,

© Wolters Kluwer Italia

«[t]he judges of the Constitutional Court shall be chosen from among members of the Judiciary from higher ordinary and administrative Courts, even if retired, university professors of law and lawyers with at least twenty years of practice».

The same requirements have to be met by **Parliament**, whose decision must be taken in Joint Chambers with a secret ballot, and based on a broad consensus of a two-thirds majority, reduced to a three-fifths majority after the third ballot. As is plain to see, the majority required is even higher than the one required for the election of the President of the Republic, which reduces to the absolute majority after the third ballot. Moreover, the nine-year term of office (reduced from the original 12 years), and the explicit non-renewability of office, reveal that the tasks of constitutional judges should be detached from any political or judicial constituency, including the President of the Republic, currently classified beside the Court as an institution of guarantee.

As the appointment procedure shows and in the light of the circumstance that each and every decision of the ItCC is taken by the whole Court, the judges of the Constitutional Court are called upon to integrate **different rationales** stemming from the organs that have contributed to their election or appointment. They act to guarantee the Constitution, even though from a standpoint that should not coincide with the role of the President of the Republic (which is 'above', but not 'outside' politics). They can repeal ordinary legislation whenever it violates the Constitution, even though they should not substitute their personal views instead of those of democratically elected representatives. Finally, they carry out a judicial function, with the awareness that constitutional justice is a *sui generis* kind of jurisdiction, which cannot be entirely reduced to ordinary judicial reasoning.

The text of the Constitution is particularly elusive as to the **functions** of the Constitutional Court. This is connected to the uncertainties that surrounded the new institution and with the risk that its action could supersede the choices taken by parliamentary majorities. As a compromise, the Constituent Assembly decided to make a list of the abstract functions that the ItCC had to carry out while delegating the concrete regulation of forms of access to the Court to future legislative choices. The result is that the normative framework of the ItCC's functions stems from different normative layers, including:

a) the Constitution and subsequent constitutional laws (Nos. 1/1948, 1/1953);
b) the ordinary legislation (Law No. 87/1953);
c) the internal rules of the Court (*Norme integrative per i giudizi di fronte alla Corte costituzionale*);

According to Article 134, the ItCC adjudicates:

- On controversies on the constitutional legitimacy of laws and enactments having the force of law issued by the State and the Regions

This is the proper domain of constitutional review of legislation, and the control of the Court can be activated in two different forms. Firstly, a judicial authority, on the occasion of a concrete controversy pending before it, can decide to suspend the proceeding and raise an incidental question to the Court. In this case, the judge is called upon to adopt a referral order, in which a basic account of the facts at stake and the reasons of the alleged unconstitutionality of a legislative rule are given (**incidental proceeding**). Or, secondly, a public authority (*i.e.*, exclusively the State or a Region) can directly challenge legislative rules in the Court because they infringe on the separation of legislative competence between the State and the Regions (Article 127). When challenging regional laws, only the State is entitled to initiate a control of flaws that are not directly related to competence issues (***principaliter* proceeding**). According to Article 123, the Constitutional Court may be called to make a control *a priori* on regional **statutes**.

- On conflicts arising from the allocation of powers of the State and those powers allocated to the State and Regions, and between Regions

Acting as an arbitrator, the ItCC is called upon to solve **conflicts** arising either among powers of the different branches of government (including each Chamber of Parliament, the Executive, the President of the Republic and even single judicial authorities) or between State and Regions regarding non-legislative acts.

- On accusations made against the President of the Republic and the Ministers, according to the provisions of the Constitution

This strictly judicial competence relates to the ascertaining of the **criminal responsibility of the President of the Republic** for the charges of high treason or of a manifest attempt to infringe the Constitution (see *I.D).5.*).

Besides these functions, with Constitutional Law No. 1/1953, the ItCC has been charged with the task to decide on the admissibility of a popular **referendum**, which means verifying whether a popular abrogation request satisfies the requirements laid out in Article 75, or is anyway consistent with other articles of the Constitution.

 © Wolters Kluwer Italia

3. Tools and Techniques of Constitutional Adjudication

The crown jewel of Italian constitutional justice, and its most recurring form of access, is the **incidental proceeding**, which is regulated by Articles 23 to 30 of Law No. 87/1953, as the prototype of constitutional review and of further proceedings pending before the Court. In its essence, this proceeding implies that a judge, during a proceeding of any type (civil, criminal, administrative, and so on), may decide to raise an incidental review before the ItCC whenever it holds that a certain legislative rule that has to be applied in the case at stake may be unconstitutional. Therefore, the relationship between the judgment before the referring judge (*giudizio a quo*) and the judgment of constitutionality is marked by a peculiar bond, in that it has a **concrete imprint** (the ItCC is called upon to verify whether the question is relevant, which means that the challenged legislative rule must be applied to solve the case), but its outcome is destined to have a **general effect** since the declaration of unconstitutionality has an *erga omnes* impact (Cerri 1978).

This peculiar relationship is the defining trait of the incidental proceeding and reveals the quintessentially relational character of the ItCC's review regarding the Judiciary. Since its first years of activity, the ItCC has shown its intention to act as the counterpart of the Judiciary whenever the interpretation and the enforcement of legal provisions adopted in the **pre-republican era** conflicted with the Constitution. Once every clause of the Constitution has been vested with binding force, and their nature of unenforceable guidelines and programmes has been abandoned (see *I.C).1* and *IV.C).1.*), the **Judgment. No. 1/1956** compelled the common judges to turn to the ItCC to verify the constitutionality of wide sectors of legislation (with particular regard to criminal law and public order regulations).

To perform such a complex task, the ItCC was called upon to find acceptance in the Judiciary, since it has always been up to common and administrative judges to raise incidental proceedings. The necessity of a viable interplay with the Judiciary emerged in the first cases, when the ItCC was faced with the need to forge **new judicial instruments**, with particular regard to the type of decisions that had to be taken. According to Article 136 of the Constitution, the possible decisions appear to be entrapped within an either/or alternative; *i.e.*, between the straight declaration of unconstitutionality and the rejection of the constitutional challenge. Since its first rulings, this rigid alternative has been progressively dismantled in favour of a more nuanced **set of alternatives**, which the ItCC has progressively established on a judge-made law basis over the next decades, in terms of a fully-fledged decisional toolbox (Ragone/D'Amico 2023 at 290).

From an historical perspective, the first alternative to the acceptance/rejection alternative is the notion of the **interpretative decisions**. With this kind of ruling, the ItCC moves from the assumption that the issue raised by the judge can be put into a different light whenever a distinction is made between the text of the legal provision at stake and the different interpretations thereof. Once a legal *provision* can be interpreted in different ways, and thereby produce different meanings (*norms*), the judge is entitled, with the guidance of the ItCC, to enforce the meaning that is more consistent with the Constitution. In these cases, the ItCC is called to adopt 'interpretative rejection decisions' (*sentenze interpretative di rigetto*), which steer judicial activity towards the interpretation of a legislative provision that reconciles its different meanings with the constitutional text without the necessity of a declaration of unconstitutionality.

The main difficulty with this kind of decision is that rejection decisions (*sentenze di rigetto*) are not binding for the Judiciary as a whole (*erga omnes*), so other judges may decide not to follow the arguments of the ItCC. On some occasions, these have been deemed to violate the *domain reservé* of the Court of Cassation in the interpretation of **ordinary law**, whereas the role of the ItCC should be to ascertain the interpretation and the meanings of the **Constitution**. The initial response of the ItCC to this reaction of ordinary courts was to adopt 'interpretative declarations of unconstitutionality' (*sentenze interpretative di accoglimento*), whose main scope was to quash the interpretations put forth (mainly) by the Court of Cassation, with the *erga omnes* effect provided for by decisions of unconstitutionality (*sentenze di accoglimento*). Beyond this variety of formulae, interpretative decisions had a deep impact on the structure and the rationale of the Italian model of constitutional review of legislation, since they highlighted the necessity for the ItCC and the judiciary (and the **Court of Cassation**, in particular) to cooperate in the interpretation and the enforcement of the Constitution. The review of legality (presided over by the Court of Cassation) needs to be constantly driven and qualified by the interpretation of the Constitution put forth by the ItCC. At the same time, the constitutional interpretation of the ItCC would risk being ineffective if those meanings were detached from interpretive practices emerging in the 'living law' (*diritto vivente*), mainly stemming from the case law of the Court of Cassation (BARSOTTI ET AAL. 2016).

Whereas interpretative decisions aimed at regulating the coexistence of the ItCC and the Judiciary, further varieties of judgments had to be explored concerning the safeguarding of the relationships between the ItCC and **Parliament**. As in many other systems, the main problem of this relationship involved the opportunity and limits of intervention of Constitutional Courts in cases of **legislative omissions,** which give rise to constitutional infringements. Within the context of

 © Wolters Kluwer Italia

a constitutional text that is deeply entrenched with positive obligations in the field of social policies like the Italian one, legislative omissions and shortcomings may be more threatening for the normative force of the Constitution than an explicit (active) violation. Unlike other systems of constitutional review, the Italian one showed an increasing willingness to enter into the legislative domain, moving from the assumption that the enhancement of constitutional provisions, however legislative or judicial, may differ in degree, but not in substance (Modugno 1981).

Given these premises, the ItCC paved the way towards a practice of '**manipulative judgments**', whose main function is to fill the legislative gaps with judicially elaborated content, and whose introduction is deemed to be mandatory under the Constitution. In other words, whenever a legislative provision is challenged because it omits to prescribe something, the gap can be filled by the ItCC, insofar that the omission amounts to an unreasonable legislative framework (a certain benefit is granted to category A and not to category B, even though A and B are similar in many respects) and the gap-filling activity does not leave the ItCC with any political discretion as to the solutions that can be taken (the extension of the benefit to B must be consistent with the conditions applied to A). When this happens, the ItCC must declare a certain legislative provision to be unconstitutional, 'in that it omits to prescribe' constitutionally necessary content.

Manipulative judgments are the preferred grounds of **reasonableness** (see *I.B).4.* and *III.A).2.b.1.*), in that the violation of the principle of equality, and the consequent employment of the reasonableness test has often amounted to a legislative framework that has not treated equal situations alike (or *vice versa*). To solve these problems, the ItCC forged a wide set of judicial responses, which range from the above-mentioned '**additive decisions**' (*sentenze additive*: a certain rule is unconstitutional in that it omits to prescribe something) to 'substitutive decisions' (*sentenze sostitutive*: a certain rule is unconstitutional in that it prescribes X rather than Y). More nuanced alternatives require that the legislative gap is not filled with a precise rule, but with a general principle that is up to the common judges to enact in practice (and sometimes the principle is not judicially enforceable but works as a *caveat* for Parliament).

As has been clarified, manipulative judgments should not be adopted when the gap-filling activity implies **political discretionality**, since the decision of the ItCC does not find any kind of reference in legislation concerning the means and the addressees of the rule that is allegedly called upon to fill the gap. In other words, the ItCC is not equipped with the power to adopt a completely new rule (that is reserved to Parliament). Rather it can correct a legislative assessment that has omitted to rule on a specific issue or that has given a partial response to a more general

© Wolters Kluwer Italia

problem. There might be situations in which the ItCC is prevented from adopting manipulative judgments, since a certain situation, which is *per se* unconstitutionally regulated, cannot be solved outside of a political appreciation that is demanded to the parliamentary lawmaker because the ItCC is prevented from choosing from among different alternative solutions that are all equally compatible with the Constitution. When this happens, the question raised by the judge is declared inadmissible (since too much political discretion calls for legislative intervention), but the legislative shortcoming may be declared to be at odds with the Constitution. These kinds of decision work, therefore, as '***warning decisions***' (*sentenze monito*), because Parliament is made aware that it has a duty of intervention.

Experience shows, however, that this duty is not enforceable, and Parliament often remains silent in complying with warning decisions. In recent times, constitutional shortcomings related to the inactivity of Parliament have been tackled by the ItCC with a new decisional instrument, which has been defined in terms of **prospective unconstitutionality** (*sentenze a incostituzionalità prospettata*). When the ItCC ascertains that the regulation of a certain topic is unconstitutional, but the remedies thereto imply the exercise of a political discretion that is, *prima facie*, outside of the Court's appreciation, the Court changes the handling of the case and raises an order that gives a certain time to Parliament to fill the gap (or introduce a new regulation related to the topic at stake) according to more or less strictly binding rules. Once the suspension time is over (and the term for the legislator has expired), the Court may decide to deal directly with legislative novelties if Parliament has been responsive to the previous order, or to demand the evaluation to the referring judge as to the necessity of a further review (this alternative has been followed in the case concerning life imprisonment without parole in Orders Nos. 97/2021, 122/2022 and 227/2022). If Parliament does not comply with the request of the Court within the given deadline, the Court itself is authorised to give effect to its previous ruling by «partially re-writing legislation accordingly to the constitutional principles» (Cartabia/Lupo 2022 at 198). This decisional module has been employed in a case concerning the criminal treatment of assisted suicide (Order No. 207/2018 and Judgment No. 242/2019) and the criminal treatment of libel by the press (Order No. 132/2020 and Judgment No. 150/2021).

The panoply of judicial responses that the ItCC has been able to forge in recent decades (most of them being outside of any legislative framework regulating its action) may appear, at first sight, to be a sign that the Court has expanded its action by largely interfering with the room of *manoeuvre* of both Houses of Parliament (with manipulative decisions) and other jurisdictions (mainly with interpretative decisions). Such a view, however, risks overlooking that the characteristics of

 © Wolters Kluwer Italia

the ItCC are peculiar if compared with the role traditionally assigned to constitutional courts in other countries, in that it is not immediately detached from the enhancement of the Constitution as put forth by the parliamentary lawmaker, while maintaining a close connection with the Judiciary and the methods of judicial enforcement (TEGA 2021). In simple terms, its main role is to reconnect and reconcile **the judicial and political enforcement of the Constitution**. As the different typology of decisional modules shows, it is thus quite impossible to sharply separate the discretional areas reserved for parliamentary politics and those reserved for the Constitutional Court, since they both fall under the domain of the Constitution. At the same time, even the rigid separation between the judicial tasks of the ItCC and of the Court of Cassation, as to primacy in legal interpretation, is blurred, because constitutional interpretation cannot be fully detached from legislative enactment (and *vice versa*).

All of this explains why the role of the ItCC has been largely placed outside some of the dominating narratives about constitutional justice (such as the doctrine of the *counter-majoritarian difficulty*) and its **relational character** has been highlighted, within which cooperation, interdependence, interaction with both Parliament and the Judiciary largely prevail over hierarchy, separation and competition (BARSOTTI ET AAL. 2020).

4. The Constitutional Court and its Commitment to European Integration

The ItCC's deeply rooted entrenchment with the Judiciary and the Parliament has favoured a similar cooperative attitude when dealing with European and supranational adjudication, mainly in the field of **fundamental rights**.

As will be more extensively discussed in *II.B).3.*, with regards to both European Union law and the European Convention on Human Rights, the more recent approach of the ItCC towards the inputs stemming from European law, reveals the willingness of the Constitutional Court to enter into a dialogue with the European Courts sitting in Strasburg and Luxemburg, while maintaining its role of ultimate guardian of the Constitution.

With regard to **EU law**, the growing acceptance of the doctrines of direct effect and of primacy (fully established with Judgment No. 170/1984) has not prevented the ItCC from recently engaging in a fruitful relationship that has focused on the direction and limits of judicial and normative integration of supranational law into the Italian legal order. After 2008, when the ItCC issued, for the first time, a preliminary reference to the Court of Justice of the EU, the intensity of the relationships between the two Courts significantly increased. On one hand, the ItCC declared itself committed to a «spirit of **loyal cooperation**» because of its being part of the judicial system established at the EU level by Article 19 TEU (Judgment No. 54/2022), as is demonstrated by the increasing number of **preliminary references** raised in recent years (Orders Nos. 103/2008, 207/2013, 24/2017, 117/2019, 182/2020, 216 and 217/2021). On the other hand, this openness to cooperation and judicial dialogue has **not implied a steady acceptance** of each and every input coming from Luxemburg, as is demonstrated by those judicial sagas in which the ItCC successfully promoted a reversal of the previous approach of the ECJ about some debated issues (on retroactivity of criminal sanctions, see Order No. 24/2017 and Case 42/17, *M.A.S. and M.B,* and on the right to silence in administrative proceedings leading to substantially criminal sanctions, see Order No. 117/2019 and C-481/19, *DB*).

In a similar vein, the ItCC prompted growing compliance with the decisions of the **European Court of Human Rights**, particularly after recognising the ECHR's capacity to bind ordinary legislation following Article 117, para. 1, even though its enforcement at the internal level must be presided over by the ItCC itself, which must verify whether rules and principles stemming from both the Convention and the decisions of the ECtHR are not at odds with the Constitution (Judgments Nos. 348 and 349/2007). Since 2007, the ItCC has repealed internal pieces of legislation on countless occasions, because they conflicted with the decisions of the ECtHR, even in cases not directly concerning Italy (among others, Judgment No. 200/2016). At the same time, as in EU-related issues, compliance with ECtHR's rulings has not prevented the ItCC from highlighting the contribution it may give from the standpoint of its role as the guardian of the Constitution. With regards in particular to the enforcement of ECtHR's decisions, the ItCC is occasionally called upon to assess whether and to what extent their content (which stems from **concrete cases** and situations) can be vested with the ***erga omnes* effects** of its rulings. In a highly controversial passage of Judgment No. 264/2012, the ItCC clarified its different position, *vis-à-vis* the ECtHR, by emphasising the necessity that the protection of fundamental rights that it has to promote must take account of its systemic nature, unlike the fragmented approach of a case-by-case jurisdiction. Moreover, with Judgment No. 49/2015, a further much debated *caveat* is made as to the internal effects of ECtHR's judgments, concerning their nonbinding nature in constitutional adjudication when they do not stem from a 'well-established case law'.

With regard to both European Courts, the ItCC has thus showed a growing commitment toward openness and relationality, while seeking to constantly reconnect a similar attitude to its main task to preserve the Constitution and its founding principles.

 © Wolters Kluwer Italia

REFERENCES

ALLEGRETTI, U. [1989], *Profili di storia costituzionale italiana. Individualismo e assolutismo nello stato liberale* (Bologna, il Mulino).
AZZARITI, G. [2005], *Critica della democrazia identitaria. Lo stato costituzionale schmittiano e la crisi del parlamentarismo* (Roma-Bari, Laterza).
BARSOTTI, V., AND OTHERS [2016], *Italian Constitutional Justice in Global Context* (Oxford, Oxford University Press).
BARSOTTI, V., AND OTHERS [2020], *Dialogues on Italian Constitutional Justice: A Comparative Perspective* (Abingdon, Routledge).
BARTOLE, S. [2012], *La Costituzione è di tutti* (Bologna, il Mulino).
BERTI, G. [1975], 'Articolo 5', in BRANCA G. (ed) *Commentario alla Costituzione. Principi fondamentali* (Bologna-Roma, Zanichelli-Il Foro italiano).
BRADLEY, A. & PINELLI, C. [2012], 'Parliamentarism', in ROSENFELD, M. & SAJÓ, A. (eds), *Oxford Handbook of Comparative Constitutional Law* (Oxford, Oxford University Press).
CAMERA DEI DEPUTATI [2022], Servizio Studi, XVIII Legislatura, La produzione normativa: cifre e caratteristiche (28 settembre 2022), available at www.camera.it/.
CARLASSARE, L. [2005], 'Costituzionalismo e democrazia nell'alterazione degli equilibri', in *Studi in onore di Gianni Ferrara* (Torino, Giappichelli).
CARTABIA, M. & LUPO, N. [2022], *The Constitution of Italy. A Contextual Analysis* (Oxford/New York/Dublin, Hart).
CERRI, A. [1978], 'Il profilo tra argomento e termine della questione di costituzionalità', 23(1) *Giurisprudenza costituzionale*.
CHELI, E. & SPAZIANTE, V. [1977], 'Il Consiglio dei ministri e la sua presidenza: dal disegno alla prassi', in RISTUCCIA S. (ed), L'istituzione Governo: analisi e prospettive (Milano, Comunità).
CHELI, E. [1978], 'Il problema storico della Costituente' in ID., *Costituzione e sviluppo delle istituzioni in Italia* (Bologna, il Mulino).
CIVITARESE MATTEUCCI S., AND OTHERS [2021], 'Italy: Legal Response to Covid-19', in KING, J. AND OTHERS (eds), *The Oxford Compendium of National Legal Responses to Covid-19* (Oxford, Oxford University Press).
COSTA, P. [1985], *Lo Stato immaginario. Metafore e paradigmi nella cultura giuridica italiana fra Ottocento e Novecento* (Milano, Giuffrè).
CRISAFULLI, V. [1958], 'Aspetti problematici del sistema parlamentare vigente in Italia', 9(1) *Jus*.
CRISAFULLI, V. [1960], 'Gerarchia e competenza nel sistema costituzionale delle fonti', 9(3) *Rivista trimestrale di diritto pubblico*.
CRISAFULLI, V. [1984], *Lezioni di diritto costituzionale. II.1 L'ordinamento costituzionale. Le fonti normative* (Milano, Giuffrè).
ELIA, L. [1961], 'Appunti sulla formazione del Governo', republished in ID., *Costituzione, partiti, istituzioni* (Bologna, il Mulino, 2009).
ELIA, L. [1970], 'Governo (forme di)', in *Costituzione, partiti, istituzioni* (Bologna, il Mulino, 2009).
ESPOSITO, C. [1948], 'Commento all'art. 1 della Costituzione', in ID., *La Costituzione italiana. Saggi* (Padova, Cedam, 1954).
ESPOSITO C. [1960], 'Capo dello Stato', republished in ID., *Diritto costituzionale vivente* (Milano, Giuffrè, 1992).
FARNETI, P. [1983], *Il sistema dei partiti in Italia 1946-1979* (Bologna, il Mulino).
FERRARA, G. [1974], 'La pari dignità sociale (appunti per una ricostruzione)', in *Studi Chiarelli* (Milano, Giuffrè).
FERRARA, G. [2000], *Gli atti costituzionali* (Torino, Giappichelli).

FERRARA, G. [2009], 'Sulla democrazia costituzionale', in *Scritti in onore di Lorenza Carlassare* (Napoli, Jovene).
FIORAVANTI, M. [2021], *Lezioni di storia costituzionale* (Torino, Giappichelli).
GALLIGAN, D. J [2013], 'The People, the Constitution, and the Idea of Representation', in GALLIGAN D. J., VERSTEEG M. (eds), *Social and Political Foundations of Constitutions* (Cambridge, Cambridge University Press).
GRIGLIO, E. [2022], *Parliamentary Oversight of the Executives. Tools and Procedures in Europe* (Oxford/New York/Dublin, Hart).
LA PALOMBARA, J. [1987], *Democracy Italian Style* (New Haven, Yale University).
LUPO, N. [2015], 'I "governi tecnici" nell'esperienza repubblicana italiana', 14(1) *Ventunesimo Secolo*.
LUPO, N. & PICCIRILLI, G. [2017], 'Conclusion: 'Silent' Constitutional Transformations: The Italian Way of Adapting to the European Union', in LUPO, N. & PICCIRILLI, G. (eds), *The Italian Parliament in the European Union* (Oxford and Portland, Hart).
MARTUCCI, R. [2002], *Storia costituzionale italiana* (Roma, Carocci).
MODUGNO, F. [1981], 'Corte costituzionale e potere legislativo', in BARILE P., AND OTHERS (eds), *Corte costituzionale e sviluppo della forma di governo in Italia* (Bologna, il Mulino).
MORTATI, C. [1946], *La Costituzione di Weimar* (republished in 2019, Milano, Giuffrè).
MORTATI, C. [1975], 'Articolo 1', in BRANCA, G. (ed) *Commentario alla Costituzione. I principi fondamentali* (Bologna-Roma, Zanichelli-Il Foro italiano).
PALADIN, L. [1986], 'Presidente della Repubblica', in *Enciclopedia del diritto* (Milano, Giuffrè).
PALADIN, L. [1995], *Diritto costituzionale* (Padova, Cedam).
PALADIN, L. [1996], *Le fonti del diritto italiano* (Bologna, il Mulino).
PANUNZIO, S. P. [1979], 'Esperienze e prospettive del referendum abrogativo', in *Attualità e attuazione della Costituzione* (Roma-Bari, Laterza).
PICCIRILLI, G. [2018], 'Il ruolo europeo del Presidente della Repubblica', in IBRIDO, R. & LUPO, N. (eds), *Dinamiche della forma di governo tra Unione europea e Stati membri* (Bologna, il Mulino).
RAGONE, S. & D'AMICO, G. [2023], 'The Evolution and *Gestalt* of the Italian Constitution', in VON BOGDANDY, A., AND OTHERS, *The Max Planck Handbooks in European Public Law. 2 Constitutional Foundations*, Vol. 2 (Oxford, Oxford University Press).
REPETTO, G. [2018], 'Appunti per uno studio sui rapporti tra garanzie costituzionale e indirizzo politico nell'esperienza repubblicana', 23(3) *Diritto pubblico*.
RESCIGNO, P. [1966], *Persona e comunità* (Bologna, il Mulino).
RESCIGNO, G. U. [1967], *La responsabilità politica* (Milano, Giuffrè).
RIVOSECCHI, G. [2018], 'I riflessi dell'Unione europea sul rapporto governo-Parlamento e sull'organizzazione interna del Governo' in IBRIDO, R. & LUPO, N. (eds), *Dinamiche della forma di governo tra Unione europea e Stati membri* (Bologna, il Mulino).
ROMANO, S. [1909], 'Lo Stato moderno e la sua crisi', trans. in CROCE, M. (ed) [2023], *Law, Necessity and the Crisis of Modern State* (Abingdon, Routledge).
ROMANO, S. [1946], *L'ordinamento giuridico* (2nd ed., Firenze, Sansoni), trans. CROCE M., *The Legal Order* (Abingdon, Routledge, 2017).
SAITTA, A. [1964], *Alle origini del Risorgimento: i testi di un celebre concorso* (Roma, Istituto storico italiano per l'età moderna e contemporanea).
TEGA, D. [2021], 'The Italian Constitutional Court in its context. A narrative', 17(3) *European Constitutional Law Review*.

 © Wolters Kluwer Italia

Part II

Italy and the EU

An ever closer Union is the EU's (informal) motto, quoted in the treaties' provisions ever since the Preamble of the EECT in 1957. It offers the sense of the European project's dynamic nature as well as the scope of the Union (or, as it has been said, its *telos*), as represented by the steady integration of Member States.

The evolutionary nature of the integration process is not unidirectional. In some 60 years since the Rome Treaties, the EU's powers have increased, as have the attributions and influence of EU institutions. These processes were fostered by formal amendments to the treaties approved over the years, and the evolution of informal practices among the European institutions.

The same process has also involved the Member States, which have been transformed over time through their EU membership. The domestic legal systems of EU Member States have also changed in significant ways due to the transfer of powers to the supranational level and the parallel reorganization of statehood. In the words of Peter Lindseth, European integration may be considered a consequence of «the post-war constitutional settlement of administrative governance at the national level», namely a new understanding of traditional state structure, necessarily open to international law and cooperation with other States.

To understand this process, its starting point, and the results of this evolution, it should be remembered that behind the original idea of European integration there was the strong adhesion to a specific set of political ideals. Not by chance, Adenauer, De Gasperi and Schuman were all part of the same political family as Christian Democrats (and German speakers as one of their mother tongues). All of them worked towards the precise aim of securing peace and increasing living conditions in their countries, to prevent the involution of post-war democracies. Hence, at the time of the signing of the Treaties of Rome, the six founder Member States had some structural features in common: they were all based on a parliamentary system and thus were experiencing similar

© Wolters Kluwer Italia

dynamics between their legislatures and governments. This is an important point of reference because it also influences the way in which citizens perceive the institutional balance among EU institutions.
Italy has been and still is part of this process. As a founder member of the ECs since the beginnings and then of the EU, it has contributed to the shaping of continental integration. In turn, its internal structures and procedures have been deeply influenced by seventy years of continuous exchanges with European institutions and the implementation and application of EU law.
In the following paragraphs, the aim is to provide a sense of the importance of Italy and the ECs/EU to one other: the significance of the Italian contribution to the definition of the EU's most fundamental aspects and, in turn, the real depth of the transformation of the Italian constitutional system as a consequence of multiple European influences.
This Part is structured as follows.
Section A) analyses those specific ideas, instruments, theories and experiences that now constitute **parts of the backbone of the EU and that owe to Italians an important part of their origins**.
Section B) reverses the perspective, highlighting how much the Italian legal order has been transformed in its process of Europeanisation. Its institutions, its system of the sources of law, the way to protect of fundamental rights and its economic development have been decisively influenced by EU Membership.
Finally, **Section C)** looks at the **interaction between the two legal orders**, focusing on their respective autonomy and their further development in the broader global scenario.

 © Wolters Kluwer Italia

A) THE ITALIAN CONTRIBUTION TO EUROPEAN INTEGRATION

In the analysis of the **mutual influence** developed in seventy years of Italian EU membership, the focus will be placed first on the Italian contribution to the European construction. It will be highlighted what Italy gave in terms of **intellectual proposals** as well as of **institutional instruments and practices** to contribute to the integration project that became parts of the backbone of the European framework. They comprise **Altiero Spinelli**'s original intuition, that of conceiving of a (federal) Europe before anyone else; the procedural design that introduced the main tools for legal integration, such as the instrument of the **preliminary reference**; the theoretical systematisation of the balance that exists between European law and national constitutional constraints, such as the doctrine of the so-called **counterlimits** (*controlimiti*); and finally, the proposal for a **cooperative** (and, as it had been recently defined by Daniel Sarmiento «seductive») **attitude to the judicial dialogue** between national constitutional courts and European courts, which is preferred to the more adversarial approaches developed by others (and significantly the German *Bundesverfassungsgericht*).

1. Foundations: The Ventotene Manifesto and beyond

A famous quote from Pietro Calamandrei refers to the birthplace of the Italian Constitution in the mountains where the *partigiani* fought and died for a free and dignified Italy in the liberation of Italy following the tragic years of the fascist regime. Similarly, if one wants to find the **birthplace of European integration**, they should visit **Ventotene**, a wild and charming **island in the Tyrrhenian Sea**, where **in 1941 Altiero Spinelli and Ernesto Rossi** wrote their pamphlet entitled *For a Free and United Europe. A Draft Manifesto* during their detention as anti-fascist prisoners.

The year 1941 thus saw the origins of the European ideal but was also, paradoxically, the darkest phase of World War II: Nazi Germany was occupying most of the western and central part of the continent and even invading the eastern part with the so-called *Operation Barbarossa*; Japan was cementing its claims and furthering its expansion in the Pacific, and the USA was still not directly engaged as the attack in Pearl Harbor would only occur at the end of that year. At this time, the most likely future scenario was an overwhelming victory of the Tripartite Pact and the collapse of European democracies.

However, a small group of **anti-fascist intellectuals** who had been deported to Ventotene began debating their hopes for the post-war period, revealing an outstanding capacity to maintain a clear mind in such difficult conditions.

The **Ventotene *Manifesto*** has **an explicit federalist perspective**, denouncing the limits of «a balance of independent European States» and of the principle of classical international law of non-intervention in internal matters, indeed

© Wolters Kluwer Italia

identifying in each national constitution a «vital interest» for other European countries as well. These ideas were stressed even further. Not only did it advocate for the rejection of competing sovereignties, the *Manifesto* also drew attention to the limits of international cooperation mechanisms witnessed in the previous decades. At the basis of its proposal there was the conception of a new form of statehood and, indeed, a new approach to sovereignty in more limited and open terms.

This ideal heritage reverberated in Article 11 of the Constitution that epitomized the ECs' aims some years prior to its foundation. In it can be found the repudiation of war, linked to the constitutional principle of openness, the acceptance of the limitations of state sovereignty in the name of «peace and justice among nations». Not surprisingly, it would constitute the main reference for the participation of Italy in the ECs/EU.

The original content of the Ventotene *Manifesto* was later echoed by the **Schuman Declaration (1950)**, which clarified the instrumental nature of cooperation between France and Germany with regard to the aim of maintaining peace.

> The pooling of coal and steel production should immediately provide for the setting up of common foundations for economic development as a first step in the federation of Europe, and will change the destinies of those regions which have long been devoted to the manufacture of munitions of war, of which they have been the most constant victims.
>
> The solidarity in production thus established will make it plain that any war between France and Germany becomes not merely unthinkable, but materially impossible. The setting up of this powerful productive unit, open to all countries willing to take part and bound ultimately to provide all the member countries with the basic elements of industrial production on the same terms, will lay a true foundation for their economic unification.

On the contrary, the objective of combining the fundamental raw materials for heavy industry – coal and steel – had the declared aim of **making the war «materially impossible»** once the economies of the two main European countries became interdependent. As in the Ventotene *Manifesto*, in the Schuman Declaration too the traditional means of international law were considered insufficient to achieve the ambitious aims it proposed, indicating that «for a transitional period» it was necessary to have **a broad mechanism of the harmonization and convergence of individual state economies**, to be implemented under the arbitration of a subject that was to be identified by **mutual agreement**. Thus, briefly, the principle was established whereby cooperation between states was coordinated by an external body, the bearer of purely 'unitary' or 'supra-state' interests.

Even prior to their beginnings, the ECs were conceived as a different subject from traditional international law, with an instrumental nature designed for

© Wolters Kluwer Italia

definitively political, rather than economic purposes. This design was created in the early 1950s on raw materials and sealed in 1952 with the establishment of the European Coal and Steel Community (ECSC). In order to strengthen the military relationship between the contracting States, it should have immediately followed up by a **European Defence Community** (EDC), a natural continuation of this design. However, the EDC treaty was rejected at the stage of its ratification by the French National Assembly, thus constituting the first of many setbacks in the process of European integration, which was nevertheless not to be halted.

The reaction to this first failure was the relaunch of continental integration with the EEC and Euratom, maintaining the idea of the crucial importance of economic integration in a broader perspective. This **gradualist approach** can first be traced back to another great protagonist of the commencement of the integration process, **Jean Monnet**, to whom the idea of the so-called «*Europe de petits pas*» is owed, i.e., the progressive construction of the results of convergence between the Member States.

Gradualism, however, should not be interpreted as a renunciation of the **constitutional ambitions of the European project**, but rather as an exercise in pragmatism, a way in which to continue practising the same objectives. This is the basis underlying the «ever closer union», which is contained in the preamble to the Treaty of Rome of 1957 and which subsequent Treaties were to expand upon, and which still today constitutes the founding basis of what is defined as the process of European integration, indicating its evolutionary nature. This gradual approach was also explicitly embraced by the Italian Government in the Report that accompanies the bill for the authorization of the ratification of the Rome Treaties (A.C. 2814, II leg., at 45), in which they are referred to as being «not perfect, albeit necessitating the instrument for their improvement» and requesting for this purpose «the will of Governments and commitment of the citizenry». This document already contained the undisguised **constitutional ambition**, which anticipated the possibility of the direct election of a European Parliament, together with the idea of a future transfer of European sovereignty to this assembly.

Yet Italy maintained its attitude towards a constitutional evolution of the integration process. A confirmation of this can be found in the **advisory referendum held on 18th of June, 1989**, on the occasion of the election of the European Parliament. Italian citizens were asked to vote on an issue which included the request to transform the then-existing Communities «into an actual Union, with a government accountable to the parliament» and to attribute to the latter the mandate «to establish draft European Constitution to be directly submitted to the ratification of the competent bodies of the Member States». The referendum, which took place only a few months prior to the fall of the Berlin Wall – but which was conceived with a spirit that already looked further ahead – was remarkably successful, with a turnout of over 80% and consensus higher than 88% of the voters. Its impact on the European level can be considered marginal, as no such mandate was given and no «European Constitution» was debated because of that. However, the simple fact that it was held, the participation that it triggered and the consensus reached in the population are good indicators of what was the sentiment in Italy some 30 years after the beginning of the European integration.

The Italian position has undergone some notable changes in subsequent years. This does not seem to be due to the evolution of the political context and, in particular, to the emergence of Eurosceptic political parties. On the contrary, the growing **Euroscepticism** in national politics seems to be rather the cause of a change in Italy's attitude towards European integration, an effect of the change in Italy's position within the European framework. The Italian perspective on European integration has had two notable turning points. The first concerns the **Maastricht Treaty** when, with a view to adopting the single currency, macroeconomic requirements were introduced which were difficult to reconcile with the management of the national budget, which had until that point been inclined towards deficit spending policies. Indeed, the moment at which Italy's European membership began to constitute not only a source of economic development but also a significant source of macroeconomic constraints may be identified to have been at the very start of the 1990s. The second turning point can be identified as being the progressive **enlargement** of the number of Member States. Over time, the 6 founding states were joined by Great Britain, Denmark, Ireland, Greece, Portugal, and Spain, as well as – in the mid-1990s – Austria, Finland, and Sweden. The real change then occurred with the 2004 enlargement in which 10 new States, mostly from Central and Eastern Europe, joined the EU. It was then completed in the subsequent years with further adhesions, all from countries from the former Eastern bloc. This new geographical arrangement of Europe, together with Italian progress in its decades-long EU membership, gave Italy a very different position to that which it held at the end of the 1950s. Indeed, from a comparatively undeveloped and poor country, particularly in its South, fifty years later Italy presented itself as one of Europe's most advanced countries, especially in its Northern regions. The consequence of this was also a **radical change of positioning** with respect to the potential for the attraction and use of the significant European funds that aimed to achieve territorial cohesion and the structural development of the Member State. These funds had already been significantly drained by the German reunification process and at this point were being mainly allocated to the new Member States.

The combination of these two trends lead to a dual change of perspective for Italy. In the light of the evolution of the European integration process, there was a widespread loss of consensus within public opinion due to the drop of its output legitimacy (which is the capacity of improving life conditions of the citizens). In short, over recent years, belonging to the EU has no longer been perceived to be

 © Wolters Kluwer Italia

an opportunity or source of greater well-being, as was previously the case, but is rather seen as a cost that is difficult to tolerate considering the considerable constraints that membership imposes.

The overall result of this has been the **emergence of populist and Eurosceptic political parties**, which in recent years also started to hold significant positions in the Italian government. However, here it will be the way in which Italy's long membership of the EU has deeply influenced party politics and contributed to the domestication of the more extreme parties by including them in both national and European responsibilities that will be discussed.

2. Instruments: Symmetries Between Incidental Proceedings and Preliminary Reference

The Italian contribution to Europe's formation was not merely intellectual and political. **Italian lawyers** have long been an essential part of the community of scholars and legal practitioners who have contributed to the legal design of the ECs (PAVONE 2022).

The importance of the **preliminary reference** mechanism in the evolution of European integration has long been established up to the point of indicating the **«judicial» nature of Europe's construction** (STONE SWEET 2004). The current design of this fundamental tool was reached also thanks to the contribution of the Italian delegation in the drafting of the Rome Treaties, when there was an extensive revision of the preliminary reference as regulated before.

In the 1951 Paris Treaty, the preliminary reference mechanism was limited to assessing the validity of the deliberations of the High Authority (Article 41). The drafters intended to make a clear distinction between the powers of national judges and those of the European Court of Justice (ECJ), leaving untouched the jurisdiction of the former and involving the latter only in cases of possible treaty violation by a European act of secondary rank. This procedure proved to be largely unsatisfactory. Not only did it remain unused in practice, without a single reference issued by national courts in the period between 1952 and 1957, but it was also unfit to sustain the development of the integration process. As it was limited to the assessment of the validity of the deliberations of the High Authority, it aimed to enforce the ECSC Treaty over the action of other institutions. Therefore, its results could only have sanctioned the integration progresses, and had no potential for furthering it more significantly.

It was only with the 1957 Treaties that the possibility of a preliminary reference for the **uniform interpretation of community law** (both concerning the treaties and acts of secondary law) was added. A crucial role in this regard was played by the Italian delegation, and in particular by **Nicola Catalano** (later a key member of the ECJ), who elaborated the procedure **based on the incidental proceeding in accessing the ItCC** that had been drafted just few years earlier in the Law No. 87/1953 (see *I.E).3.*). The proposal was modelled on the basis of Article 23 of Law No. 87/1953, as an ordinary and necessary instrument of dialogue between common judges and the sole interpreter of the Constitution.

The addition of an interpretative capacity to the ECJ for national referrals has been fundamental to European integration. Indeed, it constituted the primary means by which some of the core principles of EU law could be asserted, such as direct effect and primacy. Most of the ECJ's landmark cases were decided on the basis of this procedure, including ***van Gend & Loos*** **(1963) and** ***Costa/ENEL*** **(1964)**.

The monopoly of the ECJ's interpretation of European Law was the premise for its uniform application, and the mechanism enabling the referral of cases for preliminary rulings constitutes its most distinctive and effective feature.

There are clear **symmetries between the Italian system of access to constitutional adjudication and the process for requesting a preliminary ruling by the European Court**.

One key similarity is the **centralized nature of the scrutiny**. Just as the Constitutional Court is the only judge of the constitutionality of domestic laws, so the ECJ is the sole institution that is entitled to interpret European sources. This confirms the necessity of the unification of institutions in both legal orders, with a court that embodies the unifying nature of the codified *constitutional* document. Although the actual application of European law is diffused (and performed by ordinary – national – judges) it is only the Court of Justice that may be considered to offer a «secure and reliable» interpretation of the Treaties. A further consequence of this has been the attribution to a common institution of the interpretation of the treaties, thereby avoiding the possibility of a differentiated interpretation that relies on national institutionalism and national legal traditions.

Secondly, both tools can be activated **by all judges**. In contrast to other systems (e.g., the *question prioritaire de constitutionnalité* introduced in the French system in 2008, which is limited to the highest judges, such as the Court of Cassation and the Council of State), in both the Italian and the European systems the idea is to make the instruments of judicial dialogue accessible at all stages of the application of law.

In brief, there is in both approaches an **underlying idea of relationality**, meaning the insufficiency of the individual judge (and the individual legal system) in comprehensive adjudication. The result is the creation and development of **legal interdependence between national and European legal orders.**

The autonomy of the ordinary judge, both in the national context as well as in the European legal order, is of utmost importance; however, autonomy alone is

 © Wolters Kluwer Italia

not necessarily sufficient when higher values come into play. Such higher values may include the compatibility with constitutional principles (and fundamental rights), in the first place, and the uniform application of European law (and thus equality among Member States in respecting common obligations) in the second.

There are also differences between the two remedies regarding the question of constitutionality (brought before the ItCC) and preliminary reference (before the ECJ).

The effects of the decisions are different. The **ItCC is directly entitled to declare the unconstitutionality** of the law infringing the Constitution. The **ECJ is called upon 'only' to clarify the interpretation to be given to European law**, and it is up to the national judge to take the consequences of that interpretation (if necessary, by the non-application of conflicting domestic norms). This difference is inherent in the autonomy that will necessarily be attributed to each legal order. It is, however, consistent with the approach that the ECJ fosters regarding granting primacy (rather than supremacy) of EU law over national law: as will be said more in detail below, at the end of a long elaboration by the ItCC, EC/EU law is not considered to be hierarchically higher than national law. It claims for its priority within the matters conferred to the European level. Conflicting national law will not be repealed or annulled. It will be set aside by the priority granted to EU law.

3. Theories: Legal Pluralism, Dualism, Counterlimits

Italian literature was well-equipped to frame the theoretical complexities of several different legal systems co-existing and overlapping in a variety of ways. As early as 1917-18, Santi Romano – arguably the most influential Italian legal scholar of the twentieth century – in his *L'ordinamento giuridico* (The Legal Order) put forward a twofold theory: institutionalism, which affirms an intrinsic correspondence between societal organization and legal norms, unified in the socio-legal notion of 'institution'; and legal pluralism, which considers the coexistence of several social organizations and, as a logical consequence, of different legal systems to be physiological. This, in turn, begged the question of how this pluralism, and the conflicts that could ensue, should be managed. In answer to this, it should be said that Romano still had great confidence in the traditional state as the overarching legal institution. Today, Romano's volume (translated into English only in 2018 but widely circulated in other languages for decades) is a cornerstone of the theories current today which explain supra- and international legal integration in terms of pluralism (one the most recent examples of work following this line of thinking is the theory of inter-legality elaborated by Klabbers/Palombella 2019).

Notwithstanding the strong political will to create the ECs, the exceptionally advanced legal integration entailed by them has proven to be challenging both in theory and in practice, namely in the courts. Therefore, the Italian approach to European legal integration has involved **substantial critical reflection**. **The ItCC has also progressively assumed a crucial role** in shaping the approach and in setting the conditions in which Italy participated in the European process.

The text of the Constitution did not provide for a proper European clause. The political situation in the 1950s and 1960s (during which there was a deep division between the major political parties regarding Italy's place in the international scenario) would not have allowed for a constitutional amendment to be added to it. The constitutional amendment procedure requires a two-thirds majority, and until 1970 the other option for approval, through an absolute majority plus a popular referendum, was not available, as the rules for the latter were still absent until the approval of the Law No. 352/1970. Furthermore, until the late 1990s, general opinion allowed for the amendment of the constitution with only a large parliamentary majority, although on certain subjects this was impossible to achieve.

In light of this situation, **the Italian approach to legal integration within the ECs could not be based on a modification of the constitution that legitimized it**. In the absence of the potential for amending the black letter of the Constitution, the ItCC achieved a similar goal through the **progressive interpretation of the existing norms**, granting them an evolutionary (and rather innovative) content in comparison with the original one. Over time, the ItCC significantly changed its position, recognizing the autonomy of EC law from public international law and its different interactions with domestic law.

Most of the vocabulary that was used in the scholarly debate, and which continues to be used to describe the approach to legal integration in the ECs, and later in the EU, was in fact created by **Paolo Barile**, an influential interpreter of the Italian constitutional evolution for many years. To him we owe many key expressions, such as the **«European journey» of the ItCC** or «counterlimits», both of which derive from the progressive refinement of the case law and his innovative interpretative work regarding constitutional texts (Barile 1973).

This depiction of a «European journey» that is fundamentally **evolutionary in nature** was proposed to reflect the development of the Court's positioning, observed in the adaptation of domestic categories to the specific needs of European integration. This process consisted of **a certain number of steps** and, upon each of them, the ItCC refined its understanding of EC law, its status in the Italian legal order and, consequently, the criteria necessary for the resolution of clashes between EC and conflicting domestic law.

In the name of the Italian legal order's **dualistic nature**, the composition of the conflicts existing between international law and domestic law requires an

 © Wolters Kluwer Italia

instrumental premise, consisting of the **transformation of the foreign legal order into a domestic rule**. The former takes the nature, the rank and the status of the domestic norm enabling its entrance into the legal order. This passage is necessary for the use of those categories that a domestic court can handle in a dualistic system. In this framework, international treaty law is considered as having the same rank of national legislation, in the name of the legislative authorization for the purpose of ratification that is provided for in Article 80.

At the beginning of this journey, the ItCC demonstrated significant **resistance** to accepting the novelties that were already emerging from the ECJ's case law. If the latter had already stated the direct effect and the primacy of EC law in light of the early case law elaborated by the ECJ, the ItCC was still unable to find any significant difference between public international law and European law. Community norms were treated in Italy exactly like international ones, specifically as international treaties, and so to be understood as having the same rank of the domestic legislation that ratified it.

The most important decision of this phase is **Judgment No. 14/1964**. This was based on the same principal litigation of the ECJ case *Costa/ENEL*. The conclusions of the ItCC, in this case, could not have been more different from those of the European court. In transforming EC law in domestic legislation due to the rank of the act that authorized the ratification of the ECT, the conflict was perceived as being between two (domestic) legislative sources, which could be solved through ordinary **chronological criteria**. Consequently, with a significant paradox, the application of EC law was ensured only *vis-à-vis* domestic norms that were older than the law authorizing the ratification of ECT, thus jeopardizing the uniform application of European law.

The second step of the ItCC's European journey came some 10 years later. It was also most probably the decisive step as it was on this occasion, in **1973**, that the Court found **Article 11 to be the constitutional reference for European integration**. Following the same dualist approach, the identification of a constitutional basis for the application of EC law in the domestic legal order implied that it shared the same constitutional rank. In this context, the necessary consequence of the conflict with domestic legislation was the latter's unconstitutionality, which was a direct result of the application of the general hierarchical criteria.

The solution proposed in the ***Frontini* Judgment (No. 183/1973)** had multiple and uncertain implications. The outcome was the granting of the application to EC law. Thus, at least at first glance, it could be interpreted as being closer to the approach pursued by the ECJ. Nevertheless, it was not only the underlying motivation that was different (as it was based on the hierarchal superiority of EC law and not on its primacy due to its necessary uniformity), but its procedures and its

© Wolters Kluwer Italia

consequences had further problematic aspects. As for the procedures, the **unconstitutionality of the domestic law that conflicted with EC law** meant that the application of the latter depended on its involvement with the ItCC. Due to the centralized system of constitutional adjudication, only the ItCC could have been capable of resolving such conflicts, thus delaying the application of EC law to the constitutional judgment, and thereby **depriving the ordinary judges of their autonomy in ensuring the primacy of the application of EC law**. Secondly, the effect of a decision of unconstitutionality is the annulment of conflicting legislation, which is something that is not requested by the ECJ. In the event of a subsequent modification of EC law, annulled domestic law could no longer be applied, although no such conflicts exist any longer.

The most important contribution to the European debate of this journey has been the doctrine of **counterlimits** (*controlimiti*), another expression that Paolo Barile proposed. It is the result of an elaboration on the wording of Article 11 Const., indicating the existence of the **limits to those «limitations» (to sovereignty)** – these are the «*counter-*» limits – that **Italy is willing to accept to pursue «peace and justice among Nations».**

The ItCC has never used the exact word «counterlimits» in its decisions related to European integration. To date, albeit in international public law, this wording was in fact explicitly used in the *Ferrini* case (Judgment No. 238/2014), confirming that counterlimits became a general doctrine for the ItCC. However, ever since the *Frontini* case, the entire role of the ItCC in relation to European integration has been shaped around the potential it offers for the identification of a violation of counterlimits, denoting the detection of whether, and how, EC/EU law may determine an infringement of the Italian Constitution's core values up to the point at which its application may be ruled out. Interestingly, the doctrine of counterlimits was proclaimed by the ItCC **one year prior to the *Solange* judgment** issued by the German Federal Constitutional Court, thereby contributing to the circulation of an Italian model to the conditional acceptance of the primacy of EC law and its relationship with the protection of fundamental rights as enshrined in the national constitution.

The capacity of the ItCC to assess counterlimits was later confirmed and detailed in the subsequent ***Granital* judgment (No. 170/1984)** in which, significantly, the **judge rapporteur was Antonio La Pergola** (prominent lawyer, later President of the ItCC, Minister of EU affairs, MEP, member of the ECJ and Advocate General). In this landmark case, the ItCC affirmed a new principle and reiterated part of what had already been stated in *Frontini*. On the one hand, it confirmed Article 11 as the basis for the introduction of the domestic legal order of EC law. However, in contrast to *Frontini*, it did not derive from this basis any necessary hierarchical superiority based on national law. Instead of

© Wolters Kluwer Italia

the invalidity of domestic legislation conflicting with EC law, the ItCC discovered **a new equilibrium** through the establishment of a **division of competences between national and EC law**, requesting the **disapplication of domestic law** in the sectors that were attributed to the European level.

The reasons leading to this further change of approach by the ItCC are to be found also in the evolution that was taking place in the case law of the ECJ. Just in between *Frontini* and *Granital*, the ECJ had released the fundamental *Simmental* Judgment (case C-106/77) in which it claimed, within the principle of conferral, the primacy of European law notwithstanding the rank and the status of the conflicting domestic norm.

> «by virtue of the principle of primacy of Community law [...] the national judge, charged with applying [...] the provisions of Community law, has the obligation to ensure the full effectiveness of these rules, disapplying, if necessary, on his own initiative, any conflicting provision of national legislation, without having to request or wait for its prior removal by legislative means or by any other constitutional procedure».

This shift to the further **criteria of the competent lawmaker** implied a decisive difference in the role of national judges: this was to detect the potential conflict between national and EC law, but they also possessed the authority to solve these conflicts, without the necessity of the prior involvement of the ItCC. National judges were granted the power of the disapplication of national legislation in order to be able to secure full application of EC law. Only in the event of potential conflicts with the fundamental principles of the Constitution, the inviolable rights of the person or, in general, when counterlimits were at stake, was there a requirement to raise the issue of constitutionality, similarly to what was generally expected after the *Frontini* case.

In brief, the core of the doctrine' of counterlimits is the following: the **primacy granted to EU law is not absolute** and the principle of openness entailed in Article 11 must be balanced with the further **supreme principles of the Constitution**, later defined by the same ItCC as those principles that cannot be modified even through a constitutional amendment (Judgment No. 1146/1988). The role of the ItCC in enforcing these principles is latent, in the sense that the ItCC claims to have this capacity even without a significant practice. The ItCC was careful to recall the existence of this supervisory role in the interactions between legal systems in later decisions. For example, in **Judgment No. 232/1989 (*Fragd* case)** the ItCC was keen to underline its powers in this respect. While recognizing the improvements in the protection of fundamental rights by the ECs (which already at that time constituted an «integral and essential part of the community legal system»), the ItCC reaffirmed its role in checking the compliance of EC law with the fundamental principles of the Italian constitutional order, with specific regard to the **inalienable rights of the human person**. That statement was followed by the recognition that «what is highly improbable is still possible», as the premise for the necessity of preserving the arbitrary role of the Court for the sake of the integrity of Italian constitutional (supreme) principles.

The potential for the application of counterlimits may be described as a sort of reserve power on the part of the ItCC that has been developed as a general doctrine of Italian dualism. It has been applied not only to international public law (as said, in the Judgment No. 238/2014), but also in cases concerning the relationship with the Vatican State (Judgment No. 18/1982). In both occasions, the fundamental right of **access to justice was enforced as a supreme principle of the Italian Constitution**. The openness of the legal order is thus limited to the aim of ensuring the integral protection of individual rights.

In conclusion, the Italian contribution to the European debate on the relationship between core constitutional values and European law concerns the mutual interdependence of the two legal orders. The doctrine of counterlimits aims to reconcile the inherent openness of the contemporary state with an acknowledgement of its boundaries, to allow a nation-state to participate in European integration and, at the same time, to assert its most fundamental values, such as the inviolable rights of its citizens.

4. Experiences: Constructive Judicial Dialogue with the ECJ

The ItCC's European journey did not end with the *Granital* judgment. The acceptance of a division of competences at the national and European levels did not signify the full embrace of the position that the ECJ has fostered since the decisions of *Van Gend & Loos* and *Costa/ENEL*.

In particular, the ItCC was for many years **resistant to participating in any dialogue with the ECJ** through the instrument of the **preliminary reference**. Like many other constitutional courts (Claes 2015), the notion of being required to depend on another subject to be able to define its own judgments led the ItCC, for a long time, to fail to consider using this instrument. Indeed, at least until the mid-1990s, the ItCC offered only confused arguments in support of its refusal to directly engage with the ECJ. Firstly, it considered that issuing a question about the interpretation or the validity of EC law was merely a **possibility**, even though it was a court of last, indeed only, instance (Judgment No. **168/1991**). It even **denied its eligibility to access it at all**, asserting that it was not included in that definition of «court or tribunal of a Member State» as per Article 234 ECT, based on its previous jurisprudence in the field of judicial organizations (**Order No. 536 /1995**).

 © Wolters Kluwer Italia

In line with the *Granital* doctrine, in cases of **dual preliminarity**, the ItCC asked ordinary judges to issue the preliminary reference first, and then to potentially raise a question of constitutionality, if relevant, once any doubts concerning the interpretation of EC law had been clarified, where doubts concerning constitutionality persisted. Otherwise, when issues were brought to its attention that also concerned aspects of compatibility with EC law, these were always declared inadmissible, precisely because it was first deemed necessary to activate dialogue with the ECJ through the tool of preliminary reference (e.g., Order No. 319/1996).

However, it was evident that this approach could not be sustainable in the long run. First of all, the idea of deferring to the main trial judge for the issue of a preliminary reference first was completely unacceptable in cases of **principal proceedings**, i.e. when it was not the judges who referred the matter to the ItCC, but rather the Government or the Regions (Cartabia/Weiler 2000).

Not by chance, it was in this context exactly that the ItCC raised its **first preliminary reference (Order No. 103/2008)**. The motivation that the ItCC gave was a sort of acknowledgement that previous decisions had been somewhat mistaken, even though it claimed a sort of continuity. In particular, the ItCC confirmed its exclusion from the national judiciary, qualifying itself as the **supreme constitutional guarantor**. However, the ItCC supported its decision regarding the activation of dialogue with the ECJ as its decisions cannot be appealed, rendering it a body of last (actually only) instance. Moreover, it further supported the argument (rendering it even more EU-friendly) by stating that «were it not possible to make a preliminary reference [...] in constitutionality proceedings where the court has been seized directly, the general interest in the uniform application of Community law [...] would be harmed».

Five years later, the ItCC issued a **further preliminary reference**, the first one in an **incidental proceeding (Order No. 207/2013)**. This occurred because the question of interpretation concerned an EU directive that did not have direct effect, enacted in the national legal order via delegated legislation. The referring judge doubted the constitutionality of the subsequent legislative decree and raised a question of constitutionality for the purpose of checking its compliance with Article 76 Const. (via comparison to the delegating law). In this context, only the ItCC was in the position to apply the EU directive, at the time of using the delegating law as an interposed norm in the judgment on the legislative decree.

However, even after Order Nos. 103/2008 and 207/2013, the European journey of the ItCC cannot be considered as concluded. On the contrary, they both appear to be perfectly compliant with the *Granital* doctrine, due to the absence of judges who could refer a preliminary question to the ECJ, and also because judges involved in the affair were not called to apply the European provision subject to interpretative doubt (an activity that only the ItCC could have exercised when dealing with the question of constitutionality).

In some way, even the subsequent reference for a preliminary ruling in relation to the so-called ***Taricco* saga** (Order No. 24/2017) did not seem to deviate from the doctrine that has been defined in the case law of the ItCC since 1984. Indeed, although the tone of the order was extremely harsh, as if to indicate an ultimatum made by the ItCC to the ECJ, its procedural contours are perfectly consistent with the theoretical framework defined at the time (PICCIRILLI 2018). Ordinary judges had recognized a possible violation of the counterlimits and, precisely in line with the *Granital* doctrine, could do nothing but involve the ItCC by issuing questions of constitutionality that used Article 11 Const. as the parameter for the decision. In light of the parameter used, the ItCC was unable to declare the questions raised inadmissible, because – following *Granital* – it was one of those cases in which the compatibility of European law with counterlimits was questioned.

The real rupture with the *Granital* doctrine occurred with the subsequent **Judgment No. 269/2017**. As will be discussed later (at *II.B).3.b.*), in this decision the ItCC proposed an inversion of the remedies in cases of dual preliminaries where there exists an overlap between the fundamental rights protected by the Italian Constitution and those rights contemplated in the Charter of Fundamental Rights of the European Union (**CFREU**). With this proposal, also in light of the subsequent refinements of this new approach, the ItCC is promoting a constructive dialogue with the ECJ, one which has been particularly appreciated in scholarly debate. Unlike the «revolt and frustration» of the German Federal Constitutional Court and the «pragmatic resignation» of the Spanish one, the way the ItCC is now handling this tool appears to be significantly more promising (SARMIENTO 2021). Instead of claiming an absolute and exclusive monopoly (as the former does) or taking for granted a definitive transfer of the power of adjudication (as in the second approach), the ItCC proposes itself as an equal interlocutor, with a view to the constitution of a network for the protection of fundamental rights. The German approach appears perhaps rather illusory in a system that is inspired by the European composite constitution, and excessively passive the Spanish one. **The Italian proposal is more «seductive»**, as it opens a dialogue with the ECJ with a view to collaborative schemes, suggesting real practicable solutions.

However, behind a formal openness to dialogue, the ItCC continues to play a pivotal role in the relations between Italy and the EU according to a rigidly dualistic model. The *Taricco* saga had already demonstrated the extent to which the ItCC, while activating the preliminary reference, essentially asked the ECJ several rhetorical questions, to which it obtained the expected responses. Indeed, in its final judgment (No. 115/2018) the ItCC went even further, asserting its point of view in disagreement with the ECJ, but only once the dialogue was over.

 © Wolters Kluwer Italia

In the end, the ItCC showed how it is possible to practice counterlimits, without, however, explicitly stating them (GALLO 2019).

With the subsequent Order No. 117/2019, the ItCC opened another season in its European journey. This was the first preliminary reference on the validity of an EU measure made by ItCC, concerning the verification of the interpretation of a directive and, alternatively, its compliance with the CFREU. This attitude towards the ECJ is particularly representative of the Italian way of managing the relationship with Luxembourg. It was not a continuous challenge of the **right to have the last word**, nor a passive abdication to the *fait accompli* of an ECJ as the reference organization in the relationship between states and the EU level. The aim of the ItCC is to consolidate a network for the protection of fundamental rights, defining its role as the final stage of the national system and the first point of contact between it and the EU legal system.

B) EUROPEAN DRIVERS IN THE INNOVATION OF THE ITALIAN LEGAL ORDER

In this section the focus will be inverted. After having analysed the Italian contribution to the construction and the evolution of the EU, the focus will shift to the **influence that the European membership had in the evolution that the Italian legal order**. The latter appears deeply transformed and many of the changes that can be registered have to be read as a consequence of its participation in the European integration.

The analysis will focus on four different dimensions: the institutional system, the sources of law, the protection of fundamental rights and economic integration.

1. The Institutional System

Following the order in which constitutional bodies are tackled by the Constitution in its Second Part, attention will be paid on the novelties related to the Parliament, the President of the Republic, the Government and the Regions, following the order in which they are mentioned in the Constitution. No specific focus will be made on the judiciary and on the ItCC, as they are largely addressed in the paragraphs devoted to the protection of fundamental rights (at *II.B)3.*).

1.a. The Europeanisation of Parliamentary Functions

Parliaments are perhaps the most **reluctant** constitutional branches in respect of their relationships with processes such as **internationalisation or Europeanisation**. They traditionally constitute the *fora* of **national representation** and the places of **exercise of state sovereignty**. It is therefore natural for them to resist any attempt of rethinking statehood or the sharing of legitimacy.

© Wolters Kluwer Italia

Inherent to the nature of parliamentary bodies are structural characteristics that lead them to act as natural locations for discussion and exchange. As has been authoritatively remarked since the times of Hegel, they traditionally act as **intermediate institutions between the government and the people**, a sort of *portico*, namely a middle space that is not yet part of the buildings where public power is exercised and is still accessible by the people in the streets.

Moreover, the process of European integration has always been characterised by a real or presumed **democratic deficit**. European institutions have attempted to respond to this in two different ways over time. In the first phase, an attempt was made to recognise **an ever more incisive role for the European Parliament**, which since 1979 has been directly elected by the citizens of all the Member States. Decision-making procedures have been progressively amended in order to increase the role of the EP. Then, in the second phase, starting from the 2000s, this empowerment of the European Parliament began to be considered unsatisfactory with regard to increasing the level of democratic participation of citizens. Thus, also in response to the widespread discontent and loss of public opinion with respect to the integration project of Europe, **National Parliaments** (hereafter 'NPs') were therefore **directly involved**, becoming recognised as considerable powers of direct intervention in the vital decisions of the EU.

The decisive step in this direction was taken by the **Lisbon Treaty**, also defined (perhaps, with some excessive emphasis) as **the Treaty of Parliaments**. Among its many institutional innovations, the Lisbon Treaty expanded the application and renamed as the **ordinary legislative procedure** the one previously known as 'codecision', i.e. the one in which the European Parliament acts on an equal basis with respect to the Council. Moreover, it has recognised NPs, granting them extensive powers with regard to important segments of the institutional life of the Union, both by incorporating initiatives that were in the meantime launched by the Commission, and through a profound innovation of the relationship between European and national institutions.

A further innovation introduced by the Lisbon Treaty consisted of adding to the Treaty on European Union (TEU) a **Title specifically dedicated to democratic principles (Articles 9-12)**. Of particular importance is Article 10, which affirms the **foundation of the Union on representative democracy**. Its purpose is not only to further reaffirm the European Parliament's capacity to represent European citizens, but also to anchor the activity of Governments in the Council and in the European Council to the relationship they have with the respective parliaments. Furthermore, Article 12 TEU expressly refers to the **contribution of NPs to the good functioning of the EU**, thus linking their role to European policies, regulated in the TFEU.

 © Wolters Kluwer Italia

The new **powers of the NPs** established by the Lisbon Treaty can be organised into three different categories: those based upon a direct mention in the Treaties; those indirectly deriving from the Treaties' provisions referring to national constitutional procedures; and those that derive implicitly from the provisions of the Treaties that specify the powers of national governments, and that have the potential to be developed in a dialogue between the executive and the representative body (especially in Member States, like Italy, which have parliamentary forms of government).

Some powers of NPs that are based on a direct mention in the Treaties existed also prior to the Lisbon Treaty but were limited to **passive rights to be informed** upon regarding the draft European acts under discussion in Parliament and the Council. With the Lisbon Treaty – and in particular due to **Protocols Nos. 1 and 2** – NPs have been called upon to actively contribute to the implementation of the **principles of subsidiarity and proportionality** (Articles 5 TEU and 69 TFEU). In the matter of the shared competencies between EU and Member States, NPs are empowered to report possible violations of those principles, requesting the Commission to re-evaluate its initiative. Furthermore, NPs hold specific powers in key facets of the institutional life of the EU: in participation with their representatives in the **Conventions for the reform of the Treaties**, according to the ordinary procedure (Article 48 TEU); intervening in the discussion regarding the accession of new Member States (Article 49); discussions with EU institutions concerning decisions related to family law with cross-border implications (Article 81(3) TFEU); and in the adoption of regulations on Eurojust and Europol (Articles 85 and 88 TFEU).

NPs are indirectly involved in a series of complex procedures which have a first phase at the European level and a second one within the Member States. There are many references in the Treaties to such **Euro-national procedures** when the finalisation of a decision taken by EU institutions needs to be approved by the Member States **in accordance with their respective constitutional requirements**. These procedures address some strategic areas such as, among others, the initiative aimed at the establishment of a common defence (Article 42(2) TEU); the ratification of Treaty amendments and the approval of revisions in simplified form (Article 48(4) and (6) TEU); the approval of agreements subsequent to the accession of new Member States (Article 49); the decision to leave the EU (Article 50); the adhesion to the ECHR (Article 218(8) TFEU); the adoption of a «uniform procedure» or «principles common to all Member States» for the election of the European Parliament (Article 223); and the determination of the Union's resources (Article 311(3)).

Finally, NPs may acquire a further role in those cases when Treaties grant national governments the power to delay decisions or to refer some specific

© Wolters Kluwer Italia

dossier from the Council to the European Council. This mechanism (informally termed the *emergency brake*) may be activated in the following cases: when «important aspects» of an individual Member State's social security system may be affected by the adoption of measures related to the freedom of movement for workers (Article 48 TFEU); and also when «fundamental aspects» of an individual Member State's criminal justice system may be affected by the adoption of a directive on some selected issues (Articles 82(3) and 83(3) TFEU). Although no parliamentary power is explicitly envisaged in these areas, the dynamics of the parliamentary form of government can lead to a dialogue between the NP and the government responsible for declaring the application of the **emergency brake** at the European level. For example, the Italian legislation implementing this power foresees that a parliamentary motion can be approved for the purpose of providing the government with indications on how to act in the European Council.

In short, the Lisbon Treaty grants powers to the NPs concerning matters such as defence, democracy, fundamental rights, economic resources, membership of the Union and the *constitutional* rules of the latter. These may be considered amongst the most delicate issues with which the EU deals, especially in relation to the mutual relationships between its Member States and the prospects for its constitutionalisation. The contribution of NPs to the good functioning of the EU is therefore extremely concrete. Furthermore, **NPs are co-protagonists of the constitutional avenues for the further development of integration** (BESSELINK ET AAL. 2014).

The involvement of NPs in these decision-making processes deserves attention not only because it shapes their emerging European role, but also because it is significant in relation to the evolution of their functions within national legal orders. These new powers can also contribute to a partial **rebalancing with their respective governments**, which have certainly benefitted the most from their EU membership.

With regard to the **Italian Parliament**, the implementation of its new European powers had several difficulties. Following the ratification of the Lisbon Treaty and its entry into force on 1st of November, 2009, there was no immediate follow-up for their implementation. This was due to a complicated situation in domestic politics, with the crisis that faced the Berlusconi government and the resignation of the Minister for EU policies, as well as a long phase in which the management of the financial crisis was taking up the majority of institutional attention.

It was only in 2012 that there was a decisive initiative by the parliamentary committee on EU policies, later supported by the new Government led by Mario Monti, and in particular by the Minister for EU affairs, Enzo Moavero Milanesi. The result was the approval of Law No. 234/2012 which profoundly transformed

 © Wolters Kluwer Italia

the domestic framework of the implementation of EU law (see *infra II.B).2.c.*) and also provided a comprehensive framework for the innovations of the Lisbon Treaty.

In particular, **Law No. 234/2012** was significant for its distinctive framing of the new parliamentary powers deriving from the Lisbon Treaty on the basis of the purpose of the specific contribution that NPs give to the Euro-national procedure. When parliamentary votes are requested to support a decision taken at the European level, Law No. 234/2012 requests the approval of a law (this occurs in relation to the establishment of a common defence, simplified revisions of the Treaties, and decisions on the EU's resources: Articles 42(2), 48(6) TEU and 311(3) TFEU). In contrast, when the power of NPs is only required for the vetoing of an initiative put forward by the EU institutions (for instance, proposals to lower the majority needed for the decision in the Council or proposals concerning family law with cross-border implications (Articles 48(7) TEU and 81(3) TFEU), Law No. 234/2012 requests a simpler deliberation of the Houses. Therefore, they could pass a motion or vote more flexibly, without the requirement of the formality of the law-making procedure (Lupo/Piccirilli 2017).

Finally, with regard to powers attributed to the individual House, (subsidiarity scrutiny, political dialogue, etc.) Law No. 234/2012 provides indications regarding improved coordination between the Houses and in their relationship with the regional level. This was a wise choice that was also made for the purpose of preserving parliamentary autonomy.

1.b. The European Role of the President of the Republic

EU membership has also influenced how the **President of the Republic** exerts his role as **«head of State» and «representative of national unity»**.

This is notwithstanding the stability of the black letter of the articles of the Constitution dedicated to the President of the Republic (see at *II.B).2.a.*). However, some consequences should be expected in light of European integration. It can only be expected that consequences would follow for the role of the «head» of the Member State of a broad project of continental integration.

The Constitution stipulates that the role of the President of the Republic represents not merely the «Republic» (in the general sense) or the nation (the representation of which is attributed to the Members of Parliament), but its very «unity». In this way, its **representative function has multiple meanings**. On the one hand, it indicates that one task of the President of the Republic is to offer «representation», so to speak, in terms of mirroring the country, presenting himself as a permanent and visible symbol of national unity and identity. On the other hand, it also indicates something rather more dynamic and proactive, because as the President is unable to limit himself solely to the registration of syncretic or symbolic elements of the national community, **he also becomes the bearer and, in some sense, the builder of that identity**. This task seems to refer not only to activity within the country, but also outside of it, in a plural and, to some extent, an integrative sense with regard to all the different citizens that comprise the country whose unity is embodied in the role of the President of the Republic.

Many former Presidents of the Republic have interpreted their role in the latter direction, requesting to be able to take on a more structural **involvement in foreign policy**, to be able to ensure a continuity that the political instability of governments is not been able to guarantee. In the 1960s, President Segni and then later in the early 2000s President Ciampi made this request, recalling the «specific substantial content» of the dual role as both «head of State» and «representative of national unity» (President Ciampi precisely used these terms in his letter of 17th of May, 2000 to the President of the Council of Ministers). In short, several Presidents of the Republic have asked for a more incisive role in foreign policy, underlining their position as guarantors of the continuity of Italy's international relations. This vision seems to be consistent with the theoretical framework proposed by Paolo Barile in his identification of a «constitutional» political direction for the President of the Republic, as a guarantor of the pursuit of the «permanent» purposes of the legal order (Barile 1958).

Within this approach, which places the President of the Republic in a key role that is also outside of the legal system, the context of European integration takes on a specific importance.

In 1996 President Scalfaro addressed a message to the Parliament recalling «the commitment of foreign policy and above all advising of the importance of proceeding decisively in the march towards Europe». However, it was with **Carlo Azeglio Ciampi** that the promotion of European integration emerged as a trait that was characteristic of the presidential mandate. It was also due to Ciampi's personal history that the specific interpretation of European integration he advocated was so close in nature to federalist thought. For example, during the preparatory works of the Treaty establishing a Constitution for Europe, on 10th of February, 2004 Ciampi sent a letter to the President of the Constitutional Affairs Commission of the European Parliament (at that time, by chance, Giorgio Napolitano), to commemorate the 20th anniversary of the presentation of Altiero Spinelli's draft European Constitution, underlining a close connection with the founder of European federalists. The presentation of that project was identified as the «true starting date of the European constituent process which it is now urgent to complete» and Altiero Spinelli's commitment as a «testimony of the values that Europe embodies», for which «his enthusiasm and his tenacity in pursuing them spur us on to make the heritage of unification tenaciously desired and conquered by the Europeans bear fruit».

 © Wolters Kluwer Italia

The particular attention devoted to the aim of European integration appears to be not only a significant part of the general interest paid by Presidents of the Republic for the purpose of international relations, but **EC/EU issues seem to enjoy a particular autonomy**, as they are closely **combined with domestic politics**, and thus confirm the close interconnection between the domestic and European public spheres.

The most recent experience, relating both to the Presidency of Napolitano and the current mandate of Mattarella, **confirms the great attention paid by the Presidents of the Republic to the development of internal dynamics within the EU** and the close interrelationship with internal constitutional affairs. As an example, Napolitano decided to wait until the end of Italy's six-month presidency of the Council before delivering his resignation, thus further confirming the need to coordinate even the most personal choices of a President of the Republic with the institutional system of Europe.

Even more evident and incisive were the links between the internal dimension and the European dimension in the actions of Giorgio Napolitano throughout his «long» Presidency. This was particularly evident in **2011** for at least two reasons: firstly, the evident overexposure of the Presidency of the Republic in relation to the celebrations of the **150th anniversary of the unification of the country** (and thus through series of celebrations that related to the idea of «national unity» to be represented); and secondly, the intertwining of the events of the **political crisis of the Berlusconi Government** with those of the **economic crisis**, which exploded in the most dramatic terms and led to an even greater emphasis of the presidential role.

In that crucial year, the role of the President of the Republic appeared to go far beyond the aim of ensuring the presence and visibility of the unity of the Republic. Indeed, his/her activities were instrumental in helping to stimulate and strengthen the process of creating a collective national identity embedded within the process of European integration. Moreover, this was an especially interesting attempt, largely because it was based on cultural positions which – although shared by many and widespread across various different sections of the population – were difficult to qualify as unanimous or even agreed upon by the majority of the political parties in Parliament. On several occasions, faced with the deterioration of the relevant economic indicators, the President of the Republic intervened to establish a direct dialogue with international stakeholders and identify as recipients of his messages «European partners, international observers and the world of financial investors» (as in the declaration of 8th of November, 2011). On the eve of the summer of 2011, Giorgio Napolitano met and spoke with a large number of selected and qualified interlocutors, including the Governor of the Bank of Italy himself (and future President of the ECB) Mario Draghi, in addition to establishing the practice of meeting the President of the Council of Ministers before the latter's departure for the meeting of the European Council. That summer was then characterised by the **letter written by Jean-Claude Trichet and Mario Draghi**, warning Italy about the reforms that were necessary (see *infra* at *II.B).4.c.*).

In the following months, in the most complex and dramatic moments of that phase, Napolitano essentially guided the resignation of the fourth Berlusconi government and the subsequent appointment of the Monti government. Napolitano made at least two crucial interventions in this period which, on both occasions, were significant for the emphasis this placed upon his role as head of State from the perspective of observers outside of Italy.

The first was the announcement on 8th of November, 2011 of the **commitment of the President of the Council of Ministers to resign** his mandate the day following the approval of the budgetary law (which, moreover, presented the significant opportunity to amend it «in the light of the most recent contribution of observations and proposals of the European Commission»). The press release was issued few moments after the end of the meeting with Prime Minister Berlusconi in which the President of the Republic had announced the commitment of the Prime Minister to resign, and so essentially **leaving Berlusconi with no choice but to do so**.

The second intervention was then to reaffirm in the contents of a press release issued on the following morning, in a particularly assertive tone.

> «Considering the pressure of the financial markets on Italian public debt, which today has reached alarming levels, in my capacity as head of State I would like to clarify the following, in order to dispel any misunderstanding:
>
> 1) there is no uncertainty whatsoever about the fact that the President of the Council, Hon. Silvio Berlusconi, will resign. This decision will become effective with the approval in Parliament of the budgetary law;
>
> 2) on the basis of agreements between the Presidents of the Houses and the parliamentary groups both from the majority and the opposition, the law will be approved in the next few days;
>
> 3) consultations by the President of the Republic will therefore take place immediately and as quickly as possible to find a solution to the government crisis;
>
> 4) therefore, soon there will be either a new government able to take any further necessary decision with the confidence of Parliament, or Parliament will be dissolved to immediately start an electoral campaign.
>
> Fears about any prolonged period of governmental and parliamentary inactivity are therefore completely unfounded, since it is in any case possible to adopt emergency measures at any time, if necessary.».

© Wolters Kluwer Italia

It was this specific tone, in addition to the format of the press release, in which sections were subdivided into points that provided a further element of certainty. **Speaking in his role as «head of State»** (and thus making it clear that the actual recipients of the message were intended primarily to be the **Governments of the other Member States of the Eurozone**, as well as international financial markets), Napolitano provided reassurance regarding the rapidity in which the budgetary law was approved, the consequent resignation of the fourth Berlusconi Government and the formation of a new Government (or, alternatively, the rapid recourse to the polls, in order to avoid a period of long governmental and parliamentary inactivity).

Mattarella acted in great continuity with Napolitano, demonstrating the strength of the commitment of the Italian Presidency of the Republic to the European project.

The most remarkable moment of Mattarella's mandate so far has most probably been his intervention in the context of the long and tormented **process of forming the first Conte Government** in the spring of 2018 when **he refused to appoint Paolo Savona as Minister of Economy and Finance** due to his previous declaration in support of a swift exit from the common currency. The President of the Republic underlined Italy's status as a «founding country» and «protagonist» of the EU, as if to indicate the irrevocability of its membership.

The episode deserves attention for several reasons. From the perspective of internal constitutional law, the debate developed primarily in relation to the relationship between the President of the Republic and the President of the Council of Ministers in the appointment of Ministers, to discuss whether a potential absolute veto on specific candidates was in the former's powers. From a further and more external perspective, the President of the Republic has become the bearer of the European interest in domestic politics, prioritising a commitment to European obligations over the autonomous development of the national form of government.

The Italian membership of the EU, therefore, seems to be assumed to be a permanent aim of the constitutional order, in relation to which it is perhaps possible to rediscover the idea of a «European constitutional political direction» on the part of the President of the Republic, aimed at promoting and guaranteeing the realisation of those objectives and, indeed, the continuation and progressive consolidation of the constitutional integration of Europe. This development can also be problematic: with two different institutions (the ItCC and, now, also the head of State) fostering the European interest in the domestic arena there is always the possibility of a clash between them, in case of divergent ideas of consistency with the EU treaties.

© Wolters Kluwer Italia

However, **actual adherence to the European perspective is not acritical** and moments of harsh confrontation have taken place between the President of the Republic and the EU institutions. Indeed, with regard to recent examples, it is worth recalling the press release of 12th of March, 2020, made following statements by the President of the ECB Christine Lagarde, according to which the ECB did not have the task of controlling the spread between the government bonds of the different Member States. In those grave days, when Italy was among the first of the European countries to face the peak of infections in the **COViD-19 pandemic**, Mattarella replied harshly, stressing that he «expected, with good reason, at least in the common interest, solidarity initiatives and not moves that might hinder action»

In conclusion, despite the stability of constitutional provisions, the **growing attention to European issues by the President of the Republic** testifies to the overall evolution of the national legal system in an «ever closer» relation with the European system. The increasing interventions by the representative of national unity to **protect Italy's European membership** confirm the extent to which the latter must now be considered as a structural and, in some way, irreversible element of the Italian constitutional order.

From this point of view, and also considering the reciprocal interactions between the two levels, this evolution was most probably possible due to the distance that exists between the President of the Republic and the everyday environment of political and parliamentary consensus. The indirect election of the President of the Republic and the seven-year term of office have contributed to the maintenance of a distance from party politics, thus permitting the head of State to deal with the general needs of maintaining the system. The situation would have been quite different if a different form of government existed. Nor can significant innovations be excluded if the procedure for electing the President of the Republic were to change, or in any case, if mechanisms were to be introduced to ensure greater political communication between the parliamentary majority and the head of State.

1.c. The Presidentialisation of the Government

The Italian form of government (i.e., the mutual relationships between its constitutional bodies) has experienced constant evolution during the history of the Republic. One of the key factors that contributed to outlining the trends of this development was certainly EU membership.

The participation of the ECs has further **strengthened the position of the Government *vis-à-vis* the Parliament**, beyond what was already taking place as a result of domestic reasons. The institutional arrangement of the ECs initiated

 © Wolters Kluwer Italia

new scenarios for national administrations. Ministers have been called to **direct participation in the various configurations of the Council**, adding to their traditional administrative role a **new capacity to act as legislators in Europe**. Although European legislative procedures have evolved, with the progressive increase of the role of the European Parliament (and later with the participation of NPs: see *supra II.B).1.a*), the Council (formerly, the Council of Ministers of the European Union) has always been (and still is) a necessary branch of the European legislature. Furthermore, in several areas of EU competence, especially decisive ones such as Common Foreign and Security Policy, Justice and Home Affairs and financial crisis management, the traditional intergovernmental approach has not been replaced by more participatory instruments of the community method.

The twofold role of national executives may also be considered to be the most radical **denial of any distinction between national and European levels**. It is apt to quote here again the words of Peter Lindseth, who noted that the cooperation among the Member States of the EC/EU must be considered to be a manifestation of shared administrative governance, in which the protagonists are the governments of the Member States.

Within this general trend of the **consolidation of governmental leadership in the domestic institutional balance**, a specific evolution may be observed concerning the President of the Council of Ministers, which probably benefitted most from this evolution (Musella 2022). Far beyond its national role, the specific attributions deriving from the functioning of European institutions – and in particular its participation in the European Council – granted an undoubtedly pivotal role to the Italian head of government as a protagonist, which deeply influenced its position in domestic politics.

The parliamentary form of government was by no means an Italian peculiarity at the time at which the ECs were created. Indeed, at the time of the signing of the Treaties of Rome (which took place a year prior to the advent of the Constitution of the Fifth French Republic), **all the governments of the six founding states were dependent upon a relationship of confidence with the respective NP**. Despite this, the characteristics of Italian parliamentarianism were very specific and quite different from those of other member states, such as Germany.

Italian parliamentarianism contains a number of specific elements that renders it **structurally weak**. For example, the fact that a relationship of **confidence must be maintained in two separate Houses**, both of which are **directly elected** by the people (and, for most of the history of the Republic, elected with different electoral laws) constitutes **a unique case in comparative law**. Furthermore, from the perspective of comparative law, the role of the President of the Council of Ministers appears much weaker in comparison to its European counterparts. Unlike the role of the German Chancellor (or later, the English Premier or the

© Wolters Kluwer Italia

President of the Spanish Government), **the Italian President of the Council of Ministers is not autonomous in the choice of ministers** and also has no **power to force them to resign**. The difference is evident already from the name of the office: a chairperson of a collegial body and not formally a *Head* of the Executive. It was in fact only the prestige and personal role of a man such as De Gasperi that had the capacity to contribute a different appearance to a framework of rules that was purposely structured to render the government weak, in order to avoid any of the risks of the authoritarianism that were experienced under fascism. In any case, De Gasperi was to play a decisive role only in the initial phase of the European project. Indeed, it was his premature death that further revealed the structural instability of successive Italian governments. Furthermore, the Italian peculiarity of ensuring a weak higher government was significantly highlighted following the entry into force of the Constitution of the Fifth Republic (1958), and also with the subsequent introduction of the direct election of the President of the French Republic (1962).

This approach of maintaining a weak leadership of the Government has also been followed by the ItCC in recent times. In Judgments Nos. 262/2009 and 23/2011, the ItCC **qualified the President of the Council of Ministers to be a *primus inter pares***, i.e., placing him at the same level as other ministers, according to an approach that emphasised a collegiality of the government that was likely to have been assumed to be rather greater than was actually the case in practice.

In fact, the decades following World War II witnessed a **verticalisation of policies and a presidentialisation of the governments of Western democracies**. These are profound dynamics involving structural features of contemporary democracies related to the crisis of traditional political parties, the renovation of the consensus-building circuits, and innovation in strategies of political communication. The combination of these and other tendencies resulted in an emphasis on the role of the Executive to the detriment of the Legislature and, within governments, in the valorisation of the role and potential of the leadership (POGUNTKE/WEBB 2005).

However, the integration of Europe too has provided an institutional backbone for the realisation of these tendencies.

The creation of the **European Council**, first informally and then through its transformation into the formal institution of the European Union by the Treaty of Lisbon, enabled the **Italian Prime Minister to act on an equal footing with the German Chancellor and the President of the French Republic** in the meetings of the Heads of State and Government of the EU. The political nature of the European Council, and its institutional task of granting the EU «the necessary impetus for its development and [...] the general political directions and priorities thereof» (Article 15(1) TEU) have been further strengthened in practice. In the

 © Wolters Kluwer Italia

immediate aftermath of the entry into force of the Treaty of Lisbon, the European Council exerted a prominent role in leading the EU in the financial crisis, taking the most important and problematic decisions, and surpassing the role that had been formerly played by the Commission.

In addition to the substantial data that exists, there are a number of symbolic elements that emerge from the black letter of the Treaties that deserve attention. First of all, according to Article 10(2) TEU, the European Council is the EU institution in which the **Member States are «represented» by their Heads of State and Government**. This ability of the President of the Council of Ministers alone to represent Italy is already particularly important. Indeed, the contents of Article 10(2) TEU actually seem to integrate and enrich its position as outlined by Article 95 of the Italian Constitution, which limits its tasks to the coordination between the Ministers and the maintenance of the unity of their purposes.

This new role at the European level has also led to **interesting changes in national legislation**.

Already in 1999, as a follow-up to the evolution that began with the Maastricht Treaty and which was then continued by the Amsterdam Treaty, **legislative decree No. 303/1999** (Article 3, para 2) confirmed the **President of the Council of Ministers as the individual responsible for the «implementation of the commitments taken with the EU»**. This same provision created a department within the Presidency of the Council of Ministers specifically dedicated to EU policies, in order to centralise the relationship with the EU in a structure directly subordinate to the Head of Government. This choice made it possible for the existence of both a minister specifically responsible for EU policies (as with most governments) but also for the attribution of the same functions to an Undersecretary of State, namely a lower-degree member of the Government, lacking the status of a member of the Council of Ministers. In the most recent years, Ministries for EU policies have not actually been appointed in those governments led by Renzi, Gentiloni and Draghi. It has therefore been the direct responsibility of the President of the Council of Ministers to take authority for EU affairs in Government meetings.

A further contribution to the verticalisation of the dynamics within the Government on EU affairs is derived from the structure and competencies of the interministerial committee established for the coordination of the governmental activities on this issue. The **Committee on European Affairs** (CIAE) was created by the new general law on Italy's participation in the EU (Law No. 234/2012). It is summoned and chaired by the President of the Council of Ministers, with the aim of sharing and shaping the political position of Italy in European decision-making processes. Regions may be invited to its meetings, emphasising its pivotal role not only among state-level ministries, but also in general as the propelling and guiding body in relations with the EU, thus further strengthening the role of the Government *vis-à-vis* the Parliament and, within it, of the President of the Council of Ministers.

This development has also been confirmed through the **innovation of parliamentary procedures**, as laid down by the same Law No. 234/2012. Article 4 of this legislation provides that the **Government reports to Parliament prior to each meeting of the European Council** and that the Chambers may vote to express resolutions with regard to the positions that the President intends to take. It is interesting that such votes usually tend to be cast by the Government in its entirety, yet in relation to the activity within a body in which the President of the Council of Ministers participates individually. Therefore, its role within the European Council not only represents a form of overexposure of the highest executive on the external side, but also brings about a procedural innovation in national law.

1.d. European Regional Blindness vs. the Federalisation Process

European membership influenced not only the Italian form of government (as has been said in terms of the mutual relationship between constitutional bodies) but had a significant impact also on its form of state (namely, the **distribution of powers among its territorial entities**).

In the same decades in which the EU consolidated its development, increasing significantly its competences and expanding the range of its regulations and directives, Italy was undergoing a parallel rethinking of the role of its territorial organisation. This latter process ended to be jeopardised by the former, in the light of an original feature of the European integration, often described as its «**Regional blindness**» (Ipsen 1966). The ECs and then **the EU do not ignore the existence of Regions** (*Länder*, *Départements*, *Comunidades autonomas* or whatever is the name of domestic territorial entities); on the contrary, it relies on them for important policies such as those based on structural funds. However, **European integration has been created and developed as a state-centric cooperation**, being empowered with competences on the basis of a unanimous agreement of the contracting parties of the Treaties, which are the states alone. The claim for primacy and the direct effect of EU law was unable to take into account differences among Member States about the potential existence of regional competences.

Italian regionalism had been suspended for long time, due to the late implementation of the relevant constitutional provisions (see *III.B).1.*). Only in the late 1960s were the necessary Laws for the functioning of ordinary regions approved. Then, during the 1970s, Regions were empowered with significant transfer of functions that increased their importance as point of reference in the territorial administrative governance.

 © Wolters Kluwer Italia

Instead, from the point of view of **law-making capacity, the Regions had very little role in the original constitutional design**. Ordinary regions had only a small part in few and not crucial issues in the framework of concurring competences, which mean within the general principles set by state laws.

After the crisis of the early 1990s, the Regions have been seen as a new resource for the innovation of the institutional system. They have been used, for example, as a test for the prospect of constitutional reform of the form of government (FASONE/PICCIRILLI 2021). Hence, in a more general constitutional reform approved **in 2001, their role in legislation has been significantly increased**. The legislative capacity of the state has been limited by enumerating its field of competences, with the idea of leaving the general residual competence to the Regions.

Some 20 years later it is necessary to point out the **poor impact of this reform**, not only because the ItCC pushed repeatedly for a re-centralisation of many competences in its case law (see *III.B).1.c.2.*). A further element that contributed to jeopardizing the redistribution of law-making competences within the national legal system was also the increasing influence of EU norms, whose areas of intervention and degree of detail had been enhanced in the same period.

Not even the latest reform of the Treaties brought decisive elements to clarify the situation. With the Treaty of Lisbon Article 4(2), the TEU affirms the duty for EU to respect:

> «the equality of Member States before the Treaties as well as their national identities, inherent in their fundamental structures, political and constitutional, inclusive of regional and local self-government».

However, **the actual impact of this provision has still to be defined by the ECJ**, also in the light of the particular activism of constitutional courts of the Member States in applying it and, to some extent, to interpret it (the latter being an exclusive task of the ECJ).

2. Sources of Law

2.a. The Slow Entrance of the EU into the Text of the Constitution

The Italian approach to the process of European integration was to **leave the text of the Constitution unchanged**, although its interpretation has progressed significantly thanks to the work of the ItCC.

However, even if not as an immediate and direct consequence of the modification of the founding Treaties, some **provisions of the Constitution do today carry explicit references to the EU**, its institutions or to the relationship between these and the Italian legal system.

© Wolters Kluwer Italia

The **first reference** to the Italian membership of the EU was inserted in the **Constitutional Law No. 1/1999.** As part of the modification of the autonomy of the Regions to adopt their own *statuti*, a **mention of the European Parliament** was added to the list of the offices that were indicated as incompatible with election to the regional assemblies (Article 122). Albeit indirectly, this reference is specific and nonetheless significant, because it constitutes the first of a series of amendments to the Constitution that took place in subsequent years.

1999 was a significant year for a further amendment to the Constitution, this time related more to the system of protection of fundamental rights within the ECHR system, rather than to the EU. **Constitutional Law No. 2/1999** is also a part of the Europeanisation of the Italian Constitution: by amending **Article 111**, it added a series of **principles about the fair trial** that had been affirmed by the Strasbourg Court. From then onwards, they were integrated into the Italian legal order as domestic constitutional principles.

Few years later, the entire **Title V of II Part of the Constitution**, concerning the relationship between territorial entities of the Republic, was the subject of a broad amendment, which was made through the approval of **Constitutional Law No. 3/2001**. Of particular interest was the modification to **Article 117, para. 1**, in which the «**constraints deriving from the EC law**» were placed side by side with the «international obligations» and with the Constitution itself, as limitations upon the exercise of state and regional legislative competence. This change, however, should not be misunderstood. The intention of the constitutional amendment was not to constitutionalise compliance with EU law, which would have resulted in the necessary unconstitutionality of conflicting domestic law. The purpose of the new Article 117, para. 1, was to place an emphasis on equality, despite the new division of the areas of competence, of state regional legislation, both of which were subject to the same type of constraints – constitutional, European and international – each operating according to their own specificities.

If these constitutional amendments with their limited or especially general purposes were only indirectly linked to Italian membership of the EU, **Constitutional Law No. 1/2012** must be considered a genuinely EU-driven amendment of the Italian Fundamental Charter. This amendment brought important and significant innovations during a particularly complex phase that resulted from the sovereign debt crisis. It impacted on **Articles 81, 97 and 119** and was the means by which Italy decided to implement the Treaty on Stability, Coordination and Governance, following the recommendation of the latter to insert such rules «preferably at the constitutional level». In any case, this was used not only for the introduction of the **balanced budget rule**, but also the principle of the sustainability of the public

 © Wolters Kluwer Italia

debt, both «consistently with the EU legal order». Here, the role of EU law (or, in any way, international law stemming from a treaty that was only signed by the EU Member States) is completely different and constitutes the origin and the context of the constitutional amendment, enhancing the coherence between domestic budgetary policies and the principles of EU Treaties.

Despite these **numerous amendments to the Constitution in which direct or indirect reference is made to the EU** or its institutions, the cardinal rule that still enables the entry of EU law into Italy remains Article 11 in its specific interpretation as provided by the ItCC, as from time to time also integrated with specific and additional provisions.

The result of the constitutional amendments listed is that it is now possible to find explicit references to Italian membership of the EU among the provisions of the Constitution related to Parliament (Article 81), as well as among those dealing with the Government (Article 97) and with the Regions and local autonomies (Articles 117, 119 and 122). However, even in the absence of references expressed in the parts concerning the President of the Republic, the Judiciary, and the ItCC, it is even for the latter quite possible to identify activities that are purely European or in any case inextricably linked to the process of continental integration. This is demonstrated by the particular **activism of the ItCC in identifying Art 11 the *European clause* of our Constitution**, as well as the fundamental role of individual judges in applying European law with priority even over national law, in the areas of competence of the former. The President of the Republic himself, despite the diversity of approaches among those who have held office in recent years, has progressively interpreted his role in the sense of ensuring Italy's solid engagement in the process of European integration, reviewing the understanding of his function as being representative of national unity (see at *II.B).1.b.*).

2.b. A New Concept of Legality

As has been illustrated, Italy's participation in European integration has profoundly changed the way in which the Italian Constitution has been interpreted (see at *II.A).3.*). This has led to changes in its content, with the progressive inclusion of elements referring to the EU and European institutions in its black letter legislation.

However, the **impact of legal sources** on the system is much broader and has led to the modification of certain structural principles of the republican legal order as a result of its integration with another legal system, based on very different principles and categories, yet endowed with autonomous law-making capacity.

One of the fundamental principles that has been the subject of a profound reconsideration in light of the interaction between the Italian and European legal systems is the **principle of legality**, and, with it, the very concepts of law and legislation.

The principle of legality has been a cornerstone of every constitutional system since the liberal era. It is an **extremely broad notion**, which has been subject to similarly diverse interpretations. It is a concept present in both the Anglo-Saxon legal traditions and in those of continental Europe, even though they have been developed and interpreted in extremely different ways. However, while the different experiences of continental Europe share some common traits, the Anglo-Saxon understanding of this principle is very different. There are profound divergences between the European idea of *Rechtsstaat* (*État de droit* in French, or *Stato di diritto* in Italian) and the Anglo-Saxon notion of the rule of law. From the wording itself, it may be seen how the European expression refers to the state, while the Anglo-Saxon expression refers to law and its objective ability to rule.

Similarly, diverse understandings of legality exist, which differ from one another in respect of the different role that is recognised in democratic dynamics. In **thinner understandings**, legality means simply that the administration operates on the basis of a pre-existing legal mandate, and thus not arbitrarily. **Thicker understandings**, on the other hand, see a different quality of legal rules deriving from formation procedures based on the democratic principle, namely of legislation passed by parliament.

The institutional framework of the EU has a relationship with democratic dynamics based on different presuppositions compared to that of nation states. If even the most recent reforms of the Treaties have underlined its foundation in representative democracy (Article 10(1) TEU), this has not been reflected in the qualification of European legislative acts.

Participation in the European Union has changed the concept of legality with respect to the structure of the system of legal sources in at least two different areas.

Firstly, the EU legal system introduced its own concepts of legality and now, also of legislation, on the basis of assumptions that differ from those of the nation states.

The **Lisbon Treaty reoganised the classification of European legal acts**. Beyond the already existing types of binding acts (i.e. regulation, directives, decisions), it introduced a further level of classification according a set of categories, including also that of **legislative acts** (Article 289 TFEU).

However, the EU's own notion of a legislative act is substantially different from that of the legal systems of its member states. First and foremost, the **distinction between legislative and non-legislative acts in EU law constitutes a hierarchical classification**. The secondary law sources of EU law (which also

 © Wolters Kluwer Italia

include delegated and implementing acts) are not organised in a pyramidal manner. Rather, it is the individual legal basis (that is, the provision of the Treaties providing the law-making power on the matter) that constitutes a legal system in its own right, within which the secondary law acts adopted in this regard are organized.

The **absence of a hierarchy**, and therefore the impossibility of considering legislative acts superior to non-legislative acts, was also confirmed by the ECJ. The latter clarified that a decision of non-legislative nature may suspend specific parts of a regulation having a legislative nature, as the respective legislative bases present in the Treaties already provide for the possibility of such interference (Joint cases C-643/15 and C-647/15). Therefore, it is not possible to create an automatic hierarchical supremacy in view of the legislative qualification of the act; this must be traced back to the reciprocal relationship between the legal bases in order to clarify the scope of the derivative acts adopted from them.

Furthermore, **the legislative qualification of any given act does not indicate its parliamentary origin**. The involvement of the European Parliament and its ability to determine the content of an act are not decisive factors in its qualification as a legislative act.

The EU legal system does not contemplate a necessary link between the legal effects of different types of legislative acts and the institutions from which they are produced. The lack of conformity between the decision-maker and the nature of legislative acts derives first from the confusion, within the same institution, of a plurality of functions that are traditionally attributed to different bodies within the forms of state government, as well as from the variability of the role of such institution in the approval procedures of acts sharing the same name. **A single institution may approve acts with different denominations and effects**. Furthermore, **acts of an identical nature (and attributable to the same category) may originate from different institutions**. Or, again, the same institutions may contribute in several ways to the adoption of acts that, despite having the same name and effects, are produced as a result of different procedures.

For example, ‘regulations’ may be approved on the basis of a proposal by the Commission, subsequent to an ordinary legislative procedure, in which the Council and the European Parliament participate in the decision-making process with equal powers. ‘Regulations’ may also be approved by the institutions themselves, albeit under a special legislative procedure, in which the European Parliament is limited to a mere consultative role. In a third possible hypothesis, the European Parliament and the Council could approve a ‘regulation’ following a different procedure that is not qualified as ‘legislative’ in the legal basis of the Treaty.

In short, it is not the parliamentary participation that makes an act as ‘legislative’, but rather the choice made at a higher level in the context of the adoption of the Treaty and the definition of the individual legal bases. It is therefore understood that the **EU's own concept of legislation is not directly connected to the democratic principle. It derives from the principle of conferral**, i.e. on the modalities defined by Treaties, in relation to each legal basis, on the procedure to be followed for the adoption of acts of secondary law (BAST 2012).

A second area in which it is possible to appreciate how participation in the EU has modified the idea of legality within the Italian legal system can be found in the fact that the **ItCC has recognised the capacity of European legal acts** (of whatever nature) to be applied in matters that the Constitution **reserves for national legislation**.

This is a well-established possibility that has developed since the judgment No. 183/1973 (*Frontini*) mentioned above (see *supra* at *II.A).3.*) and should not be underestimated. The potential for the intervention of European acts in matters reserved to legislature was confirmed in an important ruling relating to the autonomy of universities (No. 383/1998). In this decision, the ItCC permitted the intervention of European legal acts in a matter that the national constitution had reserved for the law. It also held that, in view of the effects of European acts, there was no need for further supplementation by national legislative acts.

This is a conclusion that deserves attention: the legal integration between national and European acts is not limited to the entry of legislative acts into national legal systems that are autonomously produced by European institutions. What is also changing are also the structural principles of the internal system of legal sources, which even in a dualist country like Italy sees the direct application of European legal acts even where the national constitution had indicated that this is reserved for acts passed by the national parliament, democratically elected by its citizens.

2.c. The Annual European Session

Italy has traditionally suffered from a **chronic delay in the implementation of European law**. The causes of this situation may be found in the chaotic methods of Italian law-making and in the high instability of governments. Both reasons have caused serious problems in national administrative action concerning the EU, especially in the period prior to the mid-1990s.

The delay in the implementation of European law is a problem from several points of view. First of all, it causes a lack of uniformity in its application, and this results in the loss of the ideal of «ever closer» integration among the Member States. Furthermore, it triggers countermeasures by the European institutions, and in particular by the Commission, which has the power to sanction non-compliant Member States. For many years, Italy has been the **Member State**

 © Wolters Kluwer Italia

with the lowest rate of implementation of EU legislation and policies. It has also been at the **top of the list of Member States when it comes to infringement procedures** related to the delayed or non-transposition of EC/EU law. Moreover, with the prospect of completing the Single Market in 1992, the requirement had arisen for an organisation of the instruments used for the implementation of directives, in order to avoid aggravating an already critical situation.

The institutional response to this situation was the adoption of an ***ad hoc*** **periodic instrument**, to be renewed on an annual basis, specifically aimed at **concentrating in a single bill the transposition of European law that required implementation at the national level**. Italy was the first Member State to implement a legal framework for an annual European session, creating **a model that was later followed by several other countries**.

This periodic instrument was introduced by **Law No. 86/1989**, the first framework law regulating the relationship between Italy and the EU inspired by the Ministry of European Affairs of that time, Antonio La Pergola. It also represented the consolidation of an approach to legislative programming which, at least in its intentions, has since constituted a reference model within the Italian legal system. The Italian Parliament had recently begun to experiment with something similar to the annual budgetary session, introduced with Law No. 468/1978. The latter had some fundamental features that can also be found in the Community/European session: the predetermination, in the legislation, of a timeframe to be devoted to the discussion of a specific bill, the provision of a legislative initiative reserved to the Government. The new Law was also **coordinated with a modification of parliamentary rules of procedures**, in order to establish precise specifications that would **limit the amending capacity of the Parliament** in the annual Community session, in order to prevent the transformation of an *ad hoc* bill into an *omnibus* one.

The original framework law on the relationship with the ECs/EU has been revised twice, first with **Law No. 11/2005** and finally with **Law No. 234/2012**. An examination of the progressive changes in these three laws reflects a significant change of approach to understanding the role of the national level in the dynamics of interaction with the EU. Already in the evolution of their titles, one is able to grasp several elements of interest. The first two laws (in 1989 and 2005) had almost identical titles juxtaposing the (mere) «participation» «to the [Community/European Union] regulatory process» and the «procedures for the **execution of obligations**» (in an evidently almost exclusively passive sense).

Law No. 86/1989 was entitled «General rules on Italy's participation in the community regulatory process and on the procedures for implementing European obligations»; Law No. 11/2005 «General rules on the participation of Italy in the regulatory process of the European Union and on the procedures for the execution of Community obligations».

The 2012 Law follows a different approach. It refers to Italy's **participation both in the formation and in the implementation of legislation and policies of the EU**, thereby including the implementation within a single notion of participation as in an integrated cycle.

Law no. 234/2012 is entitled: «General rules on Italy's participation in the formation and implementation of European Union legislation and policies».

Furthermore, the term «obligations», although the wording remains present in the text of the articles, has disappeared from the title of the framework law. Article 1, instead of listing the different types of obligations and constraints deriving from EU law n**ow refers to the exercise of powers deriving from membership** (and not merely participation). Again, this is a confirmation of the new approach followed by the 2012 law.

The introduction of the annual European session has to be considered of general importance, even beyond its specific impact in the improvement of the Italian performance in adapting national law to EU one. It contributed to reduce the chaotic methods of law-making, offering dedicated bills to convey homogeneous provisions, in a pre-established framework of procedural rules, set both by legislation and parliamentary rules of procedure. In other words, annual sessions, like the European one, are rare examples of coordination and programming law-making between Government and Parliament, all the more important in a legislation dominated by decree-laws.

2.d. Support to the Expansion of Delegated Legislation

One of the most tangible aspects of the **transformation of the methods of law-making** in the Italian legal system linked to participation in the EU is the enormous **expansion of recourse to legislative delegation in the implementation of European law** and, in particular, in the transposition of directives.

Legislative delegation lends itself perfectly to the process of the implementation of directives because it allows for a series of structural needs of the institutional system to be combined with the relationship between Parliament and the Government. The **implementation of the directives is mostly of great technical complexity**, and therefore **requires particular uniformity** in the drafting. However, any political knots still have the potential for resolution via parliamentary intervention, in the advisory opinion on the draft legislative decree. In other

 © Wolters Kluwer Italia

words, recourse to the delegation allows Parliament to avoid overwhelm from the quantity of directives that must be transposed. Indeed, the lack of an option for recourse to the delegation would also constitute a heavy constraint on the ability of Parliament to decide autonomously upon the management of its decision time-frames. At the same time, this procedure allows the Government (understood as the administration competent for the matter) to **maintain control over the modification of the national legislation**, which the same administrations will then be called upon to apply.

Recourse to legislative delegation allows for an **improvement in legislative workflows** for a further reason, as it also combines at the national level the role of legislator that the government exercises at the European level within the Council. This can be understood better if one avoids the categories (actually used almost exclusively in the Italian debate) of the «upstream» (*ascendente*) and «downstream» (*discendente*) phases, which represent Italian participation in the formation of European legislation and the subsequent activity linked to their transposition. This distinction is extremely useful for educational purposes, but it is not how the process really works, given that the **two phases are in fact components of a single regulatory cycle**. The administrations participating in the formation of European acts in the Council begin to prepare at an early stage by highlighting the potential impact of a proposed act on national legislation, through the drafting of correspondence tables. Following the approval of a directive, it will therefore be immediately clear which internal provisions must be amended in order to implement the new European act.

The preference for legislative delegation in the implementation of European law has been clearly evident for decades, but the latest modification of the general law of participation in the European Union has clarified that **legislative delegation constitutes *the* ordinary means of transposing EU law**. Law 234/2012 has split the annual bills for the implementation of EU law. The ordinary and necessary one is the **Annual European Law of Delegation**, containing the formal authorisation to the government to enact directives (and, if it is the case, to give execution to regulations) via delegated legislation. There may then be a further bill entitled «**Annual European Law**», introduced to the parliament whether and when there are further issues that require a follow-up in national law which can be directly enacted (meaning without the necessity to confer a delegation to the government).

The data on the creation of legislation in Italy highlights the significantly leading role that legislative delegation has achieved in recent years, which is also due to its implementation of European law.

A **focus on the figures in the last completed legislative term (2018-2022)** can help to understand the context. In total there have been 311 ordinary Laws approved by the Parliament. However, most of them were Laws following a governmental decision: 104 of them were Laws converting decree-laws and 120 authorised the ratification of international treaties. The other 87 Laws include 19 acts linked to the budget session and 5 were Annual European Laws or Annual European Laws of Delegation. In conclusion, there were some **63 pieces of ordinary legislation** including delegating laws followed by governmental implementations.

In the same legislative term there were **164 legislative decrees**, most of which (around 75%) adopted for the implementation of European directives on the basis of delegations approved in Annual European Laws of Delegation.

3. Protection of Fundamental Rights

The Europeanisation process of the Italian legal system also includes a significant development as regards systems for the protection of fundamental rights written into European law.

Over time, **international and supranational systems aimed at the protection of fundamental rights have multiplied**, both within the framework of international organisations created specifically for this purpose (namely, the Council of Europe (CoE) with the European Convention for the Protection of Human Rights and Fundamental Freedoms (**ECHR**)), and in light of the constitutional development of the EU, which led to the adoption of the **CFREU**.

This multiplication of rights catalogues and sites of adjudication has **directly and indirectly influenced the national system** of the protection of fundamental rights. This can be seen in the case law of the ItCC and the relationship between it and the ordinary courts. For a long time, the ItCC permitted individual judges to adjudicate on national constitutional rights and supranational guaranteed rights. More recently, however, there has been a clear **re-centralisation of scrutiny** by the ItCC (Tega 2022), alongside a trajectory that has perhaps not yet reached a fully defined equilibrium.

3.a. The Incorporation of the ECHR

As with the ECs, **Italy is also a founding state of the Council of Europe**, of which it has been a member since its creation in 1949. The ECHR was signed in Rome in 1950.

The status of the ECHR in the Italian legal system has long been considered on a par with that of other international treaties, which in Italy have an equal status to legislation. As it has been previously noted (see at *II.A).3.*), the **dualist approach of the Italian system** transmits the status of the act authorising their entry into Italy to legislative sources outside of the legal system. Consequently, **international treaties assume equal value with parliamentary legislation**, as

 © Wolters Kluwer Italia

Article 80 requires that the authorisation for their ratification be approved by parliament by means of a law.

This qualification of the ECHR in legislative terms has been maintained by the ItCC until quite recently. For example, in Judgment No. 188/1980, the ItCC reaffirmed the exclusion of the ECHR both from the scope of application of Article 10 (as is always the case for treaty law, even if of a general nature), and from that of Article 11 (representing no limitation of national sovereignty).

Over time, even without changing the value to be attributed to the Convention and its standing in the domestic legal system, the ItCC recognised an **atypical competence of ECHR law** (Judgment No. 10/1993), and then a capacity for reciprocal integration between the formulas describing the different catalogues of rights (Judgment No. 388/1999).

However, while the ItCC repeatedly confirmed the legislative status of the ECHR in Italy, the decisions emanating from the ordinary courts had begun to take very different directions. In particular, in the name of promoting the fundamental rights protected by the ECHR and the possibility that the ECHR could be invoked in the interpretation of rights guaranteed by the national Constitution, **some courts (including the Court of Cassation) had begun to disapply national legislation conflicting with the ECHR**, as interpreted by the European Court of Human Rights (ECtHR). Just to quote the most relevant examples, see decisions by the Court of Cassation, I sect., Judgment No. 6672/1998; Court of Cassation, United Sections, Judgment No. 28507/2005.

The result of this development risked being completely paradoxical. Firstly, there was a strong **similarity between the domestic treatment of EU law and the ECHR, without there being a similar reference to Article 11** and the limitations of sovereignty it mentions for the latter (thus the doctrine of counter-limits could also be used in this area). Secondly, the hypothesis of a disapplication of domestic law following an autonomous decision of the common courts risked completely **cutting off the ItCC** from exercising any role in the interpretation of fundamental rights.

The ItCC reacted to this risk by taking cues from the constitutional amendment that had in the meantime been added modifying the text of **Article 117, para 1**, by including, *inter alia*, **international obligations** amongst the limits placed on the exercise of legislative functions.

As we have seen, the motive for the inclusion of international obligations in this provision, together with the Constitution and constraints deriving from EC law, had the main purpose of reinforcing the equivalence between state law and regional law, in light of the equal subjection of both to the same set of constraints, each operating in its own part in a different manner (see at *II.B).2.a.*) There was therefore no desire to change the relationship between national law and international law. The ItCC did, however, consider that it could specify both precisely and individually which international treaties were to be understood as international obligations under Article 117, para 1. In such cases, those treaties must be considered as restrictions on legislation, and thus entail an indirect limitation of compatibility with the Constitution.

In other words, with the **twin Judgments Nos. 348 and 349/2007** the ItCC attributed to the **ECHR a status that was at the same time both supra-legislative and sub-constitutional, thus assuming an intermediate role between the Constitution and the law**, together with the ability to operate as an interposed norm in assessing the constitutionality of laws suspected of violating the ECHR (Repetto 2013). The violation of the ECHR by means of national law therefore entails the unconstitutional nature of this law, and thus it is only the ItCC that can pronounce on it, excluding any role of the ordinary courts in the disapplication of national law in conflict with the ECHR. A further consequence of this new framework is the **subjection of law emanating from the ECHR (and, therefore, from the case law of the ECtHR) to review by the ItCC**, which could exclude its application in Italy in order to guarantee the prevalence of superior national constitutional values. This pivotal role of the ItCC was implemented in Judgment No. 49/2015, in which it clarified that the constraints on the legislature only arise in regard to a well-established ECHR law; it then listed a series of indicators that exclude that this requirement has been met.

The 2007 judgments represent an extremely important new development. The trend of judicial decision that was focused on the disapplication of domestic law conflicting with the ECHR, combined with the possibility – as recognised since Protocol No. 11 – of individual applications on the issue of the violation of rights guaranteed by the Convention, risked completely depriving the ItCC of the protection of fundamental rights in Italy. The **activism of the ordinary courts** on the one hand and the ECtHR itself on the other resulted in a reaction from the ItCC. By elaborating on the changes that had in the meantime been made to the Constitution, the ItCC was able to create the premise for a legal balance that was not very different from that assumed by the *Frontini* Judgment (No. 183/1973) in relation to EU law. The **absence of any claim of primacy and direct effect of ECHR** law allowed this balance to be maintained.

In more recent years, **additional international treaties have been deemed as international obligations** by the ItCC pursuant to Article 117, para 1, and therefore equivalent to the ECHR as a constraint on subsequent legislation. These consist of the **European Convention on the Exercise of Children's Rights** (Judgment No. 7/2013) and the **European Social Charter** (Judgments Nos. 120 and 194/2018). For these two treaties, the same contextual conditions that had led to the differentiated treatment of the ECHR with respect to the general nature

 © Wolters Kluwer Italia

of international treaties do not seem to be present. They certainly have in common the **theme of fundamental rights** and the **structure of the provisions in terms of principles**, which are very similar to the provisions of the Constitution. However, the absence of a court and a system of protections as is the case in the ECHR system, as well as the impossibility of an individual action as provided for in Protocol No. 11 ECHR, make the distinction made by the ItCC between ordinary international treaties and international obligations under Article 117, para. 1, difficult to understand.

3.b. Competing Systems of Fundamental Rights Protection

A further milestone in the path of **integration between systems of protection of fundamental rights** at the national and European levels is a recent development in ItCC case law, which has initiated a **profound rethinking of the relationship between national and EU law** in this area. However, in order to grasp the innovation contained in the latest developments, it is necessary to briefly retrace the main steps that have led the European Union to manage fundamental rights, to the point of creating its own catalogue of them.

As we have seen (*supra* at *II.A).1.*), the EU was founded with great constitutional ambitions. However, as it was based primarily on economic cooperation, the approach of a gradual and progressive integration initially relegated the protection of fundamental rights to the background. In the **initial years following the Treaties of Rome, the ECJ explicitly excluded the existence of a system for the protection of fundamental rights** in the Community system (Joined Cases C-36, 37, 38 and 40/59 *Geitling*, 1960) as being exorbitant with respect to the competences attributed by the Treaties. Subsequently, since the early 1970s, important judgments had been made by the ECJ which, more or less directly, tended to recognise the protection of **fundamental rights as general principles of EC/EU law** (C-11/70 *Internationale Handelsgesellschaft*, 1970). However, these were initial statements that were instrumental to the pursuit of the ECs' own aims and confined within the limited competences of Europe at the time. Fundamental rights were not explicitly and directly recognised by EC/EU law, but their foundation was found in the **common constitutional traditions of the Member States and the human rights treaties to which they are a party**.

However, the requirement for a catalogue of rights specific to the ECs was beginning to be felt, and steps were taken to this end. A first significant moment **came in 1977 with a Joint Declaration by the European Parliament, Council and Commission**, which affirmed «the prime importance they attach to the protection of fundamental rights» derived from national constitutions and the ECHR, as well as the commitment of the European institutions to respect those rights in the pursuit of the goals of ECs. Even more explicitly **in 1989, the European**

Parliament decided to act alone, passing a resolution containing a fully-fledged Declaration of Fundamental Rights and Freedoms of 24 Articles containing specific rights, as well as 4 further final provisions.

With the reforms of the 1990s, the reference to fundamental rights entered the text of Treaties, while until then it was contained at most in their recitals.

In the **Single European Act**, third paragraph of the premises, the High Contracting Parties declare to be

> «determined to work together to promote democracy on the basis of the fundamental rights recognised in the constitutions and laws of the Member States in the [ECHR] and the European Social Charter; notably freedom, equality and social justice».

Then, the **Maastricht Treaty** introduced Article F (later Article 6), the second paragraph of which reads:

> «The Union shall respect fundamental rights, as guaranteed by the [ECHR], and as they result from the constitutional traditions common to the Member States, as general principles of Community law».

The real breakthrough in the drafting of a genuine catalogue of rights had, however, to wait for the new millennium, with the **adoption of the CFREU**. The importance of this change was further emphasised by the fact that it was accompanied by the launch of a new decision-making model, which would later be incorporated into subsequent Treaties. For the drafting of the Bill of Rights, the convening of an Intergovernmental Conference was deemed insufficient, as it would only have brought together the representatives of national governments, and would therefore have served merely as the sole expression of majorities. A **new type of body was therefore convened, termed the Convention**, also composed of the representatives of NPs, as well as of the candidate countries for EU membership and the European institutions. The result of the work of the European Convention was the CFREU, which was initially only **proclaimed in 2000, but not yet made effective**. At this early stage, however, European institutions had intended to consider themselves bound by the Charter regardless, even before it formally took legal effect. Additionally, some judges had actually begun to refer to it in their judgments, creating a situation that was formally and substantially unclear.

With the Lisbon Treaty, the CFREU was given binding value, and was placed on the same legal footing as the Treaties. The CJEU immediately demonstrated its intention to use it, referring to its contents even when the referring

 © Wolters Kluwer Italia

national judges had intended to limit the grounds for their appeals to the corresponding contents of the ECHR (C-92/09, *Schecke & Eifert*, 2010).

Its impact on the legal systems of Member States merits careful consideration.

As an act of EU law, the **CFREU is subject to the principle of conferral**; as such, its application is limited to areas of EU competence. However, two factors encouraged a major development of the potential of the Charter. First of all, there was the fact that the **areas of EU competence have significantly increased** over time with the successive revisions of the Treaties. Moreover, the essentially **constitutional tone of the CFREU** and its structure according to Titles encompassing a very broad scope of fundamental rights (Dignity, Freedoms, Equality, Solidarity, Citizens' Rights, Justice) make its generalised application very easy.

As for the impact of the CFREU on the Italian legal system, in the period immediately following its acquisition of binding legal force it followed the approach indicated by the ItCC in the *Granital* judgment (see *supra* at *II.A).3.*), thus being endowed the ability to disapply conflicting domestic law with the power of direct effect This state of affairs, however, exacerbated the risk inherent in the doctrine of the direct effect of EU law: by placing **the decision in the hands of individual judges as to whether or not to apply the CFREU** (and, consequently, whether or not to disapply the corresponding rights provided for by the Constitution), **the path was opened to a substantial de-centralisation of scrutiny in the area of fundamental rights**. On the other hand, the ordinary courts immediately started referring to the CFREU: according to an analytical study, between 1st of December, 2009 and 13th of December, 2018, the Charter was mentioned in over 3,400 jurisdictional rulings (Sciarra/Golia 2020). This quantitative data, combined with the structure and declared **constitutional ambitions of the Charter**, clarify the risk of assuming an **overflowing nature** (Barbera 2017).

Such a trend could not be accepted by the ItCC: after the trend that had impacted the ECHR in the early 2000s, it risked being cut off from ordinary courts with regard to the establishment of standards on fundamental rights. For this reason, with the **ground-breaking Judgment (No. 269/2017)**, perhaps the most important since the *Granital* case, it affirmed a new system of principles relating to the protection of rights between Italy and the EU. It required the ordinary courts ruling on dual preliminarity cases to **first raise the question of constitutionality, and, in view of the response, to evaluate to issue a preliminary reference to the CJEU**. Thus, when there exists doubt regarding the constitutionality and compatibility of EU law on the same rule of domestic law, the ItCC requests that it is consulted first, also reserving the right of referral of the case to the CJEU for a preliminary ruling, in the light of the practice developed since Order No. 103/2008 (supra at *II.A).4.*).

The reasons for this shift must be found in the content and purpose of the CFREU, as well as in the nature and purpose of the constitutionality review offered by the ItCC. With respect to the first, the **ItCC recognises the typically constitutional stamp of the contents of the CFREU**, which «largely intersect with the principles and rights guaranteed by the Italian Constitution». For this reason, when there are issues in which the **two catalogues of rights overlap**, the ItCC believes it must ensure the ***erga omnes* effect of its interventions**. Otherwise, giving the usual precedence to the application of EU law would lead to disapplication in the actual case only, without the possibility of deriving a declaration of unconstitutionality with general effect. Consequently, the ItCC indicates the priority of the question of constitutionality, in order to be able to ensure its essential function as the guarantor of the effectiveness of rights.

The new approach to dual preliminarity proposed by the ItCC has been progressively refined in a series of judgments subsequent to No. 269/2017. In particular, the ItCC clarified that **the priority of the question of constitutionality over the preliminary referral is not an obligation for the ordinary courts**, but a possibility (Judgment No. 20/2019). The purpose of this clarification is twofold: on the one hand, it serves to reassure the CJEU that it does not wish to jeopardise Italy's obligation of loyalty to the principle of uniformity of EU law; on the other hand, it acknowledges that the new scheme depends on the choices of ordinary courts, on which the ItCC does not have the power to impose a specific procedure. Subsequent decisions (Nos. 63/2019, 67/2022) further explained that Judgment No. 269/2017 constitutes a structural shift by the ItCC, in light of which it is particularly open to **centralising dialogue with the CJEU by means of preliminary rulings on fundamental rights** (Orders Nos. 117/2019, 182/2020, 217/2021).

However, the **response from the ordinary courts has varied**. For the most part, ordinary judges followed the new scheme of reversal of remedies, putting the question of constitutionality before the reference for a preliminary ruling. Administrative judges have appeared to be more faithful to the previous approach, with their judgments revealing a prevailing orientation towards the activation of dialogue directly with the CJEU (Gallo/Piccirilli 2023). A balance will probably only be achieved following a certain period of practice of this new approach. Surely, **the development triggered by Judgment No. 269/2017 has returned the ItCC to a leading role in the judicial dialogue on fundamental rights**, combining the multi-level development of rights protection systems and the centralised nature of the Italian system of constitutional justice (Martinico/Repetto 2019).

 © Wolters Kluwer Italia

3.c. The Decision not to Ratify Protocol No. 16 ECHR

In this path of progressive integration between systems for the protection of fundamental rights in the European legal space, Italy's decision not to proceed with the ratification (after having signed it) of **Protocol No. 16 ECHR** comes as some surprise.

The Protocol follows up on commitments that the Member States of the CoE made in 2012 with the **Brighton Declaration**. The general objectives of the latter were to strengthen the connection between national courts and the ECtHR, in order to ensure the best implementation of the Convention. This was in continuity with the streamlining of the operation of the ECtHR achieved with Protocol No 14 but required a further step to ensure greater **consistency between its decisions and implementation by national courts**. The main instrument identified for this purpose was the introduction of dialogue between the courts, through which the ECtHR could render **advisory opinions on the interpretation of the Convention** related to specific cases brought to the attention of national courts, while clarifying the **non-binding nature** of these opinions (Brighton Declaration, B.12.d).).

The commitments of the Brighton Declaration were implemented with the 2013 signing of Protocol No. 16. The Protocol provides that the possibility of prior involvement of the ECtHR is aimed at acquiring **advisory opinions on questions of principle in the interpretation or application of the ECHR**. This is a completely **new competence of the Strasbourg Court**, and for which the possibility of recourse to just satisfaction is excluded.

The Protocol merely sets out certain elements, leaving the detailed regulation of the operation of this new instrument of judicial dialogue to national implementation.

The contents of the Protocol merit some further elaboration. First of all, it makes it clear that the possibility of activating **this instrument is not to be understood as its extension to all national courts**: the Protocol specifies that it is accessible to the **highest courts and tribunals**, requiring each state - at the time of signing the Protocol, or at the time of filing the ratification - to identify in detail which national courts are to be involved (Article 10, Prot. No. 16). As for the purposes of prior involvement, these may concern both questions of interpretation and questions of application of the Convention. Therefore, national judges can turn to the ECtHR both to **decode the meaning of the provisions of the ECHR** and to **clarify the consequences** of the results of this process. In other words, the opinions rendered by the ECtHR aim to understand the purpose of the provisions of the Convention, their content and their possible limitations.

The **opinions rendered in this context are defined as advisory and are to be considered as non-binding** (Article 5 Prot. No. 16), although provision is made for their publication regardless (Article 4(4) Prot. No. 16). The non-binding nature differentiates the ECtHR's advisory opinions both from the preliminary reference to the CJEU as regards EU law the task of which is to provide the «certain and reliable» interpretation of EU law), and from the question of constitutionality to be addressed to the Italian Constitutional Court, which is obligatory and binding, in light of the centralised nature of the determination of constitutionality (see at *II.A).2.*). The purpose of the advisory opinions is thus twofold, i.e. both to **enable the national court to reach a solution on the actual case in a manner consistent with ECtHR** case law, and to **allow the ECtHR to offer abstract clarifications** of the meaning of the Convention, while leaving the usual margin of appreciation to the national authorities.

Considering these characteristics, the idea of optional prior involvement is **consistent with the nature of the ECtHR as a subsidiary jurisdiction**, which leaves the definition of the actual case to the autonomous decision of the national court. However, already the fact that ECtHR opinions also have the purpose of publication makes it clear that they are not only intended to facilitate the decision of the individual court that requested the opinion, but also have more general compliance purposes.

Italy is among the states that have signed the Protocol. Its entry into force was foreseen with the ratification by the tenth member state (which then took place on 1st of August, 2018 for those states that have done so, which includes France). **Italy, however, decided not to proceed with the ratification** of Protocol No. 16, passing Law No. 11/2021, which authorised the ratification only of Protocol No. 15, and to leave out the part containing the ratification of Protocol No. 16. This decision was made following several years of reflection, in which the **opinions of some constitutionalists**, who raised a number of critical arguments during the pre-legislative scrutiny (Luciani 2019), and to which Parliament adhered, proved to be particularly influential.

In particular, the substantial **analogy with the preliminary reference** to the CJEU was emphasised in that, in practice, there would be no significant difference for any judge who decided to request an advisory opinion from the ECtHR. This judge would still be inclined to wait for the ruling of the Strasbourg Court (and would thus need to suspend judgment until then), and it would be very difficult not to follow the opinion once received, if only because, otherwise, the decision to have requested it and the subsequent decision to have waited for it would become unreasonable acts. In light of this reconstruction of the instrument, it was considered **a risk for national law to involve an external party in a fundamental rights judgment yet to be determined**. The risk would be that of **offering the final word to authorities extraneous to Italian constitutional**

 © Wolters Kluwer Italia

system, in which the ECHR is considered to have a supra-legislative rank, but also a sub-constitutional status.

A further reason for dispute was the fact that the ItCC was not mentioned in the list of «Highest courts and tribunals» that would have been given the right to use the new procedure in the governmental bill presented to the Chambers for the authorisation of ratification. The Court of Cassation, Council of State, Court of Accounts, and the Administrative Judicial Council for the Sicilian Region were listed. The latter was certainly an error, which could nevertheless be remedied by following the procedures of Article 10 of Protocol No. 16.

The arguments reported are not unanimously shared in the community of constitutional law scholars (LAMARQUE 2021), but – at least at present – **a change of opinion and a new law aimed at ratifying Protocol No. 16 ECHR appear highly unlikely**.

An asymmetrical and paradoxical picture ensues: with the entry into force of the Protocol for those states that decided to ratify it, the **ECtHR has begun to render advisory opinions** on the basis of requests from the highest courts and tribunals of those countries. As has been mentioned, those opinions are published, and are therefore also known to Italian judges who, to some extent, will be inclined to follow them, even if they do not have the power to issue similar requests with specific reference to the cases brought before them.

4. Economic Integration

4.a. The External Bond in Structural Reforms: a Loss of Sovereignty?

Italy's participation in the **European integration process has significantly affected sovereignty in economic matters**. The main choices on fiscal and economic policy are, in fact, no longer adopted solely at the national level by the Italian Parliament and the Government but depend – to an increasing extent – on decisions made by supranational bodies within the so-called **European economic governance**. In this framework, the Italian state is bound, *de facto* or *de iure* (i.e. either through political-economic pressures or specific legal rules), to comply and implement fundamental decisions for its economic life, which are taken mainly at the European level and in compliance with European constraints.

This capacity of European institutions to bind the Italian budgetary and economic policy choices has traditionally been described as an **external bond** (*vincolo esterno*). The fortune of this term is linked to the personality of **Guido Carli**, Bank of Italy Governor from 1960 to 1975, and Minister of the Treasury from 1989 to 1992. In 1993, Carli published a famous memoir entitled «*Cinquant'anni di vita italiana*» (Fifty years of Italian life), in which he argues that **Italy's participation in international and supranational organisations**, with the consequent

© Wolters Kluwer Italia

imposition of constraints on the budgetary and economic policies, was **necessary to carry out the structural reforms** essential for the modernisation of the country. He refers, in particular, first to the accession to the Bretton Woods Agreements in 1947, then to the Single European Act that launched the Internal Market in 1987 and, finally, to the Maastricht Treaty, signed in 1992, which established the European Union. In his view, the constraints deriving from participating in these supranational fora made it possible **to counter the «animal spirits»** (*spiriti animali*) **of the Italian political parties**. For electoral consensus and logic of sharing power, Italian parties were inclined to favour unproductive spending (with adverse effects in terms of public debt and inflation) and were resistant to undertake structural reforms that would have undermined the monopolistic rents in many private sectors and the huge state intervention in the economy.

Having a highly pessimistic opinion of Italian political establishment, Carli thus suggested a positive understanding of the external bond, which he intended as an indispensable instrument to restore sound public finance and to build a competitive market economy, overcoming the massive state interventions and restrictions on competition that characterised the Italian economic system.

However, the term external bond is much more frequently understood in a negative sense.

Critics of the European integration tend to use the term **external bond to describe**, with sharp, critical tones, **the loss of sovereignty** produced by the participation in European integration at the expense of Italy. Some authoritative scholars argue that the new European economic governance is incompatible with democratic principles and may violate the fundamental characteristics of the Constitution. In their view, the Italian Parliament and Government are called upon to merely execute **decisions made by non-democratically legitimated supranational bodies**, headed **by technocrats and excessively influenced by the financial markets**. Moreover, the European institutions have, over time, allegedly promoted only **neoliberal policies**, imposing drastic cuts in public spending with severe repercussions for the Welfare State and the fundamental rights of the citizens. Not only have they removed fiscal and economic decisions from a genuine democratic control that can only be exercised at the national level (given the alleged 'democratic deficit' of the European Union), but they also compromised the realisation of the ultimate aim of the post-World War II Constitutions to promote social rights and substantial equality among citizens.

Although it is indisputable that the European institutions endorsed – and in some cases, imposed (see the case of Greece) – policies of austerity that had dramatic consequences on citizens' quality of life and often deepened the economic

 © Wolters Kluwer Italia

crisis, causing a collapse of incomes and the dismantling of social welfare, the scenario appears nonetheless to be more varied and complex (see *Paragraphs 4.b., 4.c., 4.d.*).

First, it must be acknowledged that European integration has undoubtedly meant for the Italian state reduced autonomy in determining its fiscal and economic policies. The critical decisions concerning the Italian budgetary and economic policies are nowadays the result of an extremely complex process, which directly involves the European institutions, the other Member States, the Government, and the Parliament, and develops on two different levels: the European and the national ones (see *II.B).4.c.*).

Moreover, in this process, the **financial markets** also play a crucial role, even indirectly.

Since the so-called **divorce** (*divorzio*) **between the** Italian Central Bank (***Banca d'Italia***) **and the Ministry of the Treasury** of **1981**, when the Central Bank (upon agreement with the Government) decided to act **no more as a lender of last resort**, the Italian Government must finance itself autonomously on the markets (Chessa 2016). **Wolfgang Streeck** describes this transition, typical of contemporary capitalist democracies, as a **shift from the classic tax state** – which rely on taxation – **to the debt state** – which issues bonds in order to finance public expenditure and resulting debt (Streeck 2014). When a state needs to finance itself primarily on financial markets, it must gain and maintain the trust of those markets over time. If the high level of public debt and low economic growth put its solvency at risk, fiscal consolidation policies and substantial structural reforms are needed to recover this confidence. Such policies and reforms are subject to scrutiny by market operators and rating agencies, whose consequent choices affect the decision-making process of the state indirectly. As noted (Pitruzzella 2013), the state must therefore obtain a sort of **double trust**: the **trust of its citizens**, through the democratic process **and the trust of the financial markets, through a sound and solid fiscal policy and structural reforms**. Otherwise, the loss of confidence of international markets in the financial soundness of a state may result in higher debt interests, as the interest is the price that the state pays for loans, and this price rises the more the risk of state insolvency increases.

The need to borrow from foreign lenders and financial markets in order to finance public expenditures was definitively confirmed by the Italian participation in the **European Monetary Union** (EMU), by which the **responsibility for monetary policies** – including the power to print money – has been **transferred to the Eurosystem, headed by** an independent supranational institution, **the European Central Bank** (ECB) (see at *II.C).2.*).

Ultimately, Italy's budgetary and economic policymaking is bound both by the European constraints (primarily in terms of rules, but also of confidence of the European institutions and the other Member States) and by the financial markets.

All of this makes it clear that budgetary and economic decisions can no longer be placed solely in the dialectic between the Government and Parliament, as it used to be according to the theoretical model embraced by the constitutionalism of the twentieth century. In the new European legal order, the state sovereignty in economic and financial matters is shared with supranational institutions and influenced by various actors, even outside the traditional democratic circuit.

Whereas a minority of constitutional scholars consider this evolution as a breaking of constitutional legality, the majority tend to deem this **shared sovereignty** as **consistent with the Constitution** and entirely legitimate.

In particular, **Nicola Lupo** has argued that the economic integration and the limitations of sovereignty brought about by the European economic governance are essentially based on the fundamental principle enshrined in **Article 11 of the Constitution**, which can be regarded as a «**'implicit and general' European clause**» (LUPO 2022). Such provision consents «to the limitations of sovereignty that may be necessary to a world order ensuring peace and justice among the Nations», committing the Italian Republic to promote and encourage «international organisations furthering such ends». In addition, it must be recalled that all the developments in the economic integration were not only agreed upon but also fostered by the Italian state in supranational fora. Moreover, an **amendment to the Italian Constitution was approved in 2012** (constitutional law No. 1/2012), concerning Articles 81, 97, 117 and 119, which **confirmed**, even at the constitutional level, **the participation of Italy in the European economic governance** by recalling explicitly (Articles 97 and 119) or implicitly (Article 81) the relevant European Union Law (see *II.C).4.b.* and *II.C).3.*).

Apart from these theoretical justifications, the transition to shared sovereignty in economic matters has been supported and defended even at a more **practical level**.

Some scholars have noted that **the limitations of sovereignty** introduced through economic integration **are also essential to actively protect the state sovereignty from the speculative action of financial markets**. States like Italy that have mountainous public debt and suffer from low economic growth risk to fall into a vicious circle, where the weak financial situation results in high debt interest rates and more public spending to finance the state on the markets, consequently increasing the debt and worsening the country economic situation. As occurred during the Great Sovereign Debt Crisis (2010-2011), the financial crisis of a state can also trigger a spiral of speculation on the part of the markets,

 © Wolters Kluwer Italia

which can further spread to other vulnerable states, exposing them to sovereign default risk.

Without the European constraints introduced by the reform of the European economic governance, the dependence of debtor states on financial markets would have been much more significant, and the substantial risks of default of those states would have been higher. Greater European integration on the financial and economic side thus serves to counterbalance the power of the markets and reduce the subordination of national politics to their dynamics (PITRUZZELLA 2013).

An additional aspect must be considered. **Different kinds of external bonds** (quantitative, procedural and qualitative) have **different levels of effectiveness** and produce different degrees of limitation on Italian sovereignty.

As to **quantitative constraints** (i.e. fiscal rules that require the Member State to comply with quantitative-numerical benchmarks), they **considerably reduced the room for manoeuvre for the Italian institutions**. Nevertheless, ample **margins of flexibility** in applying these rules are already provided by the relevant legal instruments, and even greater flexibility was granted to Italy over time by European bodies when interpreting and implementing such rules (see *II.B).4.b.*).

As to **procedural constraints**, they had a direct effect on the budgetary procedures at the national level, in particular after the introduction of the so-called **European Semester** in 2011. As explained in *4.c.*, the national parliamentary proceedings had to be reshaped in order to fit within the framework of Common Budgetary Timeline. However, as argued below (see *II.B).4.c.*), such procedural constraints primarily affected the distribution of power between the Government and the Parliament at the national level, rather than the overall Italian sovereignty.

As to **qualitative constraints** (i.e. specific recommendations concerning structural reforms and economic policies), they proved weak and ineffective since most of the Member States, including Italy, show a very poor implementation level. This **weak effectiveness** was confirmed over time, even though efforts have been made to make European recommendations stricter and more effective, mainly through the introduction of the European Semester (see *II.B).4.c.*). Italy and the other **Member States seem to have retained a broad discretion in defining their economic policies in qualitative terms** and with regard to their structural reforms. Only in recent years (2021-2022) an increased effectiveness of qualitative recommendations seemed to emerge, favoured by the approval of the Next Generation EU after the Covid-19 pandemic (see *II.B).4.d.*). The disbursement of European funds (loans and grants) is, in fact, conditional upon the timely implementation of the structural reforms presented in the National Recovery and Resilience Plan (NRRP), which also incorporates the recommendations addressed by European institutions to Italy within the European Semester. Consequently, Member States find themselves compelled to implement structural reforms not to lose the funds granted by the European Union through the Recovery and Resilience Facility (RRF). However, the coercive capacity of these instruments in implementing the Italian NRRP has yet to be verified.

4.b. Membership as a Financial Constraint (SGP)

Since the ratification of the Maastricht Treaty (1992), Italian membership in the European Union has entailed compliance with **financial constraints** (of quantitative type).

The establishment of the European Monetary Union (EMU), which paved the way for the creation of the Euro, and the completion of the Single Market required a high degree of convergence between the economies of the Member States and the maintenance of a sound and prudent fiscal policy. According to prevailing economic theories, **excessive structural divergences between Eurozone economies and a weak fiscal discipline could generate instability**, adversely **affect economic growth** prospects, and **cause inflation**. In a Single Market, inflation could spill over from a Member State with a weak economy (such as Italy) to States with a more solid economy (such as Germany), thus compromising price stability.

In order **to avoid such problems** and foster convergence between economies, **the Maastricht Treaty required compliance with two fundamental fiscal rules of a quantitative type**. These rules, better known as the ***Maastricht criteria***, are a **3 per cent general government deficit-to-GDP ratio** and a **60 per cent general government debt-to-GDP ratio**, or sufficiently diminishing towards and approaching that level at a satisfactory pace (as was the case of Italy).

Initially, compliance with these two fiscal rules was requested only for the accession to the EMU. Later, **with the Stability and Growth Pact** (SGP), signed in 1997, they became **permanent**, and the European economic governance was furtherly structured **to strengthen the monitoring and coordination of national fiscal and economic policies**.

The (original) SGP consists of two Council regulations, setting out legally binding provisions, and two resolutions of the European Council in Amsterdam (June 1997). The two regulations established a so-called **preventive arm** (Reg. No. 1466/97 on budgetary surveillance) and a so-called **corrective arm** (Reg. No. 1467/97 on excessive deficit procedures). **The preventive arm** of the SGP **aims to ensure**, through the definition of surveillance procedures (i.e. ex-ante supervision), **that the Member States follow sustainable budgetary policies** in the medium term. **The corrective arm** of the SGP **aims to ensure that the Member**

 © Wolters Kluwer Italia

States adopt policies consistent with European rules, outlining a procedure aimed at correcting any non-compliance with the numerical limits indicated in the European Treaties. To this end, whereas a Member State does not comply with the deficit and debt limits, a so-called **Excessive Deficit Procedure** (EDP) may be initiated along with a deadline to comply, **which basically includes and outlines an adjustment path**. As outlined by the preventive arm regulation, all Member States are each year called to submit an SGP compliance report for the scrutiny and evaluation of the European Commission and the Council of Ministers, which will clarify the country's expected fiscal development for the current and subsequent three years. These reports are called «Stability Programmes» for the Eurozone Member States and «Convergence Programmes» for the non-Eurozone Member States.

This framework was **amended for the first time**, in the sense of an overall loosening of the constraints, **in 2005** (so-called SGP II; Regulations nos. 1055/2005 and 1056/2005), in order to consider individual national circumstances better and to add more economic rationale to the rules. The new SGP focuses on **improving public finances in structural terms**, i.e. excluding the effects of a possible economic slowdown or expansion and one-off measures. A key concept in this respect is ***structural budget balance***, the actual budget balance net of the cyclical component and one-off and other temporary measures.

The most significant addition was the parameter of the ***Medium-Term Objective*** (MTO). This value varies from country to country and corresponds to **an objective of structural budget balance** – pursued through an adjustment path – **that should guarantee a safety margin with respect to the 3 per cent deficit rule** and **ensure the sustainability of public finances**. It is country-specific, in order to take account of the diversity of economic and budgetary positions and developments as well as fiscal risks to the sustainability of public finances and is defined in structural terms. MTOs range from a deficit of 1 per cent of GDP to a balance or surplus for the Eurozone Member States. Countries like Italy that have not yet reached their MTO will have to pursue an annual improvement of 0.5 per cent of GDP as a benchmark of their cyclically-adjusted balance, minus one-off measures, with higher adjustments in good economic times and lower ones in bad economic times. At the same time, the new version of the preventive arm allows temporary deviations from a country's MTO, or the adjustment path adopted to achieve it, to take account of the implementation of major structural reforms that have verifiable, long-term positive budgetary impact.

Despite these quantitative constraints, the Italian debt-to-GDP ratio in 2008 still amounted to 106,3 per cent, rapidly increasing to 116 per cent and 118,6 per cent in the following two years.

© Wolters Kluwer Italia

In 2008, the financial crisis broke, followed **in 2009 by a global economic recession**, which caused a sharp deterioration in public finances in all European countries. In particular, in the euro area, the deterioration caused by the economic crisis was associated – starting from 2010 – with **tensions among some sovereign debtors** (including Italy), which aggravated the financial crisis and caused uncertainty about the prospects of the single currency.

The inefficiency of the SGP rules in preventing the crisis triggered, in a very short time, a series of **further radical changes to the European economic governance**. It is worth mentioning that a comprehensive reform of European economic governance is currently under discussion. On 26th of April, 2023, the Commission unveiled legislative proposals to strengthen public debt sustainability while promoting sustainable and inclusive growth in all Member States through reforms and investment, addressing deficiencies and shortcomings within the existing framework.

A first series of the interventions was carried out through acts of European Union secondary law, namely the so-called ***Six Pack***, adopted **in 2011**, and the so-called ***Two Pack***, adopted **in 2013**. On the other hand, a second series was carried out with legal instruments in the realm of international law, i.e. treaties concluded by the Member States. These are the ***Treaty on Stability, Coordination and Governance in the Economic and Monetary Union*** (TSCG, also known as the *Fiscal Compact*) and the ***European Stability Mechanism*** (ESM), which are examined in more detail below (see *II.C.2.*).

The **Six Pack aims to reinforce the surveillance of national fiscal policies and introduce a new system for monitoring macroeconomic imbalances**. It consists of five regulations and one directive. Two regulations are based on art. 136 TFEU and are applied only to the Eurozone. The other three regulations apply to all Member States and are based on Articles 121 and 126 TFEU. **The Two-Pack comprises two regulations aimed at enhancing economic and budgetary oversight for euro area Member States facing,** or at risk of facing, **severe difficulties related to financial stability**. It also entails the supervision and assessment of preliminary budgetary proposals as well as the correction of excessive deficits among euro area Member States.

Overall, these legal instruments (both European and international) have pursued a threefold objective: to strengthen the SGP, both in the preventive and in the corrective arm; to incorporate into national legal systems some financial constraints established at the supranational level; and to introduce a more structured and compelling framework for the coordination of economic policies, through the Common Budget Calendar (or European Semester, see next paragraph) as well as a procedure to prevent and possibly correct macroeconomic imbalances.

 © Wolters Kluwer Italia

As **for Italy**, such legal instruments had **many significant consequences** on the Italian legal system.

First, **a new expenditure benchmark and a new rule on public debt were introduced**. According to the expenditure benchmark established in the Six Pack, public spending must not rise faster than medium-term potential GDP growth unless adequate revenues match it. On the other hand, according to the Debt Rule, the Member States such as Italy, whose debt exceeds 60 per cent of GDP, have to converge towards the objective of a balanced budget with an annual improvement in balances of at least 0.5 per cent. Moreover, they must reduce the debt to at least 1/20 of the excess over the 60 per cent threshold calculated over the last three years. Of course, these rules further reduced the room for manoeuvre for the Italian institutions in financial policy-making.

Second, compliance with the MTO was furthermore ensured by the **numerical budget rules**, which each Member State, based on Directive /2011/85/EU (Six Pack), was bound to adopt. Italy implemented the directive by approving legislative decree No. 54/2014 (which amended Law No. 196/2009 on Accounting and Public Finance).

In addition, if there is a ***significant deviation*** **from the MTO**, a procedure is initiated which can lead to financial penalties for the non-compliant Member State. The deviation from the MTO is considered significant if the country has not reached its MTO because the structural balance shows a deviation of at least 0.5 per cent of GDP in a year or at least 0.25 per cent of GDP «on an annual average for two consecutive years». The other condition is that the trend of expenditure (net of discretionary measures on the revenue side) has an impact on the balance equal to at least 0.5 points of GDP in a single year or cumulatively in two consecutive years. In this case, **the Commission issues an early warning** and lays down a **recommendation for the Council to urge it to approve a further recommendation for the State on the measures to be taken**. The **vote of the Council** is carried out **with a qualified majority** (only the countries of the euro area take part in the vote, and the country concerned is not taken into account). If the country concerned does not take adequate action within the deadline (from 3 to 5 months), the Commission can request the Council to decide or formulate a new recommendation (by a qualified majority). If this decision is not taken within a month, the Commission can again lay down a new recommendation for the Council's decision, which this time is provided with semi-automatically: if the Council does not reject it within ten days by a reverse simple majority, it is considered as approved. If, on the other hand, an interest-bearing deposit of 0.2 points of GDP is proposed for the non-complying state, then the Council, in order to reject the measure, must, within ten days, express itself with a reverse qualified majority, while a qualified majority is sufficient to make changes.

Finally, **the Fiscal Compact provoked a constitutional amendment** of the Italian Constitution (the **constitutional law No. 1/2012** mentioned above, implemented by law No. 243/2013), which, among other things, entrenched in the Charter the balanced-budget principle (Article 81, para. 1, IC). Actually, the TSCG merely stated, under Article 3, para. 2, that the rules concerning a balanced budget «shall take effect in the national law of the Contracting Parties (...) through provisions of binding force and permanent character, *preferably constitutional*, or otherwise guaranteed to be fully respected and adhered to throughout the national budgetary processes». Arguably, the decision to amend the Constitution was taken by the Italian Government (and consequently by the Parliament) in order to offer a strong guarantee of the seriousness of the country's commitment before the European partners, as well as to calm the markets in a period of intense stress on the Italian sovereign debt.

The new Article 81 IC states: «**[t]he state shall balance revenue and expenditure in its budget**, **taking account of the adverse and favourable phases of the economic cycle**. No recourse shall be made to borrowing except to take account of the effects of the economic cycle or, subject to authorisation by the two Houses approved by an absolute majority vote of their Members, in exceptional circumstances (...).».

As is clear from the text, there is plenty of **flexibility in the implementation of this fundamental rule**. First, the reference to «the adverse and favourable phases of the economic cycle» – as confirmed in the explanatory memorandum – recalls the European rules, particularly those concerning the structural budget balance and MTO. The balanced-budget rule is, therefore, to be understood in a dynamic and flexible sense, not as a strict balance between revenue and expenditure, but rather as an adjustment path towards the structural budget balance in accordance with the European constraints.

In addition, even though a **general prohibition on borrowing is introduced** in para. 2, the state can make use of **two different and broad flexibility clauses**. The government can always borrow from the financial markets (thus increasing public expenditure) «in adverse phases of the economic cycle» or, prior approval by the Parliament (by an absolute majority of the Italian MPs), «in exceptional circumstances».

Since the entry into force of the Constitutional amendment, **the Italian state has made broad use of these flexibility clauses**: the exceptional circumstances clause was activated nine times between 2012 and 2019. In order to tackle the economic crisis generated by the COVID-19 pandemic and later by the conflict between Russia and Ukraine, the clause was activated several times over the following years.

 © Wolters Kluwer Italia

However, the experience of the last 11-12 years of the new European economic governance has shown that **even supranational institutions**, when implementing the European constraints, **have broad political discretion and flexibility**. The actual enforcement of the fiscal rules depends, in fact, on the changing interaction of three subjects: the European Commission, a technocratic body which enjoys far-reaching discretion in the implementation of the SGP; the Council of the European Union, a political body, which is obviously influenced by varied national interests of Member States; and, finally, the Member State subject to the constraints, which, at the supranational level, can represent and defend its interests through both formal and informal channels. Consequently, financial constraints are far from being automatic rules because their implementation depends on highly political and discretionary choices.

Italy offered an excellent example of the flexibility of financial constraints, even in the new economic governance, in recent years. **In 2018**, after the general elections, two populist parties, the Lega and the Five Star Movement, formed a coalition Government headed by Prime Minister Giuseppe Conte. **The new Executive decided to finance current expenditure through a significant deviation from the adjustment path to the MTO** that was previously agreed upon at the European level. At the beginning of September 2018, the European Union granted Italy a deviation on the adjustment path with a deficit equal to 1.6 per cent of GDP. However, the Conte Government decided to bring it to 2.4 per cent in 2019, 2.1 per cent in 2020 and 1.8 per cent in 2021. Pursuant to Article 7, para. 2, of Regulation No. 473/2013 (the Two Pack), **the Commission requested Italy to correct the excessive deficit**, arguing that the Italian fiscal decisions amounted to a case of particularly serious non-compliance with financial policy obligations. Later, the Commission **launched for the first time infringement proceedings against Italy for excessive debt** (i.e. violation of the second Maastricht criterion) (Rivosecchi 2019).

Despite these initiatives, the **Italian Government persevered in pursuing a higher deficit**, even maintaining an often contentious dialogue with the European institutions. Therefore, the Commission launched, for the first time, the excessive deficit procedure in response to the violation of the Debt Rule (see before). In extremis (a few days before Christmas 2018), **an agreement was reached by the Government and the Commission to bring the original 2.4 per cent deficit to GDP to 2.04 per cent. The infringement proceedings and the corrective arm procedures were consequently stopped**. As is evident, even in a case of significant deviation from the MTO (which was confirmed and accepted, even if lower than the original proposal of a 2.4 per cent deficit to GDP), the European fiscal rules were not applied automatically. Their enforcement proved highly discretionary and political, the negotiations between European institutions and the

Member State having played a crucial role in the concrete definition of the constraints (Rivosecchi 2019).

4.c. Procedures of the European Semester

As has been argued by several authors (Rivosecchi 2007, Bartolucci 2021), the **European fiscal rules have essentially been transformed into procedural constraints** within the Common Budget Calendar. In this regard, the innovation that had the most important impacts on the Italian legal system is the adoption of the so-called **European Semester in 2011**. The European Semester is **a Euro-national proceeding**, i.e. it is characterized by **interventions** of both **European and national institutions and governed in part by European law and in part by national law**. In its fundamentals, the Semester is regulated by Article 2-bis of Regulation No. 1466/1997, as amended by Regulation No. 1175/2011 (Six Pack). The European Semester procedure **aims at ensuring the coherence of the economic and budgetary policies of the Member States, through an *ex ante* coordination of economic policies**. Member States adopt their budgetary and economic policy decisions in the second half of the year, taking into account the recommendations approved by the EU institutions in the first half of the year.

The European Semester can, therefore, be regarded as an attempt not only to ensure timely compliance with financial constraints, but also to guide the Member States' economic policy choices in a qualitative sense (i.e. pointing out the most urgent and remarkable structural reforms to be undertaken). Italy aligned its national proceedings to the European Semester mainly by repeatedly amending the law No. 196/2009 mentioned above on Accounting and Public Finance.

As an overview, the intertwining of the European semester and the national proceedings foresees the following phases, according to a tight time frame:

• November: presentation **by the Commission** of the ***Annual Growth Survey*** (the main tool for setting out the general economic and social priorities for the EU for the following year);

• February / March: the European Council draws up economic and budgetary policy guidelines at EU and Member State level;

• mid-April: **Member States submit the *National Reform Programme*** (NRPs, which encompass the structural reforms and economic policies) **and the *Stability and Convergence Plans*** (SCPs, drawn up under the Pact on stability and growth), taking into account the guidelines formulated by the European Council;

• The so-called ***Documento di Economia e Finanza*** (*DEF, Economic and Financial Document*, which encompasses in one single act both the *Stability Programme* and the *National Reform Programme*) must be drafted and submitted by the Government to the Chambers by the April 10th, in order that Parliament can

 © Wolters Kluwer Italia

scrutinise it before the deadline for the submission of the Stability and National Reforms Programmes to the European Commission (April 30th).

• May / early June: on the basis of the NRPs and SCPs, the European Commission lays down the economic and budgetary policy recommendations addressed to the individual Member States (so-called ***Country Specific Recommendations***);

• June: the ECOFIN Council and the Employment and Social Affairs Council approve the recommendations of the European Commission, also on the basis of the guidelines expressed by the European Council of June;

• On the basis of the recommendations made by the European authorities in the months of June-July, as well as in order to take into account changes in macroeconomic and public finance trends (compared to the forecasts of the DEF), an *up to date DEF* is approved by Parliament in late September (by 27th of September). This document is called ***Nota di aggiornamento al DEF*** (better known as *NADEF, Updating note to DEF*).

• second half of the year (so-called **national semester**): Member States approve their respective budget laws, taking into account the recommendations received. In the Italian context, the implementation phase of the objectives contained in the DEF (and in the NADEF) must be carried out through the presentation to the Chambers, by 20th of October of each year, of the **Budget Bill**. This deadline follows 15th of October, the deadline for the presentation at the European level of the Draft Budgetary Plan.

In the Annual Growth Survey of the following year, the Commission provides an assessment of the progress achieved by Member States in implementing the recommendations.

When the European Semester was introduced in the framework of the broader reform of the economic governance in 2011, many scholars feared that the tightening of the financial and procedural constraints on Italy would have made it possible for the supranational authorities to directly impose structural reforms, even against the will of the national democratically legitimated institutions. The experience of more than ten years of European Semester has proved that, to a large extent, these concerns were unfounded. The **implementation of Italy's Country Specific Recommendations has been always quite poor** and, after all, in line with the poor implementation level of other European countries. **Member States retain a large margin of discretion in implementing the structural reforms recommended by the EU**, given that many recommendations are very general (leaving ample room for manoeuvre) and the non-compliance of the most detailed has never led to significant reactions by the European institutions. The recommendation is, in fact, a non-binding legal instrument and is not backed by any effective sanction mechanism in the case of non-compliance.

Some recommendations were repeatedly addressed to Italy, without having witnessed any significant improvement over years. This was the case, for instance, of the reduction of the duration of civil proceedings/improvement of the efficiency of judicial system (2012-2020), the improvement of the effectiveness of the public administration (2012-2017, 2018-2020), and the fight against corruption (2012-2014, 2016-2019). In some cases, Italy decided to openly contradict the supranational recommendations, sometimes even adopting measures and reforms opposed to and promoted by the EU, as happened with reference to the reform of the tax system (with the abolition of the taxation on the primary residence), to the reform of the public real estate registry (never implemented), or to the pension reforms (see so-called «*Quota 100*» in 2019).

Over time, **structural reforms** recommended by the European institutions have been actually **implemented** – on the few occasions when they were fully implemented – **almost exclusively by technocratic governments** and often **under the powerful pressure of the financial markets or the political action of the European partners**, rather than under the rules and constraints deriving from Italy's participation in the European Union.

This was the case for the structural reforms listed in a **letter, signed by ECB President Jean-Claude Trichet and** his designated successor, the Bank of Italy Governor **Mario Draghi**, that the European Central Bank addressed to the Berlusconi Government in August 2011. In a situation of mounting pressure on Italian bonds, the European Central Bank demanded far-reaching reforms and fiscal tightening measures from Italy before beginning an operation to buy Italian bonds and ease the pressure of the markets. After the resignation of the Berlusconi Government in November 2011, an emergency coalition government was formed, headed by the former European Commissioner Mario Monti. Facing an extreme financial crisis, the Monti Government implemented many of the reforms listed in the letter, which ranged from the pension reform, to the labour market reform and to the abolition of the Provinces (and, however, corresponded to the commitments previously made by Italy at the European level). But it was arguably more a matter of economic and political pressure by the markets and the European partners than of implementing the EU rules.

To put it briefly, the European external bond in structural reforms is not as tight as it might seem.

Nonetheless, **the procedural constraints** of the European Semester **had a certain impact on the distribution of power between the Government and Parliament** at the national level. The **strict timetable** set by the EU law **reduces the time given to the Parliament to scrutinise and discuss the acts of the European institutions and the Government**. The Government thus gained an

© Wolters Kluwer Italia

even greater predominance in the budgetary proceedings at the national level, diminishing the fundamental function of Parliament in terms of its democratic control over the Executive.

Such negative effect was brought to light dramatically during the **approval of the Budget Law for 2019** (in the late December 2018). The Budget Bill drafted by the Government was first presented and approved by the Chamber of Deputies, with a vote of confidence on 8th of December, 2018. However, as described before, after a long negotiation with the European Commission, the Government accepted to bring the originally indicated 2.4 per cent deficit to GDP to 2.04 per cent. This meant the Government had to re-draft the whole Budget Bill according to the new parameter.

A first maxi-amendment to the bill was thus presented by the Government to the Senate budget committee in the night session of 19th of December. A second maxi-amendment was then presented to the Senate of the Republic on the afternoon of 22nd of December (shortly after 2 pm) and finally approved by the assembly, with a vote of confidence, around 2 am. In the preceding hours, the text of the bill (1.143 paragraphs / provisions) was not concretely made available neither to the budget committee nor to the MPs. On 28th of December, the Chamber of Deputies was *forced* to vote on a completely revised bill, again with a vote of confidence, only a couple of days before it would have been necessary to proceed with a provisional budget.

Arguing that such conduct on the part of the Government was unconstitutional in the way it treated the rights of Parliament and of individual MPs, a group of MPs filed a complaint to the Constitutional Court. In a highly controversial decision (**ItCC order No. 17/2019**), the **Court declared inadmissible the conflict of attributions brought before it by these MPs**. Among other reasons, the Court highlighted that «it is important not to disregard the fact that the business was conducted under time pressure due to the lengthy engagement with European Union institutions», thus somehow justifying the reduced role of Parliament with regard to budgetary proceedings on the basis of the European integration.

Apart from these unfortunate events in Italy it should be noted that **the overall Euro-national procedure lacks full democratic scrutiny**. On the one hand, at the supranational level, the so-called **economic dialogues** enhance **an exchange of views and information between the European Parliament and other EU institutions** with regard to the application of economic governance rules and with Member States, but **without conferring to the Parliament any binding instrument or significant power**. On the other hand, at the national level, particularly in Italy, there is an **increasing predominance of the Government, with a strong marginalisation of Parliament**, which is called upon to approve fiscal and economic policies largely pre-determined by the Executive. However, the reform of the European economic governance (Article 3(2) Fiscal Compact and Regulation No. 473/2013) prompted the setting up, **in 2014**, of the ***Parliamentary Budget Office*** (PBO). The PBO is an independent body responsible for analysing and assessing the Government's macroeconomic and fiscal forecasts and verifying compliance with national and European fiscal rules. By ensuring the transparency and reliability of the public accounts, the PBO may be a new powerful tool in the hand of Parliament (and the general public) in its control of the Government.

4.d. The New Perspective of Next Generation EU

Ultimately, the external bond has, therefore, always been essentially a quantitative/procedural constraint, which has never had the 'strength' to change the quality of the expenditure of the Italian state, despite the attempts made within the European Semester with Country Specific Recommendations. The approval of the **Next Generation EU** after the Covid-19 pandemic **may mark a decisive change in the perspective**.

The health restrictions adopted, albeit with variations, by all European countries to counter the spread of the Covid-19 pandemic in the two-year 2020-2021 resulted in a lockdown for many economic activities and a significant reduction in trade, generating a severe economic crisis (particularly dramatic in the countries most affected by the disease like Italy).

The primary response of the European Union to the crisis was the so-called ***Next Generation EU* (NGEU)**, whose central pillar is the Regulation No. 241/2021. The NGEU is a **massive investment plan to revive the European economy, with a budget of a total of 750 billion euros**. These investments take the form of grants, equal to 390 billion euros, and loans at favourable interest rates, equal to 360 billion euros. By using these funds, Member States are required to define and implement structural investments and reforms from 2021 to 2026. To this end, **Member States have drawn up a *National Recovery and Resilience Plan* (NRRP) which specifies, according to a very detailed timeline (with specific *targets* and *milestones*), the reforms and investments they intend to carry out by 31st of December, 2026**. The Plans must be examined and approved by the Commission and the Council.

The majority of the NGEU funding (amounting to 672.5 billion euros) is allocated within a **newly established fund** known as the **Recovery and Resilience Facility (RRF)**, governed by Regulation No. 241 of 2021.

To finance the NGEU, the European Union has planned to increase its budget by issuing – as an exception – particular European public debt securities. In this

© Wolters Kluwer Italia

way, the financing on the markets was gained on very favourable terms and then transferred to the Member States.

However, like other European instruments of financial assistance to the Member States, **the disbursement of funds is subject to *conditionality***. As has been highlighted, however, there is a significant paradigm shift (BIN/PITRUZZELLA 2021). While in the case of specific assistance programmes or the ESM, the funding aims to ensure the sustainability of public finances and the restoration of sound fiscal policy with a view to the financial stability of the Union, the NGEU aims to foster economic recovery, making the economy of the Member States more resilient and, above all, achieving social and employment objectives.

Nonetheless, the conditionality introduced in the NGEU have the **potential to make the qualitative constraints** on Member States' spending **more stringent**. According to Regulation no. 241/2021, the Country Specific Recommendations are, in fact, the benchmark for evaluating Recovery and Resilience Plans. The National Recovery and Resilience Plans shall obtain the approval of the Commission, which assessed, among other things and as a priority, the **consistency of the Plan with the Country Specific Recommendations** of the previous years (2019-2020). Consistency will then also be verified over the years (until the end of the NGEU), given that the level of implementation of the Plan will be monitored periodically for the final approval of the disbursement of the NGEU funds. Furthermore, **if one or more Member States deem that there are *serious deviations* from the achievement of the intermediate and final targets**, they may trigger a so-called **'*emergency brake*'**, thus suspending the disbursement of funds and referring the issue to the European Council.

Thus, the economic policy recommendations to the Member States are now backed by a powerful enforcement instrument. Whereas the Member State cannot prove to have implemented the structural reforms outlined in its NRRP, the European institutions may block the disbursement of the funds, which in a phase of severe economic crisis, also deepened by the outbreak of the war in Ukraine in February 2022, are vital for the European economies.

The **Italian NRRP** was **drafted by two different Governments (the second Conte government and that of Draghi)** and will be **implemented by (at least) two different Governments (Draghi and Meloni**).

The **first phase of drafting the Italian Plan was led by the second Conte Government** (based mainly on the new coalition formed by the Five Star Movement and the Democratic Party), chaired by Prime Minister Giuseppe Conte, who was one of the key proponents of the European agreement on the Next Generation EU. The mounting **tensions within the ruling coalition**, primarily concerning the Plan and its governance, triggered a government crisis in January 2021.

© Wolters Kluwer Italia

President Conte resigned after unsuccessful attempts to resolve the crisis and form a new parliamentary majority. Therefore, **the President of the Republic appointed Mario Draghi as the new President of the Council of Ministers in February 2021**. Draghi, able to count on a strong parliamentary majority, focussed his government programme on the timely conclusion of the drafting of the Plan and its correct and effective implementation. Having only a short time to draw up and submit the NRRP to the Commission (the deadline was set on 30th of April, 2021), the Italian Plan was primarily prepared by the Government, marginalising Parliament, the Regions and local authorities.

The NRRP enacts all the Country Specific Recommendations (CRSs) addressed to Italy, and they are thus specific targets and milestones of the Plan.

Looking at the **first phase of implementation of the Plan**, it appears that the **CSRs, now transferred to the NRRP, are becoming increasingly effective**. On 30th of December, 2021, the Italian Government submitted to the European Commission the documents proving the achievement of all the 51 milestones and targets programmed for 2021, requesting at the same time to receive the first instalment of funds. Among others, some significant structural reforms were carried out to improve the efficiency of the judicial system and the efficiency of the public administration, according to the CSRs. At the same time, **some specific reforms**, highly controversial for the political parties, **faced fierce opposition even under the Draghi government**. This was the case for the reform of the public real estate registry (2019 CSR, No. 1) mentioned above, or for interventions aimed at enhancing competition (2019 CSR, No. 3).

After the fall of the Draghi government in July 2022, national elections were held on 25th of September, 2022. These resulted in **a major electoral success for the right-wing coalition** that was thus able to form a **cabinet led by President Giorgia Meloni**. In the first months of government, however, **significant delays and problems in implementing the NRRP emerged**, mainly caused by the limited administrative capacity of many public implementing bodies, and resulted in blocking the payment of the third instalment of 21 billion euros. In an **attempt to reschedule the most critical target and milestones**, the executive started a **complex negotiation with the European Commission**, whose outcomes are still uncertain, aiming at partially redrafting the Plan. In July 2023, the Commission finally endorsed a positive preliminary assessment of 54 milestones and targets linked to Italy's third payment request and consented to the adjustment and postponement of one target that had not been entirely met. Furthermore, the Commission gave its endorsement for the proposed revision to the Plan related to the fourth payment request, which now requires Council approval.

 © Wolters Kluwer Italia

C) AUTONOMY OF LEGAL ORDERS: EUROPEANIZATION OF COUNTERLIMITS AND EU CAPACITY OF TREATY-MAKING

1. Italian Constitutional Identity and its Protection, a Third Wave à l'Italienne?

In a seminal 2018 essay entitled «*Judicial review in the contemporary world – Retrospective and prospective*», **Doreen Lustig and Joseph H.H. Weiler** describe the successful diffusion of judicial review in Europe and worldwide, using the **metaphor of waves**. Lustig and Weiler mapped **three different global waves of constitutional judicial review**. The **first wave** is the **horizontal spread of judicial review** among legal state orders that occurred in the twentieth century. After a series of «constitutional revolutions» within national legal orders, with two historical turning points, the end of World War II and the end of the Cold War, most countries around the world adopted a form of judicial review. During this first wave, after the Fascist dictatorship and the tragedy of the Civil and World War II, Italy introduced the judicial review of legislation in the new Constitution (1948), establishing the Italian Constitutional Court (1956). A **second wave**, which partially paralleled and overlapped the first wave, was prompted by the **emergence of transnational orders of higher law.** In Europe, these include the **European Convention of Human Rights (ECHR) and the European Union (EU)**. The gradual emergence of international law and institutions in the contemporary world resulted in the growing use of domestic courts of the international norms as a higher law within national constitutional orders, as well as in the submission of states and their internal acts to judicial review of newly established jurisdiction (e.g. the Court of Strasbourg for the ECHR or the Court of Justice of the European Union). According to Lustig and Weiler, we are now witnessing the **rise of a third wave**, which can be deemed as a **reaction to the two other waves**. The challenges posed by domestic constitutionalism and transnational constitutionalism are provocative – according to the two reputed jurists – a correction and even backlash of judicial review reflected in the third wave. In their view, this third wave could be conceived as the result of a tension between domestic (first wave) and transnational (second wave) constitutionalism. This wave shows at least **two remarkable aspects**: first, the **emergence of national courts as an instance of control and judicial review of transnational and international governance and adjudication**; and second, **the rise of a new *identitarian* seam in constitutional discourse**.

In the context of the European Union, this *identitarian* discourse has been principally stimulated by two factors (Piccirilli 2021): on the one hand, a crucial role was played by the innovation of the Lisbon Treaty, which, according to the

© Wolters Kluwer Italia

new text of **Article 4(2) TEU,** states that «[t]he **Union shall respect the equality of Member States** before the Treaties **as well as their *national identities*,** inherent in their fundamental structures, political and constitutional, inclusive of regional and local self-government». On the other hand, and more importantly, it was the case law of various **constitutional courts of the Member States** that put great emphasis on the so-called **identity review**. It is worth mentioning, along with the best-known rulings in Italy and Germany, also those in Hungary, Belgium and Poland. With the increase in European integration and the growing interaction between national and European judicial systems, identity issues began to arise, and the new framework provided by the Lisbon Treaty offered a significant legal basis for their emergence.

Even **Italian Constitutional Court has come to employ the lexicon of constitutional identity**, even though previously the relations with other legal systems followed a **different interpretative process** and the same important constitutional case law elaborated in different terms. Essentially, the Italian Constitutional Court developed a case law based on the so-called **supreme principles**, intended as limits to domestic constitutional amendments, which in the different perspective of the interrelation of the Italian order with other legal systems, were converted into the so-called **counterlimits**. As more extensively described earlier (*II.A).3.*), this concept was elaborated by the ItCC precisely regarding the relationship with the law of the European Communities. The term 'counterlimits' emerges from the wording of the Article 11 of the Italian Constitution, in order to identify those limits to oppose to the «limitations of sovereignty» to which Italy can consent on the supranational level.

As we have seen, only in 2014 was the very term 'counterlimits' actually used in the reasoning of a decision. Previously, albeit with a certain consistency in content, constitutional case law was not very clear from a lexical point of view, as the Court resorted to numerous similar or analogous expressions (FARAGUNA 2016). Recently, however, **with order no. 24/2017,** i.e. the preliminary reference order in the so-called Taricco saga, **the ItCC has** finally **introduced the new category of *constitutional identity*,** making **express reference to Article 4(2) TEU**. This decision, which proceeds with a preliminary reference to the Court of Justice of the European Union in the context of the so-called Taricco case, may be considered a turning point, an important and innovative decision in the lexicon but to be read substantially in line with the already established principles.

In the subsequent development of the Taricco saga, **the ItCC referred again to the Italian constitutional identity in the decision No. 115/2018**, which somehow put an end to the Taricco saga. Afterwards, **in order No. 117/2019**, the ItCC found **another opportunity**, in the context of a preliminary reference to the Court of Justice, **to renew its latest approach, linking the doctrine of**

 © Wolters Kluwer Italia

counterlimits to the protection of Italian constitutional identity. The latter was aligned with the same decisions which had in the past characterized the case law relating to the former. In particular, the Court reconnected the importance of the «inalienable rights of the human person» (judgments Nos 238/2014, 18/1982 and 323/1989) as elements characterizing Italian constitutional identity, without reference either to the counterlimits, or to the supreme principles.

In short, in the most recent case law of the ItCC, **constitutional identity now seems be understood as a synonym both with respect to counterlimits and supreme principles**. Thus, the Court completed a process of what may be called a **Europeanisation of the counter-limits**.

The use of the lexicon of constitutional identity in these preliminary reference orders (as in Nos. 24/2017 and 117/2019) may be a specific choice in recalling the vocabulary of the Treaties, more comprehensible to the Court of Justice. According to authoritative doctrine (SARMIENTO 2021), this solution constitutes further proof of the «**seductive**» **approach of the ItCC**. Especially in comparison with other Constitutional Courts, the ItCC has shown itself to be much less conflictual and more dialogic: the Court seeks **open recourse to the shared conceptual categories** of the supranational judicial system and construction of the dialogue in a **persuasive and non-confrontational key** so as to be able to exercise best those forms of interaction that are now indispensable within the framework of the composite Constitution of the European Union (PICCIRILLI 2021).

2. International Treaties between EU Member States

Recalling the overall framework proposed by Lusting and Weiler, it is worth stressing that the reaction to the «second wave» of judicial review does not limit itself to domestic courts. Even at the European level, **tensions emerged between the European legal order and its system of judicial review**, on the one hand, **and transnational law and international courts and tribunals**, on the other. These tensions can be detected **both in cases of international treaties concluded by the Member States which potentially interfere with European Union law** and **in cases of international treaties signed by the European Union within its treaty-making capacity** (see below). In such contexts, the scenario reaches a different level of complexity since the issues concerning the protection of the autonomy of EU law often parallel the issues concerning Member States' identity, hence generating the potential for conflicting decisions on a number of levels (national, European and international).

A first area where tension may arise is that of international treaties concluded among the Member States. In particular, whereas it is politically impossible to modify the European Treaties without unanimity among the Member States, the EU Member States tend to adopt international treaties outside the EU legal framework, conferring nonetheless additional competencies to European Union institutions. This was the case of two important treaties concerning European economic governance, the **Treaty on Stability, Coordination and Governance (TSCG)** and the **Treaty establishing the European Stability Mechanism (ESM)**. Still, these treaties raise complex issues concerning the consistency with existing EU law and Member States' commitments in the European context, threatening to affect the autonomy of the European Union law and Member States' legal orders vis-à-vis international law.

The ***Treaty on Stability, Coordination and Governance in the Economic and Monetary Union*** (TSCG, also known as Fiscal Compact) was signed at the European Council on 1-2 March, 2012. The recourse to an international treaty for budgetary measures and the coordination of economic policies was justified by the lack of unanimity among the EU Member States necessary to amend the existing European treaties. The United Kingdom and the Czech Republic opposed the amendment and did not sign the new Treaty. The TSCG incorporates and **integrates into a unitary framework some of the fiscal rules and procedures for the coordination of economic policies** that had already been introduced (or were about to be introduced) to a large extent by EU secondary law in the framework of the new economic governance (see above *II.B).3.*). Among the main contents of the Treaty, there is – as already mentioned – the **commitment of the parties to implement and introduce, within one year from the entry into force of the Treaty, the *golden rule* for which the budget of the state must be in balance or surplus**. Italy approved the Constitutional Law No. 1/2012, which introduced in the Constitution the principle of balanced budget, in compliance with the constraints deriving from the European Union (above *II.B).4.b.*).

The ***European stability mechanism*** (ESM), on the other hand, is one of the pillars of the new European economic governance system. It was set up in October 2012, following an intergovernmental Treaty (TESM) signed in February 2012 by the governments of the Eurozone Member States. In order to establish the ESM, it was necessary to amend Article 48 TEU, Article 136 of the Treaty on the Functioning of the EU (TFEU) with a simplified revision procedure. Paragraph 3 was added: «Member States whose currency is the euro can establish a stability mechanism to be activated where indispensable to safeguard the stability of the euro area as a whole. The granting of any necessary financial assistance under the mechanism will be subject to strict conditionality». The ESM was intended first to complement and then replace the transitional financial stabilisation mechanism (European financial stabilisation mechanism, EFSM, and European financial

 © Wolters Kluwer Italia

stability facility, EFSF), established initially for three years (until 31st of December, 2012) and then extended until 30th of June, 2013.

In order to fully understand the rationale behind the ESM, it is necessary to recall that, as explained above (*II.B).4.a.*), establishing the European Monetary Union entailed the definitive transferal of monetary policy from the Member states to the Union. However, **the European Central Bank**, the independent institution leading the European monetary system, **does not have all the powers of a traditional central bank**, such as the American FED or the *Banca d'Italia* before the 1981 *divorzio*. The main purpose of the ECB is to maintain price stability and the fiscal stability of the euro area. However, it **cannot act as a lender of last resort to the Member States, given the prohibition under Article 123 TFUE**. In addition, **Article 125 TFEU sets out the so-called *No bail out clause***. According to this provision: «The Union shall not be liable for or assume the commitments of central governments, regional, local or other public authorities, other bodies governed by public law, or public undertakings of any Member State, without prejudice to mutual financial guarantees for the joint execution of a specific project. A Member State shall not be liable for or assume the commitments of central governments, regional, local or other public authorities, other bodies governed by public law, or public undertakings of another Member State without prejudice to mutual financial guarantees for the joint execution of a specific project. (...)». This provision was intended to ensure that the responsibility for repaying public debt remains national and to prevent the so-called *moral hazard* of Member States which conduct irresponsible budgetary policies and count on the financial assistance of those with sound fiscal policies.

However, **when one or more Member States face a severe financial crisis and are exposed to speculation on international markets**, these **prohibitions significantly impair the potential for effective interventions on the part of the European Union** to assist the Member States in distress. With the aim of compensating what is often called a *design flaw* of European integration, temporary funds were created in accordance with Article 122 TFEU (the aforementioned EFSF and EFSM) which then evolved into a permanent instrument, the ESM.

In short, **the ESM is**, therefore, **a crisis-related intergovernmental international institution** that performs, in the perspective of the financial stabilisation of the Eurozone, the **function of lender of last resort that the ECB cannot perform** by providing financial assistance to the Member States in distress.

The mechanism has the following main features:

• access to ESM **financial assistance is granted on the basis of *strict conditionality*** under a macroeconomic adjustment programme and a public debt sustainability analysis. The policy measures to be adopted are specified in a ***Memorandum of Understanding*** (MoU), negotiated by the Commission, the European Central Bank (ECB), the International Monetary Fund (IMF) (where applicable) and the beneficiary Member State;

• the beneficiary Member State is required to implement an appropriate form of private sector participation according to the specific circumstances and in a manner entirely consistent with IMF practices;

• the ESM has an adequate lending capacity of 500 billion euros and a total subscribed capital of 700 billion euros;

• the ESM governing bodies are the ***Board of Governors***, which comprises the ***Finance Ministries of each of the 19 ESM shareholders***, and the Board of Directors;

• all **present and former members of the ESM bodies are subject to *professional secrecy***, and the officers of ESM and the other staff of ESM enjoy immunity from prosecution with regard to actions carried out in their official capacity.

The TSCG and the ESM generated a number of **legal disputes, both at the level of Member States and the European level**.

From the European perspective, the treaties posed several constitutional issues. First of all, they both provide for the participation of some European institutions, even if they operate outside the European legal order. In this way, **the European *principle of institutional balance* may be jeopardised**. This principle, enshrined in Article 13(2) TEU, demands respect for the powers conferred by the Treaties on institutions and the related division of powers and aims at preserving the very structure of the Union and its autonomy. It implies that each institution performs a specific function within the EU legal order, respecting the relations between the various EU institutions and the relations between them and the Member States. A further issue is related to the ***strong intergovernmental character* of these Treaties**, which **may reduce the control by the representative institutions** (in particular the European Parliament), increasing the democratic deficit in the supranational economic governance. Ultimately it was also argued that the ESM could be inconsistent, among other things, with the Articles 123 and 125 TFEU mentioned above.

The Court of Justice ruled on these matters in the ***Pringle* case** (Case C-370/12), introduced by a preliminary ruling from the Irish Supreme Court, **finding the ESM consistent with European Union law** (De Witte/Beukers 2013).

In brief, the Court specified that Article 123 TFEU was addressed specifically to the ECB and to the central banks of the Member States, rather than to Member States as a whole: the latter are therefore permitted to create mechanisms to grant

 © Wolters Kluwer Italia

financial stability such as the ESM. With reference to Article 125 (no bail out clause), the Court of Justice emphasized the fact that

> «the ESM will not act as guarantor of the debts of the recipient Member State by referring to the spirit of the article inserted by the Treaty of Maastricht. In fact, the latter will remain responsible to its creditors for its financial commitments».

As explained before, the rationale of Article 125 was to encourage Member States to follow a sound budgetary policy. Therefore, the Court declared that the no bail out clause is not infringed by

> «the granting of financial assistance by one or more Member States to a Member State which remains responsible for its commitments to its creditors provided that the conditions attached to such assistance are such as to prompt that Member State to implement a sound budgetary policy».

The Court of Justice also offered important **guidance for treaties concluded among the Member States that involve**, to some extent, **European institutions**. First, the Court confirmed that such international agreements could not fall within the exclusive competence of the European Union, as is the case for the ESM, which shall be placed within the area of economic policy (and not the monetary one). Second, the Member States involved need to comply with EU law when exercising their competencies under the international treaty. In addition, the Court stated that new tasks can be conferred to European Union institutions on the basis of international treaties so far as they «do not alter the essential character of the powers conferred on those institutions by the EU and FEU Treaties».

From the Member States' point of view, the primary constitutional issues were those of **democratic control over ESM decisions** (given the professional secrecy that protects the works of its bodies) and the **strict conditionality** imposed on those Member States which are granted financial assistance. These issues have been widely **discussed in Italy**, and many have feared that the recourse to ESM assistance (which the Country might need, given its weak financial situation) would lead to a temporary loss of sovereignty in fiscal and economic policies. The fierce opposition of many political parties is currently delaying the ratification of the ESM reform (which took place in November 2020), which aims to strengthen the mechanism and tighten its conditionality.

However, the **most significant legal disputes** were raised **in Germany**, where citizens, single MPs, and the *Die Linke* party issued a complaint to the Constitutional Court against the TSCG and ESM Treaty (Schmidt et aal. 2013).

The **German Constitutional Court** (*Bundesverfassungsgericht*), with a **provisional decision on 12th of September, 2012** on the constitutionality of the ESM and the Fiscal Compact (later confirmed in its judgment on 18th of March, 2014), established that the **obligation of confidentiality** imposed by the ESM Treaty on the Financial Ministers who sit in the bodies of the ESM (Article 34 ESMT) **could not be opposed to the two branches of the German Parliament, the *Bundestag* and the *Bundesrat*** (Rivosecchi 2014). It also stated that the assistance provided in the ESM cannot be automatic and cannot be transformed into an unlimited guarantee in favour of other countries. From time to time, **any increase in ESM funding must always be subject to the approval of the German Bundestag**, which has «responsibility for the budget» according to the German Basic Law (so-called *Haushaltsverantwortung*, flowing from Article 38 (1) GG, which enshrines the right to vote of German citizens).

Consequently, the German State adopted «reservations and interpretative declarations» to the Treaties in accordance with the provisional decision of the Constitutional Court. Thus, an **asymmetry has emerged between the Member States adhering to the ESM Treaty**. While the German Parliament maintains control over the increase in spending and is informed by the German government on the decisions adopted by the ESM bodies, the same does not apply to the other States (Pinelli 2014). Nonetheless, the only Member State that has not ratified the ESM reform is now Italy, since Germany proceeded with the ratification after the ruling of the Federal Constitutional Court that declared inadmissible new direct complaints (December 2022).

3. The Case of EU-Negotiated Trade Agreements

Another area in which conflicts may arise between the laws of the Member States, the European Union law and international law, and their respective judicial or quasi-judicial systems is that of EU-negotiated trade agreements.

The trade treaties of the European Union can be divided into ***mixed* and *non-mixed treaties***. **Mixed treaties fall partly within the exclusive competence of the European Union and partly within the competence of the Member States**. Non-mixed treaties are those adopted exclusively within the competence of the Union (Conconi et aal. 2021). While for the latter, the decision of the European Union is sufficient to bind all the Member States (pursuant to Article 281 TFUE), **for mixed treaties, it is necessary that the approval of the Union is followed by ratification by all the 27 Member States.** This implies that the refusal to proceed with the ratification by a single Member State can block the whole treaty, with repercussions on the whole Union and all Member States. Pending the treaty's ratification by all Member States, **the European Union can still provisionally implement it**, even if **exclusively for the part that falls under the exclusive**

© Wolters Kluwer Italia

competence of the European Union. The rest, which fall within the competence of the Member States, cannot be provisionally implemented.

This is what happened, for example, with the ***EU-Canada Comprehensive Economic and Trade Agreement* (CETA)**, a progressive trade agreement between the EU and Canada, signed in 2016. CETA is a mixed treaty and requires ratification by all Member States. Initially, the treaty's signature almost failed due to **opposition from Belgium, particularly the Wallonia region**, which must ratify international treaties according to Belgian constitutional law. The European Parliament nevertheless approved the conclusion of the CETA, and **the Council decided to start the provisional application in 2017**. In 2020, after three years of provisional application, it was the Netherlands (and, in particular, the Dutch Senate) which cast doubts on the ratification of the treaty. Dutch parliamentarians expressed concern for national interests, particularly in terms of meat quality standards and the unfair competition that Canadian producers could have exercised to the detriment of Dutch ones. While the opposition of the Dutch Senate was soon overcome in 2022, in 2020, there was a **vote against CETA by the Cyprus Parliament**, which expressed concerns about the protection of the typical halloumi cheese. More recently, a momentous **decision issued by the Supreme Court of Ireland (*Costello v. Government of Ireland and Ors.*** [2022] IESC 44) **held the proposed ratification of CETA by the Irish State as unconstitutional**. According to this ruling, the trade agreement providing for an investor tribunal which had powers to make binding and enforceable decisions that would be unreviewable by national courts, would have compromised judicial sovereignty in Ireland. Italy itself has yet to ratify the treaty, also due to the opposition of many political forces concerned about the protection of national production.

As is evident, the successful conclusion of mixed treaties depends, to a large extent, on the decisions of the Member States, which are **strongly influenced by national interests**. This often jeopardises the conclusion of this type of agreement. However, most of the trade agreements signed by the European Union are mixed treaties, also because **the European Union, through these instruments, aims not only at increasing trade exchanges but at pursuing additional purposes** (often falling outside the exclusive competence of the EU), such as safety, human rights, and higher environmental standards or fulfilment of sustainable development goals.

Defining when a treaty is mixed can be complex. Broadly speaking, the Common Commercial Policy falls within the exclusive competence of the European Union pursuant to Article 207 TFEU, and the Union has gained an increasing role in trade policy under Article 3(1) TFEU. The Court of Justice offered some guidance in its Opinion No. 2/2015 on the *EU-Singapore FTA (Free Trade Agreement)*. In the ***Singapore Opinion***, **the Court found that the investment portfolio and the Investor-State Dispute Settlement (ISDS) fell outside the scope of the European Union**. Therefore, treaties establishing ISDS must be concluded as mixed.

The issue of the ***Investor-State Dispute Settlement*** **(ISDS)** is particularly controversial. According to this mechanism, **disputes between foreign investors and states (or the EU) are transferred to international arbitration tribunals**. In this way, the national courts of the Member States involved (as well as the European ones) cease to have jurisdiction over such disputes. **In more recent agreements**, like those concluded with Vietnam and Canada, the EU replaced the traditional ISDS with an ***Investment Court System*** **(ICS), moving away from the model of private arbitrators** that characterized the ISDS to embracing the idea of a permanent court system with procedural due process guarantees, in an attempt to respond to the diffuse public criticism.

Apart from the concerns over the priority to commercial interests allegedly given by these courts or arbitration tribunals, to the detriment of the protection of human rights, the environment and labour, a crucial juridical matter at stake is the safeguarding of the **autonomy of the legal systems** concerned. The core issue is to prevent an international court or arbitration tribunal from binding, even indirectly, the national courts of the Member States (or even the Court of Justice) in the interpretation and the application of the rules of domestic law (or Union law).

In order to protect the autonomy of the European Union, the European Commission tends to follow a dualistic approach when signing such treaties. The **dualistic approach** implies a clear separation between the international agreement and the related dispute resolution mechanism established by it, on the one hand, and the legal order of the European Union and its judicial system, on the other. This type of approach was followed, albeit with variations, in the trade deals with Singapore, Vietnam and Canada (CETA), as well as in the proposals presented by the Commission in the context of the negotiations aimed at concluding the ***Transatlantic Trade and Investment Partnership*** **(TTIP)** agreement with the United States.

Among other things, autonomy is guaranteed in such treaties through the **exclusion of the direct effect of the provisions of the agreement** and the

 © Wolters Kluwer Italia

exclusion of EU law as part of the applicable law by the ISDS. Otherwise, a body outside the European Union legal framework would be allowed to apply provisions of EU law without the Court of Justice being able to offer a preliminary ruling on their interpretation. To overcome these drawbacks, some scholars have proposed a mechanism modelled on the reference for a preliminary ruling pursuant to Article 267 TFEU, by which the arbitration tribunal established on the basis of such agreements could request the Court of Justice to solve any doubts relating to the interpretation of EU rules.

However, in an influential 2018 judgment (Case C-284/16, ***Achmea***), the **Court of Justice ruled** that **the ISDS arbitration clause** in an international investment agreement between two European Union Member States (i.e. a bilateral agreement between the EU Member States) was **incompatible with the principle of autonomy of EU law**, which protects the full effectiveness and consistency of EU law and therefore demands its uniform interpretation. According to the Court of Luxemburg, such autonomy is guaranteed, under Article 19 TEU, by providing exclusive jurisdiction to the Court of Justice of the European Union. Only the Court of Justice is entitled to offer authoritative interpretations of EU law, even on the basis of the *judicial dialogue* with national courts via Article 267 TFEU (i.e. preliminary rulings). Investment arbitration can have an **adverse effect on autonomy,** as such arbitration can decide matters of EU law without being subject to the CJEU's control since arbitration tribunals are not national courts and cannot issue preliminary references.

Even though this ruling was **issued in a case of bilateral intra-EU agreement**, many scholars have argued that it might mark the end of ISDS clauses also in other trade agreements, including those negotiated by the European Union. According to an alternative interpretation, this decision may be also read in line with the previous case law of the CJEU. In an earlier pronunciation, **Opinion No. 1/2017**, the **Court reviewed the compatibility of the mechanism for the settlement of disputes provided for by the CETA** and found it **compatible with EU primary law**. The Court of Justice held that the establishment of a court or an arbitrator responsible for the interpretation of the provisions of a treaty whose decisions are binding on the EU may be compatible with EU law **as far as it has no adverse effect on the autonomy of the EU legal order** and its constitutional framework. However, in order to grant this autonomy, those tribunals cannot have the power to interpret or apply provisions of EU law, other than those of the CETA, or to make decisions which might have the effect of limiting the powers of the EU institutions as shaped according to the single European legal order.

REFERENCES

Barbera, A. [2017], 'La Carta dei diritti: per un dialogo fra la Corte italiana e la Corte di Giustizia', paper delivered in Seville on 26-28 October, 2017, available at www.cortecostituzionale.it.

Barile, P. [1958], 'I poteri del Presidente della Repubblica', 8(2) *Rivista trimestrale di diritto pubblico*.

Barile, P. [1973], 'Il cammino comunitario della Corte', 18(3-6) *Giurisprudenza costituzionale*.

Bartolucci, L. [2021], *La sostenibilità del debito pubblico in Costituzione. Procedure euro-nazionali di bilancio e responsabilità verso le generazioni future* (Padova, Cedam-Wolters Kluwer).

Bast J. [2012], 'New Categories of Acts after the Lisbon Reform: Dynamics of Parliamentarization in EU Law', 49(3) *Common Market Law Review*.

Bergonzini, C. (ed) [2019], *Costituzione e Bilancio* (Milano, FrancoAngeli).

Besselink, L. and others [2014], 'National Constitutional Avenues for Further EU Integration', Study for the European Parliament, available at www.europarl.europa.eu.

Bin, R. & Pitruzzella, G. [2021], *Diritto costituzionale* (Torino, Giappichelli).

Cartabia, M. & Lupo, N. [2022], *The Constitution of Italy. A contextual Analysis* (Oxford, Hart Publishing).

Cartabia, M. & Weiler, J.H.H. [2000], *L'Italia in Europa: profili istituzionali e costituzionali* (Bologna, il Mulino).

Carli, G. [1993], *Cinquant'anni di vita italiana* (Roma-Bari, Laterza).

Caruso, C. & Morvillo, M. (eds) [2020], *Il governo dei numeri. Indicatori economico-finanziari e decisione di bilancio nello Stato costituzionale* (Bologna, il Mulino).

Chessa, O. [2016], *La costituzione della moneta* (Napoli, Jovene).

Conconi, P. and others [2021], 'EU Trade Agreements: To Mix or Not to Mix, That Is the Question', 55(2) *Journal of World Trade*.

De Witte, B. & Beukers, T. [2013], 'The Court of Justice approves the creation of the European Stability Mechanism outside the EU legal order: Pringle', 50(3) *Common Market Law Review*.

Faraguna, P. [2015], *Ai confini della Costituzione. Principi supremi e identità costituzionale* (Milano, FrancoAngeli).

Faraguna, P. [2021], 'On the Identity Clause and Its Abuses: "Back to the Treaty"', 27(3) *European Public Law*.

Fasone, C. & Piccirilli G. [2021], 'The new «form of government» in the reforms of the Italian regional system', in Arban E., and others (eds), *Federalism and Constitutional Law. The Italian Contribution to comparative Regionalism* (Abingdon, Routledge).

Gallo, D. & Nicola, F.G. [2016], 'The External Dimension of EU Investment Law: Jurisdictional Clashes and Transformative Adjudication', 39(5) *Fordham International Law Journal*.

Gallo, D. [2019], 'Challenging EU constitutional law: The Italian Constitutional Court's new stance on direct effect and the preliminary reference procedure', 25(4) *European Law Journal*.

Gallo, D. & Piccirilli, G. [2023], 'Dual Preliminarity, Today. Evaluating the Impact of Judgment No. 269/2017 of the Italian Constitutional Court', 15(1) *Italian Journal of Public Law*.

Ipsen, H.P. [1966], 'Als Bundesstaat in der Gemeinschaft', in *Probleme des Europäischen Rechts. Festschrift für Walter Hallstein zu seinem 65. Geburtstag* (Frankfurt am Main, Klostermann).

Klabbers, J. & Palombella G. (eds) [2019], *The Challenge of Inter-Legality* (Cambridge, Cambridge University Press).

Lamarque, E. [2021], 'The Failure by Italy to Ratify Protocol no. 16 to the ECHR: Left behind but not lost', 1(1) *The Italian Review of International and Comparative Law*.

 © Wolters Kluwer Italia

Luciani, M. [2019], 'Note critiche sui disegni di legge per l'autorizzazione alla ratifica dei Protocolli n. 15 e n. 16 della CEDU', hearing to the Chamber of Deputies held on 26th of November, 2019, available at www.sistemapenale.it/.
Lupo, N. & Piccirilli G. (eds) [2017], *The Italian Parliament in the European Union* (Oxford-Portland, Hart Publishing).
Lupo, N. [2022], 'Clausole "europee" implicite ed esplicite nella Costituzione italiana', 20(4) *Federalismi.it*.
Lustig, D. & Weiler, J.H.H. [2018], 'Judicial review in the contemporary world— Retrospective and prospective', 16(2) *International Journal of Constitutional Law*.
Martinico, G. & Repetto, G. [2019], 'Fundamental Rights and Constitutional Duels in Europe: An Italian Perspective on Case 269/2017 of the Italian Constitutional Court and Its Aftermath', 15(4) *European Constitutional Law Review*.
Menegus, G. [2020], 'Gli indirizzi di massima per il coordinamento delle politiche economiche *ex* art. 121 TFUE nel quadro del semestre europeo', 13(3) *Osservatorio sulle fonti*.
Musella, F. [2022], *Monocratic Government. The Impact of Personalisation on Democratic Regimes* (Berlin, De Gruyter).
Pavone, T. [2022], *The Ghostwriters. Lawyers and the Politics behind the Judicial Construction of Europe* (Cambridge, Cambridge University Press).
Piccirilli, G. [2018], 'The «Taricco saga»: The Italian Constitutional Court continues its European Journey', 14(4) *European Constitutional Law Review*.
Piccirilli, G. [2021], 'L'"identità costituzionale" italiana nella Costituzione composita europea', 17(1) *Torunskie Studia Polsko-Wloskie*.
Pinelli, C. [2014], 'La giurisprudenza costituzionale tedesca e le nuove asimmetrie fra i poteri dei parlamenti nazionali', 12(1) *Costituzionalismo.it*.
Pitruzzella, G. [2013], Crisi economica e decisioni di governo, *Rivista AIC* 4.
Poguntke, T. & Webb P. (eds) [2005], *The Presidentialization of Politics: A Comparative Study of Modern Democracies* (Oxford, Oxford University Press).
Repetto, G. (ed) [2013], *The Constitutional Relevance of the ECHR in Domestic and European Law: An Italian Perspective* (Cambridge-Antwerp, Intersentia).
Rivosecchi, G. [2007], *L'indirizzo politico finanziario tra Costituzione italiana e vincoli europei* (Padova).
Rivosecchi, G. [2014], 'Il Meccanismo Europeo di Stabilità e il Fiscal Compact tra Karlsruhe e Lussemburgo', 34(2) *Quaderni costituzionali*.
Rivosecchi G. [2019], 'Manovra di bilancio 2019: la rientrata procedura di infrazione per debito eccessivo', 39(1) *Quaderni costituzionali*.
Romano, S. [1918], *L'ordinamento giuridico. Studi sul concetto, le fonti e i caratteri del diritto* (Pisa, Mariotti).
Romano, S. [ENG transl. by Croce M. 2018], *The Legal order* (London, Routledge).
Sarmiento, D. [2021], 'The Consob Way – Or how the Corte costituzionale Taught Europe (once again) a Masterclass in Constitutional Dispute Settlement', *EU Law Live* 54.
Schmidt, S.K. and others [2013], 'The ESM Before Courts', 14(1) *German Law Journal*.
Sciarra, S. & Golia, A.J. [2020], 'Italy: New Frontiers and Further Developments', in Bobek, M., & Adams-Prassl J. (eds), *The EU Charter of Fundamental Rights in the Member States* (Oxford-Portland, Hart Publishing).
Stone Sweet, A. [2004], *The Judicial Construction of Europe* (Oxford, Oxford University Press).
Streeck, W. [2014], 'The Politics of Public Debt: Neoliberalism, Capitalist Development and the Restructuring of the State', 15(1) *German Economic Review*.
Tega, D. [2021], 'The Italian Constitutional Court in its context. A narrative', 17(3) *European Constitutional Law Review*.

Part III

Democracy and Pluralism in Italy

Democracy is not just a matter of holding free elections. It requires multiple centres of power and, accordingly, a complex setting of different bodies to guarantee that individual liberties and rights are properly safeguarded. Italian constitutional democracy is therefore closely linked to institutional pluralism and pluralism of rights.

Part III deals precisely with the intertwining of democracy and pluralistic principles in the Italian Constitution.

In Section A, the **founding traits of democracy and pluralism** in the constitutional provisions are addressed through the perspective provided by Articles 1 and 139 of the Constitution, the former proclaiming the principle of popular sovereignty and the latter establishing the republican principle in accordance with the outcome of the constitutional referendum of 1946. The role of fundamental rights and freedoms within the constitutional fabric as bulwarks of democracy and pluralism is also highlighted. In the same Section, the **principle of equality**, in both its formal and substantive dimension, is analysed as a pillar of the democratic character of the State.

But pluralism in the Constitution is not only the cornerstone of the fundamental rights system, as Article 2 exemplifies when it states that «the Republic recognises and guarantees the inviolable rights of the person, both as an individual and in the social groups where human personality is expressed». Pluralism is also the guiding star of the entire legal system that is characterised by the coexistence of different institutions such as Regions, political parties, trade unions, religious denominations, etc.

Within this framework, Section B aims to detect the **intertwining of democracy and pluralism through the institutions provided for by the Constitution**. More precisely, Regions as expressions of institutional pluralism are analysed in the evolutionary path of constitutional reforms. Two principles informing Title V – the principle of subsidiarity and of regional autonomy – are specifically explored here in so far as they reveal a sort of dual nature

capable of enhancing pluralism or producing fragmentation depending on their concrete application. Parties and trade unions as expressions of political and social pluralism are also investigated. They perform a quite similar role within a democratic society: both of these institutions collect, bring together and represent in the public sphere the different requests of citizens, strengthening the pluralistic background of the Italian legal system through a constant dialogue between different societal components. Religious denominations as expressions of religious pluralism are dealt with, focusing on the relationship between the State and the Catholic Church, the peculiar secularism characterising the system (so-called *laïcité à l'italienne*), and the related freedom of religion and conscience.
Lastly, Section C looks at **democracy and pluralism through the lens of rights**. In fact, pluralism does not only focus on individuals but also ensures that **minorities, and groups in general**, can act through democratic tools in order to represent their interests. From this standpoint, the main instrument through which citizens can actively take part in democratic life and fully exercise the rights guaranteed by the Constitution in a pluralistic environment is via a community.
This particular dimension of pluralism is examined in this section by analysing those rights that concretely contribute to the affirmation of democracy through specific communities or social groups. Particular attention is therefore given to rights fostering **social pluralism**, i.e. freedom of assembly, association, and speech, the latter involving both the right to inform and to be informed and freedom of the media. This section also investigates rights representing **cultural, ethnic, and linguistic pluralism**, i.e. the protection of linguistic minorities and the freedom of arts and sciences.

 © Wolters Kluwer Italia

A) FOUNDATIONS

1. Taking Pluralism Seriously

1.a. The Italian Democratic Republic as a Reaction to Totalitarianism and Dictatorship: The Opening and Closure of the Constitution (Articles 1 and 139)

«The totalitarian state was our obsession. Democracy, as well as our hope, was our commitment» (BOBBIO 1995 at IX). With these words, Bobbio portrayed the deepest sentiments of the people in the post-war period, providing a sharp backdrop for the Constituents' discussions. In the aftermath of World War II, the democratic ideal re-emerged in close connection with the protection of individuals **from** all forms of **totalitarianism and dictatorship**. This observation is not only true for the newly born Republic: political scientists precisely identified in this historic moment the watershed for the beginning of a second wave of democratisation involving many (but not only) European countries (HUNTINGTON 2012).

The Constitution actually opens with this recognition in concise, yet peremptory, terms: «Italy is a democratic Republic founded on labour. Sovereignty shall belong to the people and be exercised by the people in the forms and within the limits of this Constitution» (Article 1). This provision touches directly on the heart of democracy, the core of which is the position recognised to the people. In simpler terms, with the person being at the crux of any democratic reasoning, the largest possible number of people must be charged with the essential task of choosing rulers and how they shall govern, without discrimination with respect to these fundamental choices. The democratic nature of a system is determined by the degree to which this fundamental principle is upheld. Democracy, therefore, embodies the ultimate social fabric in a system, placing the person at the starting point and at the endpoint of that system (see *I.B).3.* and *IV.A).3.*).

A more thorough reading of Article 1 of the Constitution may be helpful to grasp what the Constituents essentially meant when they mentioned the democratic republic. In the Italian Constitution, democracy is unequivocally read through the prism of **popular sovereignty**, which reflects a legal myth regarding the modern state now disputed by many legal scholars (i.e. the myth of state sovereignty). The novelty of Article 1 is that it outlines the constitutive conceptual core of democracy as requiring an organisation of public power wherein institutions, organs and their activities and functions may always be attributed, connected and traced back to **the will of the people**. Only in this way can the term *popular sovereignty* (adopted as a manifesto of modern Constitutions, with the Italian one being no exception) be properly understood and its further meanings be explored. Affirming that power belongs to the people means recognising that legitimation comes from below and that democratic authorisation is always necessary to legitimise public authority.

If this is true for the opening article of the Constitution, the same is also true for the closing one (Article 139), where the role of democracy – and the people, accordingly – is again confirmed and enhanced. As already analysed in Part I, the Republic derives directly from the referendum of 2nd of June, 1946 that led to the abolition of the monarchy. This fundamental choice made by the people became part of the last constitutional provision, which states that «The status of Republic may not be subject to constitutional amendment» (Article 139).

Thus, the entire constitutional framework rests on a kind of **symmetrical logic** – clearly emerging from the first and the last constitutional provisions – which confirms the key role of democracy in the Italian legal order. Put concisely, acknowledging the republican form as the foundation of the legal system has to be read in conjunction with its democratic character. In the Constitution the two terms – **democratic and Republic** – are **tied together**. Some legal scholars have even seen in this adjective the real constitutional novelty that explains the genesis of various other constitutional provisions, starting from the articles concerning fundamental rights up to the ban «to reorganise, under any form whatsoever, the dissolved Fascist party» (provision XII, transitional and final provisions of the Constitution). In a way, this prohibition is to be considered as imposed by acknowledging the democratic nature of the Republic, and it is the only explicit sign of militant democracy in the Italian legal order. As is well known, this specific concept was originally used to describe those democratic systems that, aware of its inherent inability or historic failure to contain fascism, introduced

 © Wolters Kluwer Italia

constitutional mechanisms that pre-emptively limited civil and political freedoms in order to preserve the essence of democracy (Lowenstein 1937 at 417).

1.b. From Popular Sovereignty to Pluralism in the Constitution

In Article 1 of the Constitution, the choice made in favour of popular sovereignty as the cornerstone of a democratic republic is closely connected to the position of the individual, as recalled by Article 2 of the Constitution.

From the reading of democracy as outlined in Article 1, it follows that the exercise of popular sovereignty requires a sufficient degree of freedom. In this light, the close bonds between the **protection of fundamental rights and** the **establishment of democracy** in the Italian Constitution can be appreciated particularly from the more general perspective of European legal systems after World War II. A constitutional environment in which freedoms are adequately protected constitutes the necessary safeguard – a kind of prerequisite – for any system to be effectively democratic. The contemporary notion of **liberal democracy** highlights precisely that fundamental rights are simultaneously part of, and a limit to, democratic discourse: a boundary never to be trespassed.

Article 2 provides a general recognition of fundamental rights. Other provisions are more specifically related to the democratic process and set out the conditions for the people to effectively take part (in direct or indirect forms) in the exercise of public power. Freedoms of speech (including dissent and criticism), assembly, association, communication and information (Articles 15, 17, 18, 21) in fact constitute the grounds on which democracy grows and develops. In turn, these freedoms allow for the meaningful exercise of the right to vote – the starting point of the democratic process in the narrower sense: free parliamentary elections depend first and foremost on the space of freedom ensured before and at the moment of voting. Universal suffrage, a fair electoral system safeguarding equal chances for minorities, the recognition of forms of direct democracy and, more broadly, everything that refers to the division of power certainly represent concrete democratic achievements, but democracy goes far beyond this.

From this perspective, first it is necessary to highlight the very special position that the principle of equality is granted in democratic regimes. Equality constitutes the very essence of democracy. Democracy and equality are somewhat **overlapping terms**: as is commonly said, 'votes are counted and not weighed', which hints at the fact that each vote is bestowed with the same value as all the others.

Many other rights come to make up the framework of pluralism, as will be analysed later on: here suffice it to mention, as a notable example, freedom of thought – which is to be protected up to the point of permitting forms of criticism and dissent, as well as giving a voice to isolated minorities – not only allows pluralism to exist but also ensures that all such plural components of society can express themselves and really participate in the political process. Pluralism is the hallmark of modern democracy.

Questions have been raised as to whether the Italian legal system is truly able to ensure pluralism. One of the most authoritative Italian scholars – Costantino Mortati – expressed doubts as to the effective respect of pluralism through a combined reading of Article 3, para. 2 («which imposes the reconstitution of homogeneity in the social structure») and Articles 2 and 5, which require the setting up of a pluralistic structure which is both vertical and horizontal (Mortati 1975 at 44). Indeed, as can be seen from reading these very first articles of the Constitution, pluralism intersects with many crucial legal issues, and its implementation is a far from obvious task.

Be that as it may, achieving pluralism is a challenging aim and democracy is a demanding, perhaps even difficult, form of government (Böckenförde 2020), as will be clear also from the following sections.

2. The Principle of Equality in a Plural Society

2.a. Introduction: Equality and Pluralism

Equality lies at the heart of pluralism in modern democracies; at the same time, it also raises central questions. The implementation of the constitutional principle of equality not only enhances and qualifies the protection of fundamental rights, but also distinguishes one political order from another. Equality is the main criterion for determining **citizens' legal capacity**, since it generally implies equal treatment in certain situations and relationships. The existence of diverse social groups itself implies that not all individuals will begin their lives **from the same starting point**. However, the principle of equality seems to force equalisation on different groups and positions, hence raising questions about the intrinsic value of pluralism. On the one hand, equality tends to homogenise and regulate diversities; on the other hand, pluralism enhances differences by protecting the specificities of groups and individuals. Thus, their coexistence seems to determine **an inherent contradiction** that only a careful reading of the principle of equality and its nuances can resolve. Such antinomy finds its solution mainly on a practical-interpretative level, underlining in particular **the interdependence** between equality and pluralism.

Within the Italian legal system, the principle of equality is established in Article 3. According to this provision: «All citizens possess equal social dignity and are equal before the law, without distinction of sex, race, language, religion and

 © Wolters Kluwer Italia

political orientation, personal and social conditions. It is the duty of the Republic to remove economic and social obstacles which, by limiting the freedom and equality of citizens, prevent the full development of the natural person and the actual participation of all workers in the political, economic and social organization of the country». The first paragraph refers to **formal equality** and contains the principle of **non-discrimination**, while the second one expresses the principle of **substantive equality**.

2.b. Formal Equality and its Tools

Formal equality essentially demands identical treatment in similar situations and different treatment in structurally distinct situation. From this perspective, **formal equality** primarily refers to **the legislator**. It prevents lawmakers from distinguishing the effects of legal provisions on the basis of their beneficiaries. In this same vein, the principle of formal equality not only requires eliminating the power to arbitrarily relieve an individual or group from observance of the law, but also implies that legislative provisions are framed in general and abstract terms. It essentially prohibits any privileged treatment of citizens by reason of their assumed greater or lesser social dignity. Formal equality, in sum, requires the legislator to recognise the **same dignity** to all, despite the diversity of their conditions. Article 3 , read in conjunction with Article 2, confers fundamental rights to all citizens in conditions of equality and therefore creates **a common legal status**, which implies the same legal capacity (see *IV.A).3.*).

Yet, preventing the legislator from establishing any kind of difference between citizens would not be desirable and even rationally possible. Legal distinctions may – and in some instances must – be introduced in a reasonable and non-arbitrary way, taking into account the specificity of each situation. In this regard, Article 3, on the one hand, identifies certain subjective characteristics that can **never** be assumed by the legislator as criteria for legal distinction, such as sex, race, language, religion, political opinion, and personal and social conditions (see also para. 2.c. on substantive equality). On the other hand, it enhances the pluralist potential of democracy allowing the lawmaker to introduce **reasonable distinctions**.

2.b.1. The Standard of Reasonableness

Therefore, it becomes clear that, in the logic of Article 3, para. 1, formal equality takes on the meaning of **reasonableness**, prohibiting arbitrary distinctions between similar situations, as well as the adoption of the same provisions in order to regulate situations that should be differentiated.

In all these cases, when the reasonableness of a legal provision is challenged, the constitutional judgment follows a **trilateral model**. For example, if legal

© Wolters Kluwer Italia

provision A may be challenged (object of the judgment) because it regulates a situation in a certain manner, while another legal provision B (*tertium comparationis*, the third element of the comparison) regulates a distinct but comparable situation in a different way, the judicial test should: i) verify whether the two situations are indeed comparable, based on the *ratio legis* (underlying purpose) of each provision; ii) if such is the case, assess whether the general principle of equality (parameter) requires regulatory uniformity or whether specific reasons justify the challenged differentiation

The standard of reasonableness has also been applied as a sort of *super-principle*. It evolved to become, to some extent, an autonomous constitutional parameter, disconnected from the strict comparison between two different elements: this occurs above all when the Constitutional Court reviews a law as unreasonable in itself, without presupposing any specific term of comparison. Within this framework, the standard of reasonableness is assumed from a teleological perspective: the Court reviews the aims pursued and the means employed by the legislator, assessing the consistency, adequacy and proportionality of the contested legislation. The Constitutional Court thus examines the effects of the legislative act by comparing and balancing the benefits deriving from the law and the related costs (that is, the sacrifices it imposes on other rights and interests). In light of these judicial uses, the standard of reasonableness appears as a concrete assessment having as its object not so much the abstract provision, but rather the specific situations regulated by law. The principle of formal equality then becomes a judgment on the **balancing of interests** made by the legislator (MORRONE 2001).

2.b.2. Constitutional Balancing

Balancing constitutional interests is traditionally a privileged area for the use of reasonableness and proportionality standards.

In the case law of the ItCC this task has been practised for a long time as an indispensable tool to implement pluralism and develop a systemic conception of rights based upon human dignity. Fundamental freedoms are never affirmed **in absolute terms**, but they are part of a complex normative framework in which other rights and interests integrate with each other. In the Constitution, every right always holds its own limits, and **balancing** is an interpretative and argumentative technique that allows for the reasonable assessment of a plurality of competing constitutional values (see *IV.B).1.c.3.*).

An example is the increasingly strict scrutiny of **legislative automatisms** by the Constitutional Court. It concerns those provisions which reconnect predetermined and mandatory legal consequences upon given conditions, preventing

 © Wolters Kluwer Italia

courts or public administrations from taking into account the peculiarities of each case in order to modulate the effects of the rule (Judgments nos. 240/1997, 78/2005, 329/2007, 56 and 185/2021). In this context, the Court considers all the relevant circumstances and insists on the impossibility of establishing once and for all a hierarchical relationship between the different elements at stake. From this standpoint, pluralism always implies a dynamic balance **not determined in abstract terms** and requires the legislator to evaluate the complexity of the individual cases, or at least to attribute to judicial or administrative bodies some leeway in appreciating this complexity **in practice**. Otherwise, the ItCC will declare the unconstitutionality of the legislative provisions which ignore the specific needs of the situation or are not flexible enough to balance the multifaceted aspects of reality (see Judgments nos. 2/1999, 253/2003, and 265/2010).

2.c. Substantive Equality and Its Tools

Article 3, para. 2, expresses the principle of **substantive equality**. Even though this further delineation could appear in contrast with the provision under para. 1, it actually constitutes the most coherent development of formal equality from a legal point of view. Substantive equality aims at removing «those obstacles of an economic or social nature, which constrain the freedom and equality of citizens». This statement requires public authorities to eliminate all **social disadvantages** impeding «the full development of the human person and the effective participation of all workers in the political, economic and social organisation of the country».

Equality does not only require uniform legal treatment. It also mandates public authorities to prevent certain groups of individuals from being effectively deprived of their constitutional rights. Removing the obstacles which constrain citizens' freedom and equality does not mean that the legislator should direct individuals towards designated goals or aim at levelling society. Rather, it requires giving citizens the tools to fully develop their personalities. In this sense, substantive equality promotes **maximum individual fulfilment** and enhances pluralism, guaranteeing that everyone can achieve full personal development in an effectively free and pluralistic society.

This task can only be fulfilled by partially derogating from the principle of formal equality. The so-called promotional legislation is indeed addressed to categories of persons who are in a position of disadvantage, and it attributes specific benefits to certain individuals excluding others. This constitutive aspect of the principle of equality clearly shows **the transition from a liberal state**, based on the formal equality of citizens, **to a welfare state**, which instead aims at systematically safeguarding their substantial freedom. Consequently, while the principle of formal equality imposes on the legislator the adoption of laws that are as general and abstract as possible, substantive equality favours the issuing of provisions that resolve situations detrimental to specific minorities. These two aspects of equality **limit and complement each other**. In this sense, substantive equality will adjust the generality and abstractness of a provision according to the specific case, while formal equality will prevent positive actions from generating unreasonably unequal treatments and consequently turning into reverse discrimination.

2.c.1. The Duty of the Republic to Remove Obstacles of an Economic and Social Nature: Promotional Legislation

The principle of equality as such is not violated if the legislator introduces distinctions that advantage particular categories of persons and allows them to enjoy the fundamental rights provided by the Constitution. The principle of substantive equality requires public authorities to eliminate those conditions that – by impeding the full development of the human person – **hinder the implementation of formal equality**.

The second paragraph of Article 3 thus contributes to fully achieving the objectives set out in the Constitution in terms of pluralism, democracy, and fundamental rights guarantees. In contemporary societies, ensuring equal treatment before the law is not sufficient in itself to safeguard pluralism. This is because there are situations that substantially diverge from each other, and certain individual or groups may find themselves at a disadvantage when exercising their rights and freedoms.

The well-known concepts of **affirmative or positive action**, although initially alien to the Italian legal tradition, were introduced into the domestic system also under the heading of **promotional legislation**.

The term **affirmative action** was originally coined in the US legal system to refer to a wide range of policies and public practices aimed at empowering and assisting individuals and groups to overcome or minimise their disadvantages and participate fully in all aspects of public life (e.g., in higher education the first decision of a long and multifaceted case-law was Regents of the University of California v. Bakke, 438 U.S. 265, 1978 in which the Supreme Court allowed the use of race as a relevant factor in University admission, if it was part of an overall evaluation of the applicant; lastly, however, on this topic, Students for fair admissions, inc. v. President and fellows of Harvard College, US 600, 2023).

Positive action is an expression adopted by the Italian legal system in the wake of EU antidiscrimination law. Article 157 TFEU ensures that with a view to ensuring full equality in practice between men and women in working life, the principle of equal treatment shall not prevent any Member State from maintaining or adopting measures providing for specific advantages in order to make it

© Wolters Kluwer Italia

easier for the underrepresented sex to pursue a vocational activity or to prevent, or compensate for, disadvantages in professional careers.

In general terms, Article 3 does not identify which inequalities are to be contrasted and therefore it leaves **the legislator free to assess** them according to the changing social context. However, in certain cases, the existence of factual situations that create inequality is directly appreciated by the Constitution itself, which then establishes promotional legislation related to particular circumstances. In these situations, the Constitution identifies a series of weak subjects or minorities who must be expressly protected through the adoption of legal provisions dedicated to them (see e.g., Articles 6, linguistic minorities; 31, mothers, children and young people; 37, women and children; see also ItCC nos. 56 and 185 of 2021, workers). The promoting attitude of the national constitutional order was also evident in 2003 on the occasion of the amendment of **Article 51**. According to this provision as amended, «Any citizen of either sex is eligible for public and elected offices on equal terms, according to the requirements established by law. To this end, the Republic shall adopt specific measures to promote equal opportunities between women and men» (see *IV.C).5.e.*). Just to give an example, consistent with this same principle, Law No. 120/2011 reserves to women a certain number of seats on the boards of listed and public companies.

In Italy the need to adopt sector-specific disciplines aimed at favouring certain groups of individuals over others is perceived with less urgency compared to other legal systems, such as the United States. This tendency can be easily explained by considering the extensive social rights that modern European welfare states, including Italy, have historically implemented to protect the most disadvantaged categories.

2.d. Equality and the Anti-discrimination Policies in the EU

Within the EU legal framework, the principle of equality enshrined in Article 3 of the Constitution corresponds to Articles 20 and 21 of the Charter of Fundamental Rights of the European Union. According to these provisions, «everyone is equal before the law» (Article 20) and «any discrimination based on any ground such as sex, race, colour, ethnic or social origin, genetic features, language, religion, or belief, political or any other opinion, membership of a national minority, property, birth, disability, age or sexual orientation shall be prohibited. Within the scope of application of the Treaties and without prejudice to any of their specific provisions, any discrimination on grounds of nationality shall be prohibited» (Article 21).

Actually, the principle of equality dates back from the drafting of the Treaty of Rome in 1957 in the form of «equal pay for equal work». Therefore, it has been

© Wolters Kluwer Italia

always considered present in the EU legal system and it has also been applied in the judicial activity of the ECJ, which has constantly recognised the principle of equality **as an integral part of the common constitutional traditions** of every member state. Yet, the implementation of this principle by the Charter of Nice represents a significant innovation for the European legal order, since it explicitly codified equality and its corollaries.

So far, the Union and the corresponding Italian constitutional provisions seem to offer **different levels of protection**. Since its first decisions, the ECJ has construed the principle of equality essentially as the prohibition of treating different situations equally and equal situations differently. As a matter of fact, according to the ECJ, equality often results in **a mere anti-discrimination law**.

The choice to not include an explicit reference to substantive equality appears consistent with the classic approach of EU law, which normally considers prohibitions of discrimination mainly from an economic angle. Within the European Union, equality has traditionally developed as a legal principle intended to satisfy the economic needs related to the proper functioning of the single market, although lately there have been some developments on this matter.

Since the entry into force of Directive 76/207/EEC on equal treatment for men and women as regards access to employment, vocational training and working conditions, the ECJ has started to receive institutional actions aimed at re-establishing equal opportunities between men and women (and beyond). Along the same lines, the treaty of Amsterdam has entitled every member state to adopt specific measures facilitating the pursuit of a professional activity by the under-represented sex or compensating for any gender prejudice in professional careers and article 13 (article 19 TFEU) authorises European institutions to take "«appropriate action to combat discrimination based on sex, racial or ethnic origin, religion or belief, disability, age or sexual orientation». Therefore, the prohibition contained in Article 21 of the Charter constitutes **a universalistic extension** of the anti-discrimination protection already in place in the EU legal system.

Following the introduction of Article 13 into the treaty of Amsterdam a series of directives have been issued in the field of anti-discrimination law. Directive 2000/43/EC implemented the principle of equal treatment between persons irrespective of racial or ethnic origin and has endowed member states with the power to maintain or adopt measures to prevent or compensate for practical disadvantages. Directive 2000/78/EC established a general framework for equal treatment in employment and occupation, prohibiting discrimination based on religion or personal beliefs, disability, age, or sexual orientation. Finally, Directive 2004/113/EC on the principle of equal treatment between men and women in the access to and supply of goods, services, social protection, and education further extended the protection against discrimination based on sex. In any case, the treaties – and,

 © Wolters Kluwer Italia

consequently, the directives that implement their precepts – simply allow the EU to remove obstacles deriving from certain personal situations. Thus, they do not entirely enable European institutions to take positive action that would eliminate inequalities originating from previous social conditions. This distinguishes the EU system from the domestic legal order.

Neither the European legislator nor the ECJ have developed **a principle of substantive equality comparable to the one envisaged in the Constitution**. In terms of pluralism, this means that in the EU legal framework, the principle of equality is basically shaped **as a form of non-discrimination**, as already mentioned. This is due not only to the lack of specific competences attributed to the EU in the field of social policies, but also to a structural difference with the Constitution that expressly recognises fundamental duties of social solidarity (Article 2).

Nevertheless, this **homogenisation** favoured by the EU approach could even enhance pluralism, acting as an integration factor within the EU legal system. Creating common conditions to align radically different contexts encourages the free movement of workers (and citizens in general), and as a result, it indirectly promotes an exchange between different cultures, thus benefiting pluralism. Still, it could be that the enactment of EU law produces a disadvantage for those individuals who are in a **«merely internal situation»**. This condition derives from the non-application to these citizens of the European rules guaranteeing economic freedom in the single market. In this manner, discrimination against groups normally protected within their national legal systems is created. Surely, these situations must be repealed by domestic institutions. The Italian Constitutional Court, for example, intervened in some cases in order to remove this special kind of reverse discrimination (see ItCC Judgments nos. 249/1995 on foreign language lecturers in Italian universities, 61/1996 on lawyers and prosecutors, 443/1997 on pasta production).

B) DEMOCRACY THROUGH INSTITUTIONS

1. Institutional Pluralism: Regions and the Italian Decentralised System

1.a. Pluralism, Democracy and Regionalism

This Section will focus on Italian regionalism that has now to be considered as the most distinctive feature of its own institutional pluralism. However, before the republican Constitution came into force, Italy was based on a different tradition of limited local autonomy. To bluntly summarize the advent of Regions in Italian institutional history one may say that they have been «grafted onto a very

© Wolters Kluwer Italia

centralised State by means of a severe surgical operation». The result appears to be **an intermediate stage** between administrative decentralisation and actual federalism (Grottanelli 2006 at 3).

As such, the Italian model constitutes a useful term of comparison for the increasing developments of regional and local identities throughout Europe, also considering the close connection of these novelties with democratic and pluralistic claims. Scotland, Catalonia and, from a certain point of view, even Brexit put together demands for greater territorial autonomy and claims for democracy and sovereignty.

The grammar of democracy is to some extent changing. Although this profound transformation certainly requires new approaches in order to understand it, still territories and local communities continue to play a crucial role in combining institutional pluralism and the concrete exercise of democracy.

1.b. Italian Regionalism, or the Domestic Variant of Federalism

As previously menrioned, the Regions did not have a significant tradition before the 1948 Constitution. More than 70 years later, the fact that their role is still debated «appears to be the consequence of a choice not made at that time, during the constitution-making process» (Caretti 2000 at 552). However, some hints in the text of the Constitution have been inserted. Significantly, Article 5 lists a set of principles defining not only the unitary nature of the State, but also the close relationship between regional and local government with the democratic principle and its implementation:

> «The Republic shall be one and indivisible. It shall recognise and promote local autonomies and implement the fullest measure of administrative decentralisation of those services which are provided by the State. The Republic shall adapt the principles and methods of its legislation to the requirements of autonomy and decentralisation».

1.b.1. The Original Constitutional Design and the Early Stages of Italian Regionalism

Italian regionalism is not homogeneous. Out of the twenty Regions constituting the Republic, five of them enjoy a **special status**, with broader and differentiated **autonomy** in comparison with the other fifteen.

Regions with special status (South Tyrol, Friuli-Venice-Julia, Aosta Valley, Sardinia and Sicily) were activated immediately after World War II, with tailor-made constitutional laws. The rationale was to **avoid secessions** (especially for

© Wolters Kluwer Italia

Sicily that was acknowledged as special even before the approval of the Constitution) and to meet **specific geographical needs**, linked to linguistic minorities near the northern borders or the undefined situation of the city of Trieste. After the recognition of Regions with special statutes, the rest of the Regions was created to cover the whole country, although these institutions enjoyed a much lower level of autonomy. The constitutional design implied a reading of the unitarian principle combined with a certain degree of **political, statutory, legislative, administrative and financial autonomy** of the Regions. Constitutional provisions on these issues were concentrated in Title V of Part II of the Constitution.

This difficult start of Italian regionalism was followed by further and problematic uncertainties. The 1948 Constitution remained unimplemented in this respect for twenty years. Only in the late 1960s was the electoral law for regional councils approved and it was then possible to summon them for the first time. Nevertheless, Regions remained almost empty boxes until the transfer of some functions to them in 1972 and 1976.

The initial structuring of the system followed the typical pattern of a **centralised unitary state**, granting limited statutory, legislative, administrative and financial autonomy to the Regions. More precisely, the allocation of legislative powers outlined in Title V gave Regions **two types of legislative powers**: concurrent powers, which covered a range of subjects explicitly listed in Article 117, para. 1, and optional-integrative powers, as outlined in Article 117, para. 2.

In both cases, the mechanism still involved the intervention of a **state law**, even for matters devolved to the Regions. In the case of areas where both the state and the Regions had concurrent powers, state laws were responsible for defining the **fundamental principles**, while regional laws focused on providing **detailed rules**, in accordance with the principles established at the state level. In the second case, Regions could expand or further specify state legislation in their areas of competence, even if without entirely replacing it. The main regional legislative competencies primarily included **local and administrative interests**, such as the organisation of regional institutions, territorial planning, construction, healthcare, education, and culture. On the other hand, **the State retained residual competences** in all areas not explicitly listed in the Constitution, particularly in relation to public finance, monetary policy, defence and foreign policy.

As for the mutual relationship between legislative and executive power at regional level (i.e. its form of government), the Constitution did not leave room for any differentiation whatsoever among the Regions. It directly stated that the President and members of the regional government had to be elected by the regional council from its members. Consequently, statutes rubber-stamped **a parliamentary form of government with an assembly-oriented tendency**, characterised by the central role of the legislature and the collegiality of the executive. Regional councils were then entrusted with numerous additional functions beyond legislation. The President was considered a mere *primus inter pares* in the executive, while the other members of the latter primarily carried out preparatory or executive commitments for the legislative assembly, serving as the intermediary between the political body and the bureaucratic apparatus.

This organisation was profoundly revised with two constitutional reforms brought by **Constitutional Law No. 1/1999** on regional statutes and the form of government and the broader **Constitutional Law No. 3/2001** that, *inter alia*, reshuffled completely the division of competences between the State and Regions.

These reforms are still vividly debated both for the impact they had on the Italian regional model and for what they failed to achieve. Specifically, they imparted a quasi-federal structure to the State without any additional significant institutional modifications.

1.b.2. The 1999/2001 Constitutional Reform

The **slow implementation** of the Constitution **weakened the Italian institutional system** and the contribution to its development from a pluralistic perspective. The principles enshrined in Article 5 remained largely unimplemented even after two subsequent constitutional amendments aiming to enact them. In the end, by delaying the implementation of those principles the result was to **prevent** the **Regions from fully acting as instruments of democratic participation**. In short, if there was ever a theoretical pattern of federalism at the origins of Italian constitutional history, this model seems to have been lost along the way (D'Atena 1997 at 9).

However, the demand for strengthening local democracy through a process of decentralisation of public decision-making had experienced a special moment in the 1990s. These claims emerged also as a partial reply to the political turmoil of that decade, when the collapse of traditional parties left room for new movements, including those asking for a federal reform and even secession. A first set of countermeasures included some legislative reforms (named after Franco Bassanini, an influential politician and legal scholar) introducing the **principle of subsidiarity** in administrative governance. This principle was seen as capable of supporting an enhancement of the democratic level of participation with a first step towards a wider federalising process - in other words, a Copernican revolution of the entire form of the state.

Article 5 was thus reinterpreted in a *subsidiary-oriented* manner: the **preference for autonomy and decentralisation** clearly expressed by Article 5 was given new life, and with it the value of the closeness of the administration to the citizens.

 © Wolters Kluwer Italia

During those years, it seemed that Italy was on the threshold of a new chapter of regionalism in which the ideals underlying the introduction of the Regions in the Constitution – and therefore also the close link between decentralisation and the democratic principle – could re-emerge in a new and innovative form.

For a few years at least, under the myth of subsidiarity, the flame of constitutional reform rekindled the spirit of the domestic 'federalising process' and its relationship with the democratic principle. However, after the initial enthusiasm waned, the Constitutional Court soon dampened the winds of change by using subsidiarity also as a procedural criterion aimed at reconfirming the national interest of the system rather than favouring local government. Over time, «the principle of subsidiarity and that of differentiation disappear[ed] from circulation» (Bin 2014 at 8).

1.b.3. Regional Form of Government and Legislative Powers in the Constitutional Reforms

Getting to the heart of the reform and analysing the **regional form of government**, the Constitutional Law No. 1/1999 aimed to address the instability of regional executives experienced under the previous regime. This reform established a temporary form of government to be followed by all Regions until the new statutes came into effect. It also outlined the boundaries of regional autonomy in determining its own form of government upon the adoption of the new statute. The room for manoeuvre ended up being extremely limited and the **vast majority of the Regions have adopted a single model**, incorporating the temporary form of government into their statutes, thereby reducing further differentiations.

The President of the Region, together with the regional **council, are elected** through **direct and universal suffrage**. **The President**, once elected, has the authority to **appoint and remove members of the regional executive**. A relationship based on **the vote of confidence** shall exist between the regional government and the council, and this confidence can be revoked at any time through a motivated motion. However, if a motion of no confidence against the President, who was elected through direct and universal suffrage, is approved, it also leads to the dissolution of the regional council. This dissolution follows **the principle *simul stabunt simul cadent*** (they will all stand; they will all fall). Similar consequences arise from the removal, the permanent impediment, the death, the resignation of the President, or the simultaneous resignation of the majority of council members.

Thanks to the new constitutional provisions, the regional form of government achieved its main objective: **stability**. Still, this happened to the detriment of the council and a parallel overall strengthening of the President of the Region. In fact, thanks to direct elections, the latter has acquired his/her own strength, which he/she lacked in the previous system: the President seems nowadays to embody the regional institution resembling a kind of **Governor**, as demonstrated by the recent health emergency due to the COViD-19 pandemic that allowed some Presidents to appear as the only voice of the Region (Fasone/Piccirilli 2022).

Constitutional Law No. 3/2001 considerably reformed the territorial allocation of **legislative powers**. Profoundly changing the original provisions, the new wording of Article 117 begins by listing the same set of limits to legislative power both of the State and the Regions: they have to comply with the principles laid down in the Constitution, with constraints deriving from EU law and with international obligations (see *II.A).3.*).

Under this composite set of limits, Article 117 lists all subject matters falling within the **exclusive legislative powers of the State**, the concurrent legislative powers to be exerted by the State and Regions and the residual powers, belonging to the regional level.

Concurrent legislative power has been redesigned from two different perspectives. The first concerns the specific areas in which regional laws can intervene. If we examine the sectors listed in Article 117, para. 3, it becomes evident that they are particularly important. They cover 20 areas, including – to name a few of the most significant – international and European Union relations; scientific and technological research; education; local governance; communication; major transport and navigation networks; national energy production and distribution; health protection; and labour safety. Many of these fields were not in the previous Article 117 list. It has been critically observed that this catalogue appears to have extended the scope of regional law beyond what was necessary, thus forecasting possible difficulties arising from this new list of competences (Bin 2001 at 619, D'Atena 2003 at 16-17). However, it is important to highlight that the catalogue cannot be given a purely literal interpretation. Instead, it must be interpreted in the context of the entire constitutional framework governing the relationship between the State and the Regions. Against this background, the constitutional reform raises issues concerning the **definition of subject matters** that often required the regulatory and clarifying intervention of the Constitutional Court.

Article 117, para. 4, introduces a new and distinct regional legislative capacity of the Regions: any fields «that are not expressly attributed to the State», and not included in the areas defining concurrent competence have to be considered as attributed to the legislative power of the Regions (**residual competence**). This wording aims at including all the fields that fall outside those which are expressly listed.

 © Wolters Kluwer Italia

The ItCC repeatedly addressed the issue of identifying these **unspecified fields**. The fact that a subject area is not expressly mentioned in either of the two lists included in Article 117, para. 2 (matters falling within the exclusive competence of the State) and para. 3 (concurrent competence) does not automatically classify it as falling under residual competence (Judgment No. 303/2003). In fact, the Court strongly opposed the theory arising from a certain regional activism and legal scholars that, in the absence of state law on certain social phenomena, Regions should have **unlimited legislative powers**. In situations where **unified interests** need protection, state regulations always take precedence over autonomist interests (Judgment No. 362/2003).

1.c. Two Pluralistic Principles and their Dual Nature: Subsidiarity and Regional Autonomy

Having briefly defined the Italian model of regionalism as a way of pursuing democracy and pluralism in the newly founded Republic – together with its contradictory implementation and the following reform – it is now possible to focus on two specific principles informing such regionalism: **the principle of subsidiarity and** that of **regional autonomy**.

The reason behind this choice is clear: they are both closely tied to pluralistic democracy and can be powerful instruments to enhance pluralism, but due to their somewhat **dual nature**, they are also capable of producing the opposite effect, as the cases examined below unequivocally reveal. Not by coincidence the ItCC has been repeatedly called upon to review the constitutionality of the state and regional legislation implementing subsidiarity and territorial autonomy, and the Court's judgments on such matters, which represent a major part of its recent case law, illustrate the complex application of these principles and – more generally – of the equally complex narrative characterising **institutional pluralism** in the Republic.

1.c.1. The Subsidiarity Principle

The principle of subsidiarity is usually presented in two different ways. **Vertical subsidiarity** concerns the distribution of power **among different levels of government** (local, regional and national) and requires that an authority placed on an upper territorial level only performs those functions and tasks that could not be adequately performed at a lower level. It is also labelled as institutional – or territorial – subsidiarity. **Horizontal subsidiarity, on the other hand,** refers to the way in which competences are allocated (or shared) **between public and private actors**. Horizontal subsidiarity is thus also known as *social subsidiarity*.

Despite these different meanings, it is still clear that both vertical and horizontal subsidiarity aim in the abstract to **enhance political and social pluralism**, with the former providing local and regional communities with regulatory and political instruments for their self-government and the latter supporting individual freedom and the organisation of social groups independently of public authorities. Such dimensions of subsidiarity – often mutually interacting – reveal a strong inclination towards a **decentralisation of competences and responsibilities.**

The subsidiarity principle, mainly in its vertical dimension, came to political prominence in Europe particularly after its formal inclusion among the core principles of the European Union in the Maastricht Treaty. As Article 5 TEC (now Article 5(3) TEU) states:

> «In areas which do not fall within its exclusive competence, the Community shall take action, in accordance with the principle of subsidiarity, only if and in so far as the objectives of the proposed action cannot be sufficiently achieved by the Member States and can therefore, by reason of the scale or effects of the proposed action, be better achieved by the Community»

Protocols No. 1 and 2 annexed to the Lisbon Treaty further implement such a principle at the European Union level.

Subsidiarity was entrenched in the Italian Constitution in the 2001 constitutional amendment. The principle was not unknown in Italy before this, however. Law No. 59/1997 on the devolution of administrative functions from the central government to sub-national institutions and governance (so-called Bassanini reform) had already specified, on the one hand, that the exercise of administrative functions should preferably fall within the competence of the authorities that were closest to the citizens (vertical subsidiarity) and, on the other hand, that the devolution of functions should be arranged so that families, associations and communities might also carry out public functions (horizontal subsidiarity). But it was only the constitutional reform which was able to **elevate subsidiarity to a constitutional principle** that is mandatory by law as well as making more consistent the demands for autonomy and decentralisation already outlined and promoted by Article 5 of the Constitution.

Although it now permeates the entirety of Title V of the Constitution, the principle of subsidiarity (in its vertical and horizontal dimensions) is **recognised expressly in Article 118**, which states:

> «administrative functions are attributed to the Municipalities, unless they are attributed to the provinces, metropolitan cities and regions or to the State, pursuant

 © Wolters Kluwer Italia

to the principles of subsidiarity, *differentiation and proportionality*, to ensure their uniform implementation» (para. 1)

and

«the State, regions, metropolitan cities, provinces and municipalities shall promote the autonomous initiatives of citizens, both as individuals and as members of associations, relating to activities of general interest, on the basis of the principle of subsidiarity» (para. 4)

While horizontal subsidiarity is also obviously an important criterion for the allocation of the exercise of public functions also involving private actors – for instance, of the roles played by families, non-governmental organisations or voluntary associations in key sectors such as education and care – the following brief analysis focuses on the vertical dimension of subsidiarity alone as a specific expression of the institutional pluralism with which this Section primarily aims to deal.

From the wording of Article 118, para. 1, it may be mainly inferred that a) **vertical subsidiarity** exclusively refers (at least textually) to the exercise of **administrative functions**; b) **municipalities**, being the governmental layer that is closest to citizens, are the authorities **preferably charged** with the exercise of administrative tasks; c) only the need for **uniform implementation** of administrative functions can justify moving the exercise of the latter to **a higher territorial level**; and d) subsidiarity is considered alongside the **principles of differentiation and proportionality** (more precisely, **adequacy**, in the Italian case). Differentiation recognizes that administrative authorities, while belonging to the same governmental level, can differ with regard to their demographic and structural features and therefore they can be treated differently. Adequacy implies an assessment of the real ability of the local authorities to exercise the function that they are required to perform. Article 118, para. 1, further develops the constitutional design already entrenched in Article 5, balancing the promotion of autonomy and decentralisation and the need for ensuring unity and uniformity.

As a matter of fact, subsidiarity, differentiation and adequacy make the distribution of competences **more elastic**, depending on a functional assessment of effectiveness carried out **on a case-by-case basis**. Moreover, they jointly work 'as a lift', as they are capable of guiding the transfer of competence from one level to another. Accordingly, the principle of subsidiarity introduces a «type of governance-based form of government» whose main characteristic is «a network of the levels of government instead of the division of powers among them» (PALERMO 2005 at 191).

Nonetheless, it is worth highlighting that in the landmark Judgment No. 303/2003, the Constitutional Court – despite the wording of Article 118, para. 1 – applied this principle to the **legislative division of powers** between the State and Regions, as well. In this judgment, the Court clearly stated that although Article 118 provides for the application of the principle of subsidiarity exclusively to the exercise of administrative functions, **the attraction of subsidiarity** to the national level inevitably also has consequences for the exercise of legislative competences. In fact, **the principle of legality** necessitates that the exercise of administrative functions is regulated and organised by a law. Therefore, if administrative functions are performed by the state, the regulatory act must be national as well. Herein lies the dual nature of the principle: although it was introduced to enhance local autonomy, as a result of its 'ascensional aptitude' (GROPPI/SCATTONE 2006 at 136), subsidiarity can end up working as a centralising mechanism able to erode regional powers, thus revealing some **unintended consequences** capable of limiting in practice the role of regional governments.

In the light of the above, one might even wonder whether subsidiarity is effectively able to foster the development of a «type of governance-based form of government» (PALERMO/WILSON 2014 at 519). However, in the same Judgment No. 303/2003, in order to protect regional and local autonomy, the Constitutional Court emphasized that when national laws encroach upon regional competences through subsidiarity, the implementation of cooperative procedures between the State and the Regions becomes necessary. These procedures aim to engage all relevant stakeholders in negotiations and achieve mutual agreements. After all, such procedural mechanisms of conciliation may partially compensate for the recentralising inclination of subsidiarity and restore a network of different levels of government that could properly work together. However, the concrete evolution of the implementation of the principle of subsidiarity provides a further example of those ups and downs of regionalism previously highlighted.

1.c.2. Pluralism and Regionalism in the Italian Constitutional Framework: Autonomy at Stake

Now, let's shift the focus to another essential principle that deserves considerable attention – regional autonomy. In exploring this principle, we find parallels with the earlier discussed concept of subsidiarity showcasing a similar dualistic nature. Indeed, the principle of autonomy operates on a twofold dimension as well. In this regard, the ItCC case law has shown that the relationship between

 © Wolters Kluwer Italia

regional autonomy and democratic pluralism is a thorny issue and that, in the Court's interpretation of the entire constitutional design, one could even distinguish between a sort of **good and bad autonomy** depending on its impact on pluralism and democracy.

To begin with, on the one hand Article 5 firmly states **the unity and indivisibility** of the Republic but, on the other, recognizes and promotes local autonomy and a**dministrative decentralisation** as one of the republic's most important tasks. The role and place of local government authorities in fostering pluralism and democracy, together with the principle of unity and indivisibility of the Republic, represents a remarkable feature of the Italian Constitution. The ItCC supported this interpretation arguing in several judgments that **local communities** – especially the Regions – in Italian legal system are «fixed reference points for its **democratic fabric**» (among many others, see Judgment No. 365/1990). Their function, as an expression of pluralism, is to enact and strengthen constitutional democracy, which is first and foremost a *pluralistic democracy* (see Judgment No. 453/1989). In this light, autonomy is an essential element of democracy, whose implementation may improve the quality of democracy in term of citizens' involvement and responsibility.

Nonetheless, on several occasions, the ItCC declared unconstitutional regional legislative acts claiming for more autonomy. At stake there were the regional attempts to assert the sovereignty of the Region (Sardinia - Judgment No. 365/2003), for a consultative referendum on independence (Veneto-Judgment No. 118/2015) and for the establishment of a regional «Parliament» instead of a regional «assembly» (Liguria - Judgment No. 106/2002; Marche - Judgment No. 306/2003). The ItCC struck down the legislative acts of the latter because the word "parliament" usually refers to the national representative assembly, while the former were declared unconstitutional because it aimed as qualifying the Region as sovereign. Moreover, in the case of Veneto, the attempt was also to raise the regional flag in public offices within the Region and to classify the *Veneto people* as a national minority.

The ItCC these legislative acts declared unconstitutional primarily because the four Regions claimed the sovereignty of the regional people but also showed a desire to display the flag as symbol of this sovereignty. Hence, the ItCC declared the unconstitutionality of the legislation for the violation of the principle of sovereignty, which belongs to the State. The main reason lies in the fact that sovereignty indicates that the State has an unlimited power that has not been empowered by a superior authority (Troper 2012), and thus, the legal and political order is not created by another and it is original. Consequently, the regional power being devolved by the State, the ItCC declared unconstitutional all the regional legislative acts that were challenged by the national government.

The result of this jurisprudence is a confirmation that the quest for **sovereignty** by subnational entities is a *taboo* in regional states. Sovereignty as an unlimited and original power is **an exclusive attribute of State**, while the regional level of government has been provided for by the Constitution and is implemented by the State itself.

An additional feature to take into account is the difference between federal and regional models, which does not lie in the **quantitative criteria** of the vertical division of powers between their constituent parts, but rather in the **qualitative features** of the latter. As **derivative** – and not original – orders, Regions can only enjoy autonomy (even a potentially strong, or special, status) and not sovereignty. The latter can only be vested in the State. Accordingly, any regional claim for sovereignty is void in a regional State like Italy.

The ItCC was guided by this reasoning, especially in Judgment No. 365/2007 concerning the Sardinian attempt to create an *ad hoc* council with the task of drafting a new statute for the autonomy and sovereignty of the Sardinian people. According to the Court, Sardinia aimed at identifying a sort of regional sovereignty. Therefore, the traditional concept of sovereignty as originality – as explained above – was used in the judgment to **distinguish federal from regional systems** and to justify the different legal statuses accorded to the State and the Regions by the Constitution, as well as to declare the unconstitutionality of the regional claim.

In the other decisions, however, the Court's reasoning appeared to be more nuanced and more focused on the domestic constitutional fabric, rather than on the issue of sovereignty/originality. Put differently, the non-originality of the Regions was not the main reason for quashing the regional claims in the majority of the judgments mentioned above. In fact, the same ItCC plainly admitted that in qualifying both the State and local autonomies as constituent parts of the Republic, Article 114 of the Constitution reveals that they share a **common origin**, both stemming from the democratic principle (Judgment No. 106/2002). Accordingly, the Court suggested that popular sovereignty can unfold and develop **in many instances and places**, not only in the State, but also in the Regions and local autonomies. In a nutshell, the Court proved to be more concerned with the identification of the people as the supreme authority of the system – popular sovereignty – than discussing sovereignty as originality. Moreover, it may be added that since popular sovereignty can be exercised at a regional level as well, such a declination of sovereignty may not be per se a reason for the unconstitutionality of the regional law at stake. Despite this, the Court declared such laws unconstitutional, most likely because, in the Court's opinion, **the regional claims for autonomy were not all expressions of pluralism**. In addition, a subsequent

 © Wolters Kluwer Italia

question is related to when and under what conditions may an autonomy claim be considered as an instrument of pluralism and a legitimate expression of popular sovereignty.

In this regard it is helpful to recall the ItCC Judgment No. 118/2015, which declared unconstitutional the Veneto Law No. 16/2014 that called for a consultative referendum in order to establish the wishes of the voters of Veneto concerning the following question: «Do you want Veneto to become an independent and sovereign Republic? Yes, or No?». The ItCC firmly stated that a given referendum was inherently contrary to «the **founding principles of the unity and indivisibility of the Republic** laid down in Article 5 of the Constitution». Furthermore, although pluralism and autonomy are constitutional principles, the Court argued that they «cannot be taken to extremes so as to result in the **fragmentation of the legal order** and cannot be invoked as justification for initiatives [...] concerning prospective secession». In the Judgment No. 81/2018, the Court declared unconstitutional the Regional Law No. 28/2016 that classified the Veneto people as a national minority because the population of a Region «cannot, on this basis alone, be categorised as a 'national minority', separate from the majority of the people», as the principle of unity and indivisibility enshrined in Article 5 prevents conceiving of the Republic as 'a material sum of minorities'. In other words, regional communities cannot result in «a division of the people into its unlikely fraction». Lastly, in the Judgment No. 183/2018, on Veneto's legislation on the regional flag, the Court acknowledged that the regional competence to define the Region's own symbols lies within the principle of autonomy enshrined in Article 5. Accordingly, the power to choose the distinguishing symbols of the regional identity «must be considered to be a core element of the region's self-government power». However, it firmly stated that a joint interpretation of Articles 5 and 12 on the national flag elevates the Italian flag «to the status of a symbol of national unity». In fact, while no longer representing the emblem of territorial sovereignty of the State within the plural democracy outlined by the Constitution, the flag has become «an instrument for identification by the Nation with its own State».

As a consequence, the Court declared unconstitutional the Veneto law only insofar as it introduced an obligation for State buildings in the geographical area of the region to display the regional flag alongside the national flag, because according to a combined reading of Articles 5 and 12, «the State may not be forced under regional legislation to use publicly any symbols [...] which the Constitution does not allow to be considered as symbolic of the entire national community».

The few examples reported above clearly reveal the key elements of the Court's reasoning: the principles of the unity and indivisibility of the Republic, which also implies the **unity of the people**. The latter may also be a valuable tool in interpreting the principle of popular sovereignty that according to Article 1 «shall belong to the people» and «shall be exercised by the people in the forms and within the limits of this Constitution». The unity of the people does not refer to the homogeneity, but to the opposite, to a **plural nature of the people** as well, where different opinions and identities may be promoted and protected. In this regard, the Constitution embodies **common and fundamental values** that are shared by different identities. In fact, the ItCC highlighted the importance of «the *bonds of solidarity* between the regional population and the rest of the Republic» within the constitutional design and how indispensable it is «to guarantee cohesion and solidarity within the Republic» (Judgment No. 118/2015).

Therefore, it has been argued, **autonomy is an instrument of pluralism** to be protected and strengthened as long as the system can derive unity from the diversity of its components (ItCC, Judgment No. 183/2018). Claims for greater autonomy could appear, *vice versa*, as a sign of separateness, self-containment, non-involvement and indifference to the other parts of the Republic. The threat is that of **fragmentation and division**, which make the Republic «a material sum of minorities». This is the border beyond which claims for autonomy cease to be an instrument for pluralism and democracy and become unconstitutional demands. In this sense, it is possible to distinguish between good and bad autonomy.

Both subsidiarity and autonomy – as implemented in the regional system – are **two-faced Janus principles**: one face is pluralist; the other is not. The functioning of the non-pluralistic face of the principles is quite different: subsidiarity can re-centralise the exercise of attribution previously decentralised, while autonomy can produce separation and fragmentation. But both reveal, on the one hand, the ongoing uncertainty characterising the Italian regional form of state and, on the other, the role that the ItCC, as a consequence, keeps playing in shaping the constitutional design.

2. Political and Social Pluralism: Political Parties and Trade Unions

2.a. Pluralism, Democracy, and Political Parties

Article 49 of the Constitution states that «[a]ny citizen shall have the right to freely establish political parties in order to contribute to the development of national policies through the democratic process». From a subjective standpoint, this norm limits the right to associate in political parties to citizens alone. Yet, both constitutional and ordinary case law has ensured the right to join political movements, excluding holding executive roles, to foreigners and stateless persons as well (e.g., Judgment No. 422/1995). Moreover, Article 98, para. 3, establishes that «[t]he law may set limitations on the right to become members of political parties in the case of magistrates, serving military staff, law enforcement

 © Wolters Kluwer Italia

officers, and diplomatic and consular representatives abroad». It is therefore the individual and not the association itself that determines national politics: citizens can actively participate in political life by deciding general policies, primarily **through the parties** to which they belong (see Judgments Nos. 43/1961, 16/1978 and, more recently, 1/2014).

In any case, Article 49, read together with Articles 2, 18 and 39 of the Constitution, places political groups at the cornerstone of democratic pluralism and qualifies parties as the main vehicle for people's political participation. The framers of the Italian Constitution saw parties as necessary instruments to intermediate, bring together and coordinate the multiple interests that inherently characterise every pluralistic society and recognised that they hold the key role in making Parliament vital and effective. In this respect, parties have to **connect civil society and institutions** by indicating a clear political direction that strengthens parliamentarianism and democracy. Political groups are «what democracy needs to keep itself alive as a political ideal» (Duverger 1961 at 43). They are, therefore, «nothing less than the channels through which the legal system links the right of citizens to express institutionally the plurality of the political views of a society with the principle of representation» (ItCC, Judgment No. 76/2007). To do this, they should not be small, unstructured movements expressing personal ambitions, but **well-structured and solid formations,** based on common beliefs and inspired by legitimate interests, which have to collect and summarise the broadest needs of a political community (Clementi 2019)

This was, in a nutshell, the assumption that dominated the debate in the Constituent Assembly on the role and functions of parties in modern states. According to the drafters of the Constitution, it would have been illusory even to imagine that a democratic regime could function **without political parties**. The constitutional relevance of political movements therefore represented a significant innovation justified not only by the historical development of the legal system – given that fascism, and totalitarian regimes in general, prohibited associating in parties – but also by the democratic nature of the Republic, essentially built on popular sovereignty.

Of course, all these aspects are **strictly linked to elections** that are at the heart of every democratic and pluralistic legal system (see above, *I.B).2.*). Voting connects individuals with public authorities and allows citizens to participate – directly or indirectly – in public functions. It is therefore through the vote that the uninterrupted **chain of democratic legitimacy** is primarily preserved, guaranteeing the derivation of authority from the people, and thus ensuring democracy despite the presence of different ideological conceptions. From a pluralistic perspective, marked by the systemic need to give voice to all corners of society,

© Wolters Kluwer Italia

one of the most significant aspects related to the right to vote concerns Italian citizenship as a requirement for exercising active electoral rights (Hine 1993 at 73). Here, the crucial question is whether **in contemporary multi-ethnic societies** with a constant and stable presence of foreigners it is still fair to exclude legal residents of a state from the possibility of expressing their personal political beliefs and orienting public decision through the vote (see *IV.A).3.d.*).

2.a.1. The Democratic Process Clause

Article 49 did not institutionalise the role of political movements in the new democratic legal order. Rather, it opted for a sort of **intermediate solution** that did not qualify parties as public bodies. Actually, the Constitution neither solved the problem concerning the *legal status* of political parties nor clarified the question related to their internal democratic structure in order to avoid creating divisions between the various ideological components of the Constituent Assembly (Sartori 2005 at 121). Against this background, political parties are not considered branches of government, they are non-recognised civil society organisations with full freedom of thought and association. Despite their **private nature**, political movements undoubtedly play a constitutional role, and parties are to be considered full-fledged private agents holding public office and influencing the concrete action of state bodies. Consistent with this approach, party structure is almost exclusively left to the agreements made between members, and, in particular, to the **statutes** that determine its internal organs, functioning, rights and duties of its members as well as the aims and purposes of the entire association,

This specific element reinforces the constitutional stipulation regarding the **democratic process** that must be followed by political parties in exercising their activities. From Article 49, and even from the debate within the Constituent Assembly, it plainly emerges that the Constitution does not refer to the internal organisation of parties, but exclusively considers their external relations with other movements. The rule contained in this provision was in fact approved following a demanding political pact made among the framers of the Constitution, according to which effective respect for the democratic process clause would be entrusted to the same political parties, finding its guarantee only in the existence of a **wide pluralism**. In this sense, the conditions required by the Constitution focus above all on the greatest possible extension of the sphere of freedom both to the party and the individuals within it «to contribute to the development of national policies through the democratic process» (Article 49) by giving voice to the plurality of instances and positions present in the society, each with their own specificity.

 © Wolters Kluwer Italia

Consequently, and in order to guarantee their autonomy and pluralism as much as possible, the drafters of the Constitution did not intend to subject political parties to state control. Nor is there any law governing party activities or organisation. In this regard, the Constituent Assembly believed that the **public regulation** of the internal democracy of political groups would risk giving rise to conflict. External supervision was gradually abandoned, essentially because of the fear of interfering with the autonomy of **minority movements**. But this choice also further reinforced the pluralistic approach that the Constitution by and large adopted towards parties. As a matter of fact, political associations are not only able to freely express their vision of society, but they can also organise themselves at their convenience, reaching more effectively the aims decided by their members and supporters (Judgment No. 79/2006).

Regulating associations that structurally need to be **flexible** enough to ensure pluralism of the highest degree is a considerably important problem, if only because it is necessary to balance the private and social nature of parties with the public functions they exercise. However, to ensure compliance with external democratic conditions at least, the parties wishing to take advantage of tax breaks for private contributions or to submit lists of candidates for the elections in the Chamber of Deputies are required to adopt a **public statute**. This document must contain certain essential elements prescribed by law in terms of the party's internal democracy and transparency towards the voters. Some limited forms of control of parties' internal organisation have been provided for in Laws Nos. 515/1993, 28/2000, and 156/2002 on political funding, which imposed limits on electoral expenses and other public contributions.

In the wake of the second party crisis at the turn of 2011-2012, Law No. 96/2012 set out a substantial reduction in reimbursements and required stricter controls on the use of public funds. This new regulation started with the clear wording of the constitutional provision concerning the democratic process clause, declaring for the first time that parties must respect the principles of pluralism in their **internal organisation** with regard above all to the choice of candidates, protection of minorities, transparency, and members' rights.

2.b.1. Anti-system Parties and Transitional and Final Provision XII

In accordance with the highly pluralistic framework of the Constitution, and given the **non-militant** character of our democracy, no limits on the ideological nature of political parties were set. The only exception is to be found in provision XII of the Constitution, which forbids reorganising «under any form whatsoever, the dissolved Fascist party», as specified in Law No. 645/1952 as amended by Law No. 152/1975.

Notwithstanding Article 48, this rule additionally imposed temporary restrictions on voting rights and eligibility for leaders associated with the fascist regime. This means that a party built around a subversive ideology can still play a fully active role in the political arena as long as its activities remain respectful of the **democratic principle** and embrace the logic behind every representative legal system, such as those of free elections, the rejection of violence, and more generally, the idea of operating fairly and transparently. The drafters of the Constitution did not introduce any generic obligation to be faithful to the values underlying the republican legal order, in contrast to the contemporary German Constitution for example. What can easily be deduced is thus a **general trust in the pluralistic process** as an instrument of political confrontation, «which can include in a free dialectical opposition even those parties that do not recognise themselves in the principles of the republican Constitution» (Judgments nos. 1/1957 and 254/1974).

While the Constituent Assembly aimed at safeguarding democracy against the deterioration of pluralism, the purpose of Article 49 must be identified as the protection of the widest and freest political dialogue between different ideas, and the **mutual recognition and legitimation** of parties in the framework of a varied society. In essence, the Constitution aims to gradually include even anti-system parties into the democratic framework. For this reason, it embraces a project of **open democracy** not imposing adherence to constitutional values but rather *to fairness* in public life. This overall long-term plan points precisely at creating a **tolerant political system** within which those accepting the method (but not necessarily the contents and values) of democracy can always compete (Judgments nos. 74/1958, 15/1973).

Within this context, provision XII constitutes a **derogation** from the principle of pluralism, which by contrast postulates a complete political representation of society. It is an exception to the freedom of association and, therefore, it is **an extraordinary provision** that must be **strictly interpreted** and oriented exclusively towards the nature of the objectives pursued by the parties. It follows that a norm of this kind cannot constitute the legal basis for restricting fundamental rights other than freedom of association – first and foremost freedom of thought – without any **proven connection in the case of the reorganisation of** the Fascist party. That is, the provision demonstrates the clear will of the Constituent Assembly to refer to anti-fascism as the ideological substratum common to all political forces emerging during World War II. The introduction of **a symbolic element of unity** precisely provided the new parties with a substantial legitimacy within the framework of a non-homogeneous society. From this perspective, provision XII may constitute a sort of *grundnorm* defining the **anti-fascist paradigm of the Constitution** and informing every part of the constitutional text. It equips

 © Wolters Kluwer Italia

the republican legal order with the values of democracy, equality, dignity of the person and international openness. Yet, from it emerges the intention to reject – courageously enough, given the historical background – the model of a *militant* democracy.

2.b. Political Parties in Italy: The Progressive Dissolution of the Constitutional Model

Until the beginning of the 1990s, the Italian political system developed around two main parties **without any real change of government**, referred to as the so-called *conventio ad excludendum*. The presence of anti-systemic groups made the ideological space extremely polarised, and divergences between parties on the extreme right and extreme left led to **more moderate governmental positions** in order to preserve the **establishment** (JONES/PASQUINO 2015)

However, the last decades of the twentieth century saw a considerable growth in social complexity. Interests have multiplied, creating conflicts within once unified political groups, and social classes have lost their typical moderating function. Alongside the crisis of ideologies, political movements have struggled to provide individuals with a **common sense of belonging**. What is more, judicial inquiries into bribery, particularly those conducted during the mid-1990s – i.e., *Tangentopoli* or Bribesville – consistently speeded up this **process of dissolution**. As a result, traditional parties have less capacity to offer a political synthesis of different voices and thus formulate specific claims, and participation noticeably changed in form (LEPRE 1993).

In this renewed context, class-based parties fragmented, shifting from sustaining general interests to supporting particular instances, and ultimately failing in their long-established role of socio-political negotiator. Hence, the model of political parties that animated the Constitution in the first phase of the Republic **progressively disintegrated**. The huge mass parties founded between the two world wars disappeared, and the progressive loss of common values easily disrupted political formations that once relied on strong and universal ideals (e.g., the Communist Party or Christian Democracy). The latter – along with the problem concerning the decay in the quality of the political class and the choice of the political representatives – further exacerbated the detachment already in place between society and the party system, finally spreading an extensive anti-political sentiment (CROUCH 2019).

More specifically, after *Tangentopoli*, new political forces emerged with the aim of **reorganising the Italian political landscape**. Among these parties, Forza Italia, a centre-right movement, initially sought to capitalise on public dissatisfaction with the corrupt traditional political movements. During the same period, the Lega Nord gave voice to the autonomist and federalist demands of northern Italy, while Alleanza Nazionale (AN) represented the post-fascist area of Italian politics. Later, Fratelli d'Italia replaced AN on the right-wing of the political spectrum. Another significant anti-establishment political force that emerged in the early 2010s was the Movimento 5 Stelle (Five Stars Movement), which positioned itself as one of the main populist entities. It promoted citizen participation through instruments of direct democracy – particularly e-democracy – and openly fought against political corruption. Since then, the Italian political landscape has been characterised by a certain degree of **fragmentation**, with numerous parties and coalitions taking turns in power. Alliances and political formations have changed over the years, but the memory of Bribesville has left a significant imprint on Italian political dynamics, leading to a heightened focus on public ethics (CHIARAMONTE/EMANUELE 2022, RUSSO/VERGETTI 2023).

Beyond the various definitions and unquestionable differences existing between the models, these new organisational forms share **an inter-class character**, and the political lines their leaders adopt frequently change. Political groups today try to intercept the rapid change of societal interests by grabbing as many voters as possible from every social class. This tendency is even reinforced by the possibility of autonomously selecting the candidates in the elections, since the representatives will be forced to act as they are expected to by the leaders who chose them. This approach, of course, denies **the classical role** that parties have to perform within a pluralistic society. If they become ideologically interchangeable and devoid of any *social glue*, political movements will no longer be able to collect, bring together and transform particular claims into sufficiently general, stable, and homogeneous interests. **This inadequacy** of modern parties to ensure political stability also has repercussions for representative bodies, as they are organised on a largely unpredictable and inconsistent basis, which inevitably leads to inefficient administration and triggers debates on hypothetical reforms of the constitutional system (COTTA/VERZICHELLI 2007).

In a pluralistic democracy, however, **the function of parties is still irreplaceable** (ItCC, Judgment No. 84/1989). More broadly, the recognition of individual freedoms (e.g., opinion, assembly, and association) constitutes the prerequisite for effectively exercising the right to vote. Meeting, discussing, and expressing informed opinions in order to compare different views allows for the formation of a position that can be expressed in political choices. Nevertheless, free political decisions are possible only if parties reinterpret diverse social interests with a certain degree of homogeneity by allowing citizens to consciously exercise their participatory right. There is thus a very close relation between **political parties, sovereignty and democracy**. If the essence of democracy results in the

 © Wolters Kluwer Italia

inviolable principle of popular sovereignty, parties will have to act as the means that make particular views into sufficiently general interests, thereby connecting public decisions and individual choices, and in this way putting pluralism into effect (Pasquino 2009 at 282).

2.c. Trade Unions: Pluralism in the Workplaces

Freedom of association in a pluralist context finds another significant corollary in the **freedom to form trade unions**. To this end, Article 39, para. 1, of the Constitution states that «trade unions may be freely established», thus explicitly affirming their pluralism. This provision openly contrasts with the single or unique model of unionism – typical of fascist corporatism – and creates practical conditions for a variety of movements to be present in the same manufacturing sector. According to the freedom of trade union principle, the Italian legal system must accord **the same set of rights to all trade unions** acting in a specific production area. Furthermore, the Republic must guarantee minimum conditions for these groups to protect the professional interests of a freely determined association of workers (Judgments nos. 1/1960, 309/1997 and 353/1993).

Against this background, the freedom of trade unions – both in its individual and collective dimension – serves a more general project of social democracy based on the recognition of pluralism and political opposition as instruments of **emancipation and empowerment** of the weakest subjects. Article 39 attributes to trade unions the main function of mediating between different societal interests and bringing them to a more general level. From this standpoint, in the workplace trade unions perform a role quite similar to that which is played by parties in the Italian society. Both of these associations in fact collect, bring together and represent in the public arena the various requests of citizens and workers, thereby strengthening the pluralistic background of our legal system through a **constant dialectic between different societal components**.

Together with other constitutional provisions – and in particular with the right to strike and principle of substantive equality – Article 39 affirms the **freedom of citizen-workers** and tends to remove those obstacles of an economic or social nature, which constrain freedom and equality. Such norms basically aim to **rebalance the positions of** those considered **disadvantaged** (i.e., between workers and employers, female workers and male workers and minors and non-minors) not only through principles that commit the legislator to implementing rules but also through constitutional provisions that are directly applicable (Judgments Nos. 70/1963 and 268/1994). On the one hand, every worker can form or join trade unions inside and outside of the workplace; they can also carry out all related and preparatory activities to protect the professional interests of an identified group.

Furthermore, pluralism of trade unions also includes the freedom to be part of any organisation **without suffering any kind of discrimination**. On the other hand, the employer must not only allow the exercise of such freedoms but also make the right itself **effective**, by taking concrete action and putting in place all the necessary measures (Judgments nos. 106/1962, 34/1985 and 344/1996).

The Constitution requires trade unions to establish their internal organisation **on a democratic basis**, which would enhance their **representative character**, and to register at local or central offices. By means of this registration, trade unions are transformed from *de facto* organisations into associations with **legal personality**. What is more, registered associations are also capable of signing collective labour agreements with legal effect for all workers belonging to the category affected by the contract. The Constituent Assembly conceived of trade unions (both for workers and employers) as playing a fundamental role in defining working conditions through **collective bargaining**. Consequently, these organisations became real **political actors** that are regularly consulted by the government on legislative provisions concerning work.

The freedom of trade unions also received a significant boost following the approval of the so-called **Workers' Statute** (Law No. 300/1970), which grants not only individual workers but also trade unions a whole series of rights to be exercised within the workplace, such as the right to carry out propaganda and proselytism, the right to assembly, and the right to undertake trade union activities. Accordingly, it also punishes anti-union conduct adopted by employers. In particular, the statute implicitly guarantees the freedom of trade unions to develop their contents, and it sets out pluralism as a form of social autonomy **not predetermined in its ends** or objectives. Law No. 300/1970, therefore, officially incorporated trade unions into the workplace by attributing to them a particular importance on the level of private relationships and more precisely towards the employers. In this way, workers become able to define a variety of aspects of their employment relationships, their different needs and their political ideologies on the basis of their specific context.

The regime envisaged by Article 39 remained **practically unimplemented** for a number of reasons including the distrust on the part of a large number of trade unions of any form of control by public authorities on their internal organisation; the high degree of unionisation; and the existence of very small trade unions that would have lost their power of veto. The constitutional provision appeared **too rigid** to contain the flexible contractual and social dynamics of trade unions within the pluralistic Italian environment. As a result, the law that should have regulated registering procedures was never approved, and trade unions are still

 © Wolters Kluwer Italia

non-recognised associations that can stipulate collective labour agreements limited only to the contracting parties, i.e. the members of the associations that sign them. Their effectiveness is thus no different from that of normal private law contracts. Despite this condition, the strong representativeness of the stipulating trade unions and some decisions adopted by the Constitutional Court have often given an *erga omnes* application to the **collective labour agreements** (see, in particular, ItCC, Judgments Nos. 105/1969, 124/1991 and 51/2015).

Actually, **their lack of legal personality** further enhances the freedom of trade unions, as the State cannot exercise any control that is not strictly limited to the lawfulness of the aims pursued, which, from this point of view, also **strengthens pluralism**. Since it is not possible for the legislator to establish in advance the binding requirements to qualify a trade union, the group that constitutes it can be determined on the basis of various reasons, including ideological, cultural, and professional ones. In the national legal system, then, there are federal unions, autonomous unions, and unions affiliated with different federations. Furthermore, those belonging to the so-called triad of the most important trade unions (CGIL, CISL and UIL) are expressions of **different political ideologies** – communist, socialist, and Catholic – which originally constituted the three building blocks of unionism.

Nonetheless, in the national labour market, the dominant paradigm is still represented by associations of workers organised by **productive sectors** or branches of industry. On the basis of this model, trade unions aim at protecting the interests of those workers who are employed in the same manufacturing area regardless of the duties they perform. For example, FIOM-CGIL, FIM-CISL and UILM-UIL are three confederate trade unions that associate all workers, such as blue-collar workers, employers, and executives operating in the metalworking field. Less widespread, but still extremely important in some specific industrial sectors, are trade unions that bring together all the workers who exercise a **particular profession**. These associations have been established in production areas where traditional unionism was considered not able to fully represent the interests of certain categories, such as air traffic controllers, bus driver, or managers of trade unions.

In recent times, however, because of the economic crisis of 2008 and the subsequent widespread insecurity affecting the labour market, **the classic model of representation ended** and **new forms of trade unionism arose** in order to protect the interests of skilled workers on the basis of both their contractual type and the companies that employed them. It was precisely to meet the needs of these subjects that the large federations left room for **new organisations** with the specific purpose of **protecting atypical employees**, by reducing their salary gap and defending their rights in a context of noticeable job mobility (see, for example,

Riders Union or Deliverance, regarding riders; Acta, regarding freelance; Baule in Piazza, Cresco, or Scena Unita, regarding entertainers)

Within the same company, **several trade unions can coexist**. Some of these unions represent the workers' interests in specific productive sectors and are distinguished by the different federations to which they belong. Others represent workers with different job roles, even within the same professional category.

3. Religious Pluralism: Religious Denominations in the Italian Constitution

3.a. Religious Matters in a Plural Society

Today it is undeniable that religious issues are at the centre of a delicate political and juridical debate in Italy as well as in all European states. There is no need to underline that the **migration flows** and **demographic changes** have pressed for new policy responses to the **increasing cultural and religious diversity** of Europe. This being so, religious diversity is growing but this statement is not *per se* synonymous with the achievement of religious pluralism. On the contrary, the guarantee of a plural religious environment is currently one of the most difficult tests for a democratic system. Therefore, religion (still) matters, and the Constitution makes an important contribution to bringing together religion, pluralism and democracy.

The Constitution covers both the **relationship between the State and religious denominations**, as outlined in Articles 7 and 8, and the extensive guarantee of **freedom of worship** foreseen in Article 19, according to which «anyone is entitled to freely profess their religious belief in any form, individually or with others and to promote them and celebrate rites in public or in private, provided they are not offensive to public morality». Article 20 is usually read together with the principle of non-discrimination and Article 8, since it requires that «no special limitation or tax burden shall be imposed on the establishment, legal capacity or activities of any organisation on the ground of its religious nature or its religious or confessional goals».

If these are the main provisions governing religious issues, current constitutional law meets the religious question through the prism of secularism (*laicità*), characterised by its own peculiar features, as will be analysed in the following paragraphs. This well-established principle stemming from the Constitutional Court case law represents a paramount framework for approaching religious issues in the constitutional setting. On the surface, this principle refers to different key elements of this field, such as state **impartiality and equidistance** with regard to religious matters, the **separation of church and State** (as specified by the autonomy of their legal orders) and a **concordat regime** to prevent conflicts

 © Wolters Kluwer Italia

between the two institutions. State impartiality and equidistance represents the very foundation of religious pluralism: even if it has been interpreted in many ways across the European landscape, our model has been studied as a unique one – the so-called '*laïcité à l'italienne*' – thus pointing to a specific reading within our legal system.

The following sections will therefore analyse the **two basic principles** governing the field of religion in the Italian Constitution: **the concordat system** – considered from the point of view of both the Lateran Pacts and the agreements with other religious denominations – and **the nature of Italian form of State**, defined as '*laico*'. Finally, some sensitive issues concerning the freedoms of religion and conscience will be analysed through the lens of pluralism.

3.b. The Unique Relationship between the State and the Catholic Church

3.b.1. The Religious Peace Debate in the Constituent Assembly

A study of the relationship between the State and the Catholic Church inevitably comes up against one of the most controversial parts of Italian history. Article 7 outlines the special treatment of the religion of the majority – Catholicism – within the legal system. Not surprisingly, this provision has been considered the real battlefield that divided Italian Constituents, and its wording clearly reflects the political debates surrounding its approval. Indeed, **the legal status of the Catholic Church** within the nascent Constitution was one of the most delicate political problems faced from both a domestic and an international standpoint.

It is clearly not possible here to retrace the ups and downs of the relationship between church and State in the nineteenth and twentieth centuries. In order to understand Article 7, however, it is necessary to recall, even if only briefly, certain defining moments in Italian history starting from the unification and the annexation of the Papal States during the Kingdom of Italy (17th of March, 1861). Not coincidentally, the main argument debated in the Constituent Assembly on this issue was the achievement of *religious peace*: but what kind of peace were they referring to?

While it is true that Italy did not experience the wars of religion typical of other European countries, the dispute began with the political unification and when Rome was declared the capital of the new Kingdom (even though the city was then part of the State of the Church).

The quest for religious peace alludes to the controversial relations between the State and the Catholic Church during the liberal period (from the mid-nineteenth century to the early twentieth century), subsumed under the label of the Roman Question (*questione romana*).

In the first article of the Albertine Statute (1848), Catholicism was recognised as the **State religion**, thus confirming the decision to create a confessional State, although freedom of religion was granted for all existing forms of worship, in conformity with the law. However, despite this theoretical framework extending *favour* to the Catholic denomination, this special treatment was **largely contradicted** by several laws adopted unilaterally by the State, such as the Sineo Act (Law No. 735/1848) that abolished all privileges for those who professed the Catholic faith and recognised the equality of all citizens.

It has thus been observed that although the wording of Article 1 of the Albertine Statute on the Catholic faith as State religion was still valid, the State «had not hesitated to sacrifice the interests of the Catholic Church whenever it was necessary to support, directly or indirectly, a national interest, such as the political unity of the country» (Lariccia 1991 at 2; Elia 2008 at 5). The State and the Catholic Church had a multifaceted and nuanced relationship extending beyond the legal provisions governing it. This contrast was resolved many years later by the Fascist regime. **The Lateran Treaty** reaffirmed Article 1 of the Albertine Statute on the Catholic State religion and was signed by Pius XI and Mussolini. But even in this case, a superficial reading of the provision does not fully take into account the intentions of either the Fascist government or the Catholic Church, or the complexity of the historical period in which the Treaty was signed (Margiotta Broglio 1966).

In the meanwhile, what happened in **Italy was not an isolated case**: in the same period, several European countries with strong Catholic majorities, affected by political crises that led to authoritarian forms of government, opted for concordat regimes. While the concordat was signed in 1929, similar pacts were signed in Austria and Germany in 1933, in Portugal in 1940 and in Spain in 1953 (following different agreements from 1941 on). Therefore, **the concordat system became the model most frequently adopted** to govern the Church's relationship with the State in Europe and is still applied in the Italian legal order today.

Not surprisingly, therefore, the position conferred to the Lateran Pacts within the Constitution soon became a thorny issue in the Constituent Assembly. This brief historical outline allows to better understand why the constituent process represented **a unique opportunity** for the Catholic Church – and, more generally, for Catholics – to re-enter, in a non-conflictual manner, a previously closed (during the liberal period) or at least controversial (during the Fascist period and World War II) political territory. In this regard, even if the concordat signed by Mussolini did not represent the best possible solution for the Roman Question, it was not the right moment to risk creating a new dispute: the relationship between the State and the Catholic Church could not be questioned in that historical moment.

 © Wolters Kluwer Italia

This stance was clearly adopted by the main Catholic representatives in the Constituent Assembly. In the debate on 23rd of January, 1946, Aldo Moro stressed the importance of religious peace in order to include Catholics in the work of reconstructing Italy after the war. Similarly, on 11th of March, 1946, Giorgio La Pira restated the importance of mentioning the Lateran Pacts in the Constitution to make the Catholic Church a «precious collaborator» of the state. Furthermore, Giuseppe Dossetti's famous speech on 21st of March, 1946 demanded that all forces – including Catholic ones – contribute to the reconstruction of the State. In his words, this cooperation would have not been possible if they were left with «an inner contrast, a kind of reserve» due to a dubious relationship with the Catholic Church on the part of the State (Pombeni 2006 at 50). De Gasperi – President of the Council of ministers from 1945 to 1953 and Chairman of the Christian Democrat Party – exceptionally intervened in the Constituent Assembly on 25th of March, 1946 to discuss a fundamental political question to be decided with the approval of Article 7 on «whether the Republic accepts the contribution of religious peace that this Concordat offers: a Concordat that in the premise is declared to be a necessary complement to the Treaty that closes the Roman question» (Constituent Assembly, 25th of March, 1946, at 631).

Although these statements were enunciated by the key actors of the Christian Democratic party, it was largely thanks to the memorable address given to the Constituent Assembly by the leader of the Communist party, Palmiro Togliatti, that Article 7 was eventually approved. Like previous Catholic political leaders, he too had decided to rely entirely on the need to maintain a religious peace and to consider the workforce united in the reconstruction of Italy without making any distinction between Catholic workers and others (Constituent Assembly, 25th of March, 1946, at 640).

In short, the approval of Article 7 did not really concern any technical details about a possible 'constitutionalisation' of the Lateran Pacts. Much more was at stake: the decision to acknowledge the Catholic presence in the Republic. It was a straightforward vote characterized by a significant historical and political weight, rather than being solely a legal matter (Elia 2005). Article 7 shows therefore **the role played by the Catholic Church in the Constituent Assembly**: religious peace was a condition accepted in order to achieve **political unity** and to heal a relationship that was fractured in the liberal era and uncertain in the fascist one. Above all, the approval of this provision shows in a unique way the pluralist fabric of the Constitution.

As a final outcome, Article 7 – beyond confirming the concordat system as a model relationship between church and State through the acknowledgement of the Lateran Pacts – recognises t**he autonomy of the two legal orders**, stating that «the State and the Catholic Church are independent and sovereign, each within its own sphere» (para. 1).

3.b.2. The 1984 Reform

The issues left unresolved by Article 7 were striking: how could the – more or less apparent – recognition of a State religion stemming from Article 1 of the 1929 Lateran Treaty coexist with the autonomy of legal orders or with other denominations defined by the Constitution as «equally free» in the new provisions? After the approval of Article 7, in fact, a lively discussion on Article 8 began in the Constituent Assembly. The first paragraph, stating that «all religious denominations shall be equally free before the law», was particularly called into question. The debate focused on **the expression of the principle of equality** in this environment given the position of the Catholic Church in Italy and the specific nature of the other different denominations. Accordingly, most of the members of the Constituent Assembly held that it was not possible to consider all denominations «equal before the law» but **only «equal in freedom»**. In this way, the principle of the **equidistance of all denominations** from the State was introduced in the Constitution but **not of their equal treatment**. In fact, Article 8, para. 3, extended to denominations other than Catholicism the principle of concordat that was provided for the Catholic Church in Article 7, para. 2, and stipulated that relations with the same were governed by **agreements (*intese*)**.

The political parties involved in the Constituent Assembly deliberately decided to postpone the issues mentioned above to future amendments of the concordat in order to adapt it to the new constitutional regime. De Gasperi himself expressed his party's willingness to support **future initiatives** in order to remedy the existing inconsistencies. Nevertheless, the concordat remained in force for many years (until 1984), and the numerous knots deliberately left tied at the time of the Constitution made their way into litigation taken before the Constitutional Court. In this context, Article 7 has been reviewed several times in order to settle conflicts between constitutional principles and specific issues relating to Church-State relations. Thus, prior to the 1984 reform, the freedom of equality provided for in Article 8 was weakly interpreted in order to legitimise situations of privilege in favour of the Catholic Church.

The long-awaited reform of the Lateran Pacts in 1984 **radically changed the constitutional interpretation of Church–State relations**. The new legal framework amended part of the special regime the previous pacts had reserved for the Catholic faith, starting with the notorious rule on the State religion. Accordingly, it represented a real turning point in the constitutional interpretation of Article 7. In this regard, what is most striking in the Constitutional Court case law following the 1984 reform is the decrease in references to Article 7 and **the preference for relying solely on** the provision of **Article 8**, often in combined reading **with the equality principle**.

© Wolters Kluwer Italia

Of course, one cannot forget that in the 1970s, significant legislative reforms (e.g. legislation on divorce and abortion) contravening Catholic doctrine were enacted, and in the 1980s, the Court enshrined the supreme principle of the *laicità* (secularism) of the state. Although it was not written in the Constitution, this was based on Articles. 2, 3, 7, 8, 19 and 20. Within this historical evolution, **the issue of legal protection in religious matters began to lose its original force**. If in the case law immediately following the Constitution's entry into force the religious question was rooted in the religion of the majority, in the 1970s, it became «**religious sentiment**» (Judgment No. 14/1973) and thus began to widen the scope of protection beyond the Catholic faith to the point that it became possible to argue about religion indiscriminately.

By and large, legal scholars have supported this evolutionary interpretation of the religious issues, but they have not always shared a rigid interpretation according to strict rules of impartiality and equidistance with respect to all religious denominations, thereby risking disregarding the current constitutional text, as well as the prominence of religious issues in a pluralist society (BARBERA 2007). To conclude regarding the interpretation of Articles 7 and 8, it is possible to pinpoint an initial phase in which the special status attributed to the Catholic Church was emphasised – undoubtedly as a result of the intent of the Constituents. In a second phase, there is instead an almost total blurring of the content of Article 7 in favour of Article 8. However, it has to be underlined that **this fundamental change in the interpretation of religious matters reflects a profound change in society**: the general Catholicism of the population has been waning, and both the legislator and the judges seem to be well aware of this. Article 7 of the Constitution and the discussions that took place in the halls of the Constituent Assembly where it was born seem much further away than the seventy years that divide then from now.

3.c. The Road to Secularism in Italy: the Principle of Laicità

As Charles Taylor pointed out some years ago, «it is generally agreed that modern democracies have to be *secular*. (…) But even in the Western context the term is not limpid. What in fact does it mean?» (TAYLOR 2011 at 34). **Secularism is a very complex term** that has been used over the centuries to describe very different legal and or political principles: sometimes it represents some kind of separation of church and state, sometimes it represents a principle of equidistance (or even neutrality) between politics and religion, sometimes it imposes a duty on the State to keep religion outside the public sphere.

All these different meanings of the term *secular* reflect the different legal and constitutional clauses that one sees concern the word. France is a secular state that promotes «freedom *from* religions» restricting religions to private life. In the US, secularism means protecting «freedom *of the* religions» from the authority of the Federal government (Ruffini 1992). In United Kingdom, the constitutional order indicates the King as the Head of the State and the Head of the Church but has no an impact on the open, pluralistic society and to the respect for multicultural religions. All these examples show that, from a constitutional point of view, secularism has to be studied in a specific contest, highlighting the historical and cultural tradition of each constitutional system.

The road to secularism in Italy has been long and uneven, largely due to the historical dominance of confessionalism (the state endorsement of the Catholic religion), recognized first in the Albertine Statute and later in the Lateran Treaty. Even if – as already pointed out – the ordinary legislation during the liberal era largely called the nature of the confessional State into question, this legacy somehow shaped the Italian journey to the establishment of a secular State. This historical context informed the approach of Italian Framers, and a *veil of ignorance* in religious matters (Ferrari 2023) characterised the approach of political actors to the place of religious freedom and secularism in the Constitution: while the rejection of state confessionalism was clear, there were still too many unknowns about the relationship between the State and the churches to be able to outline a clear regulation of secularism.

Unlike other Constitutions, such as those of France or Turkey, the Italian Constitution does not explicitly enshrine the principle of secularism. Indeed, although the republican Constitution came into force in 1948, it took several decades for the **principle of *laicità*** (the Italian adaptation of the general principle of secularism) to be recognized as a supreme and inviolable principle within the Constitution. It was only in 1989 that the Constitutional Court, in a landmark ruling (**Judgment No. 203/1989**), expressly recognized it as a **fundamental trait of the Italian form of State.**

In order to have a clearer understanding of this historic decision, it is important to recall that by the mid-1980s the landscape of religious relations in the country was already undergoing significant changes. A key development was the signing of the 1984 Palazzo Madama Agreement, which abolished the confessional principle embedded in the 1929 Lateran Treaty and completely redefined the terms of the Concordat. Such a profound paradigm shift marked a notable departure from the previous exclusive relationship between the State and the Catholic Church.

In fact, during this period, a new era of agreements between the State and non-Catholic religious denominations began, thus implementing **Article 8, paras. 2 and 3** of the Constitution that states: «Denominations other than Catholicism have the right to self-organisation according to their own statutes, provided these

 © Wolters Kluwer Italia

do not conflict with Italian law. Their relations with the State are regulated by law, based on agreements (***intese***) with their respective representatives». The first agreement was reached in 1984 with the Waldenses table (evangelical Christian denomination). Subsequently, additional agreements were established with other Christian and Jewish confessions. The *intese* were a significant step to both promote religious pluralism and ensure that the rights and privileges enjoyed by the Catholic Church were extended to other religious groups as well. This ongoing process of negotiation and agreement continues to shape the landscape of religious freedom and interfaith relations in Italy nowadays, as evidenced by the existence of 13 *intese* between the State and a variety of religious organisations.

The **1989 Judgment** should be understood within this new religious context in Italy, and it can be considered ground-breaking for various reasons. Firstly, as already mentioned, it recognizes the principle of ***laicità* as a supreme and inviolable principle of the Italian Constitution**, as such characterising the republican form of the State. Secondly, despite the absence of explicit references to the secular form of the State in the constitutional charter, the Court manages to derive this principle from a combined reading of a number of articles of the Constitution (specifically, Articles 2, 3, 7, 8, 19, and 20). This approach permitted a coherent interpretation of these constitutional provisions as a **unified *micro-system*** governing the relationship between the State and religion (Pasquali Cerioli 2023 at 86) thus harmonizing individual freedom (art. 2, 3 and 19; the s.c. *favor libertatis*) with the promotion of religion (art. 7, 8 and 20; the s.c. *favor religionis*). The Italian approach to secularism, therefore, encompasses not only the protection of **individual** freedoms, such as freedom of thought, conscience, and religion (as seen in the *favor libertatis*), but also acknowledges the **collective dimension** of religious expression and cultural heritage (as seen in the *favor religionis*). Thirdly, it enucleates a peculiar model of secularism (*laicità*) which did not imply «indifference toward the experience of religion» but represented the «State guarantee that religious freedom will be safeguarded, in a framework of denominational and cultural pluralism» (Judgment No. 203/1989). The principle of *laicità* in the Italian model of a secular State therefore goes beyond the notion of absolute neutrality or indifference of the state towards religion. It encompasses not only the **negative profile of secularism**, which includes the obligation of non-discrimination and the separation of church and State, but also the **positive profile of secularism**, which entails the obligation to effectively protect and promote religious freedom.

Since this first historic ruling, the Court has intervened to identify the corollaries of *laicità*, or better to *unveil* them. A first corollary was the **distinction of orders between State and religious denominations**, or rather between the temporal and spiritual spheres (e.g., Judgment No. 334/1996, oath in trials). Subsequently, it was recognized that religious and cultural pluralism implies «**the equal protection of the conscience of each person** who recognises himself in a faith, whatever the religious denomination to which he belongs» (e.g., Judgment No. 440/1995 on the penal protection of religious sentiment). The **State's equidistance towards religions was** then confirmed (e.g., ItCC Judgments Nos. 195/1993 and 63/2016, on places of worship; and No. 329/97 on the criminal protection of religious sentiment).

The concept of the State's equidistance or **neutrality towards religions has been explored extensively within the ECtHR case law**. To mention just two leading EctHR decisions, the *Kokkinakis* case marked the first instance in which the Court found a state in violation of Article 9 ECHR, which protects the right to freedom of thought, conscience, and religion. In this case, the Court condemned Greece for its treatment of a Jehovah's Witness, recognizing that the state had failed to maintain a neutral and impartial stance towards religious practices (case of *Kokkinakis v Greece*, Application No. 14307/88, Judgment 25th of May, 1993). Similarly, the *Sahin* case dealt with the issue of religious freedom and the principle of State neutrality: in this case, the Court addressed the ban on wearing religious symbols, specifically headscarves, in Turkish universities. The Court held that the ban violated the applicant's right to manifest her religious beliefs, emphasizing the importance of state neutrality and non-discrimination based on religion (Grand Chamber, case of *Leyla Şahin v Turkey*, Application No. 44774/98, 10th of November, 2005).

However, to return to the case law of the Constitutional Court on the issue of the State's equidistance towards religions, the Court ruled that the specific discipline agreed between the State and religious denominations under Article 8, para. 3, of the Constitution does not constitute discrimination. In this regard, the Court also held that the **government's decision to enter into an agreement with a religious confession constitutes a political act and therefore cannot be challenged**, and that the presence or absence of an agreement with the State does not affect the principles of *laicità* and equal liberty enunciated in Article 8, para. 1 (ItCC, Judgment No. 52/2016).

If this is the rich jurisprudence on the basis of which the supreme principle of *Italian-style* secularism has been constructed, one must nevertheless register the **deafening absence of the Italian Legislature** on the matter: although there has been a debate for some time in the parliamentary chambers on the adoption of a law on freedom of religion which would implement the Constitution and give effect to the principle of secularism and the right to freedom of religion, the only legislation currently in force is the **1929 law on approved cults** (*culti ammessi*), which still governs relations between the State and non-approved religions. In

 © Wolters Kluwer Italia

the face of contemporary issues such as immigration and globalization, Italy's religious geography has undergone significant changes since the first half of the twentieth century. The presence of religious communities that were relatively recent, such as Islamic organizations, has become more prominent. As a result, the provisions of Law No. 1159/1929 may not fully meet the needs of these newer religious communities (ALICINO 2017). The persistent **inertia of the Legislature** inevitably casts a shadow over the effective realisation of the principle of secularism in the Italian legal system.

Indeed, the application of the principle of secularism in everyday life in the Italian context involves various complexities, particularly in areas such as **education in public schools** and the **display of religious symbols in public spaces**. These two examples highlight the ongoing challenges and debates surrounding the practical implementation of secularism in Italy.

To understand the first issue, one can recall the substance of Judgment No. 203/1989 already analysed, which is indeed noteworthy. In this case the Constitutional Court used the supreme principle understood as a kind of *positive* secularism to justify the institution of religious education in public schools. This decision provoked considerable debate because of its implications, particularly from the point of view of a secular State. In fact, the Court justifies the institution of religious education by interpreting secularism through the lens of pluralism. It **argues that the expression of religious freedom, even through positive interventions such as religious education, can be conducive to fostering pluralism**. More precisely, the question of constitutionality concerned Article 9, para. 2, of the 1984 Agreement, according to which «The Italian Republic, recognising the value of religious culture and taking into account that the principles of Catholicism are part of the historical heritage of the Italian people, will continue to ensure, within the framework of the aims of the school, the teaching of the Catholic religion in all non-university public schools». By endorsing the inclusion of an opt-out clause and emphasizing the need for non-discrimination, the Court sought to strike a balance between the teaching of Catholic doctrine in public schools and the principle of a secular State. On the one hand, the Court's decision to uphold the constitutionality of this law reflects the recognition of the cultural and historical significance of Catholicism in Italy; on the other, it ultimately shows «an active benevolent attitude toward religious freedom» (FARAGUNA 2019 at 44) that supports the Court's understanding of the principle of *laicità*.

The issue of religious education in school curricula has also been addressed by the Strasbourg Court. A notable example of this rich case law is the *Folgerø* case (Grand Chamber, case of *Folgerø and Others v Norway*, 2007, Application No. 15472/02, Judgment 29th of June, 2007), in which the ECtHR examined the Norwegian system of religious education, which required religious education as part of the curriculum in public schools. The Court found that the lack of an acceptable alternative to religious education prevented the applicants from effectively exercising their freedom of thought, conscience and religion.

The **argument about the preservation of cultural and historical traditions** underscores the still ongoing tension around these delicate and divisive issues. It is enough to recall the heated debate surrounding the compatibility of the display of the crucifix in Italian public schools with the supreme principle of *laicità*. As is well known, the crucifix is a symbol that holds deep religious significance, particularly within the Catholic faith, and its presence in public school classrooms has been a subject of contention, particularly after the landmark ***Lautsi*** decision of the Strasbourg Court. In this case, brought forward by an Italian citizen of Finnish origin, the ECtHR firstly ruled in 2009 that the display of crucifixes in Italian public schools violated the right to freedom of thought, conscience, and religion as protected by the European Convention on Human Rights (case of *Lautsi v Italy*, Application No. 30814/06, Judgment 3th of November, 2009). The Court held that the mandatory display of crucifixes could be seen as a violation of parents' rights to ensure their children's education is in line with their own beliefs or non-beliefs, relying on a combined reading of Article 9 of the European Convention of Human Rights (freedom of thought, conscience, and religion) and Article 2 of the first Protocol to the Convention (right to education). In response to the *Lautsi* ruling, the Italian government appealed against the decision, and in 2011, the Grand Chamber of the ECHR reversed the earlier decision (Grand Chamber, case of *Lautsi v Italy*, Application No. 30814/06, Judgment 18th of March, 2011; see WEILER, 2012). The Grand Chamber held that the presence of crucifixes in Italian public schools did not breach the European Convention on Human Rights and that the display could be seen as representing the cultural, historical, and social values of Italy. It added that «a crucifix on a wall is an essentially passive symbol and ... cannot be deemed to have an influence on pupils comparable to that of didactic speech or participation in religious activities». In summary, the ECtHR's decision recognized the wide margin of appreciation for member States, treating the ban on indoctrination as the ultimate limit of State discretion.

However, despite the about-turn by the ECtHR, the debate on the presence of crucifixes in Italian public schools has continued and remerged in front of the **Court of Cassation in 2021** (United Sections of the Court of Cassation, Judgment No. 24414/2021), reigniting the dilemma regarding the neutrality of public spaces and the cultural and historical heritage of the country, thus reflecting the ongoing tension between the principles of *laicità* on the one hand, and the cultural and historical significance attached to religious symbols on the other. The case in question concerned a teacher who disagreed with a decision taken by students during a class assembly to hang a crucifix in the classroom. The conflict arose between the professor's freedom to teach and the democratic principle, as the

© Wolters Kluwer Italia

students' decision was made directly and on the basis of their own choice, without external regulatory constraints and by majority vote (CECCANTI, 2021 at 951). The Supreme Court, in a very long and complex decision, stated that the mandatory display of the crucifix, imposed by the public authorities, is incompatible with the Constitution. However, the Court also ruled that the school community has the right to decide whether to display the crucifix in the classroom. This decision was to be made considering the convictions of all members of the community and aiming to find a reasonable accommodation that respected the differing positions held within the community (VENTURA 2021).

Indeed, the principle of *laicità* within the Italian constitutional case law has been subject to various interpretations, and a clear and uniform definition of the term is not easily identifiable. Depending on the specific cases and fields involved, Italian courts have used different definitions of *laicità*, including equidistance among faiths, impartiality, non-indifference, and even neutrality. While the interpretations of this principle may vary, it does not sweep away its peculiarity, i.e. a tendency toward a *favor religionis* and its rootedness Catholic history (RAGONE/VANONI 2018).

3.d. Religious Pluralism through Rights, i.e. Freedom of Religion and Conscience

The natural corollary of the unique religious pluralism that stems from the principle of secularism embraced by the Constitution and embedded in Articles 7 and 8 is the **broadest recognition of the freedom of religion**. It is enshrined, first and foremost, in Article 19, to be read in conjunction with the ban on religious discrimination (Article 3, para. 1), but it is also indirectly protected by other constitutional provisions guaranteeing freedoms and rights to a certain extent related to religious ones: e.g., the right to assemble and form associations, the right (and duty) of parents to educate their children, the freedom of teaching, etc.

Looking at Article 19 alone, it states that «anyone is entitled to profess their religious belief freely in any form, individually or with others, and to promote them and celebrate rites in public or in private, provided they are not offensive to public morality». Therefore, **freedom of religion is a multifaceted right,** since it includes: a) the right to *profess* (both individually and collectively) a religious belief and also to *change* it any time; b) the right to *proselytise*, i.e. to attempt to persuade another individual to change his or her religion; and c) the right to *celebrate rites*, the only limitation being the respect for public morality. Furthermore, freedom of religion (like the majority of rights and freedoms) has a *negative* side to it too: the freedom *not* to believe as well as the right *not* to adhere to a religious community also fall under the scope of Article 19. Accordingly, the Constitutional Court clearly stated in Judgment No. 117/1979 that atheism shall be protected by Article 19 (and not merely by Article 21 ensuring freedom of speech). On the other hand, the same Constitutional Court declared Article 4 of the royal decree No. 1731/1930 unconstitutional, insofar as it envisaged a *de jure* adhesion of Jews to the Italian Jewish Communities (Judgment No. 239/1994). Similarly, the freedom to proselytise implies two distinct but related notions of freedom, both equally protected by Article 19: the freedom of the proselytisers to conduct proselytising activities and the freedom of the potential proselyte *not* to be interfered with by such activities. The consequence of the protection of the latter is that proselytism and religious propaganda can only be guaranteed as long as they do not entail acts of physical and psychological violence and coercion (Judgment No. 188/1975). Needless to say, the general principle of equality complements the protection provided by Article 19.

The composite nature of the freedom of religion found in multicultural and heterogeneous societies as they are today, may give rise to a diverse and complex reality where strong and different religious identities coexist often generating increasing confrontation, if not open conflict. We may consider, for example, the particularly thorny issue of the display of religious symbols at school, already analysed above, or the conflict potentially rising between a religious (or religiously oriented) organisation and a person belonging to a different religious affiliation (or an atheist) in **employment relationships**. Is the organisation allowed to use religious criteria to hire or fire people? Or would this amount to a discrimination on grounds of religion, forbidden as such according to the principle of equality? It is clear that two different rights are at odds here. On the one hand, from the standpoint of a *collective right*, religious organisations have the right to express and assert their own religious identity. On the other hand, however, from the point of view of *individual right*, an individual is free to adhere to religious affiliations without discrimination on these grounds. Which right – the organisation's or the individual's – should prevail in a case like this? Usually, secular orders adopt solutions that try to balance the competing, but equally legitimate claims at stake, admitting that religious organisations can adopt different treatments based on a person's religion or belief where, by reason of the nature of the activities that are to be carried out, the religious belief constitutes a genuine, legitimate and justified occupational requirement (see for example Article 3, para. 3, of the legislative decree No. 23/2015 implementing the European directive 2000/78/EC). It is worth mentioning, however, that the identification of a direct link between the occupational requirement imposed by the employer and the activity concerned is not an easy task and many varied and nuanced interpretations are possible (ItCC Judgment No. 195/1972, case of *Cordero*; case *Lombardi Vallauri v Italy*, Application No. 39128/05, Judgment 20th of October, 2009; ECJ *Egenberger*, C-414/16, 17th of April, 2018). Therefore, the potential for conflict still remains.

 © Wolters Kluwer Italia

The few examples mentioned above clearly reveal how much the religious question matters and affects the entirety of the ordinary life of democratic systems. As a consequence, if democracies want to prevent legal conflicts from degenerating into violence and social and political battles, they need to deal with religious issues and manage them carefully, **accommodating diversities in a balanced and reasonable manner**.

In this regard, a useful tool to reconcile specific religious stances with other positions, and ultimately to increase tolerance within the system, may be **conscientious objection**, which consists of a person's appeal to his/her individual conscience (or, more in general, to his/her morality) in order to be discharged from compliance with a piece of legislation that is considered inconsistent with her ethical convictions. Conscientious objection is, therefore, a corollary of **freedom of conscience** that is also expressly recognised in several international instruments (e.g. Universal Declaration of Human Rights, Article 18; European Convention on Human Rights, Article 9; Charter of Fundamental Rights of the EU, Article 10).

Indeed, conscience being the innermost thoughts of a person, capable of including also moral, ethical and philosophical convictions, freedom of conscience should be considered as even broader than freedom of religion or belief. In fact, freedom of conscience would imply the person's right to freely form her own conscience according to all the values a human being cherishes, whether of religious nature or not. Nonetheless, since religion is traditionally conceived of as the most essential component of the human conscience, **freedom of conscience is commonly protected in conjunction with the freedom of religion** and **conscientious objection is mainly** – albeit not exclusively – **allowed for religious reasons**, although the term *religious* is usually **interpreted broadly** (see for example the U.S. Supreme Court, Judgment *United States v. Seeger*, 1965, which, while admitting that the term 'religious' can also be referred to non-traditional religions, excludes any reference to political or philosophical values; somewhat differently, the European Court of Human Rights seems to admit conscientious objection to military service for reasons other than religious ones in the EctHR, Grand Chamber, case of *Bayatyan v Armenia*, Application No. 23459/03, Judgment 7th of July, 2011; and case of *Savda v Turkey*, Application No. 42730/05, Judgment, 12th of July, 2011). In conclusion, the range of reasons justifying conscientious objection may vary; however, what is sure is that **religion plays a fundamental role in this context**.

In Italy neither freedom of conscience in general nor conscientious objection in particular are **expressly recognised in the Constitution**. Despite this, the Constitutional Court inferred without hesitation the constitutional protection of all rights of conscience from a **combined reading** of Articles 2, 3, 19 and 21 of the Constitution. According to the Court, «the innate area of individual conscience shall be considered as the deepest legal repercussion of the universal idea of human dignity surrounding the enjoyment of rights» (Judgment No. 467/1991) and the constitutional provisions mentioned above read in conjunction with each other, bring a unitary and all-inclusive protection of conscience rights to light (Judgment No. 42/1997). Conscientious objection is explicitly **admitted at legislative level** – for *any reason* of conscience – in four cases:

a) **military service**: Law No. 772/1972 (amended by Law No. 230/1998) allowed objectors to replace conscription with compulsory civil service (as is well known, however, conscription was suspended from 1st of January, 2005 by Law No. 226/2004);

b) **abortion**: Article 9 of Law No. 194/1978 legalising abortion, introduced the right to conscientious objection for the health personnel involved in activities that are specific and necessary to perform an abortion (but not regarding activities to be conducted before and after abortion), while excluding conscientious objection when there is an immediate risk to the life of the woman;

c) **animal testing**: Article 1 of Law No. 413/1993 acknowledged conscientious objection to the use of animals for educational and research purposes;

d) **assisted reproduction technologies**: Article 16 of Law No. 40/2004 provided for the possibility of conscientious objection for health professionals, who are not obliged to take part in the procedures that are specifically and necessarily directed towards assisted reproduction (but not from assistance before and after the intervention).

Why may conscientious objection be a useful tool to manage religious diversity? As mentioned above, conscientious objection allows people to obey their consciences and, accordingly, be discharged from compliance with legal obligations when particularly sensitive issues are at stake. For this reason, conscientious objection can basically avoid dissent expressed against specific provisions by people who hold **non-mainstream ethical views** turning into open opposition and conflict. In so doing, conscientious objection makes the **coexistence** of religious disagreement with **a stable and peaceful legal order possible**. In simpler terms, conscientious objection may be helpful to deal with disagreement in order to build a sort of ***overlapping consensus*** on some **fundamental values** within the system, thus **increasing tolerance and trust between** all individuals living in it, despite their considerable mutual differences.

Nonetheless, conscientious objection also raises several **constitutional issues**, worth mentioning here briefly, merely highlighting two particularly relevant questions.

 © Wolters Kluwer Italia

First, what happens if the number of conscientious objectors is so high that this *de facto* results in prejudicing the rights of other people, even though those rights are still ensured by law? In this case conscientious objection ceases to be a merely private act of obedience of a person to her own conscience but also becomes an act impacting on the lives of the people that are the intended addressees of the services that the objector refuses to provide (a clear example of this can be found in the high number of medical practitioners objecting to abortion in Italy, close to 90% in some Regions).

Second, who (or what authority) is empowered to decide when conscientious objection may be allowed? Many legal orders expressly provide for conscientious objection in some cases but not in others. May a person raise conscientious objection in a case where she is not expressly entitled to do so by law? For example, can a civil servant object to the registration of a same-sex partnership, if the act introducing civil unions does not mention the right to conscientious objection to registration (Case of *Ladele*, issued in ECtHR, *Eweida and Others v The United Kingdom*, Applications Nos. 48420/10, 59842/10, 51671/10 and 36516/10, Judgment, 15th of January, 2013)? Or, again, can a bakery refuse to provide a wedding cake to a gay couple based on the owner's religious beliefs without any express legal provision in this respect (U.S. Supreme Court, *Masterpiece Cakeshop v. Colorado Civil Rights Commission*, 584 U.S. (2018))? Can objection to abortion be extended also to cover the morning-after pill? It is generally accepted that legislatures can decide on this matter: conscientious objection is allowed only *secundum legem*, i.e. only where it is provided for by law.

At first glance, the power of Legislatures to rule on conscientious objection might seem astonishing and at odds with the very essence of the issue. If conscientious objection is conceived of as a tool to allow the moral and ethical imperatives of personal conscience prevail over a majority decision in individual cases, why should an *external* authority, which – what is more – expresses the thought of the majority, be allowed to identify which individuals' moral *inner* reasons are worth prevailing? Personal conscience is not an objective entity: it is personal. And legislatures are not neutral: they are political bodies par excellence and work according to the majority principle. However, conscientious objection necessarily implies non-compliance with duties that are still provided by law. The Constitution, in the same Article 2, on the one hand, guarantees the inviolable rights of the person, and «expects that the fundamental *duties* of political, economic and social solidarity be fulfilled», on the other. Conscientious objection lies precisely where fundamental rights and fundamental duties meet. To what extent can legal systems give up the fulfilment of duties in the name of improvement of rights and freedoms? The issue at stake is essentially the *amount* of conscientious objection that a constitutional order can admit without jeopardising its own unity and cohesion that are guaranteed by compliance with solidarity duties. Therefore, it is not surprising that Legislatures are considered to be the best placed to strike this **extremely sensitive balance**. After all, they represent the people and are one of the instruments through which popular sovereignty is traditionally exercised.

In light of the above, it is clear that religious pluralism is today one of the biggest challenges for democratic systems. One could even say that **religious pluralism is the real testing ground for democracies**. Nonetheless, pluralism is the only path to be taken in systems that need to deal with differences and derive unity from the diversity of their components.

C) DEMOCRACY THROUGH RIGHTS

1. Social Pluralism

The special attention given by the Italian Constitution to the **protection of fundamental rights in the public sphere** is the main indication of an **open democracy.** In response to the Fascist period, the new Republic focused on the promotion of different cultures and different identities that could contribute their own ideas to pluralism and public debate, either individually, through the protection of freedom of expression, or collectively, through the recognition of freedom of assembly and association. Within this framework, the Constitution directly protects communities and social groups (Luciani 2023), not only through specific provisions recognising the principles of equality and non-discrimination, but also through social pluralism, which strengthens democracy through the protection of collective rights.

1.a. Freedom of Assembly: Sharing Ideas in Private and Public Spaces

The importance of strengthening democracy through rights is immediately evident upon reading Article 17, which protects freedom of assembly. According to this provision «[c]itizens may assemble peaceably and unarmed. No previous notice is required for meetings, including those held in places open to the public. In case of meetings held in public places, prior notice shall be given to the authorities, who may prohibit such meetings only for proven reasons of security or public safety». Its inviolability is embodied in the only limitation expressly provided: **meetings must be peaceful and unarmed**.

As is well known, freedom of assembly was already proclaimed in the Constitutions of the end of the eighteenth century. Together with the freedom of association and of speech, the exercise of this liberty is particularly relevant for the direct **participation** of people in public life. From this perspective, its protection

© Wolters Kluwer Italia

is directly rooted in the principle of pluralism granted in Article 2, para. 2, thanks to its reference to social groups. Indeed, meetings are permitted in private and in public spaces. The authorities do not have the right to intervene in advance (except for proven reasons of security and **public safety** in public spaces), but they can stop gatherings that endanger the participants, even if private meetings are held in the residences of the organisers.

By analysing Article 17 in the light of this principle some key elements emerge.

The first clue that confirms the **social nature of the freedom of assembly**, highlighting the possibility of each individual to participate in a public forum, is related to the quality of the meeting protected by Article 17. This provision does not refer to casual meetings (e.g. a queue at a shop or office), but only to organised assemblies of people who share a purpose. This is broad enough to include flash mobs, sit-ins and impromptu meetings where people gather to manifest ideas: what counts is the intention to be part of a group at a given moment, not the message conveyed.

A further element that can be interpreted in terms of the development and enhancement of democracy is represented by **the duty to give notice**. Notice is not required for private meetings and those that occur in places open to the public. It is required instead for meetings held in public spaces with the only duty being that goal of informing authorities, specifically the police, which can evaluate the possible risks and better organise the preparation and the conduct of the meetings. It is important to **reconcile the various constitutional interests involved**, among them are the freedom of movement and the protection of the right to health of persons. For this reason, notice does not involve obtaining authorisation from the police but is conceived instead as a tool that reinforces the idea of a democratic system particularly mindful of the exercise of fundamental rights in pacific contexts. Notice is **not necessary for political meetings** in order to stress the importance of assemblies that are directly linked to the exercise of political rights, hence to the promotion of pluralism and democracy. Authorities may prohibit them only for proven reasons of security or public safety.

Despite the importance of protecting public safety, especially in public meetings with a large number of participants or where the message conveyed is controversial (e.g. assemblies organised by extreme political movements against ethnic and religious minorities), authorities **cannot exercise discretion in disbanding assemblies**. Even though the law forbids bringing arms and objects that can be used as arms, according to the Constitutional Court's interpretation, the authorities can only intervene if in concrete and dangerous circumstances these objects are used to injure participants, passers-by or the police force itself and act exclusively against who behave against the law. Only reasons related to the *real* infringement of **public order** can limit freedom of assembly: accordingly, arbitrary restrictions by the public authorities dissolving meetings on the basis of their content (and not just on the basis of their conduct) are not allowed, since it would realise a form of indirect censorship.

Criminal liability rests solely on the perpetrators and on the organisers who did not give notice. The participants do not have any responsibility and hence cannot be punished.

1.b. Freedom of Association

Article 18 of the Constitution protects the freedom of association. Through this provision, the principle of pluralism becomes a **central pivotal point** for fostering the **political and institutional dialogue** mentioned in Article 5 of the Constitution.

Article 18 states that «[c]itizens may form associations freely and without authorization for any ends that are not forbidden by criminal law. Secret associations and associations that, even indirectly, pursue political aims through organisations of a military nature shall be forbidden». Similar to the freedom of assembly, the freedom of association conciliates the principle of both **personalism and pluralism**. With regard to the former, it enhances the self-determination of the person «as an individual and in the social groups where human personality is expressed», as Article 2 explicitly provides. With regard to the principle of pluralism, Article 18 enhances the deliberate decision to adhere (or not) to associations that contribute to the **free exchange of ideas at social, cultural, religious and political levels**.

Much more so than freedom of assembly, freedom of association is evidence of the change of perspective in the democratic system. In fact, while during the liberal period freedom of association was not provided for in the Albertine Statute and was considered an obstacle to individual self-determination as a reaction to the regime, when individuals were grouped according to class (see *I.A).2.*), during the fascist period the main objective was the repression of all groups that could culturally or politically threaten the stability of the government.

Thanks to the efforts of the Catholic and working-class movements in particular, the democratic republican Constitution reserves **a special place for freedom of association**, considered fundamental for strengthening pluralism and democracy. The protection of this freedom can be considered as a sort of **strategic tool** to achieve a good level of democracy and equality.

The right to freely associate without authorisation is recognised. Hence, administrative authorities only have the right to dissolve existing associations after investigations carried out by judicial authorities. There is no obligation

 © Wolters Kluwer Italia

to participate in associations, except for those that pursue a public interest, for example, professional boards, like the bar association. Ultimately, the limits to the freedom of association are laid down with the intent of ensuring the protection of this right from a pluralistic perspective, because every social group contributes to determining the general will of the people.

The Constitution expressively forbids association for **ends** that are **prohibited** to **individuals by criminal law**. This means that the purpose of the association is irrelevant to the exercise of the right: what is lawful for the individual is lawful for associations as well. As the Constitutional Court stated, freedom of association is the projection of individual freedom onto the level of collective action (Judgment No. 417/1993), a further sign of the close link between this right and the pluralistic and democratic principle, especially regarding political participation (CRISAFULLI/PALADIN 1990).

This link is particularly evident when looking at the other limitations provided in Article 18, i.e. the prohibition of **secret associations** conspiring against the democratic order and those associations that «even indirectly, pursue **political ends** by means of organisations having a **military character**». If the forbidden criminal end can be interpreted in the light of the ordinary dynamic of the democratic process, the prohibition of both secret associations and those that pursue political ends by means of organisations having a military character can be read in the light of the maintenance of democracy, thereby highlighting the political dimension.

Betting on an ***open*** **democratic system**, i.e. a democracy that does not recognize limits on dissent, the Constituents wanted to exclude associations that could secretly or indirectly subvert the democratic order. Only transparency and the internal democratic organization guarantee a frank confrontation of the ideas shared in a group, which protects the individual members and the democratic state in general. Accordingly, Article 18 aims at guaranteeing the democratic method and not the democratic *contents* of the association. Indeed, the military character of associations that pursue political ends is reminiscent of how the Fascist party rose to power. Therefore, military associations can exist if they do not contend with political issues.

Regarding **secret associations**, the law implementing Article 18 clarifies that these forms of association are forbidden only if they focus on political matters, as otherwise the principle of confidentiality that the Constitution reserves to individuals and groups would be infringed. As a matter of fact, after having discovered the existence of a Masonic Lodge named P2, which secretly conspired against the democratic order, Law No. 17/1982 was passed to regulate the matter in detail.

This aimed to ensure a better protection of the freedom of association by avoiding the judge's discretion in deciding the unnecessary dissolution of associations considered not to be truly dangerous.

Since the method and not the content is under scrutiny, it is absolutely evident how the constitutional system denies a protected democratic model – as has been already mentioned – recognising the possibility of forming political parties that pursue anti-democratic ideas. This is confirmed by reading Article 18 together with Article 49 and provision XII (transitional and final provisions of the Constitution). The first protects the right to freely associate in parties that «contribute to determining national policies through democratic process»; the second forbids the reorganisation, «under any form whatsoever, the dissolved Fascist party». On the grounds of a consolidated interpretation of this provision by the Constitutional Court, **only political parties that replicate the same structure and intent of the Fascist party can be dissolved**. In fact, in the history of the republic, there have been examples of anti-system parties, such as the MSI (Italian Social Movement), which actively participated in the political life of the country despite never repudiating the ideology of the Fascist party and the Republic of Salò.

At present, the **open attitude of the Constitution**, embodied in Article 18, is being put to the test. Problems related to peaceful coexistence require new types of regulations to address them. In the face of such new challenges, the constitutional system has to draw a difficult line between two opposite interests: the need to protect the security of individuals on the one hand, and the need to protect the pluralism of ideas and associations (including whoever tries to deny the importance of other cultures) on the other.

Two specific laws have thus been approved: one aims at reducing **racial discrimination** (Law No. 205/1993, which penalises associations that intend to incite hatred or discrimination on the basis of ethnicity, race or religious affiliation); the other aims at punishing **international terrorism** (Law No. 438/2001). Keeping in mind the open nature of the democratic constitutional system, the constitutionality of these provisions is dubious, leaving an unanswered question: does democracy grow stronger if it is protected by the state or if it is left in the hands of the community? In the following, it will be seen that this is a crucial question which also involves the freedom of speech.

1.c. Freedom of Speech

Freedom of speech is probably one of the rights most closely linked to pluralism and liberal democracy. On the one hand, in accordance with the typically

 © Wolters Kluwer Italia

liberal ideals, it aims to protect the individuals' right to freely express and disseminate their own ideas without interference by public and private powers. On the other hand, freedom of speech is also the most essential precondition for a public opinion to develop freely and self-consciously and, therefore, can be considered «the cornerstone» of every democratic system (see ItCC, Judgment No. 84/1969), a sort of «unconditional reflection» of the democratic principle and pluralism. Ensuring **dialectical confrontation between different ideas** – however challenging and uncomfortable they may be – is the pillar of an open and pluralistic society and, therefore, the necessary premise for the protection of other fundamental rights and freedoms to be continuously guaranteed and improved. Freedom of speech can be considered a **multifaceted right**. In this sense, it requires a positive commitment in order to establish and maintain a «**free marketplace of ideas**», to cite a famous, although not totally uncontroversial, American doctrine, according to which the truth can only emerge from the competition of ideas in free and transparent public discourse (U.S. Supreme Court, *Abrams v United States*, 250 U.S. 616 (1919)).

Having said this, it is not surprising that, as it was severely supressed repressed during the **fascist period**, the right to the manifestation of thought was placed at the heart of the constitutional debate. This is illustrated by the sheer length of the constitutional provision guaranteeing freedom of speech, Article 21, which consists of six paragraphs and differs considerably from the other constitutional provisions on fundamental freedoms (which are considerably shorter).

Article 21 reflects, first and foremost, the liberal nature of the right at stake. The first paragraph reveals the individual character of this freedom, and the broad protection surrounding free speech from undue interference by public powers: as it states, *anyone* has the right to express freely their thoughts, both occasionally and professionally, without distinctions between citizens and foreigners and between individuals and social groups. Furthermore, Article 21 fully protects both the individual freedom to express thoughts and its opposite: the **right to remain silent**.

It is crucial to focus on two specific aspects involving the freedom of speech: one concerning its boundaries and the other related to the means of expressing thoughts. As for the former, it is well known that although freedom of expression is a powerful instrument of democracy, it can also be used to attack both individuals and the state. What speech, then, requires protection according to Article 21? Can a distinction be drawn between legal and illegal speeches depending on their content? What limits can be legitimately imposed on freedom of expression without jeopardising the «free marketplace of ideas» and, therefore, the very essence of democracy? As a matter of fact, starting from the very first judgment

© Wolters Kluwer Italia

of the Constitutional Court it has been acknowledged that also right too must be balanced with the other constitutional rights which are guaranteed: «the concept of limit is inherent in the concept of law» (Judgment No. 1/1956).

As regards to the means accorded to anyone to express their own thoughts, the role played by the media is clear. This issue becomes even more challenging if one considers that freedom of speech includes two different components: the right **to express ideas** (the active component) and the **right to be informed** (the passive component). While the latter is not directly and expressly protected by Article 21, it is however, plainly admitted that the right to be informed is a value that may be inferred from several constitutional norms that shape the position of individuals towards public authorities (Articles 1, para. 2, 9, 33, 64 and 97 of the Constitution), and lead to the conclusion that, in order to consciously exercise political rights, citizens should be able to be fully informed (Pace 1992). A similar protection is also assured by the ECHR when it states that «everyone has the right to freedom of expression. This right shall include freedom to hold opinions and to receive and impart information and ideas without interference by public authorities and regardless of frontiers» (Article 10, par. I). In the light of this, pluralism of media becomes essential to protect freedom of expression and ultimately democracy.

1.c.1. What Boundaries?

Even mere facts can be considered manifestations of thought, whether they are true or false, and accordingly, they should also be protected. It is not surprising then that the right to report news, criticism and satire are equally protected as well as the news revealed by simple gossip. As the Constitutional Court explained, this is because freedom of speech is the right which, among all the primary fundamental rights, is decisive for democracy (Judgment No. 168/1971).

The Italian constitutional scholarship of the 1960s and the 1970s has always stressed that manifestations of thought can include various forms of **propaganda** and **apologetics**, but not speech aimed at concretely provoking illegitimate action.

Article 21 explicitly sets decency as a limit to freedom of speech (Article 21, para. 6). The boundaries of such limit are uncertain to some extent, so that it lends itself to evolving interpretations according to the sensitivities of society at any given historical moment. Nevertheless, the concept of decency has undergone a downsizing: according to constitutional case law, freedom of expression may not be limited for opinions deemed immoral; otherwise, there could be the risk of affirming public ethics that could hinder the free flow of individual thoughts.

 © Wolters Kluwer Italia

The ideas forbidden in compliance with the limit of decency would be in the first place those linked to the criminal law notion of obscenity or those acts, which according to the common sentiment, offend modesty. In particular, the Constitutional Court affirmed that these acts are the manifestations of sexuality that take place in public and are not confined to the private sphere (Judgment No. 368/1992). Secondly, since the Constitutional Court itself has provided a notion of morality that is more constitutionally oriented (in the sense of being read in the light of the principle of human dignity), the thoughts not covered by constitutional protection would be those that are placed in antithesis to the plurality of ethical concepts that coexist in contemporary society (Judgment No. 293/2000).

Implicit limits have been identified step by step in order to protect other individual rights: no one would question the need, for example, to balance on a case-by-case basis, freedom of expression with the right to honour or the right to privacy, even though these are not rights explicitly provided for in the Constitution.

Problematic is the category of **crimes of opinion**, which do not protect the subjective position of any single individual, but rather the personality of the State – such as vilification – or social (ethnic, national, religious) groups. In the first case, these crimes are viewed with great suspicion, as they would inhibit dissent, hindering the circulation of antagonistic political ideas. In the second case, the crimes of **hate speech** are at stake: they are punished only if they cause immediate tangible unrest and put the public order in danger (ItCC, Judgment No. 65/1970). At present, the attention paid towards minorities, even through the application of the hate speech provisions (art. 604 bis criminal code propaganda and instigation to commit crimes on the grounds of racial, ethnic and religious discrimination), opens the doors to the application of another type of limit, which scholarship describes as **logical limits** intrinsic to freedom of speech, i.e., manifestations of thought that would be considered irrational expressions. However, this kind of limit also applies when danger is not concrete and imminent, but only virtual and presumable. Consequently, the application of logical limits brings with it the danger of punishing opinions that harm dignity only in probabilistic terms, as it is difficult to verify the causal link between the thought expressed and effective injuries to certain individuals or groups. The Constitutional Court has never had the opportunity to clarify this point, while judiciary is expanding the boundaries of illicit expressions, mostly influenced by the European Court of Strasbourg case law. Indeed, through a broad interpretation of the clause on the prohibition of abuse rights (Article 17 ECHR) the Strasbourg Court enlarged the limits regarding hate speech. It developed the doctrine of **indirect harm** punishing all the expressions that foster stereotypes dangerous for the maintenance of the democratic system (see, *ex multis*, case of *Garaudy v France*, Application No. 65831/01, Decision, 24th of June, 2003; case *of Feret v Belgium*, Application

No. 15615/07, Judgment, 16th of July, 2009; case of *M'Bala M'Bala* v France, Application No. 25239/13, Decision, 20th of October, 2015).

1.c.2. Pluralism through Media

Although in 1946 television was not entirely unknown, and radio broadcasting played a decisive role during World War II, the framers of the Constitution decided to regulate more precisely the press, a *medium* that during the fascist period had suffered from the greatest and most hateful controls by the regime. Consequently, the heart of Article 21 is occupied by provisions concerning the freedom of the press that is meticulously regulated. Paragraph 2 categorically excludes the possibility of subjecting the press to censorship and authorisation, precisely to avoid *ex ante* controls on the content spread by newspapers. Moreover, according to paragraph 3, seizure of press is permitted only by reasoned judicial orders and for the offences expressly determined by the law on the press. These provisions that strictly govern the press show how in the past **the social dimension of the freedom of speech** has been underestimated, ignoring the influence that the media could have.

From the mid-1970s onwards, the need arose to reinterpret Article 21 in the light of the technological changes taking place, compensating for the silence of the framers of the Constitution on radio and television. In a context of increasing favour for private enterprise, there was the problem of preventing broadcasting companies from producing distorting effects. In fact, at the time, objective structural limitations prevented the development of a fully competitive audio-visual market, with the risk of concentrating enormous media power in the hands of a few. The media regime was basically duopolistic: the public service, on one hand, and the other private TV channels like, in particular, Mediaset.

Attempts to regulate the radio and television system were unsuccessful for many years, and the solutions that were finally found were not satisfactory. It would be impossible to summarise almost 30 years of legislative and jurisprudential events that marked the stages of an uneven journey. It is more interesting to mention the solutions that were found thanks to the Constitutional Court's interpretation of pluralism in these matters, both with regard to entrepreneurial activity and in terms of content.

First, the Constitutional Court reminded both parliament and the government of the duty to seek solutions that reconcile the active and the passive side of the manifestation of thought (freedom to inform and to be informed) in order to realise the democratic principle. Therefore, it has urged them to remedy the anomalous duopoly in Italy in the radio and television sector. The solution proposed by

© Wolters Kluwer Italia

the Court was based on the elaboration of concepts of **internal pluralism** on the one hand and of **external pluralism** on the other. According to the former, media companies – particularly the public service – should broadcast the greatest possible number of opinions, trends, political, social and cultural currents of thought present in society, and therefore facilitate the participation of citizens in the social and cultural development of the country. External pluralism requires a plurality of competing private media, in order to broadcast a variety of voices and ensure the citizens' right to information (Judgment No. 826/1988).

In this sense, the provisions of the radio and television laws already enacted were considered unconstitutional. These included Law No. 223/1990, the 'Mammì law'; Law No. 249/1997, the 'Maccanico law'; and Law No. 112/2004, the 'Gasparri law'. All these laws legitimised the duopoly regime, condemned by the Court. With the transition from analogue to digital system, the problem was partly solved – at least in principle – as there would be space for everybody on the air. However, critical elements have persisted regarding access to market, as the strongest entrepreneurs have an advantage.

Following the same path previously traced, the ItCC declared Law No. 28/2000 on political communication, more commonly known as the "*par condicio* law", to be compatible with the Constitution. This law regulates access of competing political forces to the media, especially during electoral campaigns, in order to prevent economically strong candidates from occupying most of the space available to spread their own political propaganda, which would consequently give them a clear advantage.

It should be clear that, until around the new millennium, the main concern was to establish a rigorous discipline of broadcasting media, strongly committing public institutions to realising full protection of the freedom of expression. With the advent of the internet age, however, the perspective changed again, bringing attention back to the individual dimension of this freedom.

1.c.3. From Freedom of Press to the Internet

Thanks to the possibility for web users to indiscriminately access the internet, the participatory aspect has been enhanced: information is no longer limited to that which is provided by professionals but can be disclosed by anyone directly. *Digito ergo sum* seems to be the motto, satisfied through free access to the network. The consequences of this change are manifold.

First, the availability of technological means is unequal and this calls for measures to bridge the so-called **digital divide**. This was already clear when the internet started to be part of the ordinary life of everyone and became even more evident during the pandemic period. Internet allowed people to continue working, studying, participating in public life and making decisions. Scholars had started to question if access to the internet could be considered as a fundamental right even before the pandemic. Some answer unequivocally in the positive (Azzariti 2011) especially by virtue of the provisions of Article 2: internet contributes decisively to the development of each person's personality both as an individual and in social groups. In relation to this, it has been proposed to insert an *ad hoc* constitutional provision, an article 21 *bis*, which would explicitly recognise a **fundamental right to internet**.

However, the recognition of the new right to the internet implies the emergence of new rights that also need to be protected: in particular, the right to be forgotten and the right to anonymity. The **right to be forgotten** has emerged thanks to EU case law (see ECJ *Google Spain SL and Google Inc. v La Agencia Española de Protección de Datos e Mario Costeja Gonzálezand*, C- 131/12, 13 May 2014), then normalised by Article 17 of EU Regulation 2016/679, which is directly applicable in Italy. On the other hand, the **right to anonymity** has not been regulated yet, but finds its basis in ECtHR case law, due to a wide interpretation of Articles 8 and 10 of the European Convention (the right to respect for private life and freedom of expression). However, there are good constitutional reasons to state the opposite. As a matter of fact, anonymity poses serious problems related to the persecution of illicit activities that are increasingly committed online, such as incitement of violence. Even Article 21, para. 3, permits the seizure of the press in case of violations of the provision concerning the disclosure of the identity of a person responsible for a crime. Some scholars assume that this provision forbids the recognition of the right to anonymity on the internet as well.

At the same time, there has a paradigm shift: the freedom to inform and be informed is no longer guaranteed through Article 21, but also through all those constitutional and European rules governing economic initiatives: nowadays, the sector of **digital rights** is regulated under the umbrella of the competition law, much more in line with the need to have flexible rules. For this reason, the para-legislative role of independent authorities is enhanced.

On closer inspection, there is a further and more important consequence, the results of which cannot easily be evaluated. The incessant and increasingly insistent requests for **online participation** are inevitably accompanied by the need to find a fair compromise between private and collective interests. The ease with which messages can be created, their speed of dissemination and the ability to hide behind online anonymity lead public institutions to focus on the limits to be placed on the dissemination of ideas by appealing to a responsible exercise of the freedom in question: just think of the hate speech that harms the

© Wolters Kluwer Italia

dignity of minority groups, which has already been mentioned. The dissemination of **hate messages online** that can impact on the peaceful human relationships raises new legal questions about the appropriate remedies that can be thought up to stop this (PITRUZZELLA/POLLICINO 2020). In this regard, in addition to the trend to increase limits to the freedom of expression, there is a tendency to extend criminal liability – that is personal – to subjects that are indirectly involved, such as the internet service providers. Among the many legal problems that arise, it is sufficient here to recall those related to the specifications of the circumstances according to which internet providers can be charged for failure to control, so as not to depart from the principle of individual criminal liability. Other issues relate to the spreading of **fake news**. As the pandemic period has shown, fake news can seriously impact on people's beliefs potentially leading to radical choices also on health matters. Similarly, misinformation generated by fake news can also have consequences on elections and can jeopardise the very same functioning of democracy. Regarding fake news, many scholars think that legal institutions should be proactive, establishing an effective public service on the internet (MANETTI 2022).

However, this season has just begun, and it is hard to predict where technological changes will lead. The decision on how to tackle these issues is still a sort of 'work in progress'. At the moment, only a feeling of dissatisfaction can be registered concerning how public authorities are dealing with the new scenario. A decade after many of the fundamental issues relating to the internet began to arise, a legislative vacuum still persists. In the absence of specific provisions governing the network as a whole, the burden of solving the problem lies with independent authorities and the judiciary. For example, instead of removing single illegal messages, judges can decide to shut down entire social network pages that convey unpleasant posts, thus applying to the internet the same rules meant for press seizure. The consequences are evident: on the one hand, such decisions would contradict the general prohibition of extending criminal provisions through analogy; on the other, they would clash with the principle of pluralism, introducing a kind of censorship that is absolutely prohibited by Article 21.

2. Cultural, Ethnic and Linguistic Pluralism

Beyond the principle of social pluralism, the Constitution plays a vital role in safeguarding communities and groups through the recognition and preservation of **cultural, ethnic and linguistic pluralism**. These facets of pluralism centre around recognizing and accepting the diverse cultural and linguistic minorities within a given society or community. Emphasizing the importance of embracing and respecting the different minority groups present within the nation, this aspect of pluralism aims to foster inclusivity, nurture an environment of acceptance, and promote the harmonious coexistence of diverse identities within the Italian legal framework.

2.a. Safeguarding Linguistic Minorities: Language as a Cultural and Ethnic Guarantee

In Italy, there are several language minorities, historically developed because of the presence of **different ethnic and cultural groups** within the country. Some notable examples of the most important linguistic minorities in Italy can be mentioned: German in South Tyrol (recognized as an official language together with Italian); French in Aosta Valley (also recognized as an official language together with Italian); Ladin in Trentino-South Tyrol and Veneto; Slovene in Friuli-Venice-Julia; Occitan in Piedmont; Catalan in Alghero (Sardinia); and so on.

According to Article 6 of the Constitution «[t]he Republic shall safeguard language minorities by means of appropriate measures». This specific provision establishes the protection of **ethnic and linguistic pluralism**. By means of this norm, the Constituent Assembly committed the new republican system to the protection of linguistic minorities in compliance with an **autonomous principle** relevant on a domestic level. From the preliminary work carried out on the Constitution, it is therefore quite easy to deduce that it is **the language** – and not rather ethnicity or culture – which represents the distinctive criterion to protect some relevant communities from dominant social groups.

This decision has had a series of significant consequences. Firstly, language is not protected as such, but as an essential means of conveying the social, cultural and ethnic dimension of a **community**. Secondly, the general principles of pluralism and equality, enshrined in Articles 2 and 3 of the Constitution, respectively, were **not** considered **sufficient** to guarantee the protection of social minorities and their cultural values. Instead, it was necessary to introduce a specific provision protecting these groups even beyond the standards of equality. This creates a discipline aimed at preserving linguistic and, more broadly, historical and cultural peculiarities, by offering such minorities a **privileged status** within the limits set by the standard of reasonableness. Thirdly, the Constitution clearly distinguishes between **two different situations**. Article 6 directly protects linguistic minorities located in the border areas or in *linguistic islands* scattered throughout the national territory. Other constitutional principles – Article 9 in particular, promoting the development of culture and the historical heritage of the nation – protect individuals who do not belong to any specific group speaking a different language but are also characterised by a *linguistic tradition* (PIZZORUSSO 1993 at 57).

 © Wolters Kluwer Italia

In this regard, the Constitutional Court affirmed on several occasions that «the protection of linguistic minorities must be considered **a fundamental principle** of the legal system» (Judgment No. 15/1996). This principle not only overcomes the liberal concepts of a basically *closed* nation state – i.e. a legal system ethnically, linguistically and culturally homogeneous with a tendency to be insular and have limited engagement with other states and the international community – but also represents «a major political and cultural reversal with respect to the nationalistic attitude of the fascist regime, indefectibly and necessarily qualifying the Republic» (Judgments Nos. 62/1992, 768/1988, 289/1987, and 312/1983). According to the Court, Article 6 established a rule that structurally characterises the **new democratic order** as well as its form of state and government. As a result, the protection afforded to linguistic minorities is more than a mere safeguard of their languages, as «it is directly intended to enhance an ethnic and cultural heritage, which in the collective feeling of the speakers is still present and vital» (Judgment No. 170/2010).

The protection of linguistic minorities is thus an expression of the fundamental principles of social pluralism and of formal and substantive equality shaping the entire constitutional system (Judgments nos. 159/2009, and 88/2011). The linguistic dimension referred to in Article 6 is «an element of fundamental importance that, together with national, ethnic, religious, and cultural factors, contributes to defining the **individual and collective identity** of persons and groups». The protection of linguistic minorities is hence considered to be the paradigmatic expression of a broader and more detailed guarantee of identities and **social pluralism** (Judgment No. 81/2018).

From this standpoint, the recognition of linguistic minorities becomes a cultural expression that connotes the legal system and therefore postulates the need for **positive action** by State and regional institutions in order to safeguard those groups in their territory. Linguistic pluralism shows the history and heritage of different cultures, reflecting the identities of peoples and nations: the more diverse the languages, the more varied the identities will be. Accordingly, this leads to various cultural specificities that represent the special features of belonging to a community with a unique identity. In the context of societies marked by growing linguistic diversity leading to cultural pluralism in its broadest sense, it is necessary that the legal order ensures **harmonious interaction**, along with the will to coexist among individuals and groups with plural and diverse cultural, ethnic and linguistic identities (PALERMO/WOELK 2003).

2.a.1. Safeguarding of Historical Linguistic Minorities

The rule under Article 6, read in conjunction with Articles 2 and 3 , is specified by a group of detailed provisions established by different sources of law. More precisely, Law No. 482/1999 introduces an organic discipline that recognises and safeguards linguistic minorities that have **historically settled in Italy**, i.e., Albanian, Catalan, German, Greek, Slovenian and Croatian minorities, as well as individuals speaking French, Franco-Provençal, Friulian, Ladin, Occitan, and Sardinian. The same act also determines funding mechanisms for specific initiatives and outlines procedures for local authorities to follow in order to ensure the safeguarding of linguistic minorities in some particular fields, including schools, universities, relations with the public administration, toponymy, and radio or TV programs.

Overall, Law No. 482/1999 defines a **closed number** of linguistic minorities, which – regardless of Italian being the official language of the Republic – are considered significant elements of the country's **national and cultural heritage**. National legislation does not protect every linguistic minority as such, but it does elevate some specific languages and cultures that have traditionally had a **connection** with certain territories. Hence, the reference to the local historical element is very significant and has a decisive impact on the procedures aimed at delimiting the territories in which the protection of minority identities and cultures works concretely.

In short, anchoring the protection of linguistic minorities to the **territorial dimension** defines «a safe and culturally formed context, from which each linguistic group will be able to move towards the world around it» (Judgment No. 62/1992). Moreover, this criterion simplifies the entire protection mechanism since the *ad hoc* provisions determining and justifying the status of linguistic minorities operate only in those geographical areas. Consequently, the affected individuals will be able to seek protection exclusively within specific territories. In this way, a tangle of regulations and procedures ensuring the protection of ethnic and cultural minorities is avoided. In conclusion, by considering the autonomy of educational institutions as well as the increased number of regional competences on this subject matter, the domestic legislation on linguistic minorities seeks **synergy between State, regional and local groups** in order to protect languages as a cultural and ethnic element of pluralism.

2.a.2. Regional and Local Protection

The procedures established by Law No. 482/1999 to safeguard recognised linguistic minorities involve various public bodies at different times and levels, creating a sort of *variable geometry* system. From the very beginning, the Constitutional Court exclusively assigned the regulatory power in this field to the **State legislator** basically because of «mandatory needs for **unity and equality**» (Judgment No. 62/1960). The Court then gradually granted a similar power to

 © Wolters Kluwer Italia

the **regional legislator** as well, albeit within certain **limits** (e.g., Judgment No. 159/2009). According to the Court, «there is no doubt that this recognition allows regional legislators to protect linguistic minorities, especially for cultural and historical reasons. However, it does not attribute to Regions with ordinary status the autonomous and indiscriminate power to identify and protect their own regional language or other minority languages, beyond what is recognised and established by the State legislator, nor – least of all – does it allow the regional legislator to identify its community as a linguistic minority to be protected according to Article 6 of the Constitution» (Judgment No. 170/2010).

Specific provisions intended to protect linguistic minorities can be found in the special statutes of Aosta Valley, Trentino-South Tyrol and Friuli-Venice-Julia (see above *I.C).8.*). The statute of Aosta Valley recognises the French and Italian languages on equal footing, by introducing total **bilingualism** not only in the drafting and communication of public documents but also in teaching and education. Correspondingly, the statute of Trentino-South Tyrol provides for an articulated system of protection for the linguistic minorities in its territory (German and Ladin), expressly inserting the safeguard of languages among the principles of *national interest* that the region is obliged to respect in the exercise of its legislative power. Finally, with regard to the statute of Friuli-Venice-Julia, it guarantees **equal rights and treatment** to all citizens, notwithstanding their linguistic group, by safeguarding their respective ethnic and cultural characteristics. This provision especially concerns the Slovenian, Friulian and Ladin minorities.

With Regional Law No. 26/1997, Sardinia guarantees and protects the «free and multiform expression of identities, languages and culture» within the Region. It considers the Sardinian language, the Catalan language in Alghero, the Tabarchino of the Sulcis islands and the Sassari and the Gallura dialects as **fundamental cultural elements** to be safeguarded. The free use of the Sardinian language is also admitted in the regional assembly and other local bodies. Similarly, with the Regional Law No. 26 /1998, Sicily adopted specific rules to protect the **cultural and linguistic heritage** of the Albanian communities settled on the island. This law entrusts the Region with signing agreements with public broadcasting services to produce news, cultural, educational and entertainment programs in Albanian or other minority languages.

In this context, **three kinds of linguistic minorities** can be identified: groups that are highly-protected by the statutes of Regions with special status; historically recognised minorities safeguarded by Law No. 482/1999; and other linguistic groups that are also safeguarded by local authorities by virtue of the pluralistic system based on diversity and cultural enhancement.

2.a.3. International Protection

In addition to constitutional protection, Italy has also ratified **international conventions and agreements** that emphasise the importance of protecting linguistic minorities. The Framework Convention for the Protection of National Minorities, ratified with Law No. 302/1997 and which entered into force the following year, aims at safeguarding the existence of national minorities by promoting their **full and effective equality** in the field of fundamental rights and creating appropriate conditions that enable linguistic groups «to preserve and develop their culture and the essential elements of their **identity**». This convention sets out principles concerning individuals belonging to linguistic minorities in the sphere of public life as well as in the sphere of freedoms relating to education, trans-frontier cooperation, and access to the media.

More specifically, the European Charter for Regional or Minority Languages considers the promotion of linguistic minorities as part of a **common cultural heritage** which contributes to the building of a Europe based on democracy and pluralism. The Charter was adopted as a convention in 1992 by the Committee of Ministers of the Council of Europe and entered into force in 1998, applying to 25 member states. Eight countries, including Italy, have signed the Charter without ratifying it yet. In 2018, the Committee of Ministers adopted changes, which entered into force a year later, in the course of the monitoring mechanism. The European Charter offers enhanced protection for regional linguistic minorities by adopting highly detailed provisions on among others, teaching and education, relations with judicial authorities, administrative bodies and public services, cultural activities and facilities, media, economic and social life.

In this regard, the Constitutional Court provided a concise examination of the main international conventions regarding the protection of linguistic minorities, stating that «international treaties, such as the Universal Declaration of Human Rights and the European Convention of Human Rights, affirmed protection of linguistic minorities as a corollary of the general principles of equality and non-discrimination. Starting from the 1990s, however, international provisions tackling **autonomously** the issue of the safeguarding of minorities, went **beyond the mere non-discrimination** and guaranteed the right to use minority languages in institutional relations, education, and culture, in order to ensure the **effective participation** of these groups in the collective life of their country» (Judgment No. 159/2009).

2.b. Freedom of Arts and Sciences

Starting with the assumption that there can be neither social nor human progress without cultural growth, the Italian legal system promotes culture in all

 © Wolters Kluwer Italia

its aspects while respecting **ideological and academic pluralism**. Within this framework, education is the individual right to receive «free and adequate education in schools of all types and levels for the expression of human personality» (Judgment No. 240/1972). More specifically, Article 33, para. 1, of the Constitution provides that «[a]rts and science shall be free and may be freely taught». Accordingly, the State cannot impose an *official* art or science, and both terms must be understood in their broadest sense, embracing any manifestation of human intellect compatible with teaching (Judgment No. 77/1964).

Freedom of teaching thus represents an expansion of the freedom of arts and sciences: it is valid for all teachers, it cannot be delegated to other individuals – nor can it be limited by representative bodies – and it guarantees the public **education system's pluralism and neutrality**. Freedom of education also includes the right to profess any theory deemed worthy of acceptance, the freedom to teach according to the scientific method that appears most appropriate, and the right to teach or research without any political, religious, or ideological constraints. The main function of education and cultural pluralism more generally is therefore to allow students to be adequately prepared corresponding to the level considered valid at a given historical moment.

However, teaching freedom must be **balanced** both with the inviolable rights of the person and the fundamental duties of political, economic, and social solidarity. The first binding limit directly derives from Article 31, para. 2, of the Constitution, according to which «the Republic protects [...] children and the young by adopting necessary provisions», and consequently embodies the need to **protect students.** Other general limits are public morality – obviously related to the type of teaching and pupils – constitutional public order, and the prohibition of devaluing or denigrating the «spiritual heritage of the Nation» (Judgment No. 201/1995). It is not possible to use freedom of education for **political propaganda** or **proselytising**. As a result, it must be **neutral**. This aspect does not prevent teachers from expressing their personal positions, but still obliges every teacher to also inform their students of opposing viewpoints (see, for example, ItCC Judgment No. 195/1972, so called *Cordero* case; and ECtHR, case of *Lombardi Vallauri v. Italy*, Application No. 39128/05, Judgment, 20th of October, 2009).

2.b.1. Establishment of Schools and Educational Institutions

These constitutional principles are confirmed by the current legislation. The legislative decree No. 297 of 1994, which forms the Consolidated Text on Education, reiterates that freedom of education, understood **as teaching autonomy and free cultural expression for every teacher**, is guaranteed. The exercise of this freedom is aimed at instructing pupils through an **open comparison of cultural positions** and guaranteeing professional autonomy in cultural, scientific and research activities. Consequently, teaching must be carried out in compliance with pupils' moral and civil conscience, but above all in a plural and democratic context, as schools and universities are groups that interact with the broader social community.

For this reason, the legal system not only guarantees **academic freedom** but also ensures that institutions of education are **autonomously organised and managed**. Subsequently, Article 33, para. 3, affirms that «[e]ntities and private persons shall have the right to establish schools and institutions of education, at no cost for the State». In this way, the State does not have a monopoly on establishing schools and educational courses, and more generally, it cannot control the cultural development of public opinion. This implies that **public authorities must respect academic freedom and the ideological and cultural pluralism of education**. From this perspective, the freedom of arts and sciences can therefore have two distinct, albeit connected, meanings. Firstly, it implies the right of private entities to establish and manage schools. Secondly, it indicates students' freedom to choose private schools.

To this end, decree of the President of the Republic No. 275/1999 expressly states that educational institutions are functionally autonomous in order to ensure cultural pluralism. Schools are entitled to **freely approve their courses and regulate teaching in compliance with freedom of education**. In this respect, Law No. 62/2000, laying down rules for school parity and the right to study and education, reaffirms that «the Italian education system is made up of state schools and private or local schools».

2.b.2. Parity of Non-state Schools

According to Article 33, para 3, «[e]ntities and private persons shall have the right to establish schools and institutions of education, at no cost for the State». This means that non-state educational institutions are considered equal and conform with the public education system. Their offerings are consistent with the educational demands of **families** and are characterised by particular requirements set out in law, such as the stipulation of an educational plan in harmony with the Constitution; the publication of their administrative budget; the obligation to hire highly qualified teachers; and an openness to all students without any discrimination. Regarding the relationship between public and private schools, the continuing **pre-eminence** of State institutions is still justified by the dutiful nature of public intervention in the field of cultural pluralism.

The attempts to overcome the constitutional prohibition on **financing private schools** through State intervention have essentially taken two paths. The first

 © Wolters Kluwer Italia

involves the Regions. They support non-state schools by exercising the regulatory competences set out under legislative decree No. 112 of 1998. The second does not directly finance non-state schools but supports students and their families in private schools in order to promote their **right to study**. From this perspective, Law No. 62/2000 on parity amongst schools and the subsequent Law No. 289/2002 tackle the issue of financing private schools in different terms: they introduce the general **notion of public schools**, which includes both State and non-state schools, and explicitly supports students through dedicated scholarships. In this way, an attempt was made to implement Article 33, para. 4, according to which «[t]he law, when setting out the rights and obligations for non-state schools applying for recognition, shall ensure that such schools enjoy full liberty and offer their pupils an education and qualifications of the same standards as those afforded to pupils in State schools».

2.b.3. Autonomy of Higher Education Institutions, Universities, and Academies

Article 33 of the Constitution qualifies the autonomy of universities and academies as a crucial tool to protect all the **cultural freedoms** enshrined in **Article 9** and exercised in a pluralistic context by the **social groups** protected under **Article 2**. More precisely, Article 33, para. 6, states that «[h]igher education institutions, universities and academies, shall have the right to establish their own regulations within the limits established by the law».

Regarding ordinary schools in particular, a distinctive feature of higher education institutions is the «inextricable connection between [their] research and teaching activities» (Judgment No. 29/1993). Universities are *par excellence* the place for cultural and spiritual formation, where scientific research and teaching, organisational and financial autonomy are significantly encouraged. This is a statement of principle that needs to be implemented at statutory and regulatory levels through coherent provisions and procedures, especially because the **autonomy of universities**, envisaged by Law No. 168/1989, is not yet fully realised in practice. In this context, the autonomy of higher education institutions must be primarily interpreted in order to guarantee **professors' freedom to research and teach** on their findings. Nevertheless, the autonomy of universities also implies that every single institution governs itself by establishing its own systems, freely electing its branches of governance, and adopting its own specific internal regulations and statutes. This is above all **regulatory autonomy**, which expresses itself both externally (i.e., towards the State and other public bodies) and internally (that is, with regard to the organisational structure).

This kind of autonomy, therefore, must not be considered in overarching and unitary terms, but as an **individual characteristic of each university**. Only in this way will it be possible to create vigorous competition between different academies and raise the bar for scientific research achievement. Higher education institutions go beyond being mere bureaucratic extensions of state authority; structured as independent bodies, they are able of **enriching the pluralistic cultural environment**. The Constitutional Court, examining once again the merits of the provision under Article 33, stated that «the State legislator must only delimit the external content of this autonomy, while professors must be guaranteed the ownership and irremovability of their academic position» (Judgment No. 423/2004). Hence, the current right of universities to regulate independently their own competence in research and teaching both on administrative and cultural levels is **inviolable**.

REFERENCES

ALICINO, F. [2017], 'The place of minority religions and the strategy of major denominations. The case of Italy', *Rivista AIC* 2.

AZZARITI, G. [2011], 'Internet e Costituzione', 17(3) *Politica del diritto.*

BARBERA, A. [2007], 'Il cammino della laicità' in CANESTRARI, S. (ed), *Laicità e diritto* (Bologna, Bononia University Press).

BIN, R. [2001], 'Le potestà legislative regionali, dalla Bassanini ad oggi', 19(4) *Le Regioni.*

BIN, R. [2014], 'Stato delle autonomie vs. governo della burocrazia', 18(1) *Le Istituzioni del federalismo.*

BOBBIO, N. [1995], *Il futuro della democrazia* (Torino, Einaudi).

BÖCKENFÖRDE, E.W. [2020], *Religion, Law, and Democracy: Selected Writings* (Oxford, OUP).

CARETTI, P. [2000], 'Il sistema delle Conferenze e i suoi riflessi sulla forma di governo nazionale e regionale', 28(3-4) *Le Regioni.*

CECCANTI, S. [2021], 'Come in Baviera: il crocifisso resta alla parete, se è la scelta della classe', 41(4) *Quaderni Costituzionali.*

CHIARAMONTE, A. & EMANUELE, V. [2022], *The deinstitutionalization of Western European party systems* (London, Palgrave Macmillan).

CLEMENTI, F. [2019], 'The Italian Constitution after seventy years between referenda, electoral laws and institutional reform: a past that does not pass?', 24(3) *Journal of Modern Italian Studies.*

COTTA, M. & VERZICHELLI, L. [2007], *Political Institutions in Italy* (Oxford, OUP).

CRISAFULLI, V. & PALADIN, L. (eds) [1990], *Commentario breve alla Costituzione* (Padova, Cedam).

CROUCH, C. [2019], 'Post-Democracy and Populism', 90(1) *The Political Quarterly.*

D'ATENA, A. [1997], 'Le Regioni, tra crisi e riforma' in PACE, A. (ed), *Quale dei tanti federalismi?* (Padova, Cedam).

D'ATENA, A. [2003], 'Materie legislative e tipologia delle competenze', 23(1) *Quaderni costituzionali.*

DUVERGER, M. [1961], *I partiti politici* (Milano, Edizioni di Comunità).

ELIA, L. [2005], 'Alcide De Gasperi e l'Assemblea Costituente', 15(2) *Astrid Rassegna.*

ELIA, L. [2008], 'Introduzione ai problemi della laicità', in *Problemi pratici della laicità agli inizi del secolo XXI. Atti del XXII Convegno Annuale dell'Associazione Italiana dei Costituzionalisti, Napoli, 26-27 ottobre 2007* (Padova, Cedam).

FARAGUNA, P. [2019], 'Regulating Religion in Italy. Constitution Does (not) Matter', 7(1) *Journal of Law, Religion and State.*

 © Wolters Kluwer Italia

FASONE, C. & PICCIRILLI, G. [2021], 'The new "form of government" in the reform of the Italian regional system' in ARBAN, E. AND OTHERS (eds) *Federalism and Constitutional Law. The Italian Contribution to comparative Regionalism* (London, Routledge).
FERRARI, A. [2023], 'La laicità importuna: laicità costituzionale e libertà religiosa' 18(5) *Stato Chiese e Pluralismo confessionale*.
GROPPI, T. & SCATTONE, N. [2006], 'Italy: The Subsidiarity Principle', 4(1) *I·CON*.
GROTTANELLI DE SANTI G. [2006], 'The Italian Variant of Federalism', in FEDTKE, J. & MARKESINIS, B.S. (eds), *Patterns of Regionalism and Federalism. Lessons for the UK* (London, Hart).
JONES, E. & PASQUINO, G. [2015], *The Oxford Handbook of Italian Politics* (Oxford, OUP).
HINE, D. [1993], *Governing Italy: The Politics of Bargained Pluralism* (Oxford, OUP).
HUNTINGTON, S. [2012], *The Third Wave: Democratisation in the Late 20th Century* (Norman Oklahoma, University of Oklahoma Press).
LARICCIA, S. [1991], 'Stato e Confessioni religiose', in *Enciclopedia Giuridica* (Roma, Istituto della Enciclopedia Italiana).
LEPRE, A. [1993], *Storia della Prima Repubblica: l'Italia dal 1942 al 1992* (Bologna. il Mulino).
LOWENSTEIN, K. [1937], 'Militant Democracy and Fundamental Rights', 31(4) *The American Political Science Review*.
LUCIANI, M. [2023], 'La Costituzione e il pluralismo' in CAPPELLINI, P. & CAZZETTA, G. (eds), *Pluralismo giuridico itinerari contemporanei* (Milano, Giuffrè).
MANETTI, M. [2022], 'Freedom of Speech and the Regulation of Fake News', in GRAZIADEI M. & TORSELLO M. (eds), *Rapports Nationaux Italiens au XXIe Congrès International de Droit Comparé - Italian National Reports to the XXIst International Congress of Comparative Law - Asunción 2022* (Napoli, Edizioni Scientifiche Italiane).
MARGIOTTA BROGLIO, F. [1966], *Italia e Santa Sede dalla Grande Guerra alla Conciliazione* (Roma-Bari, Laterza).
MORRONE, A. [2001], *Il custode della ragionevolezza* (Milano, Giuffrè).
MORTATI, C. [1975], 'Articolo 1', in BRANCA G. (ed), *Commentario alla Costituzione. Principi fondamentali* (Bologna-Roma, Zanichelli-Foro italiano).
PACE, A. [1992], *Problematica delle libertà costituzionali, Lezioni, Parte speciale* (Padova, Cedam).
PALERMO, F. & WOELK, J. [2003], 'No representation without recognition: The right to political participation of (National) minorities', 25(3) *Journal of European Integration*.
PALERMO F. [2005], 'Italy's Long Devolutionary Path Towards Federalism' in ORTINO, S. AND OTHERS (EDS), *The Changing Faces of Federalism. Institutional Reconfiguration in Europe from East to West* (Manchester, Manchester University Press).
PALERMO, F. & WILSON, A. [2014], 'The multi-level dynamics of state decentralization in Italy', 12(4-5) *Comparative European Politics*.
PASQUALI CERIOLI, J. [2023], 'Laicità', 18(2) *Stato Chiese e Pluralismo confessionale*.
PASQUINO, G. [2009], 'Political history in Italy', 21(3) *Journal of Policy History*.
PITRUZZELLA, G. & POLLICINO, O. [2020], *Disinformation and Hate Speech. A European Constitutional Perspective* (Milano, University Bocconi Press).
PIZZORUSSO, A. [1993], 'Eguaglianza (Diritto)' in *Enciclopedia delle scienze sociali*.
POMBENI, P. [2006], 'Il contributo dei cattolici alla costituente' in LABRIOLA, S. (ed), *Valori e principi del regime repubblicano* (Roma-Bari, Laterza).
RAGONE, G. & VANONI, L.P. [2018], 'From the Secularisation Theory to the Pluralistic Approach: Reconciling Religious Traditions and Modernity in Italian Case-Law' in GILES, J. AND OTHERS (eds), *Law, Religion and Tradition* (Berlin, Springer International Publishing).
RUFFINI, F. [1992], *La libertà religiosa come diritto pubblico subiettivo* (Bologna, Il Mulino).

Russo, L. & Vergetti, F. [2023], 'The general election of 2022: the return of bipolarity?', 15(2) *Contemporary Italian Politics*.
Sartori, G. [2005], *Parties and Party Systems: A Framework for Analysis* (Cambridge, CUP).
Taylor, C. [2011], 'Why We Need a Radical Redefinition of Secularism', in Butler, J. and others (eds), *The Power of Religion in the Public Sphere* (New York, Columbia University Press).
Ventura, M. [2021], 'Il crocifisso dallo Stato-istituzione allo Stato-comunità', 41(4) *Quaderni Costituzionali*.
Weiler, JHH. [2010], 'State and Nation; Church, Mosque and Synagogue – The Trailer', 8(2) *International Journal of Constitutional Law*.

 © Wolters Kluwer Italia

Part IV

Rights and Duties in the Italian Constitution

The Constitution of the Italian Republic of 1948 – as opposed to the previous one, the Albertine Statute of 1848 – specifically focuses on recognising and guaranteeing the rights of the person. The republican legal system relies on the absolute value of the person and on the expansion of rights (Bobbio 1990). This was certainly a reaction to the annihilation of human dignity that occurred during World War II, but it also entailed moving past the freedoms of the liberal tradition of the 1800s, by, for example, proclaiming political and social rights. Rights represent the founding values of the new constitutional legal system, born out of the Resistance to fascism, to which all institutions and all of society were called upon to contribute.

Following the centrality of the person, the Italian Constitutional Court recognised the vast majority of the rights proclaimed in the Constitution also to foreigners, with the exception of right to vote.

Rights, understood as a limit to and as a basis of public power, are one of the most significant elements of **constitutionalism**: a Western political, philosophical, legal and cultural movement, aimed at **limiting the State's power** through written constitutional documents, which are also principle-based and liberal democratic. It is only after World War II that rights become the main instrument to build an alternative legal order.

Take as an example the United Nations (UN) Universal Declaration of Human Rights of 1948, which can be viewed as a new order founded on human rights. The doctrine coined by the US President Theodor Roosevelt, which contributed to the creation of the UN, should also be considered. It comprises the four freedoms that everyone ought to enjoy: freedom of expression, freedom of religion, freedom from want, and freedom from fear. These examples shed light on the dual nature of rights: on the one hand, they delegitimise the old order, and on the other, they contribute to the development of a new one. Rights then became a key word in contemporary public debate and the Italian legal system is no exception.

Moving from these premises, in Section B the protection of rights is explored with particular attention. The republican Constitution established instruments that had never been seen before in the Italian legal system for the purpose

of guaranteeing rights: the rigidity of the Constitution, the reserve of legislation, the legality principle under criminal law and the review of constitutional legitimacy.
A contemporary feature of the domestic legal system (common to numerous western democracies) that is extensively discussed in Section C, is the role developed by judicial review in protecting rights and reducing inequality. The **lawmakers'** difficulties in adopting legislation and mediating conflicts rerouted the aspirations of individuals and minority groups towards having **their rights** recognised by courts that increasingly scrutinises lawmakers' discretion. This is based on the principles affirmed by **neo-constitutionalism**. Section C addresses crucial rulings taken by the Italian Constitutional Court.
The issues discussed in this last Section should be considered along with those on secularity, the freedom of expression and the freedom of association dealt with in Part III.

A) ITALIAN CONSTITUTIONALISM AS A LIMIT TO PUBLIC POWER

1. Article 2 of the Constitution

Article 2 establishes that «The Republic shall recognise and protect the inviolable rights of the person, both as an individual and in the social groups where

 © Wolters Kluwer Italia

human personality is expressed. The Republic expects that the fundamental duties of political, economic and social solidarity be fulfilled».

Article 2, in particular, moves beyond the classical German theory, postulated by Georg Jellinek, which affirms that individual rights are based on the state's self-limitation. On the contrary, inviolable rights, which are defined in Article 2, pre-exist the state and thus limit the state's power.

It lists, among the fundamental principles of the Constitution (Articles 1-12), «the substantial **precedence of the human person** (understood as the whole of his or her material as well as spiritual values and needs) as opposed to the State and the purpose of the **State to serve the person**» ('ordine del giorno' Dossetti in Atti della Assemblea Costituente [Dossetti 'resolution' at the Constituent Assembly], Subcommittee I, 9th of September, 1946, already cited in *I A, 3, I.B).3.*). In 1948 the **gap** between the **fundamental principles** sanctioned in the Constitution, which were innovative and ambitious, and the **social and legal context** in Italy was extremely wide. This backsliding was partly due to the repressive authoritarianism of the fascist regime. Because of this gap, following the Constitution's entry into force, the most important organ of judiciary, the Court of Cassation, elaborated a doctrine according to which certain constitutional provisions were merely aspirational: meaning that, since they outlined programs or established fundamental rights and principles, they were not deemed capable of immediately binding lawmakers and, as a result, would remain dormant pending their necessary legislative implementation. This doctrine effectively froze for a significant period of time the innovative power of both Article 2 and the articles concerning fundamental rights.

When the Constitutional Court (ItCC) was finally able to issue its first judgment (Judgment No. 1/1956), it **rejected this interpretation**, confirming that all **constitutional provisions are prescriptive and immediately applicable**, meaning that they trigger the unconstitutionality of a law that conflicts with them. Therefore, it is not unreasonable to link the evolution of Italian society also to the influence exercised by Article 2, then as now. Starting from the end of the 1960s, the most informed and engaged part of Italian society used the reference to Article 2 to push lawmakers to adopt liberal legislation concerning individual freedoms. Just consider the legislation that was adopted as a result of these battles: Law No. 898/1970 on divorce; Law No. 772/1972 on conscientious objection; Law No. 151/1975 on the modernisation and reform of family law; Law No. 194/1978 on abortion; Law No. 164/1982 on the legal recognition of preferred gender (BARBERA/FUSARO 2022).

This level of innovation has remained over time, allowing the Constitutional Court to use the provisions of Article 2 in two completely new, but complementary ways. Firstly, it made it possible to offer **constitutional status** also to those rights that are not specifically set out in the list of constitutional rights, but which, in the development of society and technology, acquired significant importance. From 1987 onwards, new (that is, not explicitly set out in the Constitution) inviolable rights were recognised by the ItCC (Judgment No. 561/1987). Analogously, the Constitutional Court – prior to the reform of Article 117, para. 1, of the Constitution – was able to align the domestic constitutional legal system with the European legal and cultural movement defined as the multi-level protection of rights through the reference to Article 2 (see *II.B).3.*).

2. Definitions

The Constitution explicitly recognises numerous rights and some duties (in particular, in Articles 13-54). As previously stated, these are those rights and duties that were deemed fundamental, especially in light of their denial under the fascist regime and of the atrocities committed during World War II. All contemporary written constitutions dedicate a section to the proclamation of rights and duties, with at least one exception: the Constitution of France does not set out a specific list of rights; rather, its Preamble refers to the *Déclaration* of 1789.

Many constitutions refer, explicitly or implicitly (as does Article 11 of the Italian Constitution), to the UN Universal Declaration of Human Rights of 1948 that stood as an example for numerous international Covenants on civil, political and social rights proclaimed at international level in the following decades. Moreover, the European Convention for the Protection of Human Rights and Fundamental Freedoms, better known as European Convention on Human Rights (ECHR) is mentioned in numerous constitutions. It was signed in Rome in 1950 and it acquired a growing importance due to the creation of a Court (ECtHR) whose aim is to implement the Convention and to the fact that almost all States of the European continent are part of the Council of Europe and have ratified the ECHR as well as its additional Protocols (with the exception of Vatican and Belarus).

The constitutions established since the end of the 1990s have increased the number of guaranteed rights and duties, as demonstrated by the choices made in the legal systems of South Africa and of the countries in Central and South America, but also in the EU, through the proclamation of the Charter of Fundamental Rights of the European Union (CFREU) in 2000.

This expansion was due to the **evolution of society**, which demanded the recognition of new rights, for example, from the right to personal data protection up to the proclamation in several constitutions – such as those in Portugal, Greece, Ecuador, and Mexico – of the right to internet access, which became crucial during the pandemic.

The development was linked to the central nature of the meaning of the **negative limit to political power** embodied **by rights**: immature, more fragile

 © Wolters Kluwer Italia

democracies tend to establish a wide range of rights and duties, understood as a way to **contain** possible political **regression**.

The Italian constitutional legal system distinguishes between rights, legitimate interests, and binding duties of solidarity.

2.a. Rights

Art. 2 recognises and guarantees the inviolable rights of the person: **inviolable** because they are intrinsic to human nature; **inviolable** because they existed prior to political institutions; **inviolable** because they are recognised to all individuals (not just to citizens), and **inviolable** because they cannot be amended once they have been recognised in the Constitution.

Personal freedom, **personal domicile** and the **freedom and confidentiality of communication** are defined as inviolable rights. In other cases, the Constituent Assembly used the term **right** or **freedom** without the adjective inviolable.

Historically, the following have gradually arisen from struggles for emancipation:

• those areas of 'non-interference' from government influence recognised to individuals in liberal single-class legal orders (the basis of consensus is the bourgeoisie), understood as the absence of restrictions, known as **negative** freedoms, for example, **freedom of religion**, **of speech**, **private property**;

• those areas of 'autonomy' that, in a multi-class state (in which the basis of consensus expands to the working class), allow everyone to participate in forming political power, known as **positive** freedoms, for example, **political rights**, the **right to form associations** freely and **to assemble**;

• those areas for which state power is required to **intervene** to ensure well-being and equality, known as **social rights**.

Within contemporary legal systems this distinction is no longer convincing. Indeed, **negative** freedoms also need state promotion to be guaranteed and to be made available to all citizens. Barbera used the expression **institution of liberty**, *istituzioni di libertà*, to pinpoint the complexity of the actions that are required for full enjoyment and participation of such freedoms (Barbera 1975).

Beyond the terms used, the Constitution does not identify certain rights as being more important than others. There is **no hierarchy among constitutional rights** (Cartabia/Lupo 2022).

The rights proclaimed in the Constitution (Articles 13-51) can be exercised against everyone; they are **inalienable**, that is, they cannot be transferred to others by the person entitled to the rights; they are **fundamental** and **indispensable**, *i.e.*, they cannot be renounced or dispensed with through a private agreement; and they have no statute of limitations, *i.e.*, they cannot be forfeited even where they are not exercised.

Unlike the German Basic Law, *Grundgesetz*, the Italian Constitution does not see the compliance with the liberal democratic system, *freiheitliche demokratische Grundordnung*, as a limit to the enjoyment of rights. These two Constitutions thus developed different responses to the common experience, suffered by both legal systems, of an authoritarian regime that took over the previous constitutional order. The German Basic Law deems that compliance with the liberal democratic legal system is a value that must be protected, even by limiting the enjoyment of rights if necessary. The Italian Constitution took a **different approach** through the formulation of Article 2. It would be incorrect to consider that the Constitution sets out **unlimited rights**. The **concept of a limit is inherent in the concept of a right itself**, and within the legal system, the various legal spheres must necessarily place limits on each other, so that they can **coexist** in an ordered, civil manner (Judgment No. 1/1956).

When lawmakers adopt legislation concerning rights they are always required to use the **balancing** technique to try to balance the right to privacy, for example, with concurrent constitutional rights (conflicting in some cases) such as the media's right to inform. The Constitutional Court can rule on the reasonableness of that balancing (*III.A).2.*).

For the sake of convenience, it is possible to distinguish the following based on their content: individual freedoms that protect persons as individuals; freedoms of social formations that protect persons in social groups; social rights; economic freedoms and political rights.

2.b. Individual Freedoms

The individual freedoms (also called rights of freedom) – recognised in the Constitution, mainly in Title I on Civil Relations – that derive from the liberal tradition include: personal freedom, the right to judicial protection in the form of *habeas corpus*, the right to freedom of speech, the right to freely profess one's religion or not to profess any religion, freedom of movement and domicile, the right to assembly and association (even social groups hold rights).

2.c. Social Rights and Economic Freedoms

This is a set of rights that strongly reflect the different political views that were present in the Constituent Assembly, and above all, their common plan: pursuing the strong civil, social, economic and political growth of society by affirming and developing social and economic rights. This had never been declared in Italy in such an extensive manner. The recognition of social rights within the Constitution is wider than any other constitution of the same period.

Title II on Ethical and Social Relations singles out social rights, a fundamental instrument in reducing the extremely backward nature of Italian society following World War II.

 © Wolters Kluwer Italia

These entail protections for the family – only that based on marriage between a woman and a man (see *IV.C).5.f.*); the rights and duties of parents; the right to health, as a fundamental right of the individual and as a collective interest, ensured freely to the indigent (see *IV.C).4.*); the right to free primary education; the right to establish private educational institutions; the right to receive access from the state to higher education for deserving students without adequate financial resources; and the freedom of the arts and sciences.

Title III is on Economic Relations. This recognises, as one of the innovations of the Constitution, the freedom of holding private property; the right to work, to rest and to take holidays; to strike; the right for remuneration that is commensurate to the work performed and, in any case, capable of ensuring workers a free and dignified existence; guarantees for working mothers; the right to social assistance and unemployment and disability protections. The State shall provide for the professional training of workers and shall protect Italian workers abroad. This part of the Constitution sets out the right to industrial action and the freedom to form and join trade unions, as well as private-sector economic initiatives and the right to private property.

2.d. Political Rights

Title IV on Political Rights and Duties establishes the right to vote, to associate in political parties, to present petitions to both Houses of Parliament, and the right for each gender to be eligible for public offices on equal terms.

2.e. New Rights

New rights or **personality rights** are defined as those not explicitly set out in the Constitution, but whose constitutional value has been **recognised by the Constitutional Court**. This is possible thanks to an **expansive interpretation** of Article 2 of the Constitution (Barbera 1975), according to which this Article is an **open-ended clause** that is capable of guaranteeing those rights that are not explicitly recognised by the text of the Constitution. This is also possible by making reference to other articles of the Constitution (Pace 2003), or through a combined reading of the international Covenants on rights ratified by Italy.

In most cases, these are rights already recognised in the legal system, but only by ordinary law. For example: the right to life and physical integrity (see *IV.C).2.*); the right to sexual freedom; the right to privacy and reputation; the right to informed consent; the right to honour and personal identity; the right to gender identity, as a constitutive element of the right to personal identity; the right to housing; the right to freely enjoy the status of a couple for same-sex unions (see *IV.C).5.f.*); and the right of children to know about their biological origins, with consent from the biological mother.

Apart from rare exceptions, lawmakers have not directly introduced new rights into the Constitution, mainly because of the complexity of the amending procedure, which requires not only a solid majority, but also the respect of the identity of the republican order and the untouchable core of its fundamental principles (see *I.C).2.*).

2.f. Legitimate Interests

Regarding access to justice and judicial protection, following the traditional approach of Italian Public Law, Articles 24 and 113 of the Constitution bring together **legitimate interests** with subjective **rights**. Legitimate interest is the name – coined at the beginning of the twentieth century by administrative court case law and legal scholars – indicating the situation of those individuals who can bring a judicial review claim before an administrative court. This 'situation' – vaguely resembling the standing requirement («sufficient interest») in common law administrative law litigation – is nowadays deemed as a right in all respects. However, unlike subjective rights, legitimate interests do not guarantee immediate satisfaction of one's claim. They only award a person a set of 'procedural' or 'instrumental' powers for influencing an administrative decision, including challenging such a decision before administrative courts after the decision has been made. From this perspective, the holder of a legitimate interest cannot ask a court to re-make the decision which has been challenged or to discuss the merits of that decision but only conduct a review of the process by which the decision was reached to assess whether it was flawed and should be quashed. In addition, a person can ask an administrative court for an injunction against the inaction of a public authority. Over time, the idea that legitimate interests have gained a rights-like status has been boosted by their inclusion in situations that allow individuals to ask for compensation by a public authority. For decades the courts had regularly disallowed any claim to obtain compensation for, say, the illegal refusal of permission to start an industry or the omission to consider a proposal for land development on the assumption that there is no 'right' to such decisions. In 1999 this case law was overruled by a seminal judgment of the Court of Cassation, which acknowledged that the violation of legitimate interest amounted to the infringement of a right to a correct decision-making process which could have economic consequences. Later, a statutory law introduced a specific action for compensation before administrative courts as a way of protecting citizens' legitimate interests.

2.g. Rights and Duties

Article 2 clearly specifies the connection between inviolable rights and the fundamental duties of political, economic, and social solidarity, without setting

 © Wolters Kluwer Italia

out a hierarchy between rights and duties. This connection between freedoms, rights and duties forms the basis of the achievement of the fundamental principles of the constitutional legal system. Even the choice of the terms used in the text of the Constitution is highly indicative: the **fundamental** nature of **duties is parallel** to the **inviolable** nature **of rights**.

The members of the Constitutional Assembly reformulated the emphasis placed by Giuseppe Mazzini on the importance of duty, understood as the principle that could best guide men and bind them together in brotherhood (Duties of Man, *Dei doveri dell'uomo*, published in 1860, the year before the unification of the Kingdom of Italy, Barbera/Fusaro 2022).

Unfortunately, the issue of duties is often ignored both by scholars and public opinion, especially if compared to the attention that is given to rights. Constitutional texts are also traditionally associated with the proclamation of rights more than with the guarantee of duties. This imbalance was also impacted by factors that were external to the constitutional legal system. The individualistic rhetoric that has gained significant strength over recent decades has overshadowed what would have been a necessary reflection on the issues concerning duties of solidarity, focusing rather on the individual dimension of rights.

The recurring economic crises and their consequences at the domestic level, as well as the need for environmental protection and sustainable development, demonstrate that there is a lack of mature awareness regarding the fact that the contents of rights and duties of existing persons must take into account (and must be balanced against) the rights of **future generations**.

For example, in a judgment delivered in 2021, the German Federal Constitutional Court (*Bundesverfassungsgericht*, BVerfG) urged the lawmaker to modify the Federal Climate Change Act (Bundes-Klimaschutzgesetz, KSG) to re-adapt the legislation so that it would not place disproportionate burdens upon future generations, ultimately limiting the exercise of their fundamental rights. The KSG regulated national climate targets as well as the annual greenhouse emissions allowed until 2030, but it did not contain further specifications from 2031 onwards. By invoking the lawmakers' duties of protection that arise from Article 2(2) (personal freedom) and Article 14(1) (property and inheritance) of the Basic Law, as well as the fundamental right to a decent future and the right to an ecological minimum standard of living enshrined in Article 20 a, the claimants argued that the lawmaker failed to adopt further measures to reduce greenhouse gas emissions. Even though the Court took into account that it is not ascertainable that the lawmaker violated requirements that are incumbent upon it to avert threats of catastrophic proportions (as it ratified the Paris Agreement and it approved the KSG), it also asked whether the burdens that are inherently built into this legislative framework can be justified, or if the KSG has inadmissibly offloaded reduction burdens onto the future and onto whoever will then bear responsibility (*i.e.*, future generations).

Indeed, according to the BVerfG, fundamental rights are intertemporal guarantees of freedom, and must be taken into consideration in light of this very peculiar nature. The Court finally held that the lawmaker should have taken precautionary steps to mitigate major burdens upon future generations, and urged the lawmaker to specify in greater detail how the reduction targets for greenhouse gas emissions would be adjusted for periods after 2030.

On its part, the Constitutional Court has reiterated on multiple occasions the **principle of social solidarity** that underlies duties, defining it as the principle by which individuals are called upon to act not out of utilitarian calculations or obligations imposed by authorities, but as a free, spontaneous expression of the deep social nature of the person. This is a **principle** regarded by the Constitution as **among the founding values** of the legal system, to the extent that it is solemnly recognised and guaranteed as the basis of the social coexistence conceived by the Constituent Assembly (Judgment No. 75/1992).

The Constitution sets out numerous situations that can be classified as **both rights and duties**. For example, work is both a right, pursuant to Article 4, para. 1, and a duty of material or spiritual contribution to social progress, based on Article 4, para. 2. The duty of parents to support, raise and educate their children (Article 30) is also their right. The right to receive an education corresponds to the compulsory nature of primary education, imparted for free for at least eight years (Article 34). This is also the case for voting, which is one of the most important political rights and, pursuant to Article 48 of the Constitution, also a civic duty.

What are the **duties of solidarity** mentioned in Article 2 of the Constitution? In order of appearance, and also considering those for which the actual term 'duty' is not used, the following should be included: the **duty to contribute to the material or spiritual progress of society** (Article 4); **the duty to educate** (Article 30, para. 1) and **to attend school** (Article 34, para. 2); the **duty to submit to compulsory medical treatments** and those connected with preventing infectious diseases, provided that these are expressly set out by law and are aimed at protecting the collective interest, even if they are not essential to guaranteeing the health of the individual to whom they refer (Article 32, para. 2); and the duty **to defend the Motherland** (Article 52). This duty also takes the form of performing military service or civil service, in the event of conscientious objection (Law Nos. 772/1972 and 230/1998). Mandatory military service was suspended in 2004 and was replaced by professional military service and voluntary universal civil service (which may be performed by both citizens and foreigners), without prejudice to the possibility of implementing the draft in the event of war. The **duty to contribute to public expenditure** (Article 53) essentially takes the form of the duty to pay taxes based on one's taxpaying capacity and on the criteria of progression. The **duty of loyalty to the Republic** (Article 54)

 © Wolters Kluwer Italia

takes on a different meaning with regard to the two different categories of individuals. For common citizens, this entails the obligation to respect the Constitution and the law, and punishes several offences, such as crimes against the international personality of the state. This duty is not a limit to inviolable rights nor, unlike from Germany, does it lay the foundation for the development of a *protected democracy*. On the contrary, citizens who carry out public functions are required to fulfil such functions with discipline and honour, and may have to take an oath (formulated in a different manner, for example, by the President of the Republic, by the members of the government, by magistrates or by constitutional judges).

The provision of **additional duties** (which, however, shall serve the principle of solidarity or will implement constitutionally protected principles and interests) is the **exclusive competence of the law**, as set out in Article 23 of the Constitution. As this article prohibits the exercise of any authoritative power not founded on law, it contains one of the most significant formulations of the principle of legality.

Who are the addressees of the duties set out in the Constitution? The lawmakers identify these parties not only as those who are Italian citizens: the duties of parents to their children apply irrespective of whether the parents are citizens or not, as well as the duty of contributing to public expenditure, unlike the civic duty of voting, which applies only to Italian citizens (see below).

A separate point should be made regarding the **civic duty to vote**, as defined in Article 48 of the Constitution. The Constituent Assembly dealt rigidly with two different concepts of voting: those who considered it an individual's right, successfully acquired by women only in 1946 (while men had enjoyed it since 1912) and those who considered it a duty whose non-exercise should be penalised. Currently no penalties are envisaged (they existed in the past, though very slight and mainly reputational) and the Constitution classifies voting as a **civic duty and a right of all citizens**, the free exercise of which must be guaranteed and promoted by the Republic (Article 4 of Italian presidential decree No. 361/1957).

The Italian legal system also recognises the right to vote of prison inmates who are Italian citizens, though with numerous exceptions, in line with most legal systems, as occurs, for example, also in the French legal system (ECJ, *Thierry Delvigne v Commune de Lesparre-Médoc, Préfet de la Gironde*, C-650/13, 6th of October, 2015). On the other hand, the United Kingdom and Russia (which, since invading Ukraine, is no longer part of the Council of Europe), partially or fully eliminate that right: these two legal systems were harshly condemned by the European Court of Human Rights for breach of Article 3 of Protocol No. 1 of the European Convention on Human Rights (ECHR) (*Hirst v United Kingdom (No. 2)*, Application No. 74025/01, Judgment, 6th of October, 2005; *Greens and MT v United Kingdom*, Application Nos. 60041/08 & 60054/08, Judgment, 23rd of

November, 2010; *Anchugov and Gladkov v Russia*, Application Nos. 11157/04 and 15162/05, Judgment, 4th of July, 2013).

3. The Subjective Entitlement to Rights: Citizens and Foreigners

The Constitution attributes **inviolable rights to everyone**. The rights qualified by the adjective inviolable are explicitly recognised in some cases only to citizens (for example, Articles 3, 4, 16, 17, 18, 38 and 48). On other occasions the addressee is not identified and the Constitution employs the term **everyone** (Articles 19, 21, 24, 34 and 42). In yet other cases, rights are recognised to specific categories, such as workers (for example, Articles 35, 36, 37, 38, 43 and 46) or parents (Article 30). This differentiation is partly due to the lack of standardisation in drawing up the Constitution.

Since its early judgments, the Constitutional Court has clarified that it does not consider **itself bound** to a **literal interpretation** of the subjective references set out in the text of the Constitution. In this manner, it **granted itself** the power to **extend the scope of rights** expressly **recognised** only to citizens **also to foreigners**. The action of the Constitutional Court was thus able to align the Constitution with the general trend in European and Western legal systems to close the gap between citizens and foreigners in recognising rights that are considered inviolable. This trend was also triggered by the development of international instruments of protection of the rights *of the person*, irrespective of their legal relationship with the state. The **reciprocity clause** (linked to the legal culture prior to the creation of the Republic) based on which foreigners enjoy the civil rights attributed to Italian citizens only if the same treatment is granted to Italian citizens in the foreigners' country of origin, is **no longer recognised** in any way (there are some areas of application on issues related solely to property).

Italy is the country of arrival for migration flows from Africa, while the decision to regulate immigration is assigned to national and European policy. Even **third-country nationals who illegally** reside in the country (only Italian citizens enjoy the **right to access the territory** of the State) enjoy rights, specifically the rights **connected** with the **inviolable** area of **human dignity**, such as the right to healthcare (Judgment No. 269/2010).

3.a. Individual Freedoms

The Constitutional Court has recognised to **legally residing foreigners all the rights that the Constitution recognises to the person**. At the beginning this was made possible by **referring to**

- **Article 10, para. 2**, of the Constitution, «The legal status of foreigners shall be regulated by law in compliance with international provisions and treaties»;

 © Wolters Kluwer Italia

• and **Article 2** of the Constitution, interpreted as an **open-ended clause**, which allows the guaranteeing of inviolable rights to foreigners legally resident within the national territory (Judgments Nos. 120/1967, 104/1969, 144/1970, 203/1997, 252/2001, 432/2005, 324 del 2006 and lately 148/2008).

This occurred, from Judgment No. 120/1967, regarding the fundamental **principle of equality**: though it refers to citizens (see *I.B).4.* and *III.A).2.*), it is extended to foreigners each time inviolable rights are involved. As a result of this extension, the Constitutional Court, from Judgment No. 104/1969, set out a principle defined as **equality in the field of entitlement to rights of freedom**.

However, a limited set of rights remains exclusive to citizens: the **right to vote in general elections** and the **right to access the territory** of the state can be considered as examples in this regard. They are both immediately connected **with the constitutive** elements **of the State** (the exercise of sovereignty and the territory) and therefore remain as distinctive attribution of the people (in a strict legal sense) of the State.

3.b. Right of Asylum and Ban of Extradition

Italy is one of the few European countries that proclaims a right to asylum for foreigners and stateless persons. The content of the recognition is particularly broad. A person who is denied, in his or her own country, the effective exercise of the democratic liberties guaranteed by the Constitution shall have the **right of asylum** in the territory of the Italian Republic, in accordance with the conditions established by law (**Article 10, para. 3,** of the Constitution). People **cannot be extradited** for **political offences** (with the exception of offenses committed for the purpose of destroying a group of persons based on their nation, ethnicity, race or religion), for **offences punishable** by **death penalty** in the country requesting **extradition** (Judgment No. 54/1979) or **if the individual extradited** could be **persecuted, tortured or subject to inhumane treatment** (**ban of extradition**, **Article 10, para. 4**, of the Constitution).

An implementing law, as required by the reserve of legislation set out in Article 10, para. 3, has never come into force: the norms on **refugee status** filled the void. Those norms include the Convention relating to the status of refugees (**Geneva Convention**), ratified by Italy in 1954, and other relevant international treaties, as well as all the legislation that implements the **EU directives**. Those directives develop a common policy among Member States on **refugee status**, **subsidiary protection status** (recognised to those who fear the death penalty, torture or inhumane treatment) and **special protection status** (recognised in the case of mass exodus or exceptional events), with a view to offering appropriate status to any third-country national that requires international protection and ensures compliance with the principle of **non-refoulement** (which guarantees that no one should be returned to a country where they would face torture, cruel, inhuman or degrading treatment or punishment and other irreparable harm). This principle applies to all migrants at all times, irrespective of their migration status (Article 78 of the TFEU). Even those who do not meet the requirements to be granted refugee status, but could effectively suffer serious personal injury or harm if they returned to their home country, may apply for **special protection** (see Articles 9, 18 to 20-*bis* of the Consolidation Law on Immigration).

The administrative provisions that list the States of origin that can be considered as safe are widespread within EU (Article 37 Directive 2013/32/EU on common procedures for granting and withdrawing international protection). They have been adopted also by Italy.

The refugee crisis of 2015 led to a sharp increase in the number of unauthorized arrivals on the Italian shores (Savino 2016). The ECtHR found Italy guilty of collective returns of migrants (for example, an entire vessel of migrants), as it had not assessed the varying situations and requests of the individuals on board (violation of Article 3 ECHR, *Hirsi Jamaa and Others v Italy*, Application No. 27765/09, Judgment, 23rd of February, 2012; *Sharifi and Others* v *Italy and Greece*, Application No. 16643/09, Judgment, 21st of October, 2014; *J.A. and Others v Italy*, Application No. 21329/18, Judgment, 30th of March, 2023).

3.c. Social Rights

The enjoyment of social rights in a manner that is equal to that of citizens is also ensured, as long as it complies with requirements which reasonably verify the **individual's link** with the territory. To this end, the **anti-discrimination legislation** implemented by the EU over the years has certainly been decisive. It is therefore not surprising that the ItCC in its case-law has recognized the possibility that some services are reserved for citizens or are, in any case, only for certain categories of third-country nationals due to the **intensity of the relationship they have with the supplying state**. Even in this area, however, the ItCC has worked to extend the guarantee of rights, identifying a scope of inalienable protections which belong to the *person* and which, as such, must be protected regardless of citizenship (see *IV.C).4.*).

3.d. Voting Rights

Unlike the approach discussed above, the Constitutional Court did not break with the traditional concept concerning the relationship between the entitlement to the right to vote and citizenship: **citizenship** is considered as the **constitutionally protected legal status** that specifically **entails the entitlement** to **political** rights (Judgment No. 87/1975).

 © Wolters Kluwer Italia

EU citizens residing in Italy, in virtue of the possession of EU citizenship, have the right to vote and to stand as candidates in local and European elections (based on Article 22 of the TFEU).

Regularly residing non-EU citizens may participate in local public life on the basis of the decisions of individual municipalities, but **do not have the right to vote** in local, political, or European elections. Even though Italy signed the Strasbourg Convention on the Participation of Foreigners in Public Life at Local Level in 1994, it chose not to ratify the section that grants resident foreigners the right to vote in local elections.

Public debate on the recognition of the right to vote in political elections periodically returns to the fore, and most commentators seem to support the need to **revise the Constitution**.

Somehow, and paradoxically, **Italian citizens residing abroad enjoy full electoral rights, including in general elections** where some seats (8 in the Chamber and 4 in the Senate) are reserved to them. In the light of the particular favour that Italian legislation has for attributing citizenship to descendents of Italians who had emigrated in the early twentieth century, including those who had never lived in or even visited Italy, the access to the right to vote seems to look more backwards than forwards.

However, the solution adopted by the Constitution is not the only possible one. Other constitutions presume a weaker link between citizenship and the entitlement to voting rights, while promoting (irrespective of citizenship) the person's link with the country and the specific political community. For example, following its amendment on 10th of December, 1998, Article 8 of the Belgian Constitution sets out the option for lawmakers to extend the right to vote to non-EU citizens. This is a broad approach, whereby the right to vote can be granted as a result of stable residence in a specific country which, at the same level as citizenship, can be considered as a condition that justifies the recognition of the right to vote in line with its rationale: guaranteeing that people can participate in the government of the political community of which they are a part. This approach has recently been affirmed by an increasing amount of doctrine, which considers the *status* of citizenship as less and less founded on the concept of a national identity (in this case, we refer to types of post-national or denationalised citizenship).

3.e. The Entitlement to Italian Citizenship

In connection with the above, consideration has to be given to the debate on expanding the ways in which Italian **citizenship** can be acquired. Italian citizenship is transmitted based on *iure sanguinis*, meaning having **at least one Italian birth parent** (reference to Law No. 91/1992). Dual citizenship is permitted; *i.e.* a citizenship in addition to the Italian one. Foreign nationals who are the children or grandchildren of an Italian citizen also have the right to acquire Italian citizenship. On an exceptional basis, citizenship may be transmitted via *iure soli* only if the person's parents are unknown or stateless. Citizenship can be acquired following birth as a result of **adoption**, **marriage** or **civil union**, on request and by demonstrating one's **residence** in Italy (for example, of at least ten years, or at least four years for EU citizens, or at least five years for refugees or stateless persons). Applicants must demonstrate their **knowledge of Italian** and **swear an oath** to be faithful to the Republic and to observe the Constitution and the laws of the state. Foreign nationals who were born and have always lived in Italy have the right to obtain citizenship only if they declare that they intend to acquire it within one year of reaching the legal age of 18. Citizenship may be granted for merit to foreigners who have provided eminent service to Italy.

The Law No. 91/1992 on citizenship is certainly unsatisfactory with regard to the integration of people born or raised in Italy. For this reason, the Italian Parliament has periodically discussed the possibility of expanding the criteria of *ius soli*, for example, to the one of *ius culturae*, based on which children of foreigners who were born in Italy or entered the Country by their 12th birthday would obtain citizenship provided that they legally resided on a continuous basis and regularly attended schools in Italy for at least five years (or attended long-term education and professional training programs to obtain a professional qualification).

B) PROTECION OF RIGHTS

1. Constitutional Rigidity: (Un)Amendability of Rights

According to the majority doctrine, **inviolable rights**, along with the **fundamental principles** (see *I.C).2.*) of the legal system are **unamendable**, i.e., they cannot be amended even through a revision of the Constitution, because any negative changes would constitute a **subversion** of the **constitutional structure** (this would be legitimate if requested during the formation of a new constitution). Unamendability regards both the existence and the essential content of the rights that cannot be amended, as they are founding elements of constitutional **identity**. With Judgment No. 1146/1988 the following were identified as **implicit limits** (as opposed to the **explicit limits** that are listed in Article 139 of the Constitution) to amending the Constitution: the value of **human dignity** to which the inviolable rights are connected, the principle of **popular sovereignty**, the principle of **pluralism**, the principle of the **secularity** of the State, the principle of **equality** and the unamendability of the **judicial protection** of rights.

Inviolable rights contribute to defining the specific identity of the constitutional system and, therefore, the intangible core of its founding principles. This

 © Wolters Kluwer Italia

was also recognised by the Constitutional Court in the *Taricco saga*: in this line of case law, the Court referred to inviolable rights as pushing back against the influence of the obligations deriving from EU Treaties, specifically concerning the principle of strict legality in criminal matters (Judgment No. 24/2017, on the guarantees of strict legality on criminal liability).

In truth, over the last decades, several rights set out in the Constitution have been revised, but **solely** for the purpose of providing **more safeguards** for individuals. The reference is to the repeal of the death penalty also for cases set out by the military law of war (Article 27); the addition of the promotion of equal opportunities for men and women (Article 51); and the addition of the protection of the environment and biodiversity also in the interest of future generations (Article 9).

1.a. Reserve of Legislation

The primacy of the ordinary legislation over secondary sources of law forms the basis of the legality principle and the reserve of legislation.

The reserve of legislation is a concept envisaged in many articles of the Constitution, which regards the distribution of legal power between the legislature and the executive, reserving the right to intervene on matters specific to primary sources of law.

The cases where, and manners by which, rights may be limited must be set out by ordinary law, or by acts having the force of law (legislative decrees and decree-laws), in order to limit the abuses by the executive that occurred during Fascism. The concept of the reserve of legislation acts as a **guarantee**: it ensures relatively stable, uniform norms, the constitutionality of which is overseen by the President of the Republic and the Constitutional Court. This concept requires that these norms be drawn up by the most representative political authority, transparent to public opinion and open to critical examination by the opposition. The intensity of the reserve of legislation varies (as seen in *I.C).3.* I). There is reserve of legislation when an entire matter is reserved to lawmakers, ruling out any interventions on the part of the executive unless they regard the mere execution of the law. One example of the *absolute* reserve of legislation is that guaranteeing personal freedom (Article 13, para. 1, of the Constitution): «[...] No one may be detained, inspected, or searched nor otherwise subjected to any restriction of personal liberty except by reasoned order of the Judiciary and only in such cases and in such manner as provided by the law». This provision is also accompanied by a reserve of jurisdiction which requires that measures restricting freedom be authorised in advance (or, in urgent cases, promptly validated) by a judge.

There are also situations of *reinforced* reserve of legislation, where the reference to the law is accompanied by substantive requirements regarding the

© Wolters Kluwer Italia

mandatory content of the law, such as the case of the freedom of movement (Art. 16 of the Constitution): «Every citizen has the right to reside and travel freely in any part of the country, except for such general limitations as may be established by law for reasons of health or security. No restrictions may be imposed for political reasons».

In the field of economic rights, instead, the reference to the *relative* reserve of legislation is more common (typical expressions include 'based on the law' or 'according to the law'). The law is responsible for setting out the essential or principal norms on the matter, while the executive is responsible for issuing the detailed rules.

1.b. The Principle of Legality in Criminal Law

The principle of legality under criminal law, *nullum crimen sine lege*, plays a substantial role in the Italian constitutional legal system, based on the principles of guaranteeing personal freedom and the separation of powers.

The Italian Constitution establishes the principle of legality under criminal law in Article 25, para. 2, «No punishment may be inflicted except by virtue of a law in force at the time the offence was committed. No restriction may be placed on a person's liberty save for as provided by law».

The cases envisaged by law limiting personal freedom (based on the *absolute* reserve of legislation) are the offences set out in Article 25, para. 2. That is, in order to guarantee the enjoyment of **personal freedom**, the Constitution sets a limit to the lawmakers' ability to define specific conduct as offences that can be punished through sentences of imprisonment.

The discretion of the lawmakers is limited by the **principles of legal certainty, non-retroactivity** and the **prohibition of analogy**. Thus, they shall formulate precise criminal norms with regard to the semantic clarity and intelligibility of the terms used and are likewise required to formulate the type of offence that occurs in reality (Judgment No. 96/1981). The legality principle under criminal law rules out the possibility of interpretation by **analogy**.

The criminal norms are exclusively valid *pro futuro*:

> The non-retroactivity of less favourable criminal law provides a guarantee to individuals against arbitrary persecution and expresses the requirement that the legal consequences of one's conduct under criminal law be *calculable*, as a necessary precondition for free individual self-determination: any subsequent *surprise* exacerbation of the consequences of the offence under criminal law will be at odds with this requirement (Judgment No. 230/2012).

The central nature of the **foreseeability** and **clarity** of **criminal law** in the Constitution was reiterated by the Constitutional Court with resounding impacts in the *Taricco saga* (see *II.A.3.*). From this viewpoint, legality under criminal law

 © Wolters Kluwer Italia

implements the principle of the **rule of law**, with which it shares the purpose of guaranteeing **individual self-determination** and **dignity**.

It must be said that the principle of legality under criminal law has been eroded by numerous factors, including:

• the Italian Parliament's inability to carry out a consistent, general reformulation of criminal law policy, as is extensively demonstrated by the failed reform of the criminal code of 1930 (that is, the fascist code was not completely replaced, but only changed gradually over time);

• the 'decodification' of criminal law which, in prioritising sector-based measures, were included in unsystematic and disorganised legislative documentation, resulted in extensive and confusing proliferation of crimes defined by criminal law;

• the influence of ECHR and EU law and case law which, as also demonstrated by the *Taricco saga*, may at times be extremely penetrating, managing to impact and change the concept of the reserve of legislation as well as fundamental constitutional principles (Piccirilli 2019).

These critical factors are certainly joined by the same constitutional case law which, as a reaction to legislative inertia and the impossibility of carrying out a standardisation, felt entitled, despite retaining a certain self-restraint, to intervene through *manipulative and interpretive judgments*. Two opposing types of conduct by the Constitutional Court were criticised: on the one hand, it was too weak in punishing alleged infringements of legality under criminal law, while on the other being too invasive in the reserve of legislation.

1.c. Judicial Protection and the Constitutional Review of Legislation

Traditionally, the implementation of rights in Italy owes much to the work of the ordinary and Constitutional courts, also because civil society is increasingly turning to these courts, due to their dissatisfaction with the responses or the lack of response from lawmakers. Ordinary courts decide whether to submit the question of constitutional legitimacy to the Constitutional Court through an incidental procedure; at least in terms of the referral order, ordinary judges are the only ones that are entitled to do it (see *I.E).3.* and *IV.B).1.c.2.*).

The development of judicial protection in this sense consolidated the notion of the Constitution as a legal norm that has to be applied by the courts, not merely as a manifesto of principle, or as a rulebook for the basic procedures of political bodies, but as a full-fledge and binding legal norm.

1.c.1. Common Judicial Protection

Article 24, paras. 1-2, of the Constitution states that

«Anyone may bring cases before a court of law in order to protect their rights under civil and administrative law. Defence is an inviolable right at every stage and instance of legal proceedings». The constitutional guarantee of defence allows to take legal action for all infringements of rights by public or private parties.

The constitutional principles that lawmakers are required to implement, in addition to the legality principle under criminal law, are the **pre-establishment** of the court (Article 25, para. 1), meaning the right to the certainty that the party deciding the case shall not be a judge established *a posteriori* to an event that has already occurred (Judgment No. 88/1962), the **impartiality** and **independence** (Articles 101, para. 2, 104, para. 1, 107 and 108, of the Constitution) and the **presumption of innocence** (Article 27, para. 2). Article 111 of the Constitution, revised in 1999 based on Article 6 of the ECHR, sets out the principles of a **fair trial**, which include:

- the adversarial proceedings between the parties (the possibility of cross examination of the elements of evidence) under conditions of equality between the prosecution and defence, and the obligation for the court to provide a statement of reasons;
- the reasonable duration of the trial;
- appeals to the Court of Cassation in cases of violations of the law are always allowed against sentences and against measures affecting personal freedom pronounced by ordinary and special courts;
- appeals to the Court of Cassation against decisions of the Council of State and the Court of Auditors are permitted only for reasons of jurisdiction;
- two levels of proceedings as regards merits (even though this is not set out in the Constitution). This generally means that it is possible to submit to a different judge, specifically the second instance judge, the same issue which was already resolved in the first instance.

Separate mention should be made of the extreme difficulty of the legal system in guaranteeing a reasonable duration of proceedings: due to this inability, Italy was condemned by the European Court of Human Rights due to the **excessive length** of judicial proceedings (with the resulting obligation to compensate victims). The *Pinto Act* (Law No. 89/2001), which requires **fair compensation** in the event of the failure to comply with the reasonable term (quantified as three years for first instance proceedings, two years for appeals and one year for legitimacy proceedings before the Court of Cassation), in turn revealed itself as an instrument that is unable to ensure the prompt provision of such compensation. Currently, both civil and criminal proceedings are being reformed, in order to increase their efficiency, also thanks to the funds allocated by the National Recovery and Resilience Plan (NRRP).

 © Wolters Kluwer Italia

Ordinary courts play a crucial role in protecting rights also because they decide whether to initiate **incidental constitutional procedures**, by bringing the relevant norm to the attention of the ItCC (see *I.E).3.*; Barsotti et aal. 2016, 52). The Court itself encouraged ordinary courts to make use of their own interpretative powers whenever a question of constitutionality could be resolved through an interpretation that is consistent with the Constitution (*interpretazione conforme*). As a general rule, the Court would declare inadmissible a question, if the referral order failed to explain that such a remedial interpretation was impossible (Judgment No. 356/1996). This doctrine was developed to reduce the considerable number of questions that were being referred to the Court for a decision. However, over the long term it jeopardised the incidental method of access: many constitutional problems were no longer referred to the Constitutional Court, but resolved by the ordinary courts directly, under their own initiative, by interpreting laws in line with the Constitution. From 2015 onwards (Judgment No. 221) the Court softened its position on *interpretazione conforme*: judges are no longer requested to raise only questions which are demonstrably impossible to solve through consistent interpretation. Now it is sufficient to explain that such a construction faces relevant obstacles; ultimately, only entirely inadequate attempts at consistent interpretation are sanctioned by rulings of inadmissibility. This exemplifies a first, broader sense of **re-centralisation** [Tega 2021]: the Italian Constitutional Court re-acquires occasions for adjudication on the merits of constitutional questions, which previously had been left to other judicial bodies (ordinary courts).

Italian judges, including those of the Constitutional Court, also protect rights by **applying EU law** and interacting with the EU Court of Justice through a reference for a **preliminary ruling** in the event of doubts about the interpretation or validity of the relevant EU norm. As previously noted, a reference for a preliminary ruling can overlap with incidental procedures in cases where the same norm regarding rights is suspected of infringing not only the Italian Constitution, but also EU law and the CFREU. The Constitutional Court recommends that ordinary courts should first scrutinise the norm's constitutionality, while they are always free to ask for a preliminary ruling (see *II.A).4.*).

The ordinary courts interpret national law also in light of the ECHR: the **value** of the provisions of the **ECHR**, as interpreted by the case law of the Strasbourg Court, is **higher** than that of **national laws**, but subordinate to the Constitution. The ItCC has **exclusive jurisdiction** on any declaration of the **unconstitutionality** of **legislative provisions** that are in contrast with the Constitution, provided that the Convention's rights do not, in turn, harm constitutional **norms or principles** (Tega 2012 and 2017; Judgments Nos. 348 and 349/2007, Pollicino 2008).

© Wolters Kluwer Italia

1.c.2. The Constitutional Review of Legislation

As stated in Part I, the review of constitutional legitimacy is one of the most decisive innovations in the republican Constitution. The **salience** of the ItCC in the legal system certainly derives from the specific **importance** of the **rights** that in turn express the founding values of the Republic.

In Italy, this takes the form of a **centralised review** exclusively conducted by the Constitutional Court (NARDINI 1999; FROSINI 2008; GROPPI 2008; BIFULCO/PARIS 2020), unlike many other systems of judicial review (PASQUINO 1998) in which ordinary courts also have the opportunity to review the constitutionality of a norm that is relevant in proceedings (as occurs, for example, though through different methods, in the US, Canada, Australia, Argentina, Sweden, Finland and Denmark).

Though individual complaints cannot be submitted to the ItCC to protect rights, as they can in Germany or Spain (limiting examples to European legal systems), constitutional case law has been a determining factor in the development of rights. In particular, through the instrument of incidental procedures which is in the exclusive hands of the ordinary court during all judicial proceedings, the Court may assess whether the ordinary legislation that implements constitutional rights and fundamental principles fully complies with the content of the protections set out in the Constitution. The **incidental procedure** has been particularly effective in **modernising** a significant portion of the **legal system**, while strengthening the guarantee of the content of the rights proclaimed in the Constitution, also through the broad interpretation of Article 2 of the Constitution (considered as an open-ended clause).

The ItCC may nullify the provision once and forever with general effect (*erga omnes*). The declaration of unconstitutionality results in the *pro futuro* elimination of the challenged rule from the legal system starting from the **day after** the **official publication** of the judgment. The declaration also **affects** the **judicial proceeding suspended** after the referring order that gave rise to the question of constitutionality. **Exceptionally,** the unconstitutionality **affects retroactively** (*ex tunc*) **final criminal convictions** following the judicial application of a **norm** declared as **unconstitutional**.

In 1956, the year in which it pronounced its first judgment (see *IV.C).1.*), the Court presented itself as an effective **outsider** in relation to the Italian judicial and political system (BARSOTTI ET ALL. 2016; BIAGI 2020). Article 28 of Law No. 87/1953 required the Constitutional Court to conduct its scrutiny without making any review of the use of the Parliament's discretionary power: this was a limit that the Court has interpreted in a highly flexible manner, as will be illustrated.

At that time, it was impossible to imagine the central role that the Court would gain for itself in subsequent decades, becoming the **most effective** and

 © Wolters Kluwer Italia

respected institution of the Republic, along with the President of the Republic. Confirming and maintaining the legitimacy of the review of constitutionality has always been extremely difficult. This legitimacy has been challenged ever since it was established, not just in Italy, and continues to be questioned for a wide variety of reasons in numerous legal systems in Europe and worldwide, as illustrated also in the last paragraph of this Section. As the legal fabric prior to the Republic remained applicable also after the Constitution entered into force, in its initial decades of operation constitutional case law concentrated on aligning old-fashioned, repressive and authoritarian laws to the values of liberal democratic constitutionalism developed by the Constituent Assembly. This was called the **great substitution** because the **Court substituted** the **Parliament**, which was effectively blocked by the conservative parliamentary majority. In this initial phase, it was relatively simple for the Court to declare the **unconstitutionality** of the most **harmful pre-republican legislations** in application of the values and principles set out in the Constitution.

The Court's work was further complicated when it began to examine the constitutionality of legislation adopted by republican lawmakers.

There have been no issues of public debate upon which the Court has not ruled. This is due to both the **unstructured**, **fragmented** production of **legislation** as well as the political system's inability to mediate between opposing interests and aspirations. The failure to mediate politically these interests and aspirations meant that they were then addressed to the Constitutional Court. As the interpretation and application of the Constitution are not purely technical operations, as long as the instruments for selecting and mediating interests struggle to operate, **conflicts** are bound to increase and, without **political mediation**, eventually **end up before the courts**. In this situation, the use of principles such as **reasonableness** enables the Court to take on and exercise the role of moderator of conflicts rather than the custodian of constitutional values. One of the most recent examples was the Court's demolition of the most salient aspects of legislation regarding medically assisted reproduction, or the case in which the Court recognised access to assisted suicide to a limited kind of terminal patients in the absence of legislation explicitly permitting it (see *IV.C).5.c.*).This phenomenon is labelled as the **judicial implementation** of the Constitution, that is, the interpretation of constitutional norms through the exercise of the judicial function, attributing to norms a meaning in line with the Constitution. Numerous important examples of this will be examined in Section C.

1.c.3. Limitation and Balancing of Rights and Principles

The Constitution adopts a **pluralistic** approach: both in terms of taking the form of a democracy that represents *the People*, and in terms of a catalogue of values, translated into principles and rights, which also compete with and diverge from each other. Each right is always affirmed along with its limit. In this area, **balancing** is an interpretive and argumentative technique that enables the necessary harmonisation of multiple **competing constitutional values**. The heart of constitutional justice consists of the balancing and **reasonable weighing of values**: the concept of pluralism requires that, where there is a conflict between values, they must be balanced, **without sacrificing either one of them**.

It was not by chance that, right from its first judgment, the Constitutional Court established that:

> the concept of a limit is inherent in the concept of a right [...] within the legal system, the various legal spheres must necessarily place limits on each other, so that they can coexist in an ordered, civil manner (Judgment No. 1/1956).

Rights must harmoniously coexist in their concrete application, but this coexistence is not a given, and is the fruit of balancing which entails reasonable limitations established by the competent source. As observed by the Constitutional Court, all **rights** are reciprocally balanced with each other, and their **protection** must be **systemic and coordinated**, as it would be **unacceptable** for only one of them to expand unlimitedly, exercising undue dominance **over the others**. For example, the conflicts that could concretely arise include those between the right to health, the right to environment and the right to work. In this regard, it has been said that:

> as is the case under other contemporary democratic and pluralist constitutions, the Italian Constitution requires that an ongoing reciprocal balance be struck between fundamental principles and rights, and that none of them may claim absolute status. The classification of the values of the environment and health as *primary* rather means that they cannot be sacrificed in favour of other interests, even if protected under constitutional law, and not that they are placed at the pinnacle of a hierarchically absolute order. Precisely because it is dynamic and not set in advance, the point of equilibrium must be assessed – by Parliament when enacting legislation and by the Constitutional Court upon review – according to the criteria of proportionality and reasonableness in such a manner as to ensure that their essential core is not sacrificed (Judgment No. 85/2013).

Also the rights protected by the European Convention, as applied by the Strasbourg Court, need to be balanced with the rights proclaimed by the Italian Constitution.

> Naturally, it is for the European Court to decide on the individual case and the individual fundamental right, whilst the national authorities have a duty to

© Wolters Kluwer Italia

> prevent the protection of certain fundamental rights – including from the general and unitary perspective of Article 2 of the Constitution – from developing in an unbalanced manner to the detriment of other rights also protected by the Constitution and by the European Convention. The overall result of the supplementation of the guarantees under national law must be positive, in the sense that the impact of individual ECHR rules on Italian law must result in an increase in protection for the entire system of fundamental rights (Judgment No. 317/2009).

The purpose of such operations is not to assert the primacy of the national legal system, but rather to integrate the **protection assured by the ECHR with the one given by the domestic Constitution** (Judgment No. 264/2012); this operation is guaranteed by the Court, as it performs its **unique** institutional role (Judgment No. 170/2013).

Over the years, the Constitutional Court has clearly distilled the particular unavoidable characteristics of the constitutional guarantee of rights: as constitutional rights are **not absolute**, they may and must be **balanced** with each other. As there is **no hierarchy** of constitutional rights and values, their balancing is assigned, firstly, to **lawmakers** (which conduct this balancing *ex ante*), and then, if necessary, to the scrutiny of the **Court** (*ex post*). Balancing is carried out following criteria of **reasonableness** and **proportionality** and can **never** entail the **complete** sacrifice of one of the rights or values at stake, because the **essential core** of each one must be **preserved**. The balancing may result in the **decrease** in the **protection** of a **right** only if this **corresponds** to an **increase** in the **protection** of another right, interest or value. If, in terms of its effects, a norm that sacrifices one right does not produce benefits for other interests, it is seen as **unbalanced** and **unreasonable** (Judgment No. 20/2019 on the conflict between privacy and the transparency of the public administration; Judgments Nos. 113 and 97/2020, regarding the balancing of the right to defence, the socialising purpose of the sentence, the safeguarding of public order and the safety of citizens).

1.c.4. Equality and Reasonableness

It has been said that judicial **balancing** is carried out following **criteria** of **reasonableness** and **proportionality**. What does this mean? It is important to reiterate what was stated in Part III regarding the innovative nature of the principle of **formal equality**, Article 3, para. 1, of the Constitution. This principle does not mean absolute equality of treatment. As interpreted by the Constitutional Court, it requires that the law provides **equal** treatment to situations that are **reasonably equivalent** and different treatment to situations that are **reasonably different**. Article 3, para. 1, specifically aims to prevent persons, citizens, and non-citizens, from being harmed by **arbitrary discrimination**, without, however, requiring lawmakers to set identical norms for everyone. Thus, lawmakers shall

avoid differentiated treatment that is shown to be **unreasonable** and **arbitrary**: in this sense, legislative discretion is limited by the need to adopt reasonable legislative choices. The Constitutional Court reviews the concrete application of those choices, through judgments based on the principle of reasonableness. While basing its decisions on the specific case (in incidental procedures), the Court's thinking concerns the reasonableness of the norm set by lawmakers, and consequently its judgments will have a general impact and will determine their effects on the entire legal system.

> The **proportionality test** used by the Constitutional Court and by many other European courts, as well as by the Court of Justice, requires an **assessment** as to whether the provision under review, along with the arrangements stipulated for its application, is **necessary** and **capable** of achieving legitimately pursued objectives by requiring that the **measure chosen out** of those most appropriate is the **least restrictive** of the **rights** in play and imposes **burdens** that are **not disproportionate** having regard to the **pursuit** of those **objectives** (Judgment No. 1/2014).

The efficacy of the judicial review based on reasonableness carried out by the Constitutional Court lies in the ability to concretely assess the application and results of the legislative decisions considered within the entire legal context, having a flexibility in analysis and decision that lawmakers do not have. Lawmakers make choices abstractly and have difficulty in identifying all potential inconsistencies in a panorama characterised by the significant fragmentation of legislation (Cartabia 2016). The risk, which the Constitutional Court has been rebuked for, is the possibility of placing its will above political discretion.

1.d. Protection of Rights beyond the State

Since the end of the 1990s, the judicial protection of rights has found new trajectories of growth. It was then that the specific expression of multi-level protection of rights, mentioned in *IV.A).1.*, was coined. This refers to a protection of rights that is fuelled not only through the constitutional guarantees provided at a national level, but also by those established by the **ECHR** and the **CFREU**. Legal systems became increasingly porous: the label **multi-level protection** of **rights** dates back to this period and, while proposing a highly significant change in the understanding of the guarantee of rights, was in some way reassuring, because it expressed the image of a protection that was both enhanced and well-coordinated among the different legal levels.

This has been described also as the **second wave** of development of judicial review and refers to a period in which national constitutional courts had to adjust their traditional competences to a more complex legal order

 © Wolters Kluwer Italia

(Cartabia 2014). They were charged with new duties, because to some extent they were called to serve as European law adjudicators (Weiler/Lustig 2018, while the **first wave** was characterised by the success and spread of domestic judicial review within constitutions). From this perspective, the Italian Court fits perfectly since it has been characterised by a **consistent internationalism**, understood as openness towards international organisations ensuring peace and justice among nations, enshrined in the Constitution (Article 11) and developed as a prominent feature of constitutional case law.

Nonetheless, the idea of **protection** organised in **levels** was soon demonstrated to be **simplistic**, due to the fact that the various levels of guarantee intersect, creating an intricate fabric of case law that not only mixes the tradition of civil law with that of common law, but also sees cross-fertilisation between supranational and national jurisprudence. In a few limited cases, this mixing triggers **short circuits** that run the **risk** of **weakening**, instead of strengthening, the protection of rights at national level (see *II.B).3.*).

The **particular nature** of the **constitutional protection** of **rights** lies not only in the content affirmed in the Constitution, but also in the ways in which this protection develops in the **national context**. The diversity of scenarios explains the difficulty that the Courts in charge of the single levels of protection have in dialoguing with each other. The **purposes** of **national legal systems** are **general, democratic** and **pluralistic**. The Italian legal system is based on the idea of human and social dignity, which takes the form of **multiple rights and principles**, each corresponding to an aspect of living in a society in which human personality is expressed individually or as a group. This complexity requires the Constitutional Court to ensure a **systemic guarantee** of rights, **not piecemeal across a series of uncoordinated provisions in potential conflict** with one another (Tega 2017; Judgment No. 264/2012), starting from the choices made by lawmakers regarding balancing, coordinating and protecting rights.

The Constitutional Court does not always **consider** the lists of **rights** set out in the **Constitution**, the **CFREU** or the **ECHR** to fully **overlap** (Cartabia 2009; Tega 2012), not only because they differ in content and in the level of protection that is guaranteed, but also because the former is part of a **composite constitutional architecture** that the proceedings before the Constitutional Court are required to assure through the systemic, integrated protection of rights.

From this perspective, the ItCC fits perfectly also into the **third wave** of judicial review as described by Lustig and Weiler: a wave that displays the emergence of **national courts** as an instance of **control** and judicial review of **transnational** and international governance and adjudication – in particular human rights adjudicators, whose decisions impact the work of national constitutional courts – and gives expression to a new **identitarian seam** in constitutional discourse (see *II.C).1.*). The ItCC has lived through all three of these waves, always remaining

© Wolters Kluwer Italia

immune to political conditioning and, nowadays, to populist pressures. A focus on the systemic aspect has enabled the Constitutional Court and lawmakers – where they considered the drives to expand rights, also resulting from the affirmation of international charters – to avoid experiencing passively an unquestioned expansion of areas of freedom, and instead to be active and critical of an incremental protection of rights, while always complying with the fundamental principles of the constitutional legal system.

There are numerous reasons for the **success** of the **European Court of Human Rights**, which include the introduction of individual applications (set out in Protocol No. 11/1998) and the habit of its judges to interpret the Convention as a **living instrument**. In the Italian legal system, a highly fruitful reflection on the value and influence of the ECHR was made possible by the combined effect of Article 117, para. 1, of the Constitution, as revised in 2001 (which states that «Legislative powers shall be vested in the State and the Regions in compliance with the Constitution and the constraints deriving from EU legislation and international obligations»), and through constitutional case law (since 2007, Repetto 2013). As things stand, as stated above, the **value** of the provisions of the **ECHR**, as interpreted by the case law of the Strasbourg Court, is **greater** than that of ordinary laws, but **subordinate** to the Constitution.

Turning our attention to the EU **Court of Justice**, the ECJ affirmed that fundamental rights are the centre of the **constitutional structure** that is the characterising and distinguishing feature of the European Union. The development of an integrated protection of rights, to the extent summarised herein, is captured by **Article 6** of the **TFEU** and the **concluding articles** of the **CFREU**, based on which the protection of rights in the EU derives from **two** separate **sources**: first, from the **Charter** of Fundamental Rights and, second, from the **general principles** of jurisprudence, which include the rights sanctioned by the ECtHR and those resulting from the **constitutional traditions** common to the Member States.

Specifically, following the entry into force of the Treaty of Lisbon, the CFREU should be considered as having the same legal value as the treaties. The CFREU also applies to Member States (in addition to EU institutions) exclusively in **implementing EU law**, without this resulting in the extension of the scope of application of EU law or modifying in any way the responsibilities and duties defined by the treaties, and without jeopardising the rights as they are recognised by the national constitutions, in their respective areas of application. Based on a restrictive interpretation, the Charter would apply only to national norms for the implementation of EU law (considered in the strictest sense). In fact, the most recent case law seems interested in **expanding** this application also to any **national norm** that **interferes** with the application of European law

 © Wolters Kluwer Italia

or jeopardises its **enforceability** in some way. The borders between the Charter of Fundamental Rights and national constitutions are thus being defined, both by **EU judges** and by national **constitutional courts**.

1.e. Global Constitutionalism

The experience that has been defined as the **multi-level protection** of rights is considered an impactful example by those attempting to claim the existence of a developing **global constitutionalism** and proposing that the state paradigm be abandoned in favour of the **cosmopolitan paradigm** (Peters 2006; Kumm 2009). Another important example is the enormous expansion of the EU's influence and its **erosion** of the traditional **sovereignty** of Member States (Fichera 2018). Although it is true that the EU has only those powers that the Member States have transferred to it (the principle of conferral), it is also true that once transferred, the powers are exercised by organs of the EU and claim not only **direct effect** within the Member States but also **primacy** over **domestic law**, including national **constitutions**. Starting from the existence of international adjudicators, who have established their fundamental regulations, and judicial bodies or quasi-judicial bodies, several authors have used the label **global constitutionalism**, specifically regarding the constitutional development of the EU, and even of the WTO (referring to periods now in the past, in which the WTO took on importance which has now faded, Cass 2001). These authors have emphasised the existence of typical characteristics of national constitutionalism at international level: for example, the UN Charter, the EU Treaty and the statute of WTO are interpreted as constitutions.

From this perspective, the **second wave** of judicial review corresponded to the evolution of international law into a type of global administrative law (Cassese 2006; Cassese 2017; Ferrarese 2006; Della Cananea 2011; Lustig/Weiler 2018, 328).

Global administrative law indicates that States today share their power with a huge number of **non-state actors**, most of which are **international organisations**, to whom sovereign rights have been transferred and whose exercise goes beyond the arrangements of national constitutions. Global administrative law is defined as the **principles, procedures, and review mechanisms** that are **emerging** to **govern decision making and regulatory rulemaking by formal international organizations** (such as the WTO, the World Bank, the Climate Change Regime, etc.), **informal transnational networks of domestic regulatory officials** (such as the Basel Committee of national bank regulators, De Bellis 2018), **domestic authorities** implementing global regulatory law, **hybrid public-private** and **purely private regulatory regimes** (Kingsbury et all. 2005; Cassese 2017; Casini 2022).

From a constitutional law viewpoint, it has been correctly argued that the transposition of several categories of **constitutionalism** to **global level** is basically an **illusion**: the inevitable erosion of the state's monopoly of public power over its territory and the loss of importance that the constitution suffers at a national level is not completely offset by the external culmination of several categories of constitutionalism, such as those discussed in this part of the textbook (GRIMM 2010).

2. Rights between Political Decisions and Constitutional Adjudication

For several decades now, democratically elected lawmakers have had difficulty in reaching a legislative compromise that satisfies the demands of society regarding the content of new rights, specifically the ones that are **ethically sensitive**, such as those linked to the **beginning and end of life** or to **sexual orientation**. As a result, many of these unsatisfied demands are re-routed to ordinary and constitutional courts. In the recent history of the affirmation of the rights set out in the Italian Constitution, the main players have been the Parliament (to a lesser extent), and the Constitutional Court (to a greater extent) (MUSELLA/RULLO 2020).

Many of the cases discussed in the following Section C) demonstrate this dynamic. In some instances, such as the issue of gender balance in politics, electoral lawmakers are the first to understand the problem, as opposed to the more backwards position of the courts. In others, such as abortion, Parliament intervenes by following the direction indicated by the Court with regard to balancing the foetus' right to life and the mother's right to health; and, in others, such as the law on assisted reproduction, the Constitutional Court, through a countermajoritarian function, dismantled over the years a law that was the fruit of an incorrect balancing made by the Parliament. The request from a portion of society to be able to add the maternal surname to the paternal surname was fulfilled by the Court between 2016 and 2022, faced with lawmakers who were deaf to requests for change for thirty years. On end-of-life decisions, the Constitutional Court has indicated a way forward and is waiting for Parliament to manage to reach an agreement.

This phenomenon is actually widespread in contemporary Western democracies. Also based on the principles affirmed by **neo-constitutionalism**, the role of judicial review has been **emphasised** with regard to **protecting rights** and **reducing inequality**. This has become the basis, more generally, of the **aspirations** of individuals and minority groups **to have rights**, as they are frustrated by the difficulties that **lawmakers** have in drafting legislation and **mediating conflicts**.

Associated with this trend, constitutional courts have developed the tendency to refer to their reciprocal decisions, in a sort of **trans-judicial dialogue** (SLAUGHTER 1994; FERRARESE 2009), with the aim of strengthening their argumentation. This

 © Wolters Kluwer Italia

kind of openness to alien case law in order to push for a recognition of the need for an evolution of the domestic legal approach to sensitive topics is not unusual - see, for example, the cases of death penalty or those regarding end of life.

In reaction to the role acquired by judicial review over time, also critically labelled as **juristocracy** (HIRSCHL 2004 and 2007), a particular school of legal and philosophical thought has developed in the US and UK. This strand of thought has been defined as **political constitutionalism** or **popular constitutionalism** according to the various theoretical positions expressed. Both approaches decrease the value of judicial review in favour of enhancing the role of the Parliament or of the other branches as the interpreters of the general will of the people, their needs and interests, in opposition to judicial decisions taken by technocratic elites who were not directly elected by 'the People' (WALDRON 2006; TUSHNET 1999; PUTNAM 2016; BELLAMY 2015; GOLDONI/MCCORKINDALE 2019).

Numerous criticisms have been made by those who, though they do not support political constitutionalism or popular constitutionalism, have highlighted the **overreaching** of the ordinary and constitutional **courts** in areas that should be the competence of democratically elected lawmakers (BIN 2012; MORRONE 2019; JESTAEDT ET AAL. 2020).

On a purely political level, the spread of the **neoconstitutionalist** trend is also criticised by populist movements, in the name of their anti-elitist rhetoric.

The Polish and Hungarian legal systems effectively demonstrate that the political intention to extensively weaken the independence of the power of both ordinary and constitutional courts serves not to combat elites, but to install an **illiberal regime** that is no longer actually democratic (SADURSKI 2019). The reforms that have been implemented in Poland since 2015 have impacted the independence of judicial power, primarily that of the Polish Constitutional Tribunal which, in just a few months at the end of 2021, first subjected several provisions of the Treaty on European Union (TEU) to a verification of compliance with the Polish Constitution, in order to protect the reform of the judicial systems from penalties imposed by the Court of Justice (K 3/21); and then declared Article 6 of the ECHR unconstitutional, with regard to the ECtHR's scrutiny of the legitimacy of the process for selecting national constitutional judges (K 6/21). The European Commission and Court of Justice have repeatedly found these reforms to be **against EU law**, with specific reference to the principle of the **rule of law**, proclaimed in Articles 2 and 19 TFEU and 47 of the Charter of Fundamental Rights (*European Commission v Poland*, C-619/18, 24th of June, 2019; *European Commission v Poland*, C-192/18, 5th of November, 2019; *A.K.*, C-585/18, 19th of November, 2019; *European Commission v Poland*, C-791/19, 15th of July, 2021; *W.Ż.*, C-487/19, 6th of October, 2021; *European Commission v Poland*, C-204/21, 5th of June, 2023). Following the European Court of Justice (*Hungary v European Parliament and Council of the European Union*, C-156/21,

© Wolters Kluwer Italia

and *Republic of Poland v European Parliament and Council of the European Union*, C-157/21, 16th of February, 2022), it has been decided for the **first time** to activate the regime of **conditionality,** which provides the option of **suspending EU funds** to a Member State when **breaches** of the principles of the **rule of law** are **verified** that affect, or seriously risk affecting, the sound financial management of the Union budget or the protection of the financial interests of the Union in a sufficiently direct way (Regulation EU, Euratom 2020/2092 of the European Parliament and of the Council). When the war in Ukraine broke out, given the fundamental role played by Poland in handling refugees, the Commission froze the implementation of the decision (Baraggia/Bonelli 2022).

The Court of Strasbourg also deemed that the process for appointing members of certain bodies at the head of the Polish judicial system infringed Article 6, para. 1, of the ECHR, with regard to the right to an independent and impartial court, pre-established by law. Firstly, the Polish Constitutional Court was challenged (*Xero Flor w Polsce sp. z.o.o. v Poland*, Application No. 4907/18, Judgment, 7th of May, 2021). Then came the turn of the Disciplinary Chamber of the Supreme Court (*Reczkowicz v Poland*, Application No. 43447/19, Judgment, 22nd of July, 2021). Most recently, at least to this point, the axe fell on the Chamber of Extraordinary Review and Public Affairs (*Dolinska-Ficek and Ozimek v Poland*, Application Nos. 49868/19 and 57511/19, Judgment, 8th of November, 2021).

The 2023 reform that strips the Israel's Supreme Court of the power to overturn government actions and appointments it deems unreasonable is another embodiment of the populist anti-elitist rhetoric. The Israeli Court has developed the doctrine that it may intervene in a decision that is "highly unreasonable", crafting a powerful tool in constraining governmental decisions that unduly infringe on individual rights or allow for corruption (Kretzmer 2023). Right wing politicians have created the impression that non-elected judges rule the country, and have promoted the typical populist demand that the court has the power of veto over the will of the majority.

C) CASE-LAW ON CONSTITUTIONAL RIGHTS

Both lawmakers and the Constitutional Court have played a crucial role in implementing the ambitious programme set out by the framers of the Constitution.

Firstly, the programme was ambitious because it established that the purpose of the new **liberal democratic** legal system was to promote the **centrality** of the **nature** of the **person** and her development.

Secondly, it was ambitious because it included **constitutional adjudication**, understood as the **guarantee** of **inviolable** rights, into a legal context that was

 © Wolters Kluwer Italia

certainly refined, but nevertheless antiquated compared to the changing times. That is, not everyone was ready to accept the changes represented by the fact that the Constitutional Court could review ordinary legislation. Thus, the tradition of parliamentary sovereignty was an obstacle, especially in a legal system in which the Parliament had had a tradition of almost absolute power and would have difficulty agreeing to be just one instrument among many others in implementing the rule of law; *i.e.*, just a tile in a mosaic of mutual guaranties (as Maranini, a particularly original and critical constitutional scholar, wrote clearly).

Italian judicial culture was in a phase of **generational transfer**: the most senior generations of jurists and politicians were uncomfortable with the Constituent Assembly's project, whilst only a small number of trailblazing scholars approved of it. Thus, the majority of jurists deemed that the Court would merely determine whether the content of a law ought to be delivered as an ordinary law or as a constitutional one.

This prediction turned out to be wrong. The very first years of its activity brought out a characteristic that would no longer be negated: the sensitivity of the newly created ItCC to the changed social context, and not only to the political context. The Court started operating as a more homogeneous, agile, and **efficient outsider** of a political system that was still disorientated.

The judgments of the Constitutional Court, illustrated in this Section prove:

• that, since its first ruling, the Constitutional Court has scrutinized lawmakers' discretion;

• that the interpretation of rights provided by the Constitutional Court was useful to the other constitutional powers **to fully comprehend** the guarantees set out in the **Constitution**. It has not been a rare occurrence, for example, that the State Counsel representing the government's defence has intervened in incidental procedures – to defend the compatibility of legislation with the Constitution – arguing for an extremely incorrect interpretation of constitutional provisions;

• how the Court understands the constitutional interpretation of rights: *i*) there are **no rights** that are **more important** than others; *ii*) it is often **necessary to balance** these rights because the Constitution is **pluralist** and protects principles, rights and values that may conflict with each other; and *iii*) the result of the balancing varies depending on the importance of the assets in play;

• that a **harsh dialectic** between the two interpreters of the Constitution regarding the content of the balancing of principles, rights and values may arise. There have been judgments which repeatedly eliminate a legal provision deemed to be clearly in breach of constitutional guarantees, as in the case of the legislation on assisted procreation, or judgments which, where faced with dramatic situations, lacking a law and under pressure by public opinion, temporarily **legislate** pending the Parliament's intervention. One example is the case of assisted suicide.

The order in which the judgments are presented corresponds to the order of the issues covered in Section A).

1. The Defascistisation of the Legal Order

The foundational Judgment No. 1/1956 has been mentioned many times in this textbook (the Italian *Marbury v. Madison*, if you will). It provides an example of the distinguishing capacities of the Court right from the outset, compared to other more traditional institutions within the Italian system (Parliament and the Government). In this first judgment, the Court **struck down** a fascist-era provision that **limited freedom of expression** which had remained in force for a full eight years after the enactment of the republican Constitution. This was the occasion to make clear to the public at large the innovative scope of this institution, which was ready to uphold and give effect to the fundamental rights proclaimed in the Constitution. The case also offered an auspicious opportunity to assert the breadth and exclusivity of the Court's power of judicial review over legislation and that its judicial review also extended to fascist pre-republican legislation that was not coherent with the republican value system. This activity of legislative cleansing was emphatically referred to as the **great substitution** to stress the fact that the Court was not exercising powers vested in another body but rather its own powers in order to perform highly commendable work that others [i.e., Parliament] were avoiding, whether due to inertia or opportunistic considerations. In making this choice the Court started to establish a **relationship of trust** with, and prestige amongst, the **general public**.

This judgment was triggered by the incompatibility of Article 113 (of the Consolidated Law on Public Safety, *Testo unico di pubblica sicurezza*, approved in 1931) with the free expression of thought, protected by Article 21 of the Constitution During the various criminal proceedings, the question of constitutional legitimacy had been referred by parties who had expressed their political thoughts without authorisation from the public safety authorities as required by Article 113 of the Consolidated Law.

One of these proceedings, for example, was held against two textile workers in Prato, Catani and Masi. With the support of their trade union, these two had infringed Article 113 of the Consolidated Law which required the authorisation of the public safety authorities for all types of political propaganda. The Constitutional Court argued that this norm conflicted with Article 21 according to which anyone has the right to freely express their thoughts in speech, writing, or any other form of communication and the press may not be subjected to any authorisation or censorship. Article 113 of the Consolidated Law was held to be unconstitutional because it set out *unlimited discretionary powers* of the public

© Wolters Kluwer Italia

safety authorities. In practice, this provision subordinated the enjoyment of the freedom of expression of thought to an arbitrary assessment conducted on a case-by-case basis.

The Court **rejected** the doctrine developed by the Court of Cassation – which up to 1956, had taken on the role of the Constitutional Court – recognising only an **aspirational value** to Article 21; indeed, this doctrine was proposed in the proceedings by the State Counsel for the President of the Council of Ministers. Instead, the ruling of 1956, in opposition to the more conservative portion of the judicial, legislative, and executive branches, stated for the first time that Article 21 ought to be deemed as a binding provision having immediate implementation. It was thus established that all the **constitutional provisions** are **immediately enforceable** and shall **trigger** the **unconstitutionality** of an **ordinary legislation** that conflicts with them.

Thus, it is not an exaggeration to link this judgment to the first fundamental confirmation of the legal value of the Constitution.

Judgment No. 1/1956 was also a precursor to **today's strategic litigation**: the virtuous result of the union of antifascist political forces together with a group of jurists that worked in harmony with the values proclaimed in the Constitution. It was not by chance that the counsel of the parties before the Court consisted of lawyers who would become among the most important jurists in the years to come: Piero Calamandrei, Vezio Crisafulli, Massimo Severo Giannini, Costantino Mortati and Giuliano Vassalli (Fioravanti 2017).

2. Article 2 as an Open-Ended Clause: The Ban of the Death Penalty and the Right to Life

The formulation of Article 2 aims to reiterate the centrality in the domestic legal system of the person, also guaranteeing rights that are **not explicitly set out**, such as, for example, the inviolable **right to life**. This is what the Constitutional Court confirmed in 1996, when it ruled out the possibility of extraditing a person charged with homicide to a country where that crime is punishable with the death penalty as a result of the constitutional protection of the right to life. This right, although it is not explicitly set out in the text of the Constitution, is to be considered one of the inviolable rights of the person recognised by Article 2.

> The case concerned Pietro Venezia, an Italian citizen, charged with murder in Florida, for which the Italian Ministry of Justice had issued a provision in favour of extradition. The incidental procedure was proposed by the administrative court appealed by Venezia against a set of provisions in the Italian Code of Criminal Procedure. Following the ratification of the Treaty on Extradition with the USA, the Code of Criminal Procedure established that **extradition** from Italy to a legal

© Wolters Kluwer Italia

system that envisaged the **death penalty** was **possible** provided that the State of extradition guaranteed that such penalty would **not** be awarded or that, if imposed, would **not** be carried out. Based on these provisions, both the legal authorities and the Italian Ministry of Justice believed that there was **sufficient reassurance** of the guarantee of Venezia's inviolable right to life.

With Judgment No. 223, the Court deemed the norm in the Code of Criminal Procedure to be unconstitutional, as well as the legislation that executed the Treaty on Extradition, due to **infringement** of Articles 2 and 27, para. 4, of the Constitution. The latter explicitly sets out the ban of the death penalty.

In a legal system, the Court stated, where the ban of the death penalty is sanctioned by the Constitution, the formula of *sufficient reassurance* is inadmissible. The prohibition contained in Article 27, para. 4, of the Constitution, and the values underlying it – primarily the essential right of life – imposed an absolute constitutional guarantee. The absolute character of this constitutional guarantee firstly requires that there be no norms that authorise discretionary assessments in proceedings on the degree of reliability and effectiveness of the guarantees agreed by the country requesting the extradition. Secondly, it also influences how other public bodies exercise the powers vested in them by the republican order. This is particularly true for the functions that are instrumental to international cooperation for mutual judiciary assistance. The arguments of the State counsel for the Italian government incorrectly maintained that the ban on the death penalty could not be extended as far as limiting the concept of the extradition of citizens, recognised in Article 26 of the Constitution every time this is envisaged by international agreements (although extradition is always prohibited for political crimes committed in home countries, excluding crimes of genocide).

In this judgment too, as in the previous one, the Constitutional Court' provided the executive branch with an interpretation that more correctly captures the real scope of the constitutional guarantees.

In 2007, Parliament eliminated the only exception to the ban on the death penalty, set out in Article 27 of the Constitution, i.e., the **death penalty** applied in the **military law of war**. The ban on the death penalty, as noted in Judgment No. 223, has a particular significance: this refers to a **principle** which, in many ways, can be considered Italian, as the **first State** in the world to outlaw the death penalty was the Grand Duchy of Tuscany in 1786. The part of the work of the Constituent Assembly dedicated to civil relationships affirmed that the ban is established in the constitutional system of the Republic as a projection of the guarantee provided to the fundamental right of life, which is the first of the inviolable rights of the person recognised by Article 2.

© Wolters Kluwer Italia

2.a. Rights and Duties: Vaccinations and Limitations to Self-Determination

Besides recognizing that the Republic safeguards **health** as a **fundamental right of the individual** and as a **collective interest**, and guarantees free medical care to the indigent, **Article 32** of the Constitution also provides a specific duty that goes hand in hand with the legitimate forms of **limitation of the right to self-determination**, and that ultimately embodies the spirit enshrined by Article 2, in particular the **principle of solidarity**.

Health has not only an individual dimension (it is a *fundamental right of the individual*), but also a collective one (it is a *collective interest*). This implies that, on the one hand, the right to health may be conceived as the right to physical and psychic integrity, the right to a healthy environment, the right to treatment, the right not to be treated, and the right to be informed. On the other hand, its collective dimension entails the duty of each individual not to harm or risk harming the health of others, in line with the principle that one's rights are limited by mutual recognition and by the equal protection of the rights of others (Judgment No. 218/1994 of the ItCC). It is exactly in this sense that the Constitution conceives and justifies a specific duty to undergo **mandatory health treatments** (e.g., vaccinations) if and only if the law explicitly provides so. In other words, and as the ItCC asserted, it is the purpose which pertains to health as an interest of society at large that justifies the restriction on individual self-determination (Judgment No. 268/2017). This also entails that the extent to which the right to self-determination may be limited will vary according to the need to satisfy the right to health of others: there is a proportional relationship between the individual right to health and the collective interest that finds its point of equilibrium in a pondered judgment, by the legislator and, possibly, by the constitutional judge.

The collective dimension of health is therefore guaranteed by the express provision of a specific duty for certain individuals (or the community at large) to undergo health treatment if the law expressly makes it mandatory. This is made clear in Article 32, para. 2, which provides that mandatory treatments may be enforced only through primary sources of law (**reserve of legislation**) and that any legislative discretion must nevertheless be exercised in the **respect of human dignity**. The ItCC further clarified that the reserve of legislation is satisfied if the law explicitly indicates the disease or infection that the health treatment is designed to prevent (Judgment No. 25/2023), and that mandatory treatments should not in any case have a negative impact on the recipient's health, the only exception being those consequences that normally derive from the treatment. This is justified because the temporary and minor nature of the effects makes them tolerable (Judgment No. 307/1990).

The specific duty to undergo mandatory treatments has been subject to numerous challenges before the Constitutional Court, especially in relation to mandatory vaccination.

With Judgment No. 5/2018, the Court had been asked to decide upon the legitimacy of a norm that increased from four to ten the number of free and compulsory vaccinations for minors under the age of sixteen. The Court drew attention to the requirement to **strike a balance** between the individual right to health (including the right to self-determination) and the coexistent and reciprocal right of others and the interests of the community.

The Court specified that a national law imposing a health-related treatment is not incompatible with the Constitution provided that (cumulatively): (i) the treatment is intended not only to improve or maintain the recipient's health, but also to **preserve the health of others**; (ii) the treatment is not expected to have a negative impact on the recipient's health, besides the usual and **tolerable consequences** that normally arise from its administration; and (iii) in the event of further injury, the payment of **just compensation** to the injured party is provided for, separate and apart from any damages to which they might be entitled.

Furthermore, since the issue of vaccination involves many constitutional values, their coexistence leaves ample space for **legislative discretion** in choosing the necessary means to ensure the effective prevention of infectious diseases. This discretion must be exercised according to health and epidemiological conditions, as ascertained by the responsible authorities and the constantly evolving discoveries of medical research, to which the legislature has to turn for guidance when making its choices. In other words, besides being an example of the balancing of rights and interests in a constitutional order, Judgment No. 5/2018 also exemplifies how these principles may support a data-driven judicial review of epidemiological legislation. The ItCC further confirmed this approach in two judgments concerning the legitimacy of a norm that prescribed an obligation to undergo **COVID-19 vaccinations** on all healthcare workers and practitioners, and provided that non-compliant workers would be suspended from work without pay (Judgments Nos. 14 and 15/2023).

On the one hand, the referring courts questioned whether, in light of the adverse events reported to systems of pharmacovigilance, the available vaccinations are safe enough to be prescribed, and therefore whether individual testing for COVID-19 should be considered as a viable alternative. They also questioned whether the legal consequences that were prescribed in case of non-compliance were reasonable and proportionate, especially since healthcare workers who could not be vaccinated due to certified individual medical conditions would not incur such sanctions.

 © Wolters Kluwer Italia

The ItCC held the measures to be constitutionally legitimate and confirmed its well-consolidated case law on mandatory vaccination requirements, which ultimately tries to strike a balance between the individual right to self-determination and the community's general interest for health. The Court assessed whether the lawmaker, in exercising its political discretion, kept within an area of **scientific reliability**, in light of the best knowledge attained in that historical moment, as defined by the **designated medical and scientific authorities**.

The Court also specified that the scientific data provided by these competent authorities cannot be replaced by data acquired from other sources, even if it comes from experts in the field. This seems to indicate that the lawmaker's decision can still be considered the product of political discretion, but that it has to be based *necessarily* on scientific evidence and that the reliability of that same evidence ultimately depends on its origin.

The ItCC's case law is echoed by the ECtHR in *Vavřička and Others v the Czech Republic* (Grand Chamber, Application No. 47621/13 and five other applications, Judgment, 8th of April, 2021), where the Court of Strasbourg decided on the compatibility with the ECHR of Czech legislation enforcing a general legal duty to vaccinate children against nine diseases. The applicants argued that such State interference was in violation of the ECHR, in particular Article 8 (Right to respect for private and family life) and Article 9 (Freedom of thought, conscience, and religion). In its judgment, the Court emphasised that the right to physical integrity enshrined in Article 8 is a qualified right in the sense that it may be limited for the protection of health:

> … indeed, paragraph 2 of Article 8 provides that there shall be no interference by a public authority in the exercise of this right *except such as in accordance with the law* and is *necessary in a democratic society* in the interests of national security, […] *for the protection of health* or morals, *or for the protection of the rights and freedoms of others*. Yet again, the right to self-determination may be limited (by law), as long as limitations are proportional.

The Court recognised that the Czech legislation pursued the legitimate aims of protecting health as well as the rights of others, since vaccinations protect those who receive them as well as those who cannot be vaccinated for medical reasons, and it also noted that the duty was strongly supported by the relevant medical authorities. The importance of scientific data and advice is emphasised also by the Court of Strasbourg, especially as the legislator exercises its political discretion and finds a proper balance between different rights and interests.

Lastly, and as far as Article 9 ECHR is concerned, the Court of Strasbourg created a very sharp distinction between opinions and convictions; it did not

© Wolters Kluwer Italia

consider that the applicants' critical position on vaccination constituted a conviction or belief of sufficient cogency, seriousness, cohesion, or importance to attract the guarantees of Article 9. In other words, a general critical opinion on vaccination does not constitute an expression of conviction or belief that is sufficient to obtain an exemption.

3. Individual Freedoms Recognised to Foreigners

3.a. Personal Liberty

The ItCC, has made it very clear that it does not consider itself bound – when it comes to fundamental rights – to a literal and strict interpretation of the subjective references contained in the text of the Constitution. Starting from this assumption, it felt entitled to **extend** to non-citizens the subjective scope of **constitutional freedom and rights** expressly recognised to citizens.

One of the most important interventions of the ItCC in this area is Judgment No. 105/2001, which is crucial in Italian constitutional law as it addressed some of the main questions concerning constitutional freedoms of non-citizens, in particular personal liberty.

In Judgment No. 105/2001 the ItCC scrutinized the constitutional legitimacy of the **expulsion procedure**, governed by Articles 13 and 14 of legislative decree No. 286/1998, *Consolidated Immigration Act*, as it imposes that only the order for **detention,** and not also the **coercive transfer,** needed to be validated by a judge.

The doubts of constitutional legitimacy were related to **Article 13** of the Constitution, according to which no one may be subjected to any restriction of personal liberty except by order of the Judiciary. In exceptional circumstances, and under conditions of necessity and urgency, provisional measures can be taken by the police, but they shall always be referred within 48 hours to the judiciary for validation. In default of such validation in the following 48 hours, the measure shall be revoked and considered null and void. In other words, the system provided by legislative decree No. 286/1998 was suspected of being unconstitutional because the judge's assessment was imposed only for the order of detention and not for the coercive transfer.

The Constitutional Court **rejected** the doubt. Not per se, but in the belief that even in the absence of an express provision, it is to be considered that the judicial control over the detention would also surpass the measure of the coercive transfer to the border by means of public force.

Beyond its outcome, however, it is in its premises that Judgment No. 105/2001 developed some fundamental indications on the subjective extension of the guarantees provided by Article 13 of the Constitution. The most interesting element of its reasoning is that the guarantees of Article 13 cannot be mitigated in relation

© Wolters Kluwer Italia

to citizenship status. Although there are multiple public interests affecting immigration, and despite the fact that the problems of security and public order that are connected to uncontrolled migratory flows may be perceived as serious, as stated by the ItCC in Judgment No. 105/2001, the universal character of personal liberty, as the other rights that the Constitution proclaims inviolable, cannot be affected, as they belong to individuals not as participants in a specific political community, but as human beings.

Starting from these indications, the ItCC developed solid case law (i.e., Judgments Nos. 222 and 223/2004) through which it enacted an almost universal extension of personal liberty and of the guarantees provided for by Article 13. More generally, the Constitutional Court has consolidated within its case law a principle that has been defined as **equality** in the field of **ownership of the rights of liberty**, according to which in the Italian legal system the category of the **rights of liberty** can be considered as **human rights**, which everyone enjoys, **regardless** of their **relationship** with the state.

A similar process was also followed for the extension of the **right to defence** (Article 24 of the Constitution), the universal ownership of which was clearly expressed by the ItCC. So much so that, on the basis of this assumption, the Court recognised the **right** of expelled foreigners **to return** to Italy in order to **defend themselves** in the courts (Judgment No. 492/1991). It also established the right of the addressees of measures of restriction of personal liberty to understand their content and meaning (Judgment No. 198/2000), and, finally, declared the possibility for the foreigner to appoint his/her own interpreter at the expense of the state unconstitutional (Judgment No. 254/2007). Similar problems have also been addressed in reference to freedom of assembly (Article 17 of the Constitution) and of association (Article 18 of the Constitution) which, although expressly recognised only for citizens, are now considered extended to foreigners.

3.b. Freedom of Movement

A separate consideration should be made regarding the freedom of movement (Article 16 of the Constitution). In Judgment No. 148/2008, the ItCC clarified that, as regards **entry** into and **circulation** throughout the national territory, the situation of foreigners is **not equal** to that of **citizens**, as the **State** may control and **prevent** foreigners from **entering** and **staying** in its territory, complying with the limits deriving from the generally recognised principles of international law and any international treaties applicable to individual cases (Article 10 of the Constitution). In this regard, the Universal Declaration of Human Rights states that everyone has the right to leave any country, including his/her own, and to return to his/her country (Article 13, para. 2, of the Declaration) but does **not**

establish an **obligation** for states to **allow foreigners** to **enter** their territory. Referring back to the categories described in Section A), it can be stated that **foreigners** have only a **legitimate interest** in entering the national territory. However, there are several **exceptions** to this rule:

• citizens of the European Union enjoy a right to entry based on the freedom of movement and residence set out in EU treaties;

• family members of an Italian or a foreigner residing in Italy enjoy a right to entry, based on the EU law on the right to maintain or re-unify family;

• foreigners who, in their home countries, are denied the effective exercise of the democratic freedoms guaranteed by the Constitution enjoy a right to entry (Articles 10, para. 3, of the Constitution and 14 of the Universal Declaration of Human Rights).

4. Social Rights Recognised to Foreigners: Right to Health

The extension to foreigners of *social rights* is closely linked to the **cost of rights** and it connects more immediately to the person's link with the state (the political community and its territory). This is the case of the **right to health** (Article 32 of the Constitution), from which derives the right to receive health treatment. The ItCC has been explicit in **recognising** that the Constitution **protects** the right to **health of every person regardless** of citizenship, whatever their status may be with respect to the rules governing entry and stay in the national territory.

One of the crucial moments in the recognition of this principle was Judgment No. 252/2001, in which the ItCC expressly stated that the protection of the right to health contains an **irreducible core**, protected by the Constitution, which entitles non-citizens to receive any treatment that is necessary for their health. The judgment stemmed from a doubt raised – through an incidental procedure – by the Court of Genova, which had asked the ItCC if Article 19, para. 2, of the legislative decree No. 286/1998, Consolidated Immigration Act (*Testo unico sull'immigrazione e la condizione dello straniero*), violated Articles 2 and 32 of the Constitution, as it did not expressly prohibit the expulsion of the non-citizen who entered the territory of the state illegally for the sole purpose of completing a therapeutic treatment.

The ItCC took the opportunity to express some fundamental criteria on the process of the subjective extension of the right to health and, more generally, of social rights. In Judgment No. 252, the ItCC **rejected** the doubt raised regarding the absence of an express prohibition of expulsion not because it did not agree on the merit of it, but because it was built on an incorrect assumption: that the inviolable right to health of the non-citizen who is illegally present in the national

© Wolters Kluwer Italia

territory can be protected only through the express provision of a specific ban on expulsion.

With regard to the prohibition of the expulsion of the non-citizen who needs healthcare, the ItCC took a position on a more general level: Judgment No. 252/2001 provided a principle according to which the protection of health as a **fundamental right** of the **person** must also be **recognised** to **foreigners**, whatever their position with respect to the rules governing entry and stay in the state. The aim is obviously to ensure the **effectiveness** of the right to **health**, guaranteeing that the person can stay in the national territory until the completion of the treatment. In this regard, according to the ItCC, Article 19 of legislative decree No. 286/1998 is to be considered as an implicit **obstacle** to expulsion, also in connection with Article 35 of the same legislative decree, which prescribes the prohibition of reporting to the authorities the foreigner who is present in the territory illegally and accesses health facilities.

This is what has been defined as the **core approach**: an approach based on the identification of a minimum content of rights, of which a categorical defence is ensured. **Outside** this **minimum** core, the legislator can **differentiate** the protection of social rights but only on the basis of criteria that are reasonably linked to the rationale of the service. Lawmakers can do so only by making reasonable differentiations: they are allowed to introduce differentiated regimes as long as the differentiation occurs due to a regulatory clause that is not clearly irrational or, worse, arbitrary. Using this criterion, the Court has struck down numerous provisions that bound the enjoyment of social services to the requirement of citizenship or to a particular relationship with the territory of the state.

4.a. Social Benefits

Judgment No. 432/2005 represented one of the best known and most evident applications of this orientation. The Court declared as constitutionally illegitimate the provision of a law of the Lombardia Region (Article 8, para. 2, of Law No. 1/2002), because it did not include non-citizens residing in the Region among the holders of the right to free circulation on public transport services, which was recognised to the fully disabled residing in the Region.

This judgment demonstrates how, in order to guarantee the **principle of reasonable distinction**, the ItCC must identify the rationale of the social service and, on the basis of this, review the choices relating to the identification of the categories of beneficiaries. It is this choice that must be made, always and in any case, in compliance with the principle of reasonableness. In Judgment No. 432/2005, the ItCC identified the common and unifying feature of the beneficiaries as the percentage of disability. On the basis of this common trait, the ItCC pinpointed the rationale for the benefit in the will to facilitate – through the free use of the service – access to the local public transport system in favour of a group of residents sharing the most serious condition of invalidity. The contested provision, however, guaranteed the right to free circulation not to all people with a degree of disability equal to 100%, but only to those (1) residing in the Region and (2) who hold Italian citizenship. It is, therefore, against these two additional requirements that the ItCC had to assess the reasonableness: while residence appeared as a not unreasonable criterion for the attribution of the benefit, citizenship was presented as an inconsistent condition, as there was no reasonable correlation between it and the rationale of the law. The requirement of citizenship, therefore, was not compliant with Article 3 of the Constitution, and that is why it was declared unconstitutional.

Based on the assumption made by Judgment No. 432/2005, the ItCC developed a case law in which it adopted the **criterion of reasonableness** in order to declare as **unconstitutional** the use of **citizenship** or **long-term residence** as a condition for access to social benefits in all cases in which it appeared to be completely irrelevant and, as such, an arbitrary element of distinction.

More recently, referring to the principle expressed by Judgment No. 432/2005, the Court of Appeal of Milan raised a new doubt of constitutionality with respect to a provision (this time included in a national law, Article 11, para. 3, of the legislative decree No. 25/2008) which regulated the disbursement of funds for housing support, subjecting it – only for foreigners – to the requirement of at least ten years of residence in the national territory, or at least five years in the territory of the Region. The ItCC responded with Judgment No. 166/2018, with which it annulled the provision, confirming the case law established in 2005.

In Judgment No. 166/2018, the ItCC repeated once again that any provision that imposes distinctions between various categories of people **by reason of citizenship or residence** to regulate **access to social benefits** must respond to the principle of **reasonableness** pursuant to Article 3 Constitution. The requirement of ten years of residence in the national territory or five years in the same Region constitute, according to the ItCC, a clearly **unreasonable** and **arbitrary** term for the purposes of access to the benefit attributed. If it was acceptable, in theory, that a title could be required in order to demonstrate the non-episodic or short-term nature of the stay in the territory, and if it was also true that social policies can take into consideration additional territorial roots beyond simple residence, then there must always be a reasonable correlation between the request and the situations of hardship.

One of the last episodes in this series of judgments was No. 44/2020, which demonstrated the continuing vitality of the position described above. This time the Constitutional Court annulled, ruling on the application for incidental procedure

 © Wolters Kluwer Italia

submitted by the Court of Milan, a provision of a law of the Lombardia Region which envisaged, as a condition of access to public housing, the requirement of registered residence or being employed in the area of the Region for at least five years in the immediately preceding period. This condition was held devoid of any reasonable connection with the function of the measure and, therefore, represented a violation of Article 3 Constitution, because it led to denying access to the benefit regardless of any assessment relating to the applicant's situation of need.

In 2022 the Court examined the provision that links citizens' income to the prerequisite of holding a right to stable residence in Italy (Judgment No. 19). Citizens' income did not amount merely to a benefit aimed at satisfying a primary need of the individual, but rather promoted more complex active employment policy goals, including personalised assistance in incorporation into the world of work as well as social inclusion.

The Court held that, considering the duration of the benefit as well as the result pursued (social inclusion and integration into employment), the lawmakers did not act unreasonably in exercising their discretion to reserve the measure for foreign nationals with a permanent right of residence in Italy.

5. Limitation and Balancing of Rights and Principles

The development of a right is also the product of a virtuous cooperation between the Court and Parliament.

A demonstration of this is represented by the guarantees recognised to the lawfulness of the **termination of pregnancy** (at least under certain conditions). An additional example of this cooperation is the one regarding the **balance of gender** in politics.

When, instead, this cooperation is lacking, and the dialectic between the two interpreters – the Parliament and the Court – regarding the content of the balancing of rights and principles is in conflict, this results in judgments being considered, at least by a portion of the doctrine, as **encroachments** into the area of the lawmakers which, for this reason, should be condemned. An example is the legislation on medically assisted procreation (Law No. 40/2004): a series of judgments of the Court eliminated its most characteristic content because the **balancing** carried out by the Parliament was deemed at times **to be irrational**. The result was a sort of 'rewriting' of the Law by the Constitutional Court, with a much more liberal meaning than that intended by the lawmakers.

In cases where lawmakers are unable to adopt a law, or deem that it is not yet the time to do so, on issues that society feels for particularly, the Court may find itself in a highly delicate situation. As was stated in the last paragraph of

Section A), society was led to a view of the Court as capable of **substituting** the **inertia** of lawmakers. At times, the Court has agreed to this role. It has done so always after **repeatedly asking** the lawmakers to intervene, **indicating** them a **path** to legislate in line with the Constitution (for example through orders of inadmissibility which contain a non-binding request to the lawmakers to intervene by choosing among different possible legal solutions the one they consider feasible).

This is the case of the two judgments adopted on the issue of **assisted suicide**. These were introduced by the Constitutional Court in an area in which legislation does not exist, even though the Court has requested the parliament to provide it.

This is also the case for the two judgments that, after a thirty-year wait, rewrote the norms that originally assigned children only the paternal surname.

But is this really the duty of a Constitutional Court: to warn lawmakers of their delay and, when they do not act, to intervene? This is the question most widely discussed nowadays in the vast majority of democratic legal systems.

5.a. Abortion

The termination of pregnancy is not a right explicitly provided for in the Constitution.

The outlines of its protection were traced by the Constitutional Court, and then by lawmakers who followed and developed its indications in Law No. 194/1978, For the social protection of motherhood and the voluntary termination of pregnancy.

In the Criminal Code in force in 1975 – which was adopted in 1930 during fascism – voluntary abortion was considered a crime against the lineage of race. The good being protected was the demographic interests of the state, not the integrity of the person, as had been set out in the previous Criminal Code (1889). Article 546 of the Criminal Code punished anyone who caused an abortion, even with the woman's consent, by 2 to 5 years imprisonment, even if the danger of the pregnancy for the woman's physical or psychological well-being had been verified. The same punishment was applied to the woman.

In 1972, criminal proceedings began which would lead the Constitutional Court to rule on the issue. The proceedings concerned a woman who was afflicted with serious myopia, whose doctor had recommended terminating her pregnancy due to the danger that this disease could worsen further. The criminal court questioned the ItCC on the constitutionality of Article 546.

With Judgment No. 27/1975, firstly, it was recognised that the Constitution undoubtedly protects the foetus. Article 31, para. 2, of the Constitution requires

 © Wolters Kluwer Italia

the protection of maternity and, more generally, Article 2 of the Constitution recognises and guarantees the inviolable rights of the person. The legal situation of the foetus falls within these rights, though with its own specific characteristics. As a result, the lawmakers' intervention aimed at setting out penal sanctions is justified.

Nonetheless, the Court pointed out that the constitutional protection of the foetus may contrast with the other goods that also have constitutional protection, such as the **woman's right to health**. As a result, the legislation cannot grant the former total, absolute prevalence, denying the latter appropriate protection. Nor can it be argued that the right not only to life, but also to health of one who is already a person, meaning the woman, and the safeguarding of one who is still to become a person, the foetus, are equivalent.

The **lack of proportionality** of criminal norms on abortion was the reason why the Constitution was infringed. In adopting this judgment, the Court **recommended** to lawmakers that:

• the **balancing** of the conflicting rights can be found in the **protection of the woman's life** and **health**, while, in any event, acting in a way that **saves**, when **possible**, the life of the **foetus**;

• in order to correctly implement this balancing, the lawfulness of abortion must be anchored to a prior assessment of the conditions to justify it.

In 1978 Parliament exercised its discretion, carrying out the balancing indicated by the Court, and implementing those criteria of minimum protection of the interests deemed fundamental by the Constitution, which Judgment No. 27 had clearly indicated.

With Law No. 194/1978, the Parliament thus granted the woman, the only party responsible for her choice, the possibility to access termination of pregnancy in the first trimester in the event of serious danger to her physical health or psychological well-being, in relation to her health status or her financial, social or family conditions, or to the circumstances in which the conception occurred, or to expected anomalies or deformities of the foetus. After the first trimester it is possible to terminate a pregnancy when the pregnancy or labour would be highly dangerous to the woman's life, that is when certain pathological processes, including those relating to significant anomalies or deformations of the unborn child, which constitute a serious danger for the woman's physical health or psychological well-being.

At the same time, the legislation set out an exemption for healthcare workers who had lodged a conscientious objection against abortion.

During the pandemic, the Ministry of Health classified termination of pregnancy as a health treatment that could not be postponed.

© Wolters Kluwer Italia

Nevertheless, lack of public funds has made it highly difficult, if not impossible, to implement the provision contained in the law that the healthcare facility, with the woman's consent and respecting her dignity and privacy, is required to offer support to remove the causes – above all, financial, social or family ones – that could underlie her decision to carry out the abortion.

This issue has triggered heated discussions and legal battles in all legal systems. The best-known case is that of the United States. In 1973, the Supreme Court of the United States handed down the historical judgment *Roe v. Wade*, 410 U.S. 113, which legalised abortion, though under specific conditions, recognising a right to personal privacy to women, understood as the right to freely make choices regarding the most intimate sphere of their lives. Extreme political polarisation was created around abortion, which ended up contaminating the Supreme Court itself. In 1992, the judgment *Planned Parenthood v Casey*, 505 U.S. 833, while reviewing the conclusions reached in *Roe v Wade*, confirmed its essential point, i.e., the constitutional foundation of a woman's right to voluntarily terminate a pregnancy. Instead, this same point was decidedly rejected in the recent judgment *Dobbs v Jackson Women's Health Organization*, handed down by a Court which included three (out of nine) judges appointed by President Donald J. Trump, who had politically committed to moving the ideological axis of the Supreme Court in this direction. It was not by chance that, in the meantime, President Joseph R. Biden, Jr. set up a Commission to study possible reforms of the Supreme Court (Executive Order 14023, 9th of April, 2021). In *Dobbs*, the majority argued that a right to abortion neither finds ground in the Constitution, nor is it «deeply rooted» in national history, which the Court reconstructed up to the 1970s. On the other hand, three dissenting justices pointed out that this right is an aspect of women's equality and liberty, just like the right to interracial marriage, which also has no explicit basis in the Constitution and had been fiercely opposed for a long part of American history, until *Loving v Virginia*, 388 U.S. 1 (1967). Moreover, the dissenters fear that *Dobbs* may damage the Court's legitimation as a partisan ruling, which suddenly overturned decades-old precedents at the first occasion when a majority of the judges share the same conservative ideology. It is worth noting that the separate opinion of Chief Justice Roberts – indeed, himself a conservative – did not concur with the majority in denying the constitutional protection of the right to abortion, and found that such a broad ruling was not necessary to dispose of the specific case at hand.

The topic is at the centre of attention also in Europe. The Court of Strasbourg received over 1,000 applications concerning the statutory provision for abortion in the case of foetal abnormalities declared unconstitutional by the Polish Constitutional Tribunal (22nd of October, 2020 (K1/2020). The Tribunal upheld

 © Wolters Kluwer Italia

that human life constitutes a value at every stage of its development and, as a value arising from the provisions of the Constitution, it should be protected by the legislator. The unborn child – as a human being, entitled to the inherent and inalienable dignity of the person – is recognised under law as a subject of rights and obligations who enjoys the right to life; the legal system must provide due protection for the unborn child's dignity, which constitutes a central value without which being recognised as a subject of rights and obligations would be ruled out. On the basis of these findings, the Tribunal deemed that it is possible to have a situation where one of the constitutional interests in the conflict of interests concerns an unborn child. At present an abortion can be carried out only when a pregnancy endangers the mother's life or health, or if there are strong grounds for believing that the pregnancy is a result of a criminal act.

5.b. Reproductive Rights

The Constitution does not provide the right to become parents, rather, it assures the right of children to have a family. Nonetheless, parenthood, understood as the free choice to create a family above and beyond the biological fact, is guaranteed in ordinary legislation.

With Law No. 40/2004, for the first time in the national legal system, medically assisted procreation (MAP) was recognised for heterosexual couples in potentially fertile age according to methods that guarantee the rights of all parties involved, including those of the foetus. The legislation does not allow for **surrogate** pregnancy, which is considered to cause **intolerable offence** to the **dignity** of the woman and to profoundly undermine human relations (Judgment No. 272/2017 and Court of Cassation, Judgment No. 38162/2022). A similar ban is imposed also by different Europeans legal orders (such as Germany, France, Austria, Switzerland and Northern European countries). The **altruistic surrogacy** (absence of compensation) is accessible in UK, Australia, Brazil, Canada, India, New Zealand, the Netherlands, Greece, South Africa, Portugal and in some states of the US. Commercial surrogacy is admitted in some states of the US, Russia, Ukrain and, Mexico.

The Law of 2004 was harshly criticised. Specifically, this was because it was deemed as an expression of an ethical concept of MAP and embryos that is not shared by all of society, and that clearly conflicts with the sound precedents of case law regarding the woman's right to health based on reasonable balancing and limits placed by scientific and experimental knowledge on legislative discretion, which are continuously developing and on which the medical state of the art is based.

In the words of the Court, medically assisted procreation rests on **political discretion**: the topic involves so many constitutional principle and rights, sometimes even opposing ones, that the identification of a **reasonable balancing** among them has primarily to be attributed to the lawmakers' assessment.

Nonetheless, the Court retains the ability to review the law, in order to verify whether the lawmakers' assessment resulted in an unreasonable balancing of these needs with the values that they are founded on. Once it is verified that provisions of legislation conflict with the constitutional parameters, the Court cannot avoid its duty to remedy this and must declare the unconstitutionality of such provisions.

The interests in play, as a whole, require a balancing that ensures a **fair balance** between the protection of the embryo with the protection of the need for reproduction.

This is an example of an institutional relationship which is the opposite of the virtuous one seen with regards to the termination of pregnancy. In this situation, the Court played a **counter-majoritarian role**.

Starting in 2009 (Judgment No. 151), the Constitutional Court declared the legislation unconstitutional. In particular, it held the illegitimacy of the provision that **excluded the option of the doctor to assess**, considering the woman's age and state of health, **how many embryos to produce and how many to implant**. The legislation provided for the production of a maximum of three embryos to be implanted all at the same time. The Court stated that this provision, in the absence of any consideration of the individual personal conditions of the woman, violates Article 3 of the Constitution on the dual grounds of reasonableness and equality, since the provision requires that dissimilar situations be treated identically; as well as Article 32 of the Constitution, due to the detriment caused to the health of the woman. Therefore, the protection of the **embryo** is **not** at all **absolute** but is limited by the need to **strike** a **correct balance** with the protection of the need for **reproduction**.

In 2014, with Judgment No. 162, the Court struck down the ban to accede to heterologous MAP for couples who are absolutely and irreversibly sterile or infertile.

On that occasion the Court stated that the choice to become parents and to establish a family including children amounts to an expression of the fundamental and general right of self-determination protected by Articles 2, 3 and 31 of the Constitution. Consequently, any restrictions on this freedom, including, in particular, the absolute prohibition imposed on its exercise, will only be reasonably and suitably justified if it is impossible to protect interests of equal standing in any other manner.

© Wolters Kluwer Italia

In the Judgment No. 96/2015, the Court allowed access to MAP for **fertile couples affected** (even as healthy carriers) by **serious hereditary genetic diseases** which are susceptible (according to scientific evidence) to transmitting significant anomalies and malformations to their offspring. They were also allowed to carry out **preimplantation genetic diagnosis**, fully banned by the existing legislation. The indiscriminate ban contained in the legislation was considered an element of unreasonableness (in violation of Article 3 of the Constitution), considering that the legislation permits the undeniably more traumatic method of voluntary termination of natural pregnancies as seen above.

Therefore, Article 32 of the Constitution, of which the provision under review runs afoul, was also violated, due to the absence of respect for the woman's right to health. In addition, the damage thus caused to this right has no positive counterweight, in terms of balancing, in a need to protect the offspring, which would be, in any case, vulnerable to abortion.

With Judgment of 28th of August, 2012, case *Costa and Pavan v Italy*, the ECtHR (Application No. 54270/10) had already denounced that same antinomy, affirming, on the contrary, that in the matter of MAP, the States retain a wide margin of appreciation (as already stated in Grand Chamber, case *S.H. and Others v Austria*, Application No. 57813/00, Judgment, 3rd of November, 2011).

The Law No. 40/2004 does not allow same-sex unions of women to access MAP (Judgment No. 221/2019). It also imposes penalties such as fines and licence suspensions for medical practitioners, and suspension or revocation of the authority to provide MAP services for facilities found guilty of providing MAP services to couples or individuals not qualified under the law.

The question of the constitutionality of this prohibition was rejected by the Court. Stressing the plurality of constitutional interests involved, the rapid pace of medical and scientific advancements, and the ethically sensitive nature of many of the relevant issues, the Court held that identifying a reasonable balance fell chiefly to the evaluation of the Parliament, subject only to review by the Constitutional Court to ensure that the solution was not unreasonable. Here the Court cited the ECtHR's case law stating that States have a wide margin of appreciation in areas where there is no general consensus at the European level, and also that States may legitimately limit the use of MAP procedures to the therapeutic purpose of curing infertility.

The Court did not consider the ban as discriminatory on the basis of sexual orientation, because the physiological inability to reproduce of all same-sex couples could not be equated to medical infertility or sterility in heterosexual couples of fertile age (ECtHR, First Section, case *Gas and Dubois v France*, Application No. 25951/07, Judgment, 15th of March, 2012), and was, instead, comparable to the inability to reproduce of heterosexual couples advanced in age, who were also legitimately denied access to MAP.

© Wolters Kluwer Italia

5.c. End of Life

How can the central nature of the right to life in the constitutional legal system be reconciled with the **right** to **assisted suicide**? Can the legal system establish a person's right to obtain assistance in dying from the state or from third parties?

The Constitution **does not recognise any duty to live**, but **neither** does it recognise a **right to die**. The Parliament dealt with the issue of the end-of-life, without, however, managing to adopt a legislation that was agreed upon by the majority.

In 2017 legislation was approved (No. 219) on **informed consent**, which also guarantees access to pain therapy, including deep palliative sedation, the prohibition of aggressive treatment and advance treatment directives. Based on this law, those who are kept alive artificially, also through artificial ventilation, hydration or nutrition, have the right to choose whether to accept or refuse these treatments (even once they have begun). If the patient is unconscious, their will shall prevail, as previously demonstrated through advance treatment directives, or reconstructed *a posteriori* by the court. In this sense, in the constitutional legal system, there is **no duty** to continue **living at all costs**.

For the first time, in 2018 and 2019, the Constitutional Court dealt with individuals who do not simply want to refuse treatment, but want to die, and are capable of doing so, but need assistance.

> This was the case of Fabiano Antoniani, known as DJ Fabo. As a result of a traffic accident, the young man was completely paralysed, blind, and required mechanical respiratory assistance and artificial hydration and nutrition. However, his intellectual abilities remained intact, and he was able to communicate, though with difficulty. Fabo decided to end his life, contacting a clinic in Switzerland, where assisted suicide is legal, on certain conditions. He needed someone to take him to the clinic. He was accompanied by Marco Cappato, activist and President of the Luca Coscioni Association, which advocates for euthanasia. Fabo still had the strength to bite down on the button that injected the lethal drug. Subsequently, Marco Cappato turned himself in for the crime of assisting another person to commit suicide (punished with 5 to 12 years imprisonment, Article 580 of the I Criminal Code). The referring criminal judge believed that that offence was not compatible with the central value of the dignity of the person, set out in the Constitution, a fundamental component of which is the ability of self-determination, taking by oneself the decision on how and when to end his/her life. For these reasons, the question of constitutional legitimacy was raised.

© Wolters Kluwer Italia

At this time, the Court adopted a new type of decision: an Order (No. 207/2018), which described the constitutional framework and the correct balance to pursue, suspended the judgment and gave the Parliament a year of time to pass legislation. The constitutional value of life does not exclude the obligation to comply with the patient's decision to end his/her life by stopping medical treatments, even when this requires active conduct by third parties. The absolute ban on assistance to suicide limits patients' freedom of self-determination – deriving from Articles 2, 13 and 32, para. 2, of the Constitution – in choosing treatments, including those aimed at freeing them from their suffering.

This type of order is not envisaged in Italian law. On the contrary, similar kinds of orders exist in other legal systems.

In Austria, following the judgment of 11th of December, 2020 taken by the Austrian Constitutional Court, *Verfassungsgerichtshof*, the lawmakers revised the provisions on assisted suicide, since the prohibition of assisted suicide was found to be unconstitutional because it violated the right to free self-determination inferable from the Constitution. The amendments entered into force on 1st of January, 2022. The *Verfassungsgerichtshof* delayed the effects of the ruling over time (pursuant to a specific provision of the Austrian Constitution, Article 140, para. 5) for more than one year, to allow lawmakers to intervene.

In 2019 (Judgment No. 242), after acknowledging that Parliament had not intervened, the ItCC confirmed the **partial unconstitutionality** of Article 580 of the Criminal Code on assisted suicide, establishing that anyone, such as Marco Cappato, who assists in the suicide of an informed person, artificially kept alive, affected by an irreversible illness and intolerable suffering, cannot be punished. This is allowed, provided that the death occurs in a public healthcare facility, after obtaining an opinion from the competent Ethics Committee.

Shortly thereafter, on 26th of February, 2020, the German Federal Constitutional Court (*Bundesverfassungsgericht*) also made a significant intervention in legislation on the issue of assisted suicide. In Germany assisted suicide is not completely forbidden; only professional assistance was prohibited. The *Bundesverfassungsgericht* declared the unconstitutionality of the criminal offence of the «commercial aiding and abetting of suicide» as provided for in paragraph 217 StGB (Criminal Code). According to the BVerfG, the right to suicide also includes the freedom to ask for help from others to this end, and to avail of such help, when offered. In relation to this fundamental right, reconstructed as above, the challenged norm irremediably operates as interference by the state. The criminally sanctioned ban pursuant to Article 217, para. 1, StGB of a professionally-organised service of assisted suicide makes it factually impossible for those who intend to end their lives, based on a free and autonomous decision, to avail themselves of assisted suicide carried out in an organised form, possibly offered by third parties (BVerfG, Judgment of the Second Senate of 26th of February, 2020 - 2 BvR 2347/15).

The German judgment is important because it demonstrates how, through the **judgment of proportionality**, it was possible to **profoundly impact the criminal lawmakers' discretion**.

The two Italian judgments have been harshly criticised by those who deem that the Court has been increasingly eroding Parliament's political discretion. They have been called **judgment-legislations**. There are also others who have provided a different interpretation of Parliaments' inertia: this is not understood as the inability to reach a political balance, but as an informed choice that expresses a conservative will, an intention not to intervene.

Actually, as also demonstrated by judgments taken by other foreign Courts, contemporary Constitutional Courts consider Parliaments' inertia to be no longer tolerable where the constitutional value at stake has taken such deep root in the social conscience.

Regarding the approach of the ECtHR, it has been stated that in questions concerning the end of life, Member States enjoy a wide margin of appreciation (*Pretty v United Kingdom*, Application No. 2346/02, Judgment, 29th of April, 2002; *Koch v Germany*, Application No. 497/09, Judgment, 17th of December, 2012; *Haas v Switzerland*, Application No. 31322/07, Judgment, 20th of January, 2011; Grand Chamber, *Lambert v France*, Application No. 46043/14, Judgment, 5th of June, 2015). At the same time, the ECtHR affirmed that the right of every person to decide on the time and method of the end of his or her life, provided that the person is capable of making a free decision and acting in line with that decision, is one of the aspects of the right to a private life recognised by Article 8 ECHR (*Koch v Germany*; *Haas v Switzerland*).

5.d. Maternal Surname

In the legal system, up to the judgments of the Constitutional Court of 2016 and 2022, it had never been possible to give a child also the maternal surname. The Civil Code of 1942 and the related norms always referred to the **automatic acquisition of the paternal surname**, understood as the distinctive sign of members of the family, for children born in wedlock. The same applied to children born out of wedlock if recognised by both parents, as well as for adopted children.

Since 1988, the question of the provision's constitutionality has been periodically reported to the Constitutional Court, specifically for infringement of the right to a personal identity, pursuant to Article 2 Constitution, which entails the

 © Wolters Kluwer Italia

right of individuals to be identified by using the surnames of both parents if the individual deems that they both contributed to his/her identity.

Initially, the question was declared inadmissible (Orders Nos. 176 and 586/1988) because the issue fell within the discretion of Parliament, and because the Court deemed that the equality of spouses proclaimed in Article 29 of the Constitution – «The Republic recognises the rights of the family as a natural society founded on marriage. Marriage is based on the moral and legal equality of the spouses within the limits laid down by law to guarantee the unity of the family» – was not compromised, as the passing on of only the paternal surname was a rule deeply rooted in social custom and a criteria of protection of the family unit founded on marriage (*sic*!).

In 2006 (Judgment No. 61), eighteen years later, the Court held that the automatic assignment of the father's surname to children was a vestige of an outdated family law structure and incompatible with the constitutional **principle of equality**. The referral court asked for a manipulative judgment, which would however, have, exceeded the Court's powers. Indeed, the request to exclude the automatic assignment of the father's surname in cases where parents agree to choose the mother's would open up to different possible legal solutions that only Parliament could define and decide upon. The Court did, however, once again reiterate the multiple options that Parliament was entitled to choose from and enact.

In the meantime, the ECtHR, in case *Cusan and Fazzo v Italy* (Application No. 77/07, Judgment, 7th of January, 2014), held that the «gap in the Italian legal system» that fails to allow for giving children the mother's surname only «where the spouses agree» amounts to a **violation** of Articles 8 and 14 ECHR.

> In the judgment Cusan and Fazzo v. Italy, the ECtHR affirmed that the impossibility for parents to give their children their mother's surname at birth, instead of their father's, was an infringement of Article 14 (ban on discrimination), taken together with Article 8 (right to respect for private and family life) of the ECHR, and derives from a lack in the national judicial system, for which «reforms to the Italian legislation and/or practice are to be adopted» to overcome this.

In Judgment No. 286/2016, the Court once again addressed the legal provision that every child must be given its father's surname only at birth, and cannot be given also the mother's surname, even if so requested by both parents. This time the Court acted differently.

Referring to the case law of the ECtHR, the Court struck down the legislation with particular reference to the **right** to **personal identity**:

© Wolters Kluwer Italia

> In order to achieve the full and effective realisation of the right to personal identity, which has its **primary and most immediate expression in the name,** along with the recognition of equal significance to both parents within the process of constructing that personal identity, the **child's right** to be identified from birth by the surname of **both parents** must be **recognised**. Conversely, the provision for the absolute priority of the father's surname sacrifices the child's right to identity, denying him or her the ability to be identified from birth also by the mother's surname.

The Court also found the provision unconstitutional on the grounds that it **violated** the **principle of equality** between husband and wife.

Following this judgment, the general provision assigning the paternal surname remained in force only for cases in which there was no agreement between the parents in relation to adding the mother's surname.

In 2022, with Judgment No. 131, the Court took another step forward. The new judicial rule introduced by the Court requires the assignment of both parents' surnames to children, in the order agreed upon by them, except where they agree to give only one of their surnames. Thus, also due to the pressure from the periodic referral orders that continued to bring up the issue, the Court abandoned its prudent conduct that it held up to 2006 and took action to 'rewrite' this discipline.

5.e. Gender Balance in Politics

The Constitutional Court was called upon to deal with the issue of gender balancing in politics back in the mid-1990s. In Italy very few women have held public office.

Women were extremely active participants in the Resistance to fascism, and also due to this, they obtained the right to vote for the first time at national level in the referendum of 2nd of June, 1946, and concurrently, to be elected as members of the Constituent Assembly: although out of a total of 556 members only 21 were women. Since then, the number of women in Parliament or in regional assemblies has increased very slowly, and in a highly unsatisfactory manner.

In 1993, lawmakers attempted to remedy this gap with the electoral law for the direct election of mayors and the municipal council: neither of the two genders could represent more than two-thirds of the total. This new provision was condemned unanimously by ordinary courts, the Constitutional Court (Judgment No. 422/1995) and most scholars.

A citizen of a municipality challenged the electoral process before the administrative court due to the fact that only one woman was present among the thirty-six candidates in the three competing electoral lists for the municipal

© Wolters Kluwer Italia

council elections. The court rejected the suit, and interpreted the provision as lacking mandatory value. On appeal against the judgment, the Council of State raised the question of constitutional legitimacy, deeming that:

• the norm was mandatory;
• reserved quotas for each gender in the list of candidates were incompatible with the principle of equality enunciated in Article 3, para. 1, of the Constitution, and confirmed by Article 51, para. 1, of the Constitution, which **guarantees the eligibility for public and elected offices on equal terms for any citizens of either sex**;
• the norm infringed the rights of all citizens, guaranteed by Article 49 of the Constitution, to freely establish parties to contribute to determining national policies through democratic processes.

With Judgment No. 422/1995, the Court declared the balancing measure, defined as a sort of positive action, to be unconstitutional, due to infringement of Articles 3 and 51 Constitution.

How was the Court's reasoning possible, given that Article 3, para. 2, proclaims substantial equality that allows for the adoption of promotional legislative measures to eliminate obstacles of an economic or social nature, or, more generally, to compensate for or remove material inequalities between people?

Based on the Court's reasoning, intentionally unequal legislative measures can certainly be adopted (as happened repeatedly in those years in an attempt to achieve the equality of men and women in the workplace), but these cannot directly impact the content of the rights, which are rigorously guaranteed in equal measure to all citizens as such. The measures to promote gender balances must be freely implemented by political parties, associations or groups that participate in elections. Lawmakers cannot adopt measures which, instead of removing the obstacles that prevent women from achieving specific results, attribute such results directly to them. This would be the sense of the challenged measure, which, opting to reserve **gender quotas**, allegedly infringes, regarding rights of candidates, the unchallengeable rule established by the Constituent Assembly with Article 51, para. 1, of the Constitution (which) is that of absolute equality.

Despite this resistance, the Parliament introduced measures of gender balancing into the text of the Constitution. In 2001, Article **117, para. 7,** of the Constitution provided that **regional laws should remove any hindrances to the full equality of men and women in social, cultural, and economic life and promote equal access to elected offices for men and women**. In 2003, **the duty to promote equal opportunities between women and men** was **added to Article 51, para. 1,** which already provided that all citizens of either sex are eligible for public offices and for elective positions on equal terms, according to the conditions established by law.

© Wolters Kluwer Italia

The Constitutional Court mended its ways in 2003, following the constitutional reforms of Articles 51 and 117, para 7. The Court rejected the appeal of the Counsel of State for the President of the Council of Ministers (once again an expression of a conservative, discriminatory approach) against a regional law that merely established, in a completely neutral manner, that electoral lists must include candidates of both genders and that if this did not occur, the lists must be declared invalid by the regional electoral office. The Court dismissed the appeal and saved the neutral formulation of the norm, which merely introduced a legal restriction on the choices of who forms and submits the lists. That is, the norm does not impact in any way citizens' rights, the freedom of voters or the equality of the men and women candidates' chances in winning the election, or the unitary nature of the principle of equal representation in elections (Judgment No. 49).

In 2010, with Judgment No. 4, the Court saved another regional electoral law, challenged again by the Counsel of State for the President of the Council of Ministers (once again standing out in his display of cultural backwardness). The challenged provision **introduced gender preference** into the legal system for the first time. That is, the regional lawmakers established that, **where a voter is entitled to express two votes** (preference voting), **one must be a candidate of the male gender and the other must be a candidate of the female gender**. Non-compliance of this pre-requisite would annul the second preference vote.

The process concerning gender balancing was completed with Judgment No. 81/2012. Once again, it was the regional lawmakers that made the effort to implement gender balancing, establishing in the statute of the Campania Region that the Regional executive must be formed in full compliance with the principle of balance between the number of men and women. The Court recognised that, appointing the members of the Regional executive, which is the manifestation of the political choice of the President of the Regional executive, falls within the category of so called political acts. Nonetheless, politics must comply with what is determined by the lawmakers. The act of appointing the members of the Regional executive can thus be challenged in a judicial capacity, if it infringes the legal provisions on gender balancing.

Nowadays both regional and national electoral laws include instruments for gender balancing.

5.f. Same-Sex Marriage and Parenthood

Same-sex marriage is not provided for, either by law or in the Constitution.

Marriage in the Italian legal system can be either civil or contracted in keeping with the Concordat (that is, performed in accordance with the law of the

© Wolters Kluwer Italia

Roman Catholic Church, whose civil effects are recognised following the transcription of the marriage in the civil status registers), and exclusively **heterosexual**. The Constitution, which considers the concept of marriage according to that of the Civil Code, which entered into force a few years prior, recognises the rights of the family as a natural society founded on marriage in Article 29. It is clear that the framers of the Constitution conceived of marriage **exclusively** as the union of a **man** and a **woman**.

Lawmakers' discretion on the issue of same-sex marriage was (arguably for part of the doctrine) confirmed by the Constitutional Court in Judgment No. 138/2010.

The judgment derived from the refusal of the municipality registrar to publish notice of the intention of three same-sex couples to marry. The Court ruled that the guarantees provided by Article 2 of the Constitution refer to same-sex couples, which were recognised as social formations, but not as families. This is understood as the stable cohabitation of two people of the same-sex, who are entitled to the fundamental right to live freely as a couple, obtaining, according to the law, legal recognition thereof along with the associated rights and duties. Nonetheless, it is only for Parliament to determine – exercising its discretion – the forms of guarantee and recognition for same-sex couples.

The Court however excluded that such recognition can take place exclusively through the extension of marriage to same-sex couples. The Court also excluded that Article 29 of the Constitution – which protects marriage as the foundation of family *qua* natural society – might cover same-sex marriage. When the Constitution was enacted, marriage was exclusively understood as heterosexual.

Admittedly, the decision might be interpreted differently. Scholars have divided on the issue of the constitutional admissibility of marriage. Some suggested that the Court espoused constitutional neutrality. Others found that the Court had indeed ruled on the necessity to grant a degree of legal recognition to same-sex couples, yet in a form that is different from marriage.

The matter was solved in 2014. With Judgment No. 170/2014, the Constitutional Court **excluded** the **constitutional admissibility of same-sex marriage**. This judgment established the unconstitutionality of the norm on automatic divorce following the recognition of a married trans person. In the case at hand, the marriage of an opposite-sex couple turned into a marriage of a same-sex couple as a result of one of the spouse's transition. Hence, it could not be permitted under the law. Even though the Court considered that there is a right to preserve a legal recognition of such relation, it clearly excluded that this recognition could take the form of a (same-sex) marriage. As the Court made clear, same-sex marriage is not permissible under Article 29. It left to the lawmakers the task of

© Wolters Kluwer Italia

finding a different type of legal recognition. In conclusion, the constitutional doctrine requires some legal recognition for same-sex couples (*qua* social formations and not families) but excludes the possibility of a same-sex marriage.

This reading is essentially confirmed at the ECHR level. The lack of consensus among the State parties of the Council of Europe on same-sex marriage leaves them a considerable **margin of appreciation**. However, in 2015 the Court established that Italy, which at the time did not grant any form of legal protection to same-sex couples, overstepped its margin of appreciation under Article 8 ECHR (*Oliari and Others v Italy*, Applications Nos. 18766/11 and 36030/11, Judgment, 21st of July, 2015). Interestingly, this European judgment recalled the seminal decision of the US Supreme Court (*Obergefell et al. v Hodges, Director, Ohio Department of Health et al* 576 U.S. (2015)) according to which «same-sex couples may exercise the fundamental right to marry in all States, and that there was no lawful basis for a State to refuse to recognise a lawful same-sex marriage performed in another State on the ground of its same-sex character». The ECtHR underlined the evolution of Italian society, as well as the relatively little burden that the recognition of same-sex unions would entail for the government. The Court remarked the increasing recognition of same-sex unions among the States Parties to the Council of Europe and stressed that the ItCC had repeatedly called for such protection. Hence, it found that a recognition of civil unions was due.

The findings of Oliari were, by and large, confirmed in Orlandi (case *Orlandi v Italy*, Applications Nos. 26431/12 and three others, Judgment, 14th of December, 2017) and in case *Fedotova v Russia* (Grand Chamber, Applications Nos. 40792/10, 30538/14 and 43439/14, Judgment, 17th of January, 2023). In the last case the Grand Chamber restated that the respondent State had overstepped its margin of appreciation and had failed to comply with its positive obligation to secure the applicants' right to respect for their private and family life. The Member States who do not provide for a legal recognition of same-sex couples must provide some sort of legalization.

Oliari led to Law No. 76/2016, which introduced **civil unions** in Italy.

The Law of 2016 grants a large portion of the rights and obligations deriving from marriage, even though a civil union is a different legal instrument. **Symbolical differences** are introduced. Same-sex couples are defined as a social formation and the duty of fidelity between the partners has been eliminated.

Adding to these symbolical differentiations, same-sex couples in **civil unions cannot** access **joint adoption** (Article 1, para. 2, Law No. 76/2016). However, the Court of Cassation has confirmed that there is no abstract impediment to same-sex step-child adoption, to be considered only with regard to the specific circumstances of the case (Court of Cassation Judgments Nos. 12962/2016, 12193/2019 and 38162/2022).

 © Wolters Kluwer Italia

Concerning same-sex reproduction (where a child has a biological parent and an intentional parent, meaning the person that did not provide his/her genetic material, but has given the consent to the fertilisation procedure), several different situations, sets of rules and legal instruments need to be distinguished:

• the Italian legal system does not provide for civil registries to record two men or two women as both parents of a newborn child; only the biological parent may be recorded as parent;

• if the child was born abroad, in a state which allows two men or two women to be recorded as parents, the foreign birth certificate and status may be recognized in civil registries: according to the current case law, although the system is not organized to provide for the recognition of two men/women as parents, the recognition of the foreign act is not prohibited by national mandatory rules (Law No. 218/1995);

• however, such a prohibition exists when the child was conceived through surrogate pregnancy; in this case, the intentional parent may never be recognized as parent, neither by Italian registries directly, nor through recognition of foreign birth certificates and statuses;

• nonetheless, the intentional parent may still resort to a special form of adoption. Article 44, para. 1, d), of the act on adoptions (Law No. 184/1983) allows for such adoption when pre-adoptive foster care is impossible. Under the current case law, this clause is interpreted as also applying to children who do not need pre-adoptive foster care, as they are being raised by one biological parent, and thus the intentional parent. Many national Courts belonging to legal orders that do not recognize surrogate pregnancy are following the same interpretation of their respective legislations on adoptions in the name of the best interest of the child;

• in any case, under a general rule (Article 333 of the Civil code), when a parent engages in any conduct that is harmful to a child, the competent judge may adopt any appropriate measures. This general rule has been construed as guaranteeing the preservation of significant affective relationships when a same-sex couple enters a phase of crisis, and the biological parent attempts to sever abruptly all relationships between the former partner and the child (as stated in ItCC Judgments Nos. 225/2016 and 32/2021).

In 2021 (Judgments Nos. 32 and 33), the Court investigated a highly topical issue: the lack of recognition in domestic law of a parent-child relationship between a child born from a gestational surrogacy arrangement or from heterologous MAP both performed abroad and its intentional mother or father (meaning the person that did not provide his/her genetic material, but has given the consent to the fertilisation procedure). Though these techniques are prohibited for

© Wolters Kluwer Italia

same-sex couples by Law No. 40/2004, children born by them are entitled to all the rights recognised to citizens, irrespective of the methods of their conception.

In Judgment No. 32, the case had its origins in two women who jointly assumed parental responsibility. After a crisis within the couple, the biological mother refused to let the intentional mother have any contact with their daughters.

Judgment No. 33, on the other hand, concerned the refusal of the Italian authorities to give effect to a foreign decree that recognised two Italian men, who entered into a civil partnership, as the parents of a child who was born in Canada to a surrogate mother.

In declaring in both cases that the questions under examination were inadmissible out of deference to the legislator's assessment of the appropriateness of the means to achieve a constitutionally necessary end, the Court could not but state that the continuation of legislative inertia would no longer be tolerable, so serious is the gap in the protection of the overriding interest of the child.

In 2022 (Judgment No. 79), the Court intervened on the issue of a request for adoption by the intentional parent of a child born through surrogate pregnancy (the intentional parent was part of a same-sex male couple). The Court recognised that the rule that does not establish civil relationships between the child adopted in special cases and the relatives of the adopter breaches Articles 3, 31, para. 2, and 117, para. 1, of the Constitution, the latter in relation to Article 8 ECHR. The Court stated that the protection of a **child's best interests** requires all adopted children to be **guaranteed** the **recognition of kinship** resulting from adoption.

At the end of 2022 the Court of Cassation, Judgment No. 38162/2022, ruled on the same case decided by the ItCC with Judgment No. 33/2021 (it was the Court of Cassation that raised the question of constitutionality): the Canadian birth certificate, identifying both men as parents, could not be recognized in the Italian legal system, due to the latter's radical opposition to surrogate pregnancy; only the biological father could be recognized as a parent, while his partner could only resort to the special adoption provided for in Article 44 of Law No. 184/1983, which affords legal recognition to the affective relation with the child. The child has a **fundamental right** to the recognition of the **affective relation** with the **intentional parent**.

The ECtHR has also stated that whereas Member States remain free to establish the instrument that is best suited to ensure the child's protection while balancing the various requirements that are involved, a limit to their margin of appreciation lies in the condition that the procedures established in domestic law

© Wolters Kluwer Italia

have to guarantee **effective** and **rapid implementation** in accordance with the **child's best interests** (*D. v France*, Application No. 11288/18, Judgment, 16th of July, 2020); and Grand Chamber, Advisory Opinion of 9th of April, 2019, para. 54, handed down pursuant to Protocol No. 16).

The thorny issue regarding the status of children born abroad to same-sex couples remains to be resolved also in the EU legal order, as the recent EU Commission proposal (7th of December, 2022) well shows.

The proposal is focused on the best interests and the rights of the child also born by surrogacy.

REFERENCES

BARAGGIA, A. & BONELLI, M. [2022], 'Linking Money to Values: The New Rule of Law Conditionality Regulation and Its Constitutional Challenges', 23(2) *German Law Journal*.

BARBERA, A. [1975], 'Commento all'Art. 2' in BRANCA, G. (ed), *Commentario della Costituzione. Principi fondamentali* (Bologna-Roma, Zanichelli-Foro italiano).

BARBERA, A. & FUSARO, C. [2022], *Corso di diritto costituzionale* (Bologna, il Mulino).

BARSOTTI, V., AND OTHERS [2016], *Italian Constitutional Justice in Global Context* (New York, Oxford University Press).

BELLAMY, R. [2015], 'The Democratic Legitimacy of International Human Rights Conventions: Political Constitutionalism and the European Convention on Human Rights', 25(4) *The European Journal of International Law*.

BIAGI, F. [2020], *European Constitutional Courts and Transitions to Democracy* (Cambridge, Cambridge University Press).

BIFULCO, R. & PARIS, D. [2020], 'The Italian Constitutional Court' in VON BOGDANDY, A., AND OTHERS, *The Max Planck Handbooks in European Public Law. 3. Constitutional Adjudication: Institutions* (Oxford, Oxford University Press).

BIN, R. [2012], *Order and Disorder Legal Adjudication and Quantum Epistemology*, 2 Straus Working Paper, available at www.law.nyu.edu

BOBBIO, N. [1990], *L'età dei diritti* (Torino, Einaudi), engl. transl. by CAMERON, A., *The Age of Rights* (Cambridge, Polity Press, 1996).

CARTABIA, M. & LUPO, N. [2022], *The Constitution of Italy. A contextual Analysis* (Oxford, Hart).

CARTABIA, M. [2009], 'Europe and Rights: Taking Dialogue Seriously', 5(1) *European Constitutional Law Review*.

CARTABIA, M. [2016], 'Ragionevolezza e proporzionalità nella giurisprudenza costituzionale italiana' in GIORGIS, A., AND OTHERS (eds), *Il costituzionalista riluttante. Scritti per Gustavo Zagrebelsky* (Torino, Einaudi).

CAPPELLETTI, M. [1979-1980], 'The "Mighty Problem" of Judicial Review and the Contribution of Comparative Analysis', 53(2) *Southern California Law Review*.

CAPPELLETTI, M. [1984], *Giudici legislatori?* (Milano, Giuffrè).

CASINI, L. [2022], 'Global Administrative Law', in DUNOFF, J.L. & POLLACK, M.A. (eds), *International Legal Theory. Foundations and Frontiers* (Cambridge, Cambridge University Press).

CASS, DZ. [2001], 'The 'constitutionalization' of international trade law: judicial norm-generation as the engine of constitutional development in international trade', 12(1) *European Journal of International Law*.

CASSESE, S. [2006], *Oltre lo Stato* (Roma-Bari, Laterza).
CASSESE, S. [2017], *Research Handbook on Global Administrative Law* (Cheltenham, Elgar).
DE BELLIS, M. [2018], 'Relative Authority in Global and EU Financial Regulation: Linking the Legitimacy Debates', in MENDES, J. & VENZKE, I., (eds), *Allocating Authority: Who Should do What in European and International Law* (Oxford, Hart).
DELLA CANANEA, G. [2011], *Al di là dei confini statuali*, (Bologna, il Mulino).
FERRARESE, MR. [2006], *Diritto sconfinato. Inventiva giuridica e spazi nel mondo globale* (Roma-Bari, Laterza).
FERRARESE, MR. [2009], 'When National Actors Become Transnational: Transjudicial Dialogue between Democracy and Constitutionalism', 9(1) *Global Jurist*.
FERRARI, GF. [2008] (ed), *Introduction to Italian Public Law* (Milano, Giuffrè).
FICHERA, M. [2021], 'The Idea of Discursive Constituent Power', 3(2) *Jus Cogens*.
FIORAVANTI, M. [2017], *Costituzione italiana: articolo 2* (Roma, Carocci).
FROSINI, JO. [2008], 'Constitutional Justice', in FERRARI, G. F. (ed), *Introduction to Italian Public Law* (Milano, Giuffrè).
GOLDONI, M. & MCCORKINDALE, C. [2019], 'Three Waves of Political Constitutionalism', 30(1) *King's Law Journal*.
GRIMM, D. [2010], 'The achievement of Constitutionalism and its Prospects in a Changed World', in LOUGHLIN, M. & DOBNER, P. (eds), *The Twilight of Constitutionalism?* (Oxford, Oxford University Press).
GROPPI, T. [2008], 'The Italian Constitutional Court: Towards a "Multilevel System" of Constitutional Review?' (2) *Journal of Comparative Law*.
HIRSCHL, R. [2004], '*The Political Origins of the New Constitutionalism*', 11(1) *Indiana Journal of Global Legal Studies*.
HIRSCHL, R. [2007], *Towards Juristocracy* (Cambridge-London, Harvard University Press).
JESTAEDT, M., AND OTHERS [2020], *The German Federal Constitutional Court: The Court Without Limits* (Oxford, Oxford University Press).
KINGSBURY, B. AND OTHERS [2004], 'The Emergence of Global Administrative Law', IILJ Working Paper 1 (Global Administrative Law Series), available at www.iilj.org.
KRETZMER, D. [2023], 'Israel's Constitutional Crisis', 43(2) *Quaderni Costituzionali*.
KUMM, M. [2009], 'The Cosmopolitan Turn in Constitutionalism: On the Relationship Between Constitutionalism in and beyond the State', in DUNOFF, J.L., AND OTHERS (eds) *Ruling the World?: Constitutionalism, International Law, and Global Governance*, (Cambridge, Cambridge University Press).
MORRONE, A. [2019], 'Suprematismo giudiziario. Su sconfinamenti e legittimazione politica della Corte costituzionale', 39(2) *Quaderni Costituzionali*.
NARDINI, WJ. [1999-2000], 'Passive Activism and the Limits of Judicial Self- Restraint: Lessons for America from the Italian Constitutional Court', 30(1) *Seton Hall Law Review*.
MUSELLA, F. & RULLO, L. [2020], 'The Expansion of the Constitutional Court in Italy: Ruling the Void in Times of Political Instability', 25(1) *Review of Constitutional Studies*.
PACE, A. [2003], *Problematica delle libertà costituzionali. Parte generale* (Padova, Cedam).
PASQUINO, P. [1998], 'Constitutional Adjudication and Democracy. Comparative Perspectives: USA, France, Italy', 11 (1) *Ratio Juris*.
PETERS, A. [2006], 'Compensatory Constitutionalism: The Function and Potential of Fundamental International Norms and Structures', 19(3) *Leiden Journal of International Law*.
PICCIRILLI, G. [2018], 'The "Taricco Saga": the Italian Constitutional Court Continues Its European Journey', 14(4) *European Constitutional Law Review*.
POLICE, A. [2015], 'Administrative justice in Italy: Myths and Reality', 15(1) *Italian Journal of Public Law*.

 © Wolters Kluwer Italia

POLLICINO, O. [2008], 'Italy: Constitutional Court at the crossroads between constitutional parochialism and co-operative constitutionalism. Judgments No. 348 and 349 of 22 and 24 October 2007', 4(2) *European Constitutional Law Review*.
PUTMAN, T. L. [2016], *The Court without borders* (Oxford, Oxford University Press).
REPETTO, G. [2013] (ed), *The Constitutional Relevance of the ECHR in Domestic and European Law: An Italian Perspective* (Den Haag, Intersentia).
SADURSKI, W. [2019], *Poland's Constitutional Breakdown* (Oxford, Oxford University Press).
SADURSKI, W. [2019], 'Polish Constitutional Tribunal under PiS: From an Activist Court, to a Paralysed Tribunal, to a Governmental Enabler', 11(1) *Hague Journal on the Rule of Law*.
SAVINO, M. [2016], 'The Refugee Crisis as a Challenge for Public Law: The Italian Case', 17(6) *German Law Journal*.
SLAUGHTER, AM. [1994], 'A Typology of Transjudicial Communication', 29(1) *University of Richmond Law Review*.
TEGA, D. [2012], *I diritti in crisi. Tra Corti nazionali e Corte europea di Strasburgo* (Milano, Giuffrè).
TEGA, D. [2017], 'The Italian way: a blend of cooperation and hubris', 77(3) *The Heidelberg Journal of International Law/Zeitschrift für ausländisches öffentliches Recht und Völkerrecht*.
TEGA, D. [2021], 'The Italian Constitutional Court in its context: A narrative', 17(3) *European Constitutional Law Review*.
TUSHNET, M. [1999], *Taking the Constitution away from the Courts* (Princeton, Princeton University Press).
WALDRON, J. [2006], 'The Core of the Case against Judicial Review', 115(6) *The Yale Law Journal*.
WEILER, J.H.H. & LUSTIG, D. [2018], 'Judicial Review in the Contemporary World – Retrospective and Prospective', 16(2) *International Journal of Constitutional Law*.